# Computer Literacy for IC³™

## Updated Edition

*John Preston*
*Sally Preston*
*Robert Ferrett*

Pearson Education Ltd., London
Pearson Education Singapore, Pte. Ltd
Pearson Education, Canada, Inc.
Pearson Education–Japan
Pearson Education Australia PTY, Limited

Pearson Education North Asia, Ltd., Hong Kong
Pearson Educación de Mexico, S.A. de C.V.
Pearson Education Malaysia, Pte. Ltd
Pearson Education Upper Saddle River, New Jersey

**Prentice Hall**
is an imprint of

www.pearsonhighered.com

ISBN-13: 978-0-13-503852-9
ISBN-10: 0-13-503852-9

# PROJECT 1

# TAKING A TOUR OF WINDOWS APPLICATIONS

## IN THIS PROJECT, YOU LEARN HOW TO:

- **Start an Application and Identify Common On-Screen Elements**
- **Open and Save a File**
- **Use Ribbons and Tabs (Use Menus and Toolbars)**
- **Switch Between Open Applications and Files**
- **Change Views and Magnification**
- **Close Files and Close Applications**
- **Use Help**

# WHY WOULD I DO THIS?

*Application software* are computer programs that are used to accomplish a specific set of tasks. Applications are also referred to as *programs*. *Windows-based* applications are computer programs that are written to work on a computer using a Microsoft Windows operating system. *Microsoft Office* is a suite of applications that perform tasks commonly used in an office environment, such as writing documents, managing finances, and presenting information. Whether you are using a Microsoft Office application or another Windows-based program, you will use the same basic procedures to start and exit each application and to interact with various programs. Before you can use a software application effectively, you need to know how to work with the program's on-screen elements. Microsoft Office applications use a *graphical user interface* commonly referred to as *GUI*, pronounced *gooey*, which includes windows, dialog boxes, toolbars, and menus. A mouse and keyboard are the most common input devices used to interact with the on-screen elements. In this chapter, you learn how to use each of these elements. You will also learn how to use these elements to interact with applications.

Application programs usually offer *Help* programs—installed reference tools that can assist you in using the program. A portion of the Help program is installed with the application, and you can seek additional assistance by using online resources. In this project, you will look at some of the features common to all (or nearly all) Windows-based programs. You will also explore the common Help features.

# VISUAL SUMMARY

In this project, you explore three Microsoft Office *application windows* and identify on-screen elements. You practice using on-screen elements to manipulate the software. You open a file, add your name, and print the document as shown in Figure 1.1. You learn how to switch between open files and applications, and how to change magnification and views in a document. You then save the file you changed, and close the files and application windows. Finally, you are introduced to the Help program, which can assist you in learning how to use a software program.

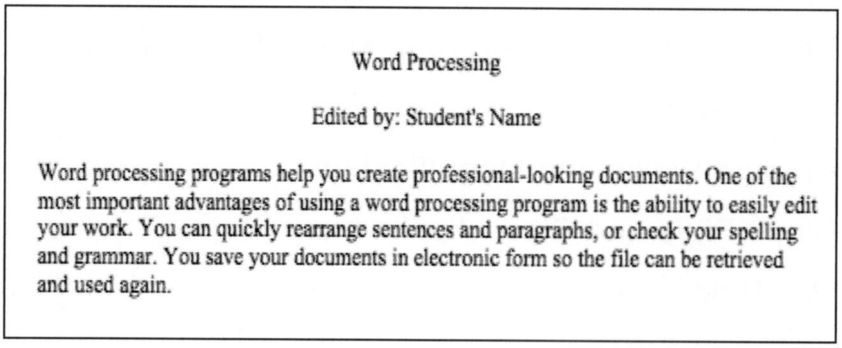

---

Word Processing

Edited by: Student's Name

Word processing programs help you create professional-looking documents. One of the most important advantages of using a word processing program is the ability to easily edit your work. You can quickly rearrange sentences and paragraphs, or check your spelling and grammar. You save your documents in electronic form so the file can be retrieved and used again.

---

FIGURE 1.1

# LESSON 1: Starting an Application and Identifying Common On-Screen Elements

To start a Microsoft Office application you typically use the Start button found on the **taskbar** at the bottom of your screen. All programs can be started in this same way. In this lesson, you start **Microsoft Office Word**—a word processing application; **Microsoft Office Excel**—a financial management application; and **Microsoft Office PowerPoint**—a presentation application.

All of these exercises can be completed with Microsoft Office 2007. Instructions throughout the lessons are based on the Windows XP operating system, running Microsoft Office 2007. Your screen may differ slightly from the figures shown, even if you are running Office 2007 or if you are running the Vista Operating System.

## To Start an Application and Identify Common On-Screen Elements

1. **Click the Start button on the left side of the Windows taskbar.** The Start menu displays.

2. **Locate and click Microsoft Office Word 2007.** The Word program might be located on the Start menu or under All Programs, in the Microsoft Office group. It may also display on an Office toolbar on the top of your screen or the Quick Launch bar at the bottom of the screen. The Word window opens to a new **document**, which is the main **work area**. The document is given a default name, such as *Document1,* as shown in Figure 1.2. This name is displayed in both the title bar and the taskbar. The work area in each application is different, but the other on-screen elements are basically the same with slight variations.

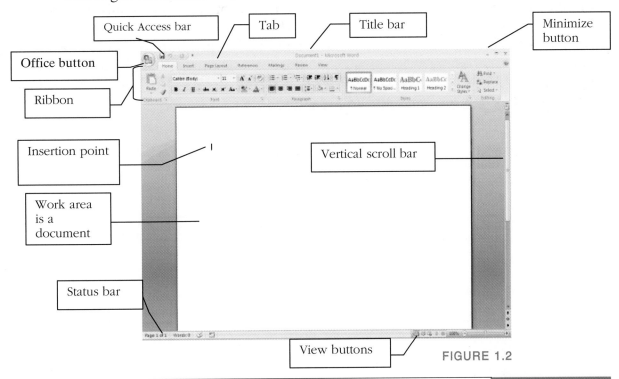

FIGURE 1.2

## If you have problems...

The Ribbon in Office 2007 has replaced the menus and toolbars in earlier versions of Microsoft Office applications. You will explore the ribbon in each project. Your work area may also look different depending on the view, zoom setting, and other variables. You can choose from several views when working in Word, and the one that is displayed is the last one that was used on that machine. This will be addressed later in this project

3. **If the window does not fill the screen, click the Maximize button in the title bar. See Figure 1.2.** Maximizing the application window expands it to fill your screen.

4. **Take a moment to locate the elements of the Ribbon and select each tab to become familiar with the application elements in the tab area.**

5. **Click the Start button on the taskbar; locate and then click Microsoft Office Excel 2007.** The Excel application opens on your screen and displays *Book1* as the default file name in the title bar.

6. **Examine your screen and locate the elements identified in the Excel window in Figure 1.3.** The same basic screen elements are displayed in both the Excel and Word applications. The Excel window displays a *worksheet* as the main work area, which is a grid of rows and columns. Rows are identified by numbers, and columns are identified by letters. The intersection of each row and column is referred to as a *cell*. Each cell is referred to by its *cell address*, which is the column letter and row number. The first cell's address is A1. Cell A1 has a dark border, which indicates that it is the *active cell*—the cell where data will display when you type.

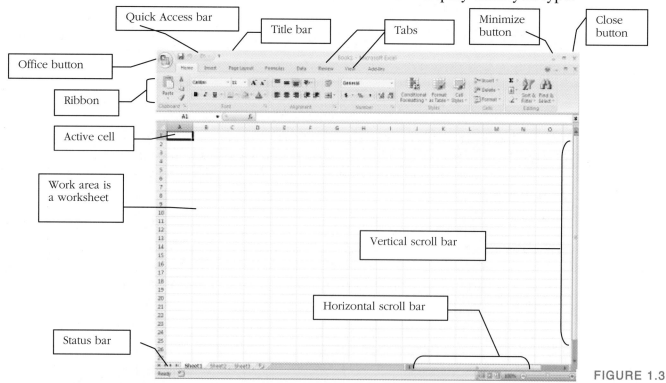

FIGURE 1.3

7. **Click the Minimize button on the Excel title bar.** The Excel application is reduced to a button on the taskbar and the Word window redisplays on the screen. The Excel program is still open, but does not display on the screen—it is minimized. This feature enables you to have several applications open at once, and move easily between the applications.

## If you have problems...

If the taskbar is hidden, you may not see the Excel button name on the taskbar. If the taskbar is hidden, move your pointer to the bottom of the screen. The taskbar will pop up. If you want to display or hide it, right-click in an open area of the taskbar and select Properties from the shortcut menu. Click the *Auto-hide the taskbar* check box to turn the Auto-hide feature on or off. The taskbar will be displayed through the end of this project and will then be hidden for the rest of the book to give you the maximum work area on the screen.

8. **Click the Minimize button on the Microsoft Office Word 2007 title bar.** The Word window is reduced to a button on the taskbar as shown in Figure 1.4.

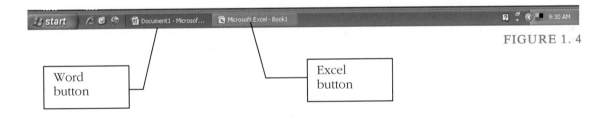

FIGURE 1. 4

Word button

Excel button

9. **Click the Start button on the taskbar; locate and click Microsoft Office PowerPoint 2007.** The PowerPoint application window opens and a PowerPoint button displays on the taskbar. The default name in the title bar is *Presentation1*.

10. **Examine your screen and locate the elements in the PowerPoint window as shown in Figure 1.5.** The main work area in PowerPoint is a *slide*. There are several *views*—ways of looking at the presentation slides in PowerPoint—that you will explore when you cover that application. Leave all applications open and continue to the next lesson

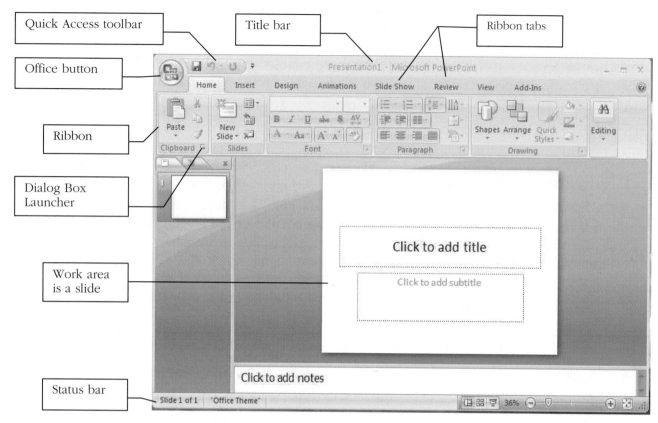

Quick Access toolbar

Title bar

Ribbon tabs

Office button

Ribbon

Dialog Box
Launcher

Work area
is a slide

Status bar

FIGURE 1.5

In this lesson, you have been introduced to a number of on-screen elements that are found in most Windows-based applications. Table 1.1 lists and describes the screen elements illustrated in this lesson.

| SCREEN ELEMENT | DESCRIPTION |
|---|---|
| *Title bar* | Displays the program icon, the name of the file, and the name of the program. The Minimize, Maximize/Restore Down, and Close buttons are grouped on the right side of the title bar. |
| *Minimize button* | Reduces the open file to a button on the taskbar. |
| *Maximize button* | Expands the application window to fill the screen. |
| *Office button* | A button that displays commands related to files |
| *Ribbon* | Contains groups of buttons for the most common commands used in applications. |
| *Tabs* | Used to access lists of commands related to a category of actions for each application. The content of the tabs vary for each application. |
| *Dialog Box Launcher* | In the lower right corner of some command groups, an icon that opens the related dialog box to which offers additional options. |
| *Application window* | Displays the open application and contains the major on-screen elements used when working with the application. |

| | |
|---|---|
| *Work area* | The area on the screen when you enter text, numbers or graphics to create a document, worksheet, or presentation slides |
| *Vertical scroll bar* | Enables you to move up and down in a file to display text that is not visible. |
| *Horizontal scroll bar* | Enables you to move left and right in a file to display text that is not visible. |
| *Quick Access toolbar* | A customizable toolbar to the right of the Office button that contains the Save, Undo, and Redo buttons |
| *Scroll box* | Provides a visual indication of your location in the work area. It can also be used with the mouse to drag a work area up and down or left to right. |
| *Insertion point* | Indicates, with a blinking vertical line, where text or graphics will be inserted. |
| *Mouse pointer* | Indicates the location of the mouse on your screen, which is independent of the insertion point. |
| *Taskbar* | Displays the Start button and the name of any open files and applications. The taskbar may also display shortcut buttons for other programs. |
| *Status bar* | Displays information about the document, worksheet, or presentation on which you are working. |

TABLE 1.1

## TO EXTEND YOUR KNOWLEDGE...

### STARTING APPLICATIONS

There are several ways to start an application. The most common is to use the Start menu, and then point to All Programs to locate the application you need. Application shortcuts can be added to the top of the Start menu or to the desktop. You can also display the Office Shortcut toolbar. Use Windows Help if you would like to use one of these shortcut methods. In this book, you will simply be instructed to start the application. You may decide on which method to use.

# LESSON 2: Opening and Saving a File

When you open an application, such as Word 2007, a new blank document displays. You can use this blank document to create a new file, or you can choose to open an existing file. After you have entered the desired information or data in your document, you will want to save it for future use or reference. The first time you save a file you will give it a name and place it in a specific storage location on your computer. Files can be saved to your computer's hard drive, a network drive, or some type of portable storage device, such as a USB flash drive, or CD. After it has been saved, you can use the Save button to save changes made to the file.

In this lesson, you open a file and save it to a folder. You then make a change to the file and save the change.

1. **Click the Microsoft Office Word button from the taskbar.** The Word window is maximized on your screen

2. **In the upper left corner of the application window, click the Office button, and then click Open.** The Open dialog box displays as shown in Figure 1.6. *Dialog boxes* are used to provide instruction to the computer. The Open dialog box is used to locate files on your computer. The default folder that displays is usually the My Documents folder on your computer's hard drive. The My Documents folder may be personalized to display the name of the registered owner of the computer.

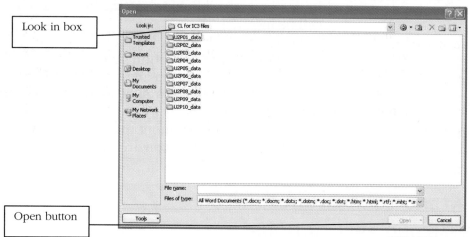

FIGURE 1. 6

3. **Navigate to the location where the student files for this book are located.** The files may be on a CD-ROM, they may be on a network drive, or they may be located on your computer or USB drive.

4. **Double-click the Student Data folder for this chapter and then click the file *CE_0101* to select it.** Double-clicking a folder opens the folder and displays its contents. Placing files in folders helps to organize your work.

5. **Click the Open button in the lower-right corner of the Open dialog box.** The *CE_0101* file opens on your screen and the file name displays in the title bar in *Compatibility Mode*—a file that can be used in Office 2003 or 2007. You can also double-click the file name to open the file.

6. **Select the Office button and then point at the Save As option.** On the right, the *Save a Copy of the document* menu displays.

7. **You have the option to save the file as a Word 2007 Document or as a Word 97-2003 Document. Click Word 97-2003 Document.** The available drives and folders for your computer display in a list.

8. **Click the arrow at the right side of the Save in box to display the list of available drives and folders. Click the drive or location where you will be saving your files.** You may save your files to a portable device, such as a USB drive, to a location on the hard drive, or to a network location.

9. **Click the Create New Folder button to the right of the Save in box and then type CE_Project1 in the New Folder dialog box; click OK.** The folder is created and displays in the Save in box. Creating folders for your files helps you organize your work so you can easily retrieve your files.

10. **Click in the File name box; hold down Ctrl and then press A to select the file name; type Sample_Word_Document.** Using two keys in combination to perform an action is a known as a *keyboard shortcut*, or shortcut key. This is a quick method of performing a task or executing a command. In this example, holding down the Ctrl key and then pressing the letter A selects all of the text in the File name box where you placed the insertion point. When text is selected, you can type to replace the selected text; this results in a new file name—*Sample_Word_Document*—as shown in Figure 1.7.

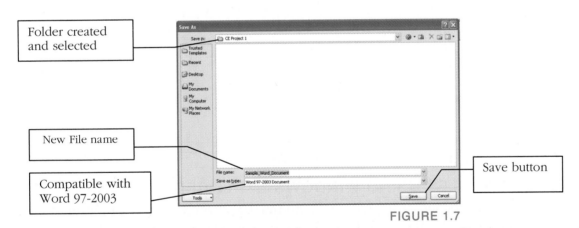

FIGURE 1.7

11. **Click Save, in the lower-right corner of the Save As dialog box.** The file is saved in a new location on your computer and the new name displays in the title bar. You can also press Enter⏎ to activate the Save command in the dialog box.

12. **Position the mouse to the right of *Edited by:* and click to place the insertion point at this location; type your name.** When you position the pointer somewhere in the text and click with the left mouse button, a flashing vertical line is inserted as shown in Figure 1.8. This is the *insertion point*. When you start typing, the text will appear at the insertion point, not at the pointer location. This is true in all application software programs. The *mouse pointer* remains on the work area portion of the screen in the shape of an I, sometimes referred to as an I-beam

---

13. **Leave the *Sample_Word_Document* open on your screen and continue to the next lesson.** The PowerPoint 2007 and Excel 2007 applications should also still be open, but minimized and displayed as buttons on the taskbar.

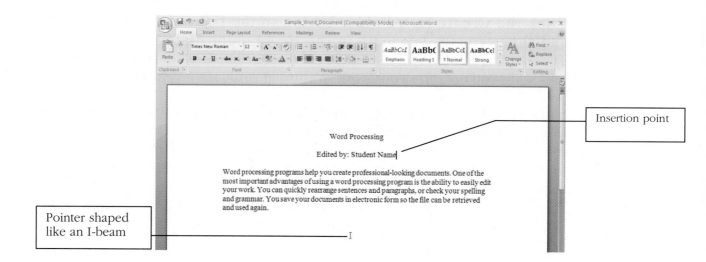

Insertion point

Pointer shaped like an I-beam

FIGURE 1.8

---

## TO EXTEND YOUR KNOWLEDGE...

### OPENING FILES USING WINDOWS EXPLORER OR MY COMPUTER

Files can be opened from within Windows Explorer or My Computer. Open My Computer, find the file, and double-click it. The application that created the file (in this case, Word) opens along with the document. If you save your files to the My Documents folder on your own computer, you can access your files by using the My Documents folder that displays on the main Start menu. Click Start and then click the My Documents folder. When your files display, double-click the file you want to use. The application used to create the file will open and the file will display.

### FILE-NAMING CONVENTIONS

File and folder names can contain up to 255 characters, including spaces. They cannot, however, include any of the following characters: < > / : " \ | * It is best to use a short descriptive name for your files. In this textbook, underscores have been used between words in a file name to facilitate transferring files over the Internet using a course management system.

## USING THE SAVE BUTTON

When a file is saved for the first time, clicking the Save button on the Quick Access toolbar opens the Save As dialog box so that you can name the file and place it within a specified location on your computer. Once a file is saved, clicking the Save button will update the file with the changes that have been made, overwriting the original file. The default location for saving files is usually set to the My Documents folder on your computer. If your computer is on a network, the My Documents folder may be different for each user who is authorized to use that computer. Always check the Save in box to ensure that you are saving your files to the intended location.

## USING DIALOG BOXES

Dialog boxes are used to tell the application software what you want to do. A dialog box can include text boxes, option buttons, check boxes, and command buttons. One of the command buttons is usually highlighted as the default choice. This means that it is the most common command that is used in that dialog box, and if you press Enter that command will be activated. For example in the Open dialog box, the Open button is highlighted and pressing Enter would open the currently selected file. Similarly, in the Save As dialog box, the Save command button is highlighted and is activated by pressing Enter.

# LESSON 3: Using the Ribbon and Tabs (Using Menus and Toolbars)

The *Ribbon* organizes commands used to work with the application into related tasks that are accessed by tabs. The commands on each tab are further organized into logical groups or categories. Most elements display an *icon*, which is an image that represents the button's function. When you click a button a command is executed. It is a quick method for interacting with an application program.

In this lesson, you learn how to use the Ribbon. Where Office 2007 differs significantly from Office 2003 and the IC3 2005 standard, the lesson titles and learning objectives from the Office 2003 version of the textbook are placed in parentheses.

### To Use the Ribbon and Tabs (To Use the Menu Bar)

1. With *Sample_Word_Document* open, click each tab on the Ribbon. Review the table below which lists the Office 2007 main tabs and the groups of the elements found in each tab. Figure 1.9 shows the Home tab.

| Tab | Groups | | | | | | |
|---|---|---|---|---|---|---|---|
| Home | Clipboard | Font | Paragraph | Styles | Editing | | |
| Insert | Pages | Tables | Illustrations | Links | Header & Footer | Text | Symbols |
| Page Layout | Themes | Page Setup | Page Background | Paragraph | Arrange | | |
| References | Table of Contents | Footnotes | Citations & Bibliography | Captions | Index | Table of Authorities | |
| Mailing | Create | Start Mail Merge | Write & Insert Fields | Preview Results | Finish | | |
| Review | Proofing | Comments | Tracking | Changes | Compare | Protect | |
| View | Document Views | Show/Hide | Zoom | Window | Macros | | |

TABLE 1.2

Quick Access toolbar

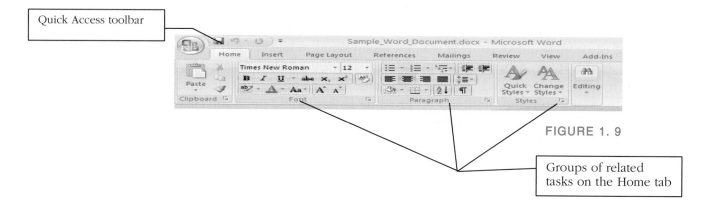

FIGURE 1. 9

Groups of related tasks on the Home tab

2. **Click the Home tab. In the Font group, click the arrow to the right of the Font button to display the list of available fonts. Move the pointer anywhere in the document and click.** When you have a menu open and want to close it, clicking outside the menu will turn it off. You can also press the [Esc] key to close a menu.

The most commonly used commands display on the Ribbon. The **Home tab** is present in all Office applications and contains most formatting commands such as Font and Font Size and basic editing commands such as Cut, Copy and Paste. The **Office button** contains the most common commands related to files such as Open, Print, and Save. The **Quick Access toolbar** is at the top of the Ribbon next to the Office button and can be customized to add buttons of your choice. Other tabs—known as **contextual tabs**—display on the Ribbon when they are needed. Some commands are common to all programs, such as Font, Header & Footer. Other commands are specific to a particular application, such as the Currency Style, Percent Style, and Comma Style formatting buttons found in Excel. Some buttons have similar purposes, but different names depending on the application.

1. **In the upper left corner of the Ribbon, point to the Office button.** When you point to the button, a ScreenTip displays as shown in Figure 1.10. This is the name of the button and the command that is executed when you click the button. A *ScreenTip* is a box that displays information about—or the name of—a screen element.

Quick Access toolbar

Office button

A ScreenTip displays when you point to the button

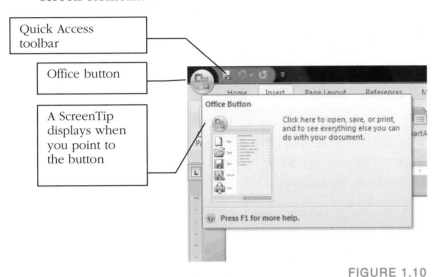

FIGURE 1.10

2. **To the right of the Office button, on the Quick Access toolbar click the Customize Quick Access Toolbar button to display the Customize Quick Access Toolbar menu. Here you can select commands to add to the Quick Access toolbar. At the bottom of the list, click Minimize the Ribbon to hide the icons and show a more traditional Office menu bar.** When you click on a tab, the Ribbon elements display for that tab.

3. **On the Quick Access toolbar, click the Customize Quick Access Toolbar button and then click to remove the check mark next to Minimize the Ribbon. Display the list again and click to place a check mark next to Open.** The Open icon displays on the Quick Access Toolbar. Print Preview and Spelling are two common tasks in Microsoft Office applications that can also be placed on the Quick Access toolbar. **Note**: The Quick Print option is a direct print command to the printer without the ability to choose printing options or a printer other than the default printer.

4. On the Home tab, in the Paragraph group, point to the Dialog Box Launcher as shown in Figure 1.11.

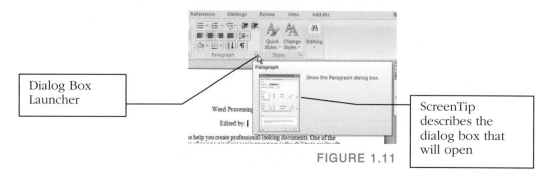

Dialog Box Launcher

ScreenTip describes the dialog box that will open

FIGURE 1.11

5. Click the Dialog Box Launcher to open the Paragraph dialog box to display a full set of options. Click the Close button to close the dialog box. Click the Page Layout tab, and in the Page Setup group, click the Margins button. A gallery displays the margin options that are available as shown Figure 1.12.

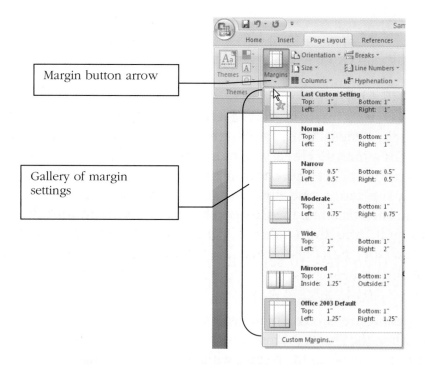

Margin button arrow

Gallery of margin settings

FIGURE 1.12

6. At the bottom of the Margins gallery , click Custom Margins to display the Page Setup dialog box as shown in Figure 1.13. Under Orientation, click Landscape and then click OK. Notice how your paper adjusts on the screen to sideways orientation. Click the Undo button on the Quick Access toolbar to return the orientation to portrait.

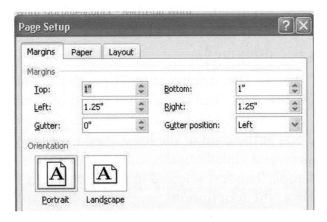

FIGURE 1.13

7. **Click the Insert tab, and in the Illustrations group click Shapes.** The Shapes gallery displays as shown in Figure 1.14.

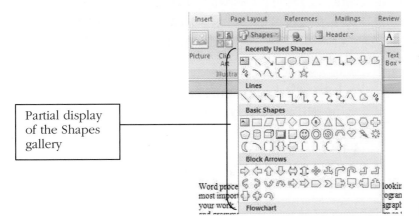

Partial display of the Shapes gallery

FIGURE 1.14

8. **Under Basic Shapes, click a shape in the first two rows. The gallery closes and the mouse pointer displays a + on the document. In an open space on the document, click and hold the left mouse button and drag downwards to the right and then release the button.** The shape is inserted into the document. The Drawing Tools Format tab displays on the Ribbon. This is a *contextual tab*, one that is hidden until an object is selected. The Drawing Tools Format tab provides more options for formatting the shape.

9. **Move the mouse pointer over the colors in the Shape Styles group to see the fill color change. On the Format tab in the Shadow Effects group click the Shadow Effects button and point to various effects to see the preview in the document. On the Format tab in the 3-D Effects group click the 3-D Effects button and point to various effects to see the preview in the document. Note:** The ability to display changes on the screen—known as *Live Preview*—is a new feature of Microsoft Office 2007.

10. Click in the document to close the Drawing Tools Format tab. Click to select the object you inserted, and then press the ⌗Delete⌗ key to remove it from the document.

11. Select the first line in the document. Click the Home tab, and in the Font group click the Font button arrow. A list of available fonts displays (see Figure 1.15). The fonts above the line are the default fonts used in Word 2007. The vertical scroll box at the right of the list is used to quickly scroll the entire list of fonts, which is arranged alphabetically. Each font displays in its own style so you can see how it will look. The text selected in your document will preview the font style as you scroll over the font options.

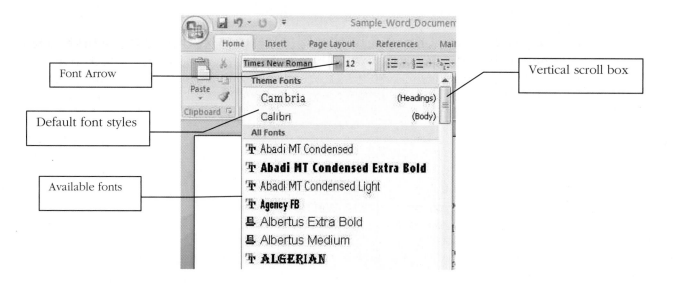

FIGURE 1.15

12. Click the Font arrow to close the list.

13. Click the Office button, point to Print, and then in the list on the right-click Quick Print. When you click the button, the active file is sent to the printer that is connected to your computer. Most toolbar buttons provide a one-click method to execute a command. Leave the document open for the next lesson.

# LESSON 4: Switching Between Open Applications and Files

Windows applications allow multiple files and multiple applications to be open at the same time. This enables you to share information between files and across applications. For example, you may have information in a document that you need for a slide presentation, or you may have a chart in Excel that you want to include in a Word document.

In this lesson you will learn how to switch between open documents and between applications.

## To Open Multiple Files in an Application and Switch Between the Files

1. **With Word open on your screen, on the Quick Access Toolbar, click the Open button.** (This assumes you put the open icon on the Quick Access Toolbar in an earlier lesson. If not, click the Office button and then click Open.) The Open dialog box displays. The folder where you saved your most recent file should be displayed.

2. **Navigate to the location where the files for this chapter are located; click the *CE_0102* file to select it, and then click Open.** On the taskbar, notice that two taskbar buttons display for the open Word files as shown in Figure 1.16, indicating that two documents are open. Depending on the resolution on your screen, and the number of buttons already displayed on the taskbar, each file may have its own taskbar button.

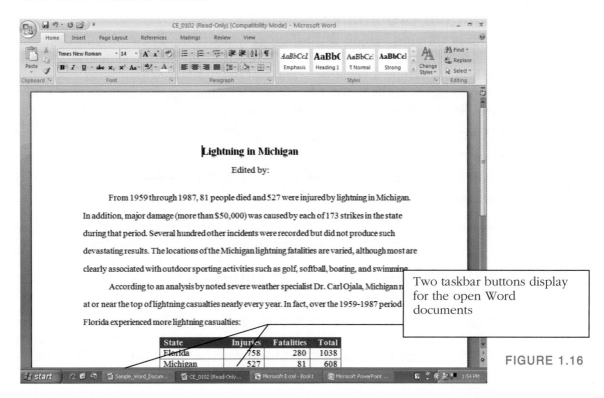

Two taskbar buttons display for the open Word documents

FIGURE 1.16

### FILE EXTENSIONS

*File extensions* are letters that follow the file name and identify the type of software that was used to create the file. If file extensions are turned on, the Word files will display .doc in the title bar following the file name for files created using earlier versions of Word. For Word 2007 the file extension is .docx. This is a feature that is controlled in Windows. To display file extensions, using Windows XP open My Computer, click the Tools menu and select Folder Options. Click the View tab and then clear the check mark from *Hide extensions for known file types*. Click OK and the extension *.doc* or *.docx* will display on the title bar the next time you open a file. Close My Computer.

3. **Click the Office button.** The Recent Documents menu is a list of the recently open Word documents. Both *Sample_Word_Document* and the *CE_0102* document are listed. Several documents can be opened at one time, and you can use the Window menu to move between the open files.

4. **From the displayed list click** *Sample_Word_Document* **to display it on your screen.** The *CE_0102* document remains open, but the *Sample_Word_Document* becomes the active document.

5. **Click the** *Microsoft Office Word – CE_0102.doc* **button on the taskbar.** The *CE_0102* document returns to your screen. You can use the Window menu or the taskbar to switch between open files.

## If you have problems...

Depending on your screen resolution or your computer configuration , you may see one taskbar button that displays *Word (2)* and includes an arrow on the right of the button. When several files and applications are open at the same time, the operating system collects the files from the same application on one button. The number on the application button indicates the number of files that are currently open for that application. Click the application button to display a list of the open files, and then click the file you want to make active.

Just as you switched between open files within an application, you can also switch between files that are open in different applications.

### To Open Multiple Files in an Application and To Switch Between Applications

1. **Click the Microsoft Office Excel button on the taskbar.** The Excel window displays a blank worksheet.

2. **Click the Open button on the Quick Access toolbar and navigate to the folder where the student files for this project are stored; click the** *CE_0103* **file and then click the Open button.** An Excel worksheet displays on your screen name as shown in Figure 1.17. If the file extensions are turned on, *.xls* displays following the file name. If this was a 2007 file, the file extension would be *.xlsx*

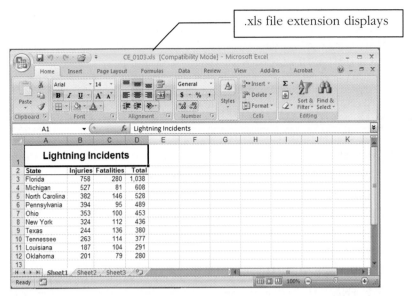

.xls file extension displays

FIGURE 1.17

3. Click the Microsoft Office PowerPoint button on the taskbar; click the Office button and then click Open.

4. Navigate to the folder where the student files for this project are stored, click the *CE_0104* file, and then click the Open button. A PowerPoint presentation file displays on your screen. If file extensions are on, then *.ppt* displays following the file name in the title bar. If this presentation had been saved, or created, as a 2007 file the extension would be *.pptx.*

## If you have problems...
If you get an error message that you cannot open the file, click OK to acknowledge the message. Display the Open dialog box again, navigate to the folder where the student files are store and select the file named *CE_104_2007*, and then click Open.

5. Click the *Microsoft Office Word – CE_0102* button on the taskbar to display the Word file.

6. Click the *Microsoft Office Excel – CE_0103* button on the taskbar to display the Excel file. In this manner, you can switch between open files in different applications. This creates a more efficient work environment, where you can share information between files and between applications. Later in this unit you will learn how to copy information from one type of file to another.

## TO EXTEND YOUR KNOWLEDGE...

### ANOTHER WAY TO SWITCH BETWEEN FILES AND APPLICATIONS
You can also move between open files by holding down Alt and then pressing Tab. A box displays a button for each open file. The currently selected file displays with a blue border. If you release Alt, the currently selected file will become the active file on your screen. While holding down Alt, each time you press Tab the selection moves to the next button displayed and the application and file name displays under

the buttons. If you have multiple windows open, you can hold down Alt and tap Esc to switch between active windows.

## LESSON 5: Changing Views and Magnification

In each application, there are several ways to look at or view a file. Different views emphasize different aspects of the file and give you several options for working with your document. For example, in PowerPoint you can look at one slide at a time so you can focus on the content of that particular slide, or you can look at several slides at once to get an overview of the flow of the information in the presentation. Each application offers a Print Preview view that enables you to see how the file looks before it is printed. In Word, you can view your file in a Print Layout view, which shows the margins around the edge of each page, or you can use the Normal view, which does not display the margins, resulting in more text on the screen. Each view has its own purpose, and which view you choose to use is often a matter of personal preference.

You can also change the magnification of the file that is displayed on your screen. A change in magnification results in more or less of the available data being displayed. This feature is particularly useful in Excel where a worksheet is often wider than the width of one screen. How much of the file displays on the screen is also a function of the screen resolution that is set on your monitor. In general, the higher the resolution, the more you will be able to see of the file.

In this lesson you will look at different views of the Word document, and change the magnification.

### To Change Views and Magnification

1. **On the taskbar, click the *Microsoft Office Word – CE_0102* button. On the Ribbon click the View tab.**

2. **On the View tab, in the Document Views group, confirm that Print Layout is selected.** The Print Layout view displays the top, bottom, right, and left margins. This gives you a better indication of the position of the text on the page, as shown in Figure 1.18.

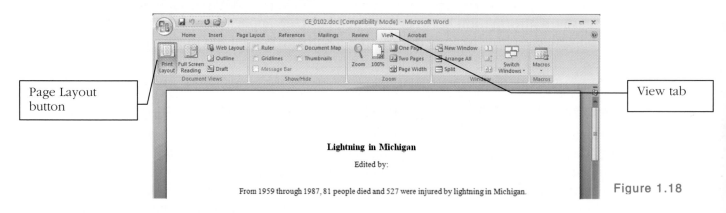

Figure 1.18

Using Productivity Software

3. **On the View tab in the Document Views group click Draft.** The document is displayed in a draft format. Some of the elements will not show. This format is used for quick and easy editing of the document.

4. **In the Document Views group click Outline.** The document is displayed in outline format and an Outlining contextual tab displays on the Ribbon. **On the Outlining tab in the Close group click Close Outline View to return to Page Layout view.** The view buttons are also available at the bottom of the document window as shown in Figure 1.19.

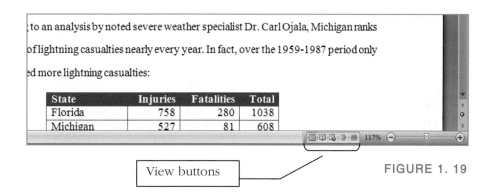

to an analysis by noted severe weather specialist Dr. Carl Ojala, Michigan ranks

of lightning casualties nearly every year. In fact, over the 1959-1987 period only

ed more lightning casualties:

| State | Injuries | Fatalities | Total |
|-------|----------|------------|-------|
| Florida | 758 | 280 | 1038 |
| Michigan | 527 | 81 | 608 |

117%

View buttons

FIGURE 1. 19

5. **In the right end of the Status bar, click and drag the slider in the Zoom Level box to approximately 75%, as shown in Figure 1.20.** The Zoom buttons control the magnification of the document that is displayed. It does not affect printing; it only changes the screen display. The Zoom percent that displays in the box is determined, in part, by your screen resolution.

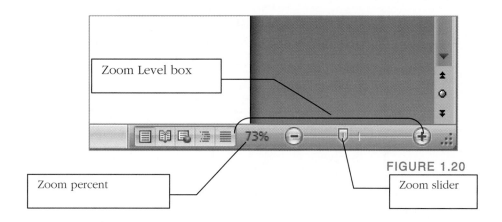

Zoom Level box

73%

FIGURE 1.20

Zoom percent

Zoom slider

6. **Right-click the Status bar at the bottom of the MS Word 2007 Window.** The Customize Status Bar menu displays a list of available options as shown in Figure 1.21. Check marks indicate selected items. These options can be placed on the status bar for easy reference. Notice that word count is checked by default to track the number of words in your document. Overtype/Insert mode will be discussed later.

Check marks indicate selected options

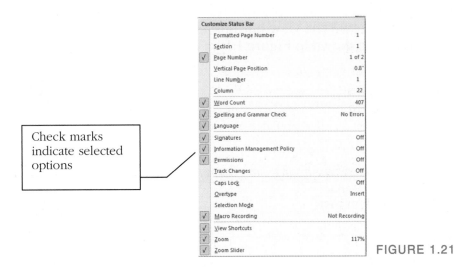

FIGURE 1.21

7. **Click in the document to close the Status menu. On the View tab in the Document Views group click Full Screen Reading.** This view displays the text in a reading layout format and adjusts the spacing of text on the page to increase readability. Your screen might display the document on two pages as shown in Figure 1.22, or as one page.

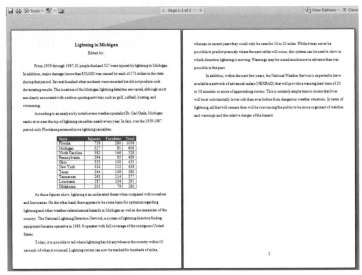

FIGURE 1.22

Using Productivity Software

8. Click the View Options button on the Reading Layout toolbar, and review the options available for the Reading Layout View. Click Close to return to the Page Layout view.

### USING THE BUTTONS ON THE TITLE BAR

The buttons at the right end of the title bar are used to minimize, maximize/restore down, or close an application. Display Office menu, and then click Close to close an open document rather than the application window

## LESSON 6: Closing Files and Closing Applications

You can close a file while leaving an application open, enabling you to work on other files within that application. In many applications, you can have several files open at once, such as the two Word files that are currently open. When you are done working, click the Office button and then click Close to close a file, or click the Exit button in the lower right corner of the Office menu to close an application. You can also click the Close button located at the right end of the title bar. If you close an application while a file is open, and have not saved the file since your last change, a message will display, prompting you to save your changes.

### To Close Files and Close Applications

1. **Click the Microsoft Office Excel button on the taskbar to display the Excel file, and then click the Close Window button at the right end of the tab bar.** The Excel file closes while the application remains open on your screen. You can open another file and continue working in Excel, or you can close the application

2. **Click the Close button at the right end of the title bar.** The Excel application closes and the Word window redisplays on your screen.

3. **Click the Microsoft Office PowerPoint button on the taskbar. Click the Office button and then in the lower right corner of the list click the Exit PowerPoint button.** The PowerPoint application closes along with the PowerPoint file. Because you had not made any changes to the file, it closes without any further prompts. If you had made an unsaved change, a message box would display to ask if you want to save the changes. The Word file should now be displayed on your screen.

4. **Click the Office button and then click Close. If prompted, save changes to the document open.** The current Word file closes and the second file displays on your screen.

5. **Use either method you practiced to close the second Word file, but leave the Word application open.**

## LESSON 7: Using Help

Learning how to use any application software is a building process, just like learning how to dance, play the piano, speak a foreign language, or do math. You start out by learning the basics and then build on those skills by adding more complex tasks. As with most learning processes, you will remember those things that you use every day and find it harder to remember the skills or techniques that are used less frequently. Even after you have acquired a level of proficiency in using a software program, you need to know what to do when you get stuck or when you cannot remember how to do a particular task.

Fortunately, software programs provide a wide variety of Help resources to assist you. The following is a list of available Help resources and the order in which they should be utilized:

- Offline help within software (such as operating systems and applications)
- Printed documentation
- Online help available via the Internet (including a software manufacturer's online Help Web sites and product user-group Web sites)
- Help desk for your organization
- Help desk of the product manufacturer

To become a self-sufficient user of software, first search the Help program installed with the software. It you cannot find what you need in the installed Help program, look for printed documentation from the software manufacturer, or find a good reference book on the software. Most software vendors also offer additional help on their Web sites. Many companies, such as Microsoft, let you connect to their Web site directly from within the software by use of a special online Help button. After you have connected to a Web-based Help site, you can search by topic or keyword(s). Often there is a user group that posts questions and responses from other users or from software specialists. These discussions provide a wealth of information about little-known problems or peculiarities of the software. Sometimes software user groups are part of the software vendor's Web site; other times they exist independently of the vendor. By searching the Internet you can usually locate a user group related to the software you are using.

If you are not able to find the help you need on your own, then you can seek help from a professional. Many companies provide computer support to staff members through a company help desk. Help desk personnel are trained to respond to questions about the software they support and to assist you in using the software. Oftentimes, problems you might encounter are unique to the particular installation protocol that is used at your company, or may be related to network, hardware, or other non-software-related issues. It is always good to check with your help desk to see if the problem you are experiencing has been reported as a problem by others. Most companies have a policy that requires you to use their help desk before turning to the software vendor's help desk. As a last resort, most software vendors provide a help desk to support their software. Before you call the software vendor's help desk, you want to make sure you have tried to find the answer yourself. Some software vendors charge for this service, or you have to pay a membership fee to be able to call to get help.

In this lesson you will learn how to use the installed Help program that is part of the Microsoft Office applications. Several methods can be used to start the Help process. You will also use the web-based Microsoft Office keywords Online Help function.

## To Get Help Using the *Type a Question* for Help Box

1. **With Word still open on your screen, double-click the Help button on the right end of the tab bar, click in the Search box and type** How do I find Clip Art? The Help program will look for keywords in your question and try to come up with answers. You do not have to add a question mark to your question. You do not need to phrase your search as a question; you could simply type *find clip art* (see Figure 1.23).

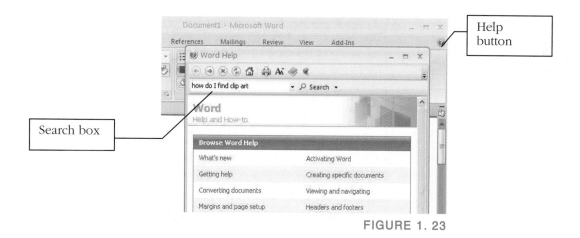

FIGURE 1. 23

2. **Press** (Enter⏎). The Search Results task pane opens and displays a list of results. The ones that are most likely to provide the information you need are nearest the top of the list (see Figure 1.24). Text that appears in blue indicates a **hyperlink**. When you click a hyperlink it provides additional information or a definition. When the pointer is positioned on a hyperlink it is shaped like a hand. If you are connected to the Internet, the list that will display will be longer and in a different order.

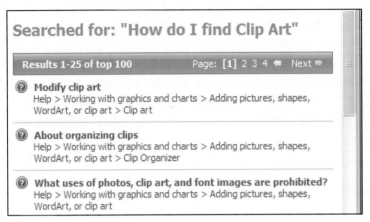

FIGURE 1.24

3. **Scroll down the list and click the *Find a clip* topic.** You might have to scroll the vertical bar to locate the topic. A Word Help window opens and provides details on the requested topic (see Figure 1.25).

FIGURE 1.25

4. **Click the Maximize button on the right end of the Help window title bar, and then click the first hyperlink text *Search for a clip*.** The Help topic expands and displays additional information.

5. **At the top of the screen, on the right side, click Show All** to display the rest of the hyperlinked text. A scroll bar displays so you can scroll the Help topic. Colored text indicates definitions of the preceding text which is shown in blue,

such as *natural language searches*. Items shown in bold text are names of on-screen elements. At the top of the window is a printer button. When clicked, this button prints the topic displayed. Notice that the Show All button now reads Hide All, as shown in Figure 1.26, which would hide all of the hyperlinked text in the Help window.

Print button

Hide All button

FIGURE 1.26

6. **Leave Word Help open for the next lesson.**

Most Help programs also include a table of contents, which is an organized listing of topics, similar to a table of contents in a book

### To Get Help Using the *Type a Question* for Help Box

1. **With the Help box open, on the toolbar click the Home button.** The Word Help home page displays. Here you can begin a new search by selecting one of the search topics. You could also begin a new search by typing a new topic in the *Search* box.

2. **On the toolbar, click the Show Table of Contents button, if necessary, to display the table of contents pane. Scroll through the Table of Contents.** Most Help programs offer a table of contents that organizes topics into logical categories. If you need to locate specific information, it is usually easier to use a keyword search.

3. **In the Table of Contents pane, click on any Book icon next to Creating specific documents.** A list of topics found under this category is displayed as shown in Figure 1.27. A book icon indicates a group that, when clicked, will display another list. A question mark icon indicates a Help topic.

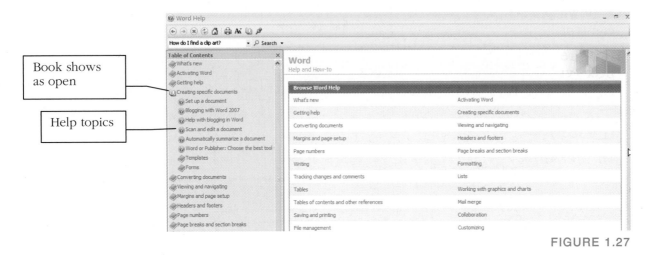

FIGURE 1.27

4. **At the top of the list in the Table of Contents pane, click** *What's new.* A list of new features displays.

5. **Click** *Top Tips for Word 2007* **and read the displayed information.**

6. **Click the Back arrow to return to the list of features.** Leave Word Help open and continue to the next part of this lesson.

There will be times when you can't find an answer using the installed application Help program. When this happens, most application software companies offer online help that enables you to search through a larger and more up-to-date Help resource. It also enables you to look at a particular topic and see what kinds of problems and questions other people have been having. The Microsoft online Help program is a dynamic environment that changes frequently. Chances are excellent that the screens you see will not match the ones shown in the figures in this lesson. The procedures for obtaining help may even be different. Use this lesson as a guideline for how online Help works, and then follow the on-screen instructions once you are online.

1. **Make sure you are connected to the Internet. Scroll to the bottom of the Word Help and How-to pane on the right. Under More on Office Online, click the Downloads link.** Your Web browser opens and displays the Microsoft Office Online Downloads Page. The panel on the left several categories of downloads. There is a search box at the top of the screen and a box where you can type keywords.

2. **On the Office Online Web page click the Clip Art tab. In the Clip art box type** Ideas **and click the Search button.** The Search page displays with related categories similar to those you found in the Word 2007 search results.

3. **On the title bar click the Close button. Open the Word Help window, if necessary.**

4. **In the More on Office Online area, click Training.** Your Web browser opens and displays the Microsoft Office Online training page.

5. **In the Training box, type** Microsoft Office PowerPoint **and click the Search button.** A list of PowerPoint-related training topics is displayed.

6. **Click** *Up to speed with PowerPoint 2007.* An overview of the topic is presented to let you know what you will learn in this training tutorial. If your computer speakers are turned on, you will hear an overview of the training topic you selected.

7. **Click the Close button to close your browser. Click the Close button in Help. Close Word.**

## USING ONLINE HELP FROM THE SEARCH TASK PANE

If you are connected to the Internet when you use the Help program within an application, the Help function will automatically connect to the related Microsoft Web site for that application. Online topics related to your question or keywords will be included in the Search Results task pane.

## SUMMARY

In this project, you were introduced to some key concepts about using application software. Each application has a work area where you enter text, numbers, or graphics. The work area varies between applications but the tools used to interface with the software have the same elements such title bars, scroll bars, ribbons, tabs, and groupings. Once you learn how to manipulate the Ribbon in one application, you can use the same techniques in other Office applications.

You practiced opening and closing applications and opening and closing files within Word, Excel, and PowerPoint. You moved between files and applications by use of the taskbar. You added your name to a Word document, saved the file with a new name and then printed the file..

Finally, you learned how to access the Help program that comes with software applications. You used the *Type a question for help* box, the table of contents, and online Help for the Word program.

You can extend your learning by reviewing concepts and terms, and by practicing variations of skills presented in the lessons. Use the following table as a guide to the numbered questions and exercises in the end-of-project learning opportunities.

## KEY TERMS

| | | |
|---|---|---|
| active cell | icon | ScreenTip |
| application software | insertion point | scroll box |
| application window | keyboard shortcut | slide |
| cell | Live Preview | status bar |
| cell address | Maximize button | tabs |
| contextual tabs | Microsoft Office | taskbar |
| dialog box | Microsoft Office Excel | title bar |
| Dialog Box Launcher | Microsoft Office PowerPoint | vertical scroll bar |
| document | Microsoft Office Word | views |
| file extensions | Minimize button | Windows-based |
| graphical user interface (GUI) | mouse pointer | work area |
| Help | Office button | worksheet |
| Home tab | Programs | |
| horizontal scroll bar | Quick Access toolbar | |
| hyperlink | Ribbon | |

## SCREEN ID

Label each element of the screen shown in Figure 1.28.

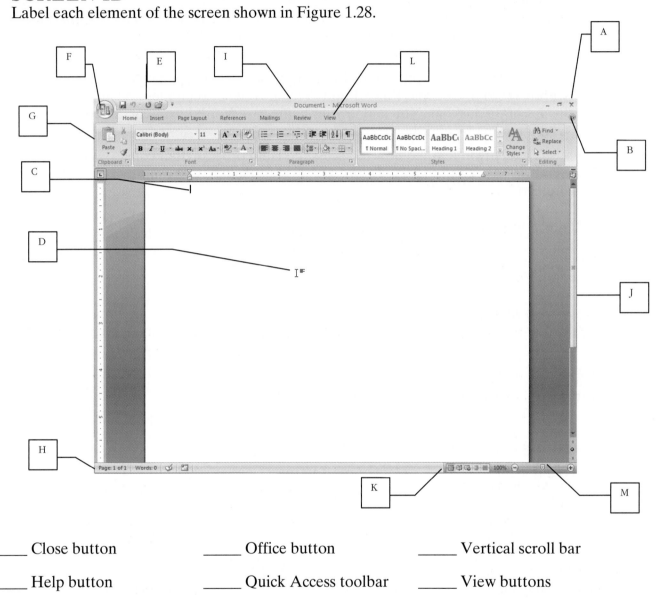

_____ Close button     _____ Office button     _____ Vertical scroll bar

_____ Help button     _____ Quick Access toolbar     _____ View buttons

_____ Insertion point     _____ Ribbon     _____ View tab

_____ Mouse pointer     _____ Status bar     _____ Zoom bar

_____ Title Bar

# MULTIPLE CHOICE

## Circle the letter of the correct answer for each of the following.

1. The work area in a PowerPoint application is a _____. [L1]
a. document
b. slide
c. worksheet
d. template

2. To open a file, click the _____ and chose Open. [L3]
a. Home tab
b. Quick Access button
c. Office button
d. View button

3. Computer programs that are used to accomplish a specific set of tasks are known as _____. [L1]
a. operating software
b. windows
c. universal programs
d. application software

4. Commands that are used to tell the computer what you want to do are commonly found on _____ and _____. [L3]
a. title bar and status bar
b. Ribbon and Office button
c. taskbar and scroll bars
d. templates and task pane

5. When you save a file the Save As dialog box is used to _____. [L2]
a. place the file in a specific storage location on your computer
b. give the file a name
c. save the file
d. all of the above

6. To move between open files or in applications you can _____. [L4]
a. click the Window menu and then click the file you want to display
b. click the file on the taskbar
c. click the file on the task pane
d. a and b only

7. To change the magnification of a document on your screen drag the _____ slider to the percent magnification you want to use. [L5]
a. Customize
b. View
c. Zoom
d. Preview

8. When you close a file, _____. [L6]
a. the application closes automatically
b. the file is saved automatically
c. if you have made changes to the file, a prompt displays asking if you want to save the changes
d. you must save your file before it can be closed.

9. If you want to learn how to create a table in Word, the first method you should try is to _____. [L7]
a. use the installed Help program
b. call your mom
c. call the software manufacturer
d. call your company's help desk

10. Which of the following would be the quickest method to use if you needed help saving a file? [L7]
a. Crabby Lady Help Desk
b. Keyword search
c. User Help Desk
d. Table of contents

# DISCUSSION

1. What are the advantages of using a suite of software such as Microsoft Office? What are the disadvantages? Have you used other software programs? How do the user interfaces for those programs compare to Microsoft Office? If you need to buy new software, how important is a familiar user interface in your purchase decision? [L1—L4]

2. In this project, you examined the Ribbon for commands that Microsoft applications have in common. Examine the three application windows for Word, Excel, and PowerPoint again and identify some differences. What buttons or commands exist in Word that you do not find in Excel or PowerPoint, and vice versa? [L1, L3, L5]

3. Explain the difference between clicking the Save button on the Quick Access toolbar and choosing Save As from the File menu. Provide examples of situations when you would use each command. [L1, L3]

## SKILL DRILL

Skill Drill exercises reinforce project skills. Each skill reinforced is the same, or nearly the same, as a skill presented in the project. Detailed instructions are provided in a step-by-step format. All of these exercises can be completed with Microsoft Office XP or later versions. Instructions throughout the exercises are based on the Windows XP operating system, running Microsoft Office 2007.

### 1. Opening and Saving a Microsoft Office Excel File

In this project you practiced opening a Word file and saving it with a new name in a new folder. You have been told that this works the same in other applications so you decide to practice with the Excel file.

1. Click the **Start** button on the taskbar and then click **Microsoft Office Excel.**

2. Click the Office button and then click Open. Click the drive where the student files for this textbook are stored.

3. Navigate to the folder where the student files for this project are stored. Double-click file *CE_0103* to open it. The Excel file displays on your screen.

4. Click the Office button and then click **Save As.** Navigate to the drive where your CE_Project1 folder is stored; double-click it to open it.

5. Click in the **File name** box. Press [Ctrl] + [A] to select the file name. Type Lightning_Incidents and then click **Save.**

6. Click in cell **A14**, type your name, and then press [Enter↵].

7. Drag the **Zoom** slider to approximately 200%. The magnification of the worksheet is changed. Depending on your screen resolution some of the data may no longer be visible on your screen. Close the file and close Excel, or continue to the next exercise.

## 2. Using the Office Menu and Key Tip Shortcuts

You want to learn more about using the Ribbon to understand how the tabs are organized and how they work. You are particularly interested in using keyboard shortcuts. You have worked with Word the most, so you decide to try using another application.

1.  Open **Excel** and then press the ⎇Alt key and observe the Key Tips that display next to the tabs and next to each command on the Quick Access toolbar. These can be used to access commands, rather than click with the mouse.

2.  Type Ⓗ and observe the Key Tips that display next to each of the commands on the Home tab. Press ⎋Esc once to remove the Key Tips from the Home tab.

3.  With the tab Key Tips still displayed, type Ⓜ to display the Formula tab and the Key Tips that can be used to access the commands on this tab. In this manner you can navigate though the tabs and the commands. This is especially useful if your mouse stops functioning, or if you prefer using the keyboard. Press ⎋Esc twice to remove the Key Tips.

4.  Press ⎇Alt + Ⓕ to display the Office menu.

5.  Examine the commands that are listed. Notice that Key Tips display next to the commands on the Office menu. You can type a letter from the display and activate the command.

6.  Type the letter Ⓞ and the open dialog box opens as the Office menu closes.

7.  Close the Open dialog box.

8.  Click the **Office** button and then at the bottom of the menu click the Excel Options button. The Excel Option dialog box displays. Review the options for Popular.

9.  In the left panel, click **Save**. Observe the Default file location to see where files are stored by default.

10. In the left panel click **Customize**. This customizes the Quick Access toolbar above the Ribbon in the application window. Review the options available. Some are common operations done in Excel such as Open, Save, Undo, and Redo. However there may be other commands that you do more often.

11. Click the Cancel button to close the Excel Options dialog box without making any changes.Click the Office Button and then click Close. Click No if asked to save Book1. Close Excel.


## 3. Using the Ribbon

You have learned that the Ribbon displays in each of the three applications you have used. You want to learn more about the Ribbon tabs and button commands and how to use them effectively. You decide you will use PowerPoint to explore the tabs.

1.  Start **PowerPoint**.

2.  Click the **Design tab**. In the **Themes group,** point to one of the theme buttons. Wait a moment to see the  effect displayed on the title slide. Move your mouse pointer over other themes and after a brief delay the slide will change to display the new theme.

3. Click the **Home tab** and in the **Drawing group** click the **Shapes** button. Select any of the objects in the gallery. Place the cross hairs anywhere in the title slide and click and drag the mouse down and to the right to draw the object.

4. Click the **Insert tab**, and in the **Text group** click **Text Box**. Click anywhere on the title slide. Notice that the ribbon displays the Home tab because this is where you select font and font size. Type your name in the text box.

5. Click the **Animations tab** and in the **Transition to This Slide group** point to one of the buttons on the left side of this group to display a slide transition for the slide on your screen. Move your mouse pointer over the buttons in the Transistions to This Slide group and observe the effect on the appearance of the slide. Click one of the options.

6. On the **Animation tab** in the **Transition to This Slide group** click the arrow on the right side of the **Transition Speed** box, and then click **Slow**. Point to the transition buttons again to see how the transition has slowed.

7. Click the **View tab**, and in the **Color/Grayscale group**, click **Grayscale**. Observe that the slide shows what it will look like if printed on a non-color printer. On the **Grayscale tab** in the **Close group** click **Back to Color View**.

8. Click the **Slide Show tab** and in the **Set Up group** click **Set Up Slide Show**. Observe the options available in the Set Up Show dialog box. Click the **Close** button without making any changes.

9. Click the **Review tab** and in the **Proofing group** click **Spelling**. Click **OK** to close the spelling completed box.

10. Click the **Office** button and then click **PowerPoint Options**. Scroll through the options for PowerPoint. Notice that some of the options are similar to those you viewed earlier. Others are specific to PowerPoint. Click **OK** to close the PowerPoint Options box without making changes. Close PowerPoint without saving the file.

## 4. Using Microsoft Help to Learn More About Switching Between Files and Changing View

You have practiced switching between files and applications using the taskbar. You would like to understand this process better and decide to use the Microsoft Help program. You elect to use PowerPoint Help and compare it with the same question using Excel Help. You would also like to see what the view options are for Excel and for PowerPoint.

1. Make sure you are connected to the Internet so you can use Microsoft Online Help.

2. Open **PowerPoint**; click the **Help** button on the right-end of the tab bar (or press F1). Type Switching between open files, and then press Enter ↵.

3. Click the topic **Show or hide multiple program buttons on the Windows Taskbar**.

4. Click the **Show All** button and read the instructions.

5. Open **Excel** and click the Help button. Type Switching between open files, and then press Enter ↵.

6. Click the topic **Show or hide multiple program buttons on the Windows Taskbar** (the same choice you chose in PowerPoint) and compare the responses.

They are identical because this function is controlled by the Windows Operating System, not the application program.

7. Follow the instructions to Show a single program button by using the taskbar properties.

8. On the taskbar, click the **Microsoft Office PowerPoint** button; press $\boxed{\text{F1}}$ The Microsoft Office PowerPoint Help task pane opens and a Search box displays.

9. Type PowerPoint Views in the Search box and then press $\boxed{\text{Enter} \leftarrow}$.

10. Locate and click the topic **Understanding the main views in PowerPoint 2007** and read the Help window. Identify the areas on your PowerPoint window that are discussed in the Help topic for changing views in PowerPoint.

11. Click the **Microsoft Office Excel** button on the taskbar, click the Help button .

12. Type **Excel Views** in the Search box, and then press $\boxed{\text{Enter} \leftarrow}$.

13. Locate and click the Help topic **Create, apply, or delete a custom view**. By comparing the description in Help you can see that views in Word, PowerPoint, and Excel are very different.

14. Close Help and then close both applications.

## CHALLENGE

Challenge exercises expand on or are somewhat related to skills presented in the lessons. Each exercise provides a brief narrative introduction, followed by instructions in a numbered-step format that are not as detailed as those in the Skill Drill section.

Each exercise is independent of the others, so you may complete the exercises in any order.

### 1. Creating Folders for Other Applications

You created a folder for the first project in the Common Elements Unit that you used to save your file. You can perform some operating system functions, like creating folders, from within an application's Save As dialog box. You decide you want to practice this process by creating folders for the other applications.

1. Start **PowerPoint** and from the Office menu click **Save**.

2. In the Save As dialog box, click the **Save in** arrow and navigate to the drive and *CE_Project1* folder you created in this lesson. Do not open the folder.

3. Click the **New Folder** button on the Save As dialog box toolbar, type PP_Project1 in the New Folder dialog box, and then press $\boxed{\text{Enter} \leftarrow}$. The Save in box displays the new folder name—PP_Project1—indicating that it is the active folder. You need to go up one level to continue making new folders at the same structural level as the CE_Project1 folder.

4. Click the **Up One Level** button on the dialog box toolbar.

5. Click New Folder, type PP_Project2, and then press [Enter←]; click **Up One Level**.

6. Repeat this process to create another folder named PP_Project3; close the Save As dialog box.

7. Open **Excel** and display the Save As dialog box. Click the **Save in** arrow and navigate to the drive and *CE_Project1* folder. Do not open the folder. You should see your three PowerPoint folders displayed. You can create folders from within any application's Save As dialog box and then open the folders regardless of the application you are using, because creating folders is part of the Windows Operating System file management program.

8. Using the same procedure, create three folders for your Excel files labeled EX_Project1, EX_Project2, and EX_Project3.

9. Repeat this process and create three folders, similarly labeled, for your Word projects. (Hint: You do not have to open Word to do this.)

10. Close the Save As dialog box and then close Excel and any other open applications

## 2. Recovering Microsoft Office Files

You do not have an uninterruptible power supply on your computer system, but you do have a surge protector. If you lose power, you want to know how you would recover your files after the power returns.

1. Open any of the three applications you have been using and begin using Help. Type: recover files and then press [Enter←].

2. Select the topic **Automatically save and recover Office files,** read the contents. You decide you want to see how often your computer is set to recover files, but the Help Window does not tell you where to find this feature.

3. Type: autorecover in the Search box, and then press [Enter←].

4. Click the topic that tells you how to change the interval for automatic file recovery.

5. Read the Help topic and then follow the directions to see how your computer is set. If you are using a computer lab or other public computer, do not change this setting. If you are working on your own computer, change the setting to a time of your choice. Keep in mind that Auto Recover is not a substitute for saving your files on a regular basis.

6. Close the dialog box and close the application.

## 3. Changing Zoom Settings in Different Views

The Zoom slider can be used in any application to increase the magnification of the work area on your screen. The choices vary, however, depending on the application and the view that is currently selected.

1. Open **Word** and open the file *CE_0102* from the student folder for this textbook.

2. Click the **Web Layout** button from the status bar, if necessary, and then on the **View tab**, in the **Zoom group**, click **Zoom** and select **100%**.

3. Change to **Print Layout** view. Notice that the Zoom percentage changed.

4. On the **View tab**, click **Zoom** and then click **Two Pages**. The document displays on two pages. Here you can get a good view of the layout of the document. Depending on your screen size and resolution you may not be able to read the content.

5. In the **Zoom group** click **One Page**. The document returns to a larger magnification. In the Web Layout view you cannot view the document on two pages.

6. Return to **Print Layout** view and and in the Zoom dialog box change the **Zoom** to Whole Page. This displays one whole page at a time, rather than two. Again, it may be too small to read the content.

7. Change the Zoom to Text Width. This view and magnification gives you a larger view of the document content, while still displaying the top and bottom margins.

8. Move the pointer to the top edge of the document until you see two facing arrows and the ScreenTip displays *Double-click Hide (Show) White Space*. Double-click to hide the white space. The white space in the top margin is hidden.

9. Double-click the top edge of the document again to show the white space. Close the file, and close Word.

## DISCOVERY ZONE

Discovery Zone exercises require advanced knowledge of topics presented in *Essentials* lessons, application of skills from multiple lessons, or self-directed learning of new skills. Each exercise is independent of the others, so you may complete the exercises in any order.

### 1. Using Help to Find the Software Version

This book was written using Microsoft Office 2007, which has some features that may not be available in earlier versions, such as the Reading Layout view in Word. If you use different computers, it is important to know the version of the software that is installed on the computer. In some software, there may be some file compatibility issues between different versions.

You will check the version of the software that is installed on the computers at your school's computer lab and on another computer of your choice, at home, at work, or in another public computer lab.

Open **Word.** Display the Office menu and at the bottom of the list click the **Word Options** button. Click **Resources, About Microsoft Office Word 2007,** and then click **About.** The version is usually the year and it displays following the name of the software near the top of the dialog box, for example in Microsoft Office Word 2007—12 is the version number. This displays as a decimal number in parentheses, and indicates the last update that has been downloaded to your software. Write down the year and version of the application that displays in the dialog box. Repeat this process for Excel and PowerPoint. Using another computer at home, school, work, or elsewhere, repeat this process and see if the installed Microsoft Office software is the same in both locations.

Using online Help, see if you can determine what differences there may be between the versions of the software.

## 2. Using the View Button in the Save As and Open Dialog Boxes

The Save As and Open dialog boxes display the files on your computer, or on various types of portable storage devices, such as a USB drive or CD-RW. Both of these dialog boxes include a Views button that allows you to control the way the files are displayed. In this Discovery Zone exercise you will practice changing the Views in the Save As and Open dialog boxes. To do this you will work in Word, but it works the same in the other Microsoft Office Applications.

Open **Word**. Display the Office menu and then click **Open** . Navigate to the student folder for this project. You will see two files displayed— CE_0101 and CE_0102. At the bottom of the dialog box, in the Files of type box, it displays Microsoft Office Word Documents. Click the Files of type arrow and then click **All Files**. Now the Excel file—CE_0103—and PowerPoint file— CE_0104—are also listed. Notice the difference in the application icons.

Depending on how your computer is set, the names of the files may display or they may display as icons. On the dialog box toolbar, click the Views arrow and then click Details. Additional information is displayed about each file: Name, Size, Type, and Date Modified display as column headings. This information can help you sort and search your files

# UNIT 2: USING PRODUCTIVITY SOFTWARE

## Microsoft Office 2007

## Project 2: Creating and Editing Files

### LESSON 1

**Creating and Saving Files**

| | |
|---|---|
| 2-1.2.6.1 | 2-1.2.6.3 |
| 2-1.2.6.2 | 2-1.3.2.1 |

### LESSON 2

**Opening Files Using Windows Explorer**

| | | |
|---|---|---|
| 2-1.2.7.1 | 2-1.2.10.1 | 2-1.2.10.3 |
| 2-1.2.7.3 | 2-1.2.10.2 | 2-1.2.10.4 |

### LESSON 3

**Navigating Around Open Files**

| | |
|---|---|
| 2-1.3.1.1 | 2-1.3.2.1 |

### LESSON 4

**Performing Simple Editing**

| | | |
|---|---|---|
| 2-1.3.2.1 | 2-1.3.7.1 | 2-2.1.19.1 |
| 2-1.3.3.1 | 2-1.3.7.2 | 2-2.1.19.2 |
| 2-1.3.3.2 | | |

### LESSON 5

**Navigating Longer Documents**

| | | |
|---|---|---|
| 2-1.3.1.3 | 2-1.3.5.1 | 2-1.3.6.1 |

### LESSON 6

**Inserting, Selecting, Deleting and Replacing Text**

| | | |
|---|---|---|
| 2-1.3.2.1 | 2-1.3.3.4 | 2-2.1.2.1 |

### LESSON 7

**Copying Text**

| | |
|---|---|
| 2-1.3.3.6 | 2-1.3.3.7 |

### LESSON 8

**Moving Text and Using the Undo and Redo Commands**

| | |
|---|---|
| 2-1.3.3.3 | 2-1.3.3.7 |
| 2-1.3.3.5 | 2-1.3.4.1 |

# PROJECT 2

# CREATING AND EDITING FILES

IN THIS PROJECT, YOU LEARN HOW TO:

- **Create and Save Files**
- **Open Files Using Windows Explorer**
- **Navigate Around Open Files**
- **Perform Simple Editing**
- **Navigate Longer Documents**
- **Insert, Select, Delete, and Replace Text**
- **Copy Text**
- **Move Text and Use the Undo and Redo Commands**

# WHY WOULD I DO THIS?

Files can be created by starting with a blank work area, an existing document, or a *template*—a predefined spreadsheet, document, or presentation that is provided with the software package. Which method you use depends on the type of document or file you need to create, and whether a file or template already exists that can be used as a basis for creating another file.

Part of the writing process is to review and edit your work, both as you write, and as a proofing function after the file is complete. With a computer file it is quick and easy to make changes, whether it is to fix typographical errors or to delete, change, or add more information to the file. Before you can make changes to a file you need to know how to move around the work area. The vertical scroll bar moves the work area up and down on your screen, while the horizontal scroll bar moves it left and right. Keys on the keyboard move the insertion point up or down on the screen, or you can use the mouse to reposition the insertion point—the location in your file where you begin to type. To correct errors as you type use ←Bksp and Delete, or use the Spelling & Grammar tool to help correct spelling and grammar mistakes. As you review your document you may need to insert, delete, or replace text, numbers, or graphics. To do this you first select the text that will be affected. You can also copy data and paste it in another location, or move data from one location to another. All of these basic tools help you produce professional and accurate results, whether you are working with a Microsoft Office Word document, a Microsoft Office Excel spreadsheet, or a Microsoft Office PowerPoint presentation.

In this project, you learn how to create files using a template and using a blank document. You open an existing file and practice some simple navigation and editing techniques. Then you open a longer document and practice additional navigation techniques. You learn how to select text using various methods, and then insert, delete, and replace text. Finally, you learn how to copy text and place it in another location in the same file and in a new file, as well as how to move text from one location to another within the same file.

# VISUAL SUMMARY

In this project you practice creating and editing documents, and moving around in a window. First you are introduced to templates when you create and complete an Expense Report using an Excel template. Then you start with a blank work area in Word and create a document. You practice navigating a window using scroll bars and buttons and learn how to select parts of your document so you can make editing changes. You practice editing techniques on two Word documents where you copy, move, and alter text. The results of your work will look similar to the documents shown in Figure 2.1.

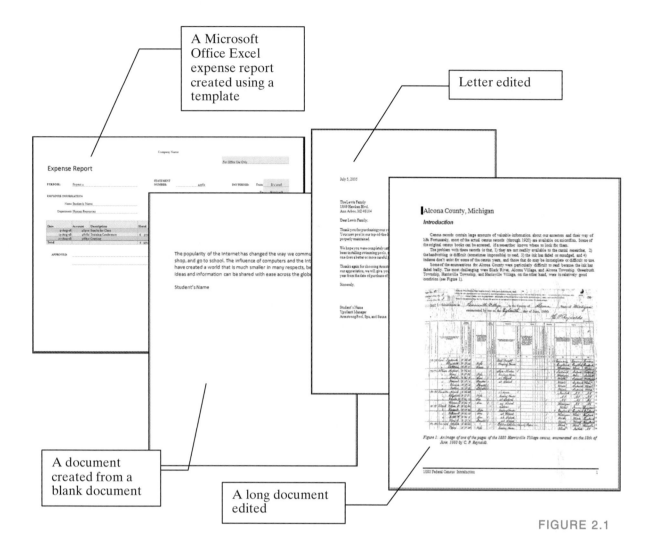

FIGURE 2.1

## LESSON 1: Creating and Saving Files

A template provides a preformatted pattern which has been designed for a specific purpose, such as a thank you letter or a letterhead style available in Word, or an expense report or balance sheet available in Excel. Some templates use a wizard to gather information for the file, others present you with a formatted work area in which you enter data and then save the file. You can also create a file from scratch by using a blank document, spreadsheet, or presentation. In this lesson, you will create an expense report using an Excel template, and then you will create a simple Word document starting with a blank document.

All of these exercises can be completed with Microsoft Office 2007. Instructions throughout the lessons are based on the Windows XP operating system, running Microsoft Office 2007. Your screen may differ slightly from the figures shown, even if you are running Office 2007, or if you are running the Vista operating system. Files will be saved in 2003 compatibility format.

1. **Start Excel 2007.** A blank worksheet displays.

2. **Click the Office button, and notice that on the right side of the menu a list of recently opened files display (if any). Click** *New*. The New Workbook dialog box displays. In the left panel, two categories— *Templates and Microsoft Office Online*—display lists of templates that are available for use. When you create and save an Excel file, you save a *workbook*. By default a new workbook consists of three worksheets, but it can contain dozens of worksheets or a single worksheet. The number of worksheets that can be in a single workbook is limited only by the capacity of your computer's memory.

3. **In the left pane, under the** *Templates* **category, click** *Installed Templates*. The installed templates display in the middle of the dialog box.

4. **Click the displayed Templates and look at the preview in the right side of the dialog box.** Several template options are available, as shown in Figure 2.2. The templates that display on your screen may not match the figure exactly.

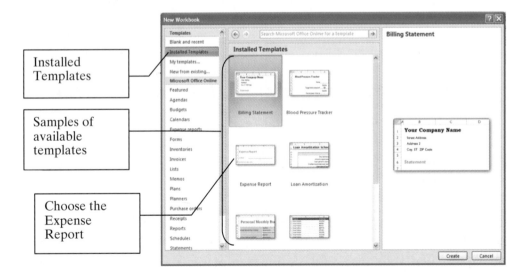

FIGURE 2.2

5. **Click** *Expense Report*, **which selects the template, and then click Create.** The *Expense Report* workbook opens.

6. **On the Status bar, click the Normal View button. Change the zoom if necessary so that you can see the entire width of the worksheet on the screen, and then examine the form.** This template is used to report expenses. Notice that there is a bordered rectangle in the space next to *Purpose*. This is the active cell—the position at which you will begin entering data. Column labels are included in the body of the form—Date, Description, Lodging, and so forth. See Figure 2.3

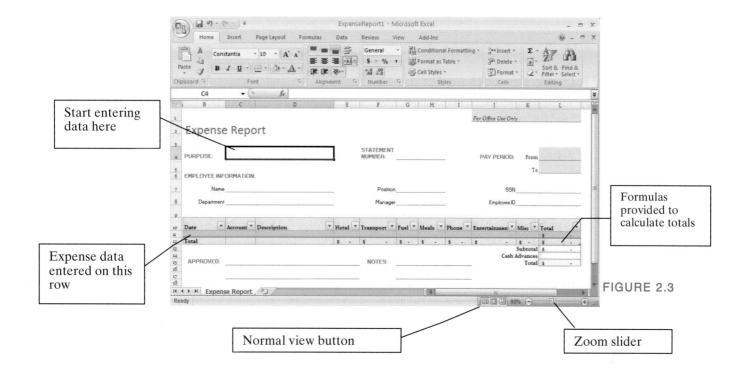

Start entering data here

Expense data entered on this row

Formulas provided to calculate totals

FIGURE 2.3

Normal view button

Zoom slider

7. **In the Purpose cell type:** `Project 2` **and press** `Tab`. The purpose of the report is entered. A *field* is a predefined area where a specific type of data is entered. You can use the tab key to move from one field to the next as you enter data into the expense report form.

8. **Press Tab two times to move to the Statement Number and then type:** `43562` **and Press** `Tab` **four times to move to the** *From* **field.** A ScreenTip may display with a message that informs you about the type of information that belongs in this field.

9. **Type:** `8/1/05` **and press** `Enter ↵` **to move to the** *SSN* **(Social Security Number) field; type** `500-77-9999` **(Do not enter your own Social Security Number).**

10. **Use Tab, keyboard arrow keys, or click the appropriate cell in the form to select the cells. Refer to the table below and fill in the remaining information.**

| To | 8/30/05 |
| --- | --- |
| Name | Type your name in the cell |
| Position | Trainer |
| Department | Human Resources |
| Manager | Mark Pryor |
| Employee ID | 123456 |

The top part of the expense report is complete

11. Click the cell under *Date*. Enter the information that follows. As you enter information for the expenses, not all categories or fields will be completed for each entry. Press ⊡Tab as necessary to skip empty fields. When you reach the end of a row, press ⊡Tab to advance to the next row.

| Date | Account | Description | Hotel | Transport | Fuel | Meals | Phone | Entertain | Misc |
|---|---|---|---|---|---|---|---|---|---|
| 8/9/2005 | 48900 | Snacks for class | | | | 54.80 | | | |
| 8/15/2005 | 46780 | Training Conference | 375.00 | 369.00 | | 295.30 | | | |
| 8/27/2005 | 56850 | Copying | | | | | | | 78.95 |

Notice that as you enter monetary values, the shaded areas at the right of each row and end of the columns display the totals of the columns or rows. Compare your screen with Figure 2.4.

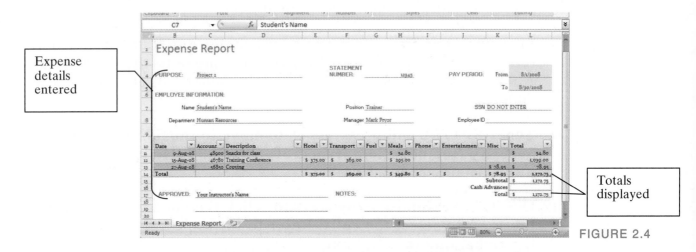

FIGURE 2.4

Expense details entered

Totals displayed

12. Click next to *Approved*, type your Instructor's name, and then press ⊡Enter↵.

13. Click the Save button on the Quick Access toolbar. Because this file has not been saved previously, the Save As dialog box opens.

14. Click the Save in arrow and navigate to the drive and folder where you are saving your files.

15. Click the Create New Folder button on the Save As toolbar, type: `CE_Project2` and then click OK. A new folder is created for the second Common Elements project and it becomes the active folder displayed in the Save as box.

16. Click the File name box, press ⌈Ctrl⌋ + ⌈A⌋ to select the default name, type Expense Report. Click the Save as type arrow and click Excel 97-2003 Workbook. Click Save. The student files used in this unit are saved using the Office 2003 file types to make them compatible with the Office 2003 version of this textbook.

17. In the Compatibility Checker dialog box, click Continue. The file is saved in your folder and the name displays in the Excel title bar.

18. Click the Office button, point to Print, and then from the list on the right click Quick Print; close the file and close Excel

---

## TO EXTEND YOUR KNOWLEDGE . . .

### SAVING A TEMPLATE

Templates can be used over and over again. When you saved the completed expense report, it created a separate file for the completed workbook. The original template is preserved and can be used again. You can also create your own templates and save them in the templates folder for use by yourself or others. Templates are handy for repetitive tasks, and where uniformity of presentation is important, such as completing standard forms and reports.

---

### To Create and Save a File Using a Blank Document

1. **Start Word 2007.** A blank document displays on your screen. In many applications, as soon as the application opens, there is a blank work area displayed where you can begin to type

2. **Type the following. As you type, do not press ⌈Enter ↵⌋, rather let the text wrap from one line to the next.**

The popularity of the Internet has changed the way we communicate, find information, shop, and go to school. The influence of computers and the Internet have created a world that is much smaller in many respects, because ideas and information can be shared with ease across the globe.

*Wordwrap* is a feature of many computer programs where the text that is entered moves to the right until it reaches the right margin. When a line runs out of room for the next word it moves that word to the next line, continuing across each line and down the page, wrapping text from one line to the next.

---

## If you have problems...

If you make mistakes while you are typing, you may see some red or green wavy under-lines to indicate a spelling (red) or grammatical (green) or (blue) contextual error. These topics will be covered a little later. For now, ignore any errors. You will learn how to correct simple typing errors in the next lesson.

3. **Press [Enter ⏎] twice and then type your name.** When you press [Enter ⏎] you end a paragraph and move to the next empty line. When you press [Enter ⏎] twice, a blank line displays between the paragraphs creating a visual separation (see Figure 2.5).

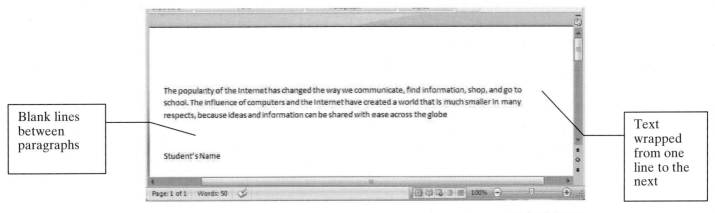

Blank lines between paragraphs

The popularity of the Internet has changed the way we communicate, find information, shop, and go to school. The influence of computers and the Internet have created a world that is much smaller in many respects, because ideas and information can be shared with ease across the globe

Student's Name

Text wrapped from one line to the next

Page: 1 of 1    Words: 50        100%

FIGURE 2.5

4. **Click Save on the Quick Access toolbar.** The Save As dialog box displays. The first line of the text you type displays as the default file name in the File name box. The file name is highlighted—the background is blue and the text is white—which means the text is selected and anything you type at this point will replace the selected text.

5. **Type: Internet Popularity to replace the default name in the File name box. Note:** If the title is not selected, press [Ctrl] + [A], and then enter the file name

6. **Click the Save as type arrow and click Word 97-2003 Document. The file will be compatible with older versions of Word. If necessary, click the Save in arrow and navigate to the *CE_Project2* folder where you are saving your files for this project; click the Save button in the Save As dialog box.** The file is saved and the new file name displays on the title bar.

7. **From the Office menu point to Print, and then click Quick Print to print your document if required by your instructor. Close the file and close Word.**

### USING A DESKTOP SHORTCUT

When you save a file, you can save a link to it on your desktop, known as a *desktop shortcut*. The actual file, however, is stored in a folder on your hard drive. A shortcut is not the same as the file—it is merely a quick way to open the file. Saving a file to the desktop creates a shortcut icon on your desktop, which you can click to open the file and its related application. If you want to send the file to someone else by attaching it to an e-mail, you must use the actual file, not the desktop shortcut. The person receiving your e-mail cannot use a shortcut to open a file that is stored on your computer. To locate a file that you have saved to the desktop, open the file and then choose File, Save As. Click the Save in arrow and examine the displayed list to see the folder and the path to that folder on your hard drive. In most cases, it will be stored in the Documents and Settings folder, or My Documents folder, depending on the version of the operating system and application software you are using.

# LESSON 2: Opening Files Using Windows Explorer

You can use several methods to open files. In addition to opening files from within an application as you did in Project 1, files may also be opened through a file manager program such as Windows Explorer. When you double-click the file name, it will open the application that was used to create the file and then open the file on your screen. It is also possible to create a shortcut to a file on your desktop and use that shortcut to open the file.

In this lesson, you open a file from within Windows Explorer.

### To Open a File Using Windows Explorer

1. **Right-click the Start menu and then click Explore on the displayed list.** The Start Menu explorer window opens and displays the drives and folders that are available on your computer. Because every computer is different, the drives that are available on your computer may vary from those shown in Figure 2.6. The way the file and folders are displayed may also differ depending on the operating system that is installed on your machine and the view set for your computer.

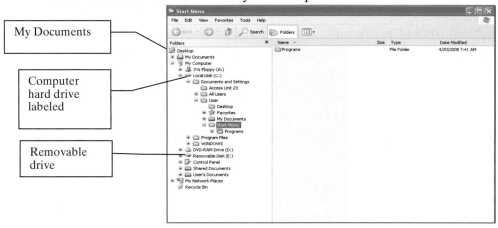

FIGURE 2. 6

2. **Click the drive where the files for this textbook are located and navigate to the folder where the student files for this Project 2 are stored.**

3. **Locate the file *CE_0201* and then double-click the file name.** Word opens and the file displays on the screen as shown in Figure 2.7.

FIGURE 2.7

4. **Display the Office menu, click Save As to open the Save As dialog box; type `Lewis Letter` in the File name box.**

5. **Navigate to the folder where you are storing the files for this chapter, and then click the Save button.** Leave the *Lewis Letter* document open to continue to the next lesson. Because this document was originally created in Word 2003, it opens in compatibility mode and the default choice of file type is Word 97-2003 when you save it.

---

## TO EXTEND YOUR KNOWLEDGE . . .

### RESOLVING COMMON PROBLEMS RELATED TO WORKING WITH FILES

Data files consist of characters and numbers that are encoded for storage according to a standard such as ASCII, EBCDIC, UTF-8, UTF-16, UTF-32, or XML. In addition to these characters and numbers, each application might include proprietary codes for special functions such as formatting. The codes used by Word may be different from those used by a competing application program such as WordPerfect. To make matters more complex, a company may add features to its application program that include codes that are not recognized by older versions of the same program. If you have trouble opening a file it may be due to one of the following problems:

♦ The operating system does not know what application program to open to read the proprietary codes in the file.

♦ The file was created by a newer version of the application program and it contains codes that the older version does not recognize.

♦ The file was saved using an encoding standard or language that is not recognized by the application.

- The file is corrupted, which means that something happened to the storage medium and some of the binary numbers have been erased or are not readable.

## PROBLEMS RELATED TO FILE EXTENSIONS

The Windows operating system tries to minimize some of these problems by using a period followed by a three or four-character code called a file extension at the end of each file name to identify which application is associated with the file. When you install a new application program, it registers the codes for its files with Windows. If you double-click a file name, Windows looks for the file extension. If the file has an extension, Windows looks into its list of extensions to see what application is associated with that extension, starts the application, and then instructs the application to open the file. For example, Word 97-2003 uses .doc to identify its files and Word 2007 uses .docx. This system works pretty well, but it can break down if one of the following situations occurs.

- The file is renamed without the file extension. Windows can be set to hide the file extensions for known file types or it can be set to display them all. If a file name is displayed with its file extension, the extension must be included when you rename the file. For example, if the file *MySummerVacation*.doc were renamed *WhatIdidThisSummer,* without the file extension, it would not be associated with Word. However, if the files are displayed with the extensions hidden you could rename *MySummerVacation* as *WhatIdidThisSummer* and Windows would automatically add the extension for you without showing it. To avoid this type of problem, always include the file extension when you rename a file if the original file has its extension displayed.

- A new application has expropriated the file extension. Some files may be used by several different application programs. Two examples are Web page files that end with *.htm* and graphics files that end with *.jpg.* If you install a new application that uses either of these types of files, it may ask if you want it to be the default program for these types of files or it may simply go ahead and change the Windows file that associates extensions with applications. From that moment onward, when you double-click one of these files the new application program will start instead of the previous program. To avoid this problem, do not agree to allow a program to be your default application for a certain type of file when you install it or change the Windows file that associates the applications and file extensions.

- The file extension is missing or misspelled. If you are in an application program and choose to open a file, the list of files displayed in the dialog box is usually restricted to the list of files that have the associated file extension. If the file you are looking for does not have the right extension it will not be listed unless you change the *Files of type* option to *All Files.* If that is the only problem, you can still open the file.

## THE FILE CONTAINS PROPRIETARY CODES THAT THE APPLICATION DOES NOT RECOGNIZE

Application programs include special features that distinguish them from their competitors. To keep ahead of the competition and to continue to improve the performance of their products, companies add new features and release new versions of their application programs every few years. Unfortunately, these features use codes that are not recognized by the competition or by earlier versions of the same program. Most companies make sure that new versions of their application programs can open files that were created by older versions even though they may not use the obsolete codes. These applications are backwardly compatible. If you have a file that contains proprietary codes that your application program cannot read, you may be able to open the file using one of the following techniques:

♦ Install a conversion program. Run your application's installation program again and look for optional conversion programs that translate the proprietary codes of other brands of application program into ones your program can read. This method would not work for applications that came out after your installation disc was created.

♦ Download and install a conversion program from the company's Web site. Many companies make conversion programs available that will translate the newer codes into codes that may be read by older versions of the software. These programs may be downloaded from the company's Web site and installed on your computer. Microsoft offers a compatibility pack to use with older versions of Word that work with Word 2007 files.

## THE FILE WAS SAVED WITH A DIFFERENT ENCODING STANDARD OR LANGUAGE

Most computers use the ASCII standard but a popular line of IBM mainframe computers use the EBCDIC encoding standard. A conversion program must be used to translate the basic binary numbers from one to the other before applications can open them. Older file encoding standards such as ASCII and EBCDIC work well with the Latin alphabet that is used in English and several other European languages. Newer encoding standards such as UTF-8, UTF-16, and UTF-32 are backwardly compatible with ASCII but contain codes for almost all the characters in the world's written languages. If a file was saved with one of the newer UTF standards, it may contain characters in a language that is not recognized by your application. You may be able to solve this problem by running the installation program for your application and looking for optional language add-ins that will recognize these characters.

## THE FILE IS CORRUPTED

There are special programs that can read damaged files and recover some of the data if you get this error message. Prevention is much easier than curing the problem. If your file is stored on magnetic media, some of its data may be lost if the media is exposed to magnetic fields. Keep your floppy disks away from magnets, including the strong magnets in music speakers. The data on optical discs may be lost if the plastic disc is scratched or it may be hard to read if the surface is dirty. When using flash drives, be sure to close all files and the programs that they used before removing the drive. Click the storage device icon in the tray area of the task bar to ensure that it is safe to remove the drive before doing so.

Protect the discs during storage and clean them carefully if they are dirty. In some cases your application program can repair some of the damage and open the file but if you get this error message it is usually too late to recover the data easily. Make backup copies of important files to reduce the risk of loss.

# LESSON 3: Navigating Around Open Files

Before you can edit a file, you need to know how to move around in the work area, referred to as *scrolling*. Scrolling can be done with keys on your keyboard, or with your mouse. To move the insertion point from one location to another use the ***arrow keys*** to move up, down, left, or right in the text, or use the ***navigation keys***— PgUp, PgDn, Home, or End. With the mouse, use the horizontal and vertical scrollbars to move the contents of the window horizontally and vertically on the screen so you can see a different part of your work area. Using the scrollbars, however, does not move the insertion point. Therefore, you would need to click the mouse to move the insertion point before you could make changes to the file. The horizontal scrollbar moves the work area left and right and is used infrequently in Word documents. It is used more frequently in Excel worksheets where it is common for information to be in an area of the worksheet that is not visible on the screen. The vertical scrollbar is used frequently as a quick way to move up and down through a file. Each scrollbar contains a scroll box—a small box or rectangle in the scrollbar between the arrows at each end of the scrollbar. Drag the scroll box up or down in the vertical scrollbar to move to another part of the file. Knowing how to effectively move around in a file enables you to enter and edit text much faster.

In this lesson, you practice using the horizontal scrollbar to move the document up and down on your screen, and the arrow keys to move left and right one character at a time, up and down one line at a time, and up and down one page at a time.

## To Navigate Around Open Files

1. **With the *Lewis Letter* document open, click the arrow at the bottom of the vertical scrollbar several times to scroll down the letter.** Notice that the screen scrolls up one line at a time. If you click the arrow and hold down the mouse button, your screen scrolls rapidly. Also notice that the insertion point does not move; rather, you can see a different portion of the letter on your screen (see Figure 2.8).

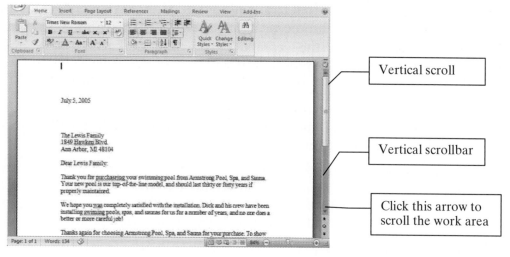

FIGURE 2.8

2. **Position the pointer on the blank line between the first and second full paragraphs in the body of the letter and click once with the left mouse button.** The insertion point is moved to the beginning of the blank line. The mouse pointer appears as an I-beam on the document and as a white arrow when on the toolbars or at the left edge of a document.

3. **Press ⬆ on your keyboard four times.** Notice that the insertion point is now just below the salutation. Using an arrow key changes the location of the insertion point in your document. If needed, the text showing on your screen will scroll up or down so that you can continue to see the insertion point.

4. **Press PgDn to move down one screen.** Notice that the insertion point moved and only the end of the document displays. The PgDn and PgUp keys move the view one screen at a time and also move the insertion point (see Figure 2.9).

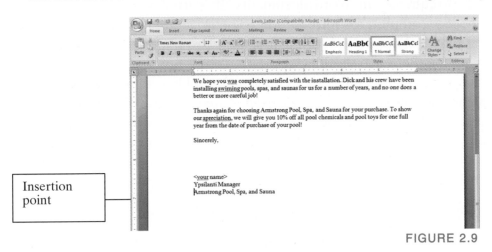

Insertion
point

FIGURE 2.9

## If you have problems...

The settings on your computer may change the way the above steps work. For example, the Zoom setting and View selection could make the first full paragraph only two lines long. In that case, only press ⬆ three times. Also, if your monitor is set for very high resolution, or if you have a very large monitor, you may see the entire document on the screen. This would make the PgDn and PgUp steps unnecessary.

5. **Press PgUp to move up one screen.** Notice that the top of the letter displays and the insertion point moves back near the top of the letter. This feature is very helpful for editing longer documents.

6. **Drag the scroll box on the vertical scrollbar down until you see the end of the letter.** This action moves the text displayed on your screen, but it does not change the location of the insertion point. You need to click at the point where you want to begin to type to move the insertion point to that location.

7. **Hold down Ctrl and press Home. Release both keys.** This combination of keys, or keyboard shortcut, can be used to move back to the top of the file. Notice that the insertion point also returns to the top.

8. Leave the *Lewis Letter* document open to continue to the next lesson.

---

TO EXTEND YOUR KNOWLEDGE . . .

### MORE INFORMATION ABOUT THE SCROLL BOX

Each scrollbar includes a scroll box, which lets you know your location in the document—it is at the top of the scrollbar when you are at the beginning of the document and at the bottom of the scrollbar when you are at the end of the document. When the document is displayed in Print Layout view, the size of the scroll box, relative to the length of the scrollbar, gives you an idea of how the currently visible portion of the document compares in size to the document as a whole (a small box) represents a large document). One of the quickest ways to move through a large document is to drag the scroll box up or down. As you scroll through a multipage document, a ScreenTip next to the scroll box displays the current page number.

### OTHER WAYS TO NAVIGATE IN A FILE

In this lesson, you practiced just a few of the navigation techniques used to move around in a file. The following table lists common keyboard shortcuts. Most of these work in a similar fashion in most Microsoft Office applications.

| TO MOVE | PRESS THE FOLLOWING KEYS |
|---|---|
| To the beginning of a file | Ctrl + Home |
| To the end of a file | Ctrl + End |
| To the beginning of a line | Home |
| To the end of a line | End |
| To the beginning of the previous word | Ctrl + ← |
| To the beginning of the next word | Ctrl + → |
| To the beginning of the current word (if insertion point is in the middle of a word) | Ctrl + ← |
| To the beginning of the next word (if the insertion point is in the middle of a word | Ctrl + → |
| To the beginning of the current paragraph | Ctrl + ↑ |
| To the beginning of the next paragraph | Ctrl + ↓ |
| Up one screen | PgUp |
| Down one screen | PgDn |

Table 2.1

# LESSON 4: Performing Simple Editing

When you create a document, you may make typographical errors that you want to correct immediately. You may also want to change a document when you proofread it. You can correct errors in several ways. The two most common methods are to use the [←Bksp] and [Delete] keys. The [←Bksp] key removes—clears—text to the left of the insertion point, and the [Delete] key removes text to the right of the insertion point. When you type new text, it is inserted at the insertion point and the existing text is moved to the right. You can also overtype text to replace it as you type. You can do this by pressing the [Insert] key to turn on or off the overtype mode in most applications.

Spelling and grammatical errors in a document tend to reduce the credibility and effectiveness of the message. Most Microsoft Office programs have two ways to check spelling and grammar. The first method reviews the completed document and gives you flexibility in checking and correcting. The second lets you correct spelling and grammar as you type.

In this lesson you learn to edit text using the [←Bksp] and [Delete] keys, as well as how to use a shortcut menu to quickly correct spelling and grammatical errors. Finally, you use the overtype feature to replace existing text.

## To Edit Text Using the Backspace and Delete Keys

1. With the *Lewis Letter* open, scroll the document so that you can see the last paragraph before *Sincerely*; click just to the left of the word *toys*, in the second sentence of the last full paragraph.

2. Press [←Bksp] once. Notice that the insertion point moves to the left and removes the space between the words *pool* and *toys*.

3. Press [←Bksp] four more times. The word *pool* is removed from the sentence, as shown in Figure 2.10

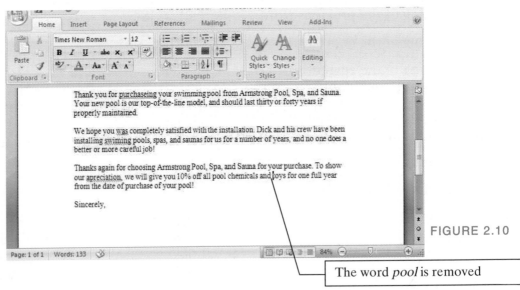

FIGURE 2.10

The word *pool* is removed

4. Press [Delete] once. The letter t of toys, located just to the right of the insertion point, is removed. However, note that the insertion point did not move.

5. **Press** Delete **three more times.** The entire word *toys* is now removed. Do not remove the space to the right of the word.

6. **Type: accessories at the insertion point.** The new word is inserted at the insertion point and the existing text is moved to the right as shown in Figure 2.11.

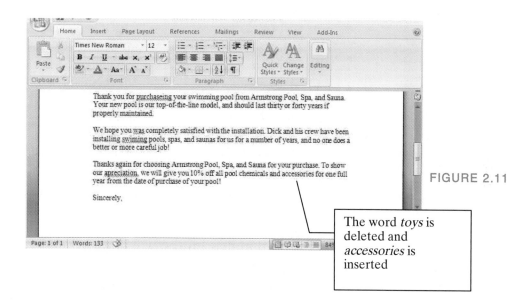

FIGURE 2.11

The word *toys* is deleted and *accessories* is inserted

Word includes a spelling and grammar option that marks suspected errors in your document. When you type a word that is not in the Microsoft Office dictionary, the spelling option highlights the word with a red wavy line. The dictionary includes thousands of words, including many proper names. Just because a word is not found does not necessarily mean it is misspelled—it could be a proper noun, a technical term, or an unusual word. Green wavy lines indicate a grammatical error. In addition, Microsoft Office 2007 can be set to check for contextual errors such as using the word there instead of when their to mean possession. These are flagged with blue underlines. The spelling option is included with Microsoft Office applications and works in a similar manner in each application. In Word and PowerPoint, the spelling option is set, by default, to mark errors as you type. In Excel, the program does not identify errors until you select the option—it does not mark errors as you type. All of the programs use the same dictionary.

## To Correct Spelling and Grammar Errors

1. **Locate the misspelled word** *purchasing* **in the first paragraph; move the pointer onto the word and click with the right mouse button.** A shortcut menu opens. The top section of the shortcut menu contains a suggestion for replacing the misspelled word as shown in Figure 2.12. The suggestion is correct.

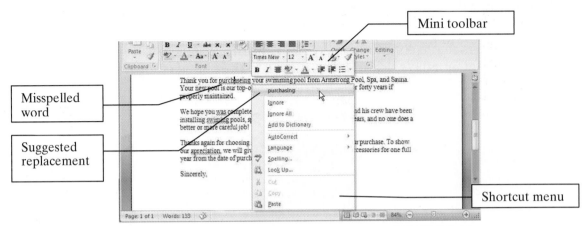

Mini toolbar

Misspelled word

Suggested replacement

Shortcut menu

FIGURE 2.12

2. **Move the pointer over the word** *purchasing* **in the shortcut menu.** The suggested replacement word is selected.

3. **Click the selected word with the left mouse button.** The misspelled word is replaced with the correctly spelled word and the shortcut menu closes. (**Note**: Throughout this book, when you are asked to click the mouse button it will refer to the left mouse button. The right mouse button will be specified.)

4. **Scroll up if necessary and right-click the word** *Hawken* **in the address line.** The shortcut menu opens with suggestions, but none of the suggestions are correct. This is an example of a word that is not in the dictionary, and is still correct.

5. **Select Ignore All from the menu.** You have instructed the program to ignore all further occurrences of this word in this document. The red wavy line disappears. A purple dotted underline may display under the address. This is known as a ***recognizer***, which means that the program recognizes this as an address. Recognizers flag names, dates, and addresses as items that you may want to add to your Outlook program—the Microsoft Office personal management program.

6. **Right-click the word** *was* **in the second full paragraph.** This word is underlined with a green wavy line, which indicates a grammatical error. There is a disagreement between the subject—*you*—and the verb—*was*.

## If you have problems:

If a wavy green line does not appear, click the Office button, and then at the bottom of the menu click, Word Options. In the panel on the left click Proofing and then click the check box next to *Check grammar with spelling* and click OK.

7. **Click** *were* **in the shortcut menu to select it.** This action replaces *was* in the sentence and the green wavy underline is removed.

8. **Continue to right-click on the next two errors that are marked with a red wavy line and select the correct spelling for each word from each**

**shortcut menu.** The spelling and grammatical errors identified by the Spelling and Grammar program are corrected as shown in Figure 2.13.

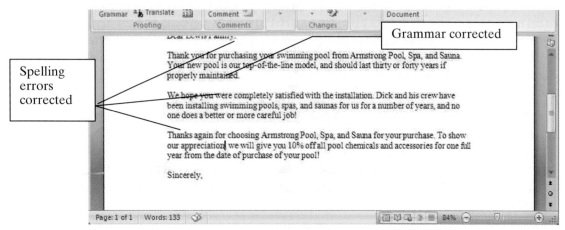

FIGURE 2.13

9. **Click the Save button from the Quick Access toolbar; continue to the next lesson with the *Lewis Letter* document open.**

---

TO EXTEND YOUR KNOWLEDGE . . .

### ADDING WORDS TO THE PROGRAM'S DICTIONARY

When the program identifies a word that is not in the dictionary, you have the option of adding the word to the dictionary on the computer you are using. This is very useful if you are in an industry that uses a lot of words that are not already in the dictionary, such as medical terms. Be very careful! If you add a misspelled word to the dictionary, it accepts the word in the future without warning. In general, do not add words to the dictionary if you are using someone else's computer or are working in a computer laboratory.

### OTHER TYPES OF ERRORS MARKED BY THE GRAMMAR TOOL

The grammar program marks a range of grammatical errors including two spaces between words and the same word twice in a row. These flags help you proof your document for spacing and other typing errors. The grammar settings are controlled in the Word Options dialog box, under Proofing. You can change the settings to check for formal versus casual language usage and two spaces between sentences. It is customary with word processing programs to only use one space between sentences.

---

In any computer program, certain default settings determine how the program operates. In Microsoft Office applications, when you start typing in the middle of existing text, the existing text is moved to the right as you type, and the new text is added at the insertion point. This is known as the *insert mode*. You can also type over existing text to replace it as you type—known as the *overtype mode*.

---

1. With the Lewis Letter document open, at the bottom of the window, right-click the status bar. On the displayed Customized Status Bar menu, notice that Overtype does not have a check mark next to it, and also notice that Insert displays to the right of Overtype. Click Overtype to add this button to the status bar. A button labeled Insert displays on the status bar, because the default setting is *insert*. This button can be used to toggle between Insert and Overtype mode.

2. On the status bar, click the Insert button to change it to Overtype. Click to the left of *<your name>* near the end of the letter; type your name to replace this placeholder text. If necessary, use Delete to remove any remaining placeholder text. As you type, the name you type replaces the <your name> placeholder. Notice that Overtype displays on the status bar at the bottom of the window, as shown in Figure 2.14. This indicates that the overtype feature is active.

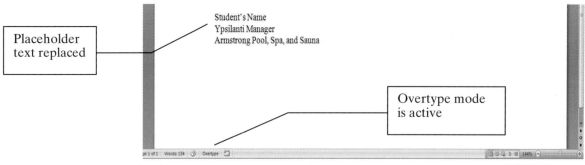

Placeholder text replaced

Student's Name
Ypsilanti Manager
Armstrong Pool, Spa, and Sauna

Overtype mode is active

FIGURE 2.14

3. Click the Overtype on the status bar to return to the insert mode. This is a toggle button; it can be used to turn on or off the overtype feature. In general, it is best to leave this feature in the insert mode unless you need to use it specifically to replace existing text in a form or other document.

4. Click the Save button on the Quick Access toolbar to save your changes. Display the Office menu, point to Print, and then click Quick Print to print the letter.

5. From the Office menu click the Close button to close the *Lewis Letter* file. Leave Word open for the next lesson.

## LESSON 5: Navigating Longer Documents

You have practiced using the scrollbar, scroll box, and keyboard shortcuts to navigate through a short document. When you are working with a larger document, there are some additional tools that will help you navigate through the file. Use the *Go To command* to navigate a document by page, section, image, or some other type of object that may be in your document. Below the vertical scrollbar, you can use the Next arrow to move to the next page or object that has been specified by using the Select Browse Object button, and the Previous arrow to move to the previous page or object.

The *Find command* is used to locate a word, phrase, or specific formatting style. This helps you quickly move through a document to locate text that may need to be changed. Once the specified text is located, the *Replace command* can be used to replace the found text if necessary. With the Find and Replace dialog box, a *global search*—a search of the entire document—can locate all instances of the specified value, so it can be changed throughout the document. In this lesson you will practice using the Go To command and Find and Replace dialog box.

## To Navigate Using the Go To Command

1. **Open *CE_0202* and save it as `Alcona_Census` in your folder for this chapter.** The document that displays is about Alcona County, Michigan, census tracking.

2. **Point to the Next button at the end of the vertical scrollbar as shown in Figure 2.15.** A *Next Page* ScreenTip displays to indicate that clicking this button will move you to the next page in the document. This is a quick method for moving through a document by page, section, heading, image, or some other specified object in your document. The ScreenTip changes to reflect the type of object by which it will browse your document.

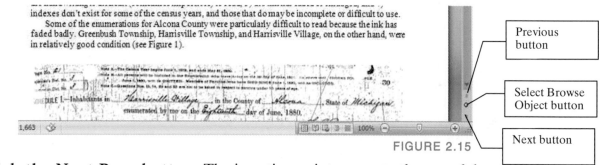

FIGURE 2.15

3. **Click the Next Page button.** The insertion point moves to the top of the second page in the document.

4. **Click the Next Page button again.** The insertion point moves to the top of the third page. Notice that it shows Page 3 of 4 on the status bar as shown in Figure 2.16.

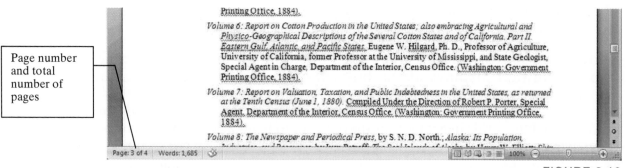

FIGURE 2.16

5. **On the Home tab, in the Editing group click the Find arrow, and from the displayed list click Go To.** The Find and Replace dialog box opens with the Go To tab displayed as shown in Figure 2.17. Here you can browse your document by typing a page number in the *Enter page number* box, or you can select the type of object by which you want to browse the document browse the document.

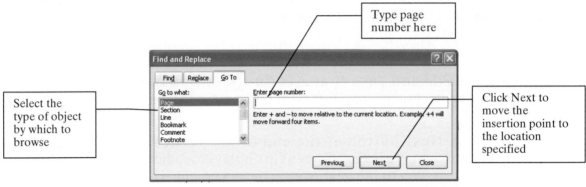

FIGURE 2.17

6. **Click the Enter page number box, if necessary, and type 1. Click Go To.** The first page of the document displays and the insertion point moves to the top of the first page.

7. **Click Close to close the Find and Replace dialog box; click the Select Browse Object button near the end of the vertical scrollbar.** A palette of buttons displays as shown in Figure 2.18. Each button represents a different type of object by which you can browse through your document. The two rows of buttons may be reversed on your screen.

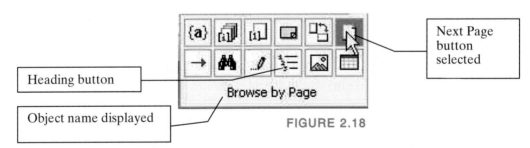

FIGURE 2.18

8. **Move your mouse pointer over each button and observe the name of the button that displays at the bottom of the palette, and then click the Browse by Heading button.** The insertion point moves to the left of *Introduction*, the next heading in the document. Notice that the Next and Previous buttons are blue—this indicates that they are set to browse by something other than by page.

9. **Point to the Next button at the bottom of the vertical scrollbar.** The ScreenTip displays *Next Heading*. The ScreenTips for the Next and Previous buttons change to reflect the type of object that has been selected for browsing.

This change occurs whether the selection is made using the Select Browse Object button or the Go To dialog box.

10. **Click the Next button two more times to move the insertion point to the next two headings.** The insertion point moves to the left of *Non-population census schedules.*

11. **Click the Select Browse Object button on the vertical scrollbar and then click the Browse by Page button.** The insertion point moves to the top of the next page—page 3. The Next and Previous buttons are displayed in black again, and when they are next used, they will browse the document by page.

12. **Press** ⌨Ctrl + ⌨Home **to return to the top of the document.**

## To Use Find and Replace

1. **Press** ⌨Ctrl + ⌨F. The Find and Replace dialog box opens with the Find tab displayed. This dialog box can also be accessed by choosing Edit, Find on the menu bar.

2. **Type microfiche in the Find what box and then click Find Next.** The first occurrence of *microfiche* is highlighted at the top of the second page of the document as shown in Figure 2.19. When text is highlighted in this manner it is selected—which enables you to delete, format, copy, or replace the text.

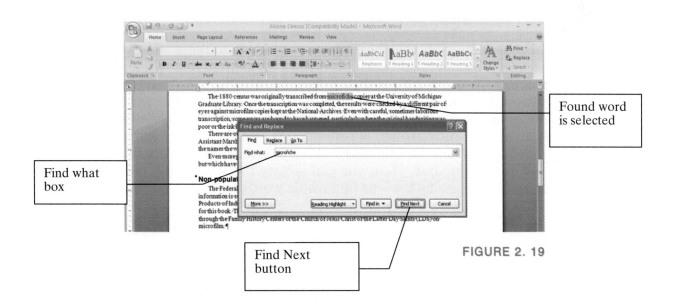

Found word is selected

Find what box

Find Next button

FIGURE 2. 19

3. **Click the Replace Tab in the Find and Replace dialog box.** On the Replace tab, the *Find what* box displays the word you are trying to find, and the *Replace with* box is available to enter a replacement word or phrase.

4. **Click in the Replace with box, type** `microfilm` **and then click Replace.** The word *microfiche* is replaced with *microfilm* and a message box displays to inform you that it has finished searching the document. If the word *microfiche* had been found again, the Find command would have moved to and selected it. Then you could again click the Replace button. In this manner, you can continue to find and replace each occurrence of a word or phrase in a document.

5. **Click OK to acknowledge the message, and then close the Find and Replace dialog box.**

6. **Click the Select Browse Object button at the end of the vertical scrollbar, and then click Browse by Page button on the displayed palette.** The Find and Replace command functions like the Go To command—it locks the item you have been searching for into the Select Browse Object button. After using the Find and Replace dialog box it is a good practice to change the Select Browse Object button back to Browse by Page, so it will browse by page the next time you use the Next and Previous buttons.

7. **Press** Ctrl + Home **to move the insertion point to the top of the document; click Save to save the changes made. Leave the *Alcona Census* document open for the next lesson.**

---

TO EXTEND YOUR KNOWLEDGE . . .

### USING THE REPLACE ALL COMMAND

The Find command searches your document looking for specific text or formatting. You can review each occurrence of an item that is found and replace it if needed, or you can do a global replacement of the specified text or format. Be cautious, however, when using the Replace All command because it could have unintentional consequences. If the word you are looking for is part of a larger word or words—such as *man* is contained within the word *manners*—replacing it could result in errors. To help narrow your search, use the More button in the Find and Replace dialog box. Here you can specify that the search must match case—upper and lowercase letters—or find whole words only.

---

# LESSON 6: Inserting, Selecting, Deleting, and Replacing Text

In most cases, the first draft of a document is written quickly to record your initial thoughts. During the proofing and editing process, you may want to expand on the existing text and add new ideas to your document, or simply change a word or a phrase. If you allowed the computer to wrap the text at the end of each line when you created the document, the program automatically adjusts the existing text to make room for whatever text you insert.

You have practiced using Backspace and Delete to delete one character at a time. If you want to remove words, phrases, sentences, or even whole paragraphs, first select the text you want to change. Selecting text is the process of highlighting areas of text so that the text can be edited, formatted, deleted, copied, or moved. Word recognizes a selected area of text as one unit, to which you can make changes. You can select text and delete the existing word or phrase and then insert its replacement, but it is faster to combine these two steps and simply select the old word or phrase and type in a new one.

In this lesson, you learn how to insert, select, delete, and replace text. First you insert new text in the *Alcona Census* document. The process of inserting text begins with placing the insertion point in the exact location where you want to insert text.

## To Insert Text

1. **With the *Alcona Census* document open, click to the right of *available* at the end of the second sentence in the first paragraph of the Introduction section.** The pointer should be between the *e* and the period that ends the sentence.

2. **Press [Spacebar] and then type: on microfilm.** The new text is inserted at the insertion point and the existing text moves to the right, wrapping down the paragraph as necessary.

3. **Click to the left of *Greenbush Township* in the second sentence of the third paragraph of the Introduction section.** There is a single space following the first sentence and the insertion point should be to the right of the space.

---

### If you have problems...

When you are first learning to use the mouse, you may sometimes place the insertion point in the wrong location. You can use the right and left arrows on the keyboard to move the insertion point one character at a time to the right or left, or the up and down arrows to move up or down one line at a time. You can also insert spaces by pressing the spacebar key when needed.

---

4. **Type: The most challenging were Black River, Alcona Village, and Alcona Township.** Make sure you add a space after the new sentence as shown in Figure 2.20.

---

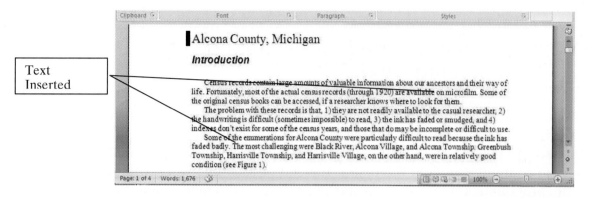

**Text Inserted**

| Alcona County, Michigan

*Introduction*

Census records contain large amounts of valuable information about our ancestors and their way of life. Fortunately, most of the actual census records (through 1920) are available on microfilm. Some of the original census books can be accessed, if a researcher knows where to look for them.

The problem with these records is that, 1) they are not readily available to the casual researcher, 2) the handwriting is difficult (sometimes impossible) to read, 3) the ink has faded or smudged, and 4) indexes don't exist for some of the census years, and those that do may be incomplete or difficult to use.

Some of the enumerations for Alcona County were particularly difficult to read because the ink has faded badly. The most challenging were Black River, Alcona Village, and Alcona Township. Greenbush Township, Harrisville Township, and Harrisville Village, on the other hand, were in relatively good condition (see Figure 1).

Page: 1 of 4 | Words: 1,676 | 100%

**FIGURE 2.20**

To delete text, you first select it. You can select text using either the mouse or the keyboard. To use the mouse, click at the beginning of the text you want to select, hold down the left mouse button and move the mouse over the area of text that you want to select. The text will be highlighted—the characters display in white and the background in black—as you move the mouse. Release the left mouse button when you have selected the intended text. Then you press ⌞Delete⌟ to clear the text from the document.

## To Select and Delete Text

1. **Click the Next Page button at the end of the vertical scrollbar to move to the top of the second page.** *About this transcription* displays at the top of the page as the heading of the next topic.

2. **Click to the left of the word *originally* in the first sentence of the first paragraph; hold down the left mouse button and drag the mouse to the right until the word *originally* (excluding spaces) is selected. Release the mouse.** The process of dragging the mouse highlights the text and displays the text in white and the background in black as shown in Figure 2.21. Selecting text takes a steady hand. If you are not satisfied with your result, click in a blank area of the document and try again.

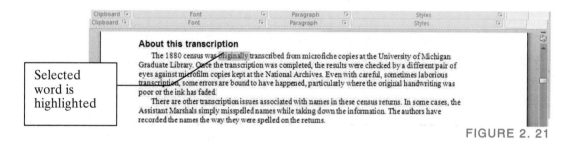

**Selected word is highlighted**

**About this transcription**

The 1880 census was originally transcribed from microfiche copies at the University of Michigan Graduate Library. Once the transcription was completed, the results were checked by a different pair of eyes against microfilm copies kept at the National Archives. Even with careful, sometimes laborious transcription, some errors are bound to have happened, particularly where the original handwriting was poor or the ink has faded.

There are other transcription issues associated with names in these census returns. In some cases, the Assistant Marshals simply misspelled names while taking down the information. The authors have recorded the names the way they were spelled on the returns.

**FIGURE 2. 21**

3. **Press ⌞Delete⌟.** The word is deleted, and the extra space is automatically removed.

4. **Click at the beginning of the third paragraph under the *About this transcription* section, to the left of *Even more problems cropped up.***

5. **Drag to the right to select the entire sentence including the period at the end, and then press ⌞Delete⌟.** The selected phrase is deleted.

Rather than selecting text, deleting it, and then typing something new, you can combine these steps. After selecting text, typing replaces the selected text with the characters that are typed.

1. **Click to the left of the word** *transcription* **in the first sentence of the second paragraph and drag to the right until you have selected** *transcription issues*. Two words are selected. You will replace this text, but you do not have to delete it first—anything you type will replace the selected text.

2. **Type:** `problems`. **Add a space, if necessary.** Notice that when you typed the first letter, all of the selected text was replaced.

3. **Move the pointer over the word** *happened* **in the last sentence of the first paragraph and double-click the mouse button.** The entire word is selected as shown in Figure 2.22. Double-clicking text takes a steady hand. You must hold the mouse perfectly still between clicks. If you are not satisfied with your results, click in an open area and then try again. **Note:** When you double-click a word, the Mini toolbar displays.

Selected word is highlighted

Phrase replaced

Mini toolbar displays

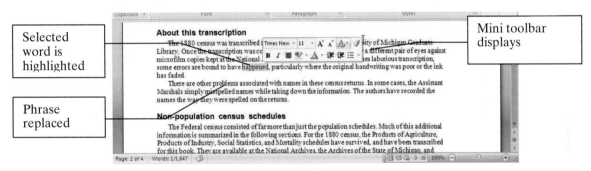

FIGURE 2.22

4. **Type:** `occurred`. The old word is replaced.

5. **Position the pointer over the paragraph that follows the** *Non-population census schedules* **heading and triple-click.** The entire paragraph is selected as shown in Figure 2.23. In this manner you can quickly select a paragraph.

Entire paragraph is selected

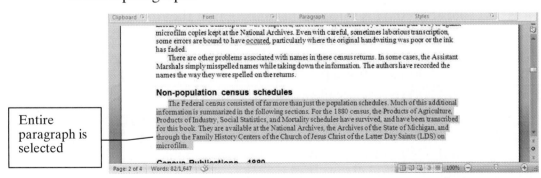

FIGURE 2.23

6. **Hold down** Ctrl **and press** A. The entire document is selected. This is a quick technique to use if you want to change a format that would affect the whole document.

7. **Click anywhere in the document to deselect the text; click the Save button and leave the** *Alcona Census* **document open to continue to the next lesson.**

### SELECTING TEXT

When you position your mouse pointer in the margin to the left of text, the pointer changes to a right-pointing arrow. The right-pointing arrow enables you to select the text you are pointing at. The left margin of a document is known as the *selection bar*. Table 2.2 lists several methods you can use to select text.

| TO SELECT | DO THIS |
| --- | --- |
| A portion of text | Click to position the insertion point at the beginning of the text you want to select, hold down Shift, and then click at the end of the text you want to select. Alternatively, hold down the left mouse button and drag from the beginning to the end of the text you want to select. |
| A word | Double-click the word. |
| A sentence | Hold down Ctrl and click anywhere in the sentence. |
| A paragraph | Triple-click anywhere in the paragraph; or, move the pointer to the left of the line, into the margin area. When the pointer changes to a right-pointing white arrow, double-click. |
| A line | Move the pointer to the left of the line. When the pointer turns to a right-pointing white arrow, click once. |
| One character at a time | Position the insertion point at the left of the first character, hold down Shift and press → or ← as many times as desired. |
| A string of words | Position the insertion point to the left of the first word, hold down Shift + Ctrl, and then press → or ←. |
| Consecutive lines | Hold down Shift and press ↑ or ↓. |
| Consecutive paragraphs | Hold down Shift + Ctrl and press ↑ or ↓. |
| The entire document | Hold down Ctrl and press A or move the pointer to the left of the line. When it turns to a right-pointing white arrow, triple- click. |

Table 2.2

# LESSON 7: Copying Text

When a section of text needs to be repeated from one location to another in a document, or from one file to another, rather than retyping the text, use the *copy* command. Copying text places it in the *Office Clipboard* or *Clipboard*—a temporary storage location in Microsoft Office applications. Then use the *paste* command to add the text in the new location. The text you copied remains in its original location, and is added to the new location in the document. This saves typing the text again.

In this task, you learn to copy text and paste it to another location in the same document, and then copy a block of text to another document

## To Use Copy and Paste

1. **Press ⌨Ctrl + ⌨Home to return to the top of the document, and then press ⌨Ctrl + ⌨F to display the Find and Replace dialog box.** The Find and Replace dialog box displays with the Find tab selected. In this case you need to find a phrase so you can select it. You will then copy the phrase so it can be pasted in another location.

2. **In the Find what box type Washington: and then click Find Next; click the Close button on the Find and Replace dialog box title bar.** The first occurrence of *Washington:* is located and selected.

3. **With *Washington:* selected, hold down ⌨Ctrl and ⌨Shift, and then press ⌨→ five times to select the phrase *Washington: Government Printing Office*, including the comma at the end of the phrase.** This phrase was left out of several of the census publications that are listed in the document (see Figure 2.24).

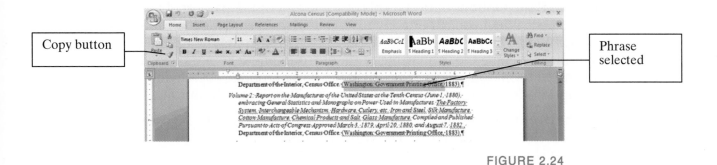

FIGURE 2.24

4. **On the Home tab, in the Clipboard group, click the Copy button.** The selected text is copied to the Office Clipboard.

5. **Press [Ctrl] + [F] to display the Find and Replace dialog box; type: Volume 11 and then click Find Next. Read the message box that displays.** A message box, as shown in Figure 2.25, informs you that *Volume 11* was not found in the selected phrase. Because the phrase you copied— *Washington: Government Printing Office,*—is still selected, the Find command first searches within the selection to look for the text you are now trying to find. The message also asks if you want it to continue to search the rest of the document.

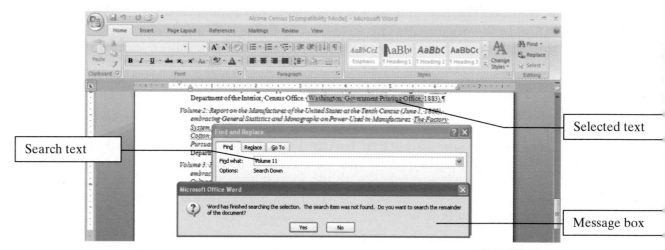

Search text

Selected text

Message box

FIGURE 2.25

6. **Click Yes in the message box to continue the search.** *Volume 11* is found and selected.

7. **Close the Find and Replace dialog box; click between the left parenthesis and *1885* in the last line of the *Volume 11* publication.**

8. **On the Home tab, in the Clipboard group, click Paste.** The copied phrase— *Washington: Government Printing Office,*—is pasted at the insertion point. The Paste Options button displays at the end of the paragraph after you paste the text. When you cut or copy text, you are also copying the formatting of that text. When you paste it, you have the option of keeping the original formatting, matching the formatting of the surrounding text in the new location, or removing all formatting. To do this, click the Paste Options button and choose one of the options from the list. For now, ignore the Paste Option button.

9. **Click between( and *1886* in the last line of the *Volume 12* publication and click the Paste button.** The copied phrase remains in the Office Clipboard and is available to paste in other locations.

10. **In a similar manner, paste the copied phrase, within the parentheses, to the left of the date, on the last line of the publications for *Volume 13* and *Volume 14.*** The copied phrase is added to the four publications as shown in Figure 2.26.

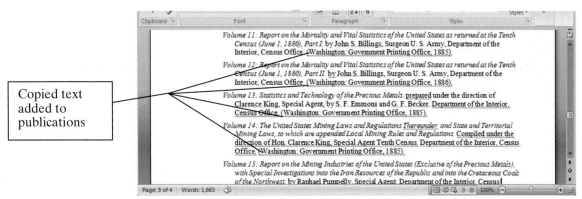

**Copied text added to publications**

FIGURE 2. 26

11. Save the *Alcona Census* document and leave it open for the next part of this lesson.

Copied text can also be pasted into another file or another application.

## To Use Copy and Paste

1. Drag the vertical scroll box up to the beginning of the *Census Publications* list.

2. Click to the left of *Volume 1* to position the insertion point at the beginning of the publications list.

3. Drag the vertical scroll box down to the bottom of the document.

4. Hold down [Shift] and click at the end of the list of publications. Release [Shift]. The list of publications is selected as shown in Figure 2.27. Clicking at the beginning of the publication list positions the insertion point at the beginning of the area you want to select. It is important to use the scrollbar to locate the end point, and then hold down [Shift] before clicking the mouse again. This keyboard shortcut is a quick way to select a large block of text that may span several pages.

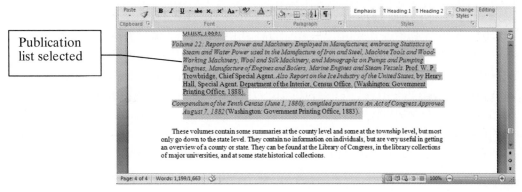

**Publication list selected**

FIGURE 2.27

## If you have problems...

If you click somewhere else in your document, the insertion point moves, and the selection of the publication list will not be complete. Click at the beginning of the publications, scroll to the end of the list, and try again.

5. **On the Home tab, in the Clipboard group, click the Copy button.** The block of text is stored in the Office Clipboard.

6. **On the Home tab, in the Clipboard group, click the Dialog Box Launcher.** The Clipboard task pane displays on the left of your screen as shown in Figure 2.28. The Clipboard can hold up to 24 items. The first few words of the copied text—the most recent item—displays on the Clipboard. The default setting for the Office Clipboard is to replace items in the Clipboard each time a new item is added. To collect several items, the Clipboard task pane must be open. This is a setting that can be changed, however, so that the Office Clipboard will collect items even if the Clipboard task pane is not showing. To make changes to the Office Clipboard settings, click the Options button at the end of the Clipboard task pane.

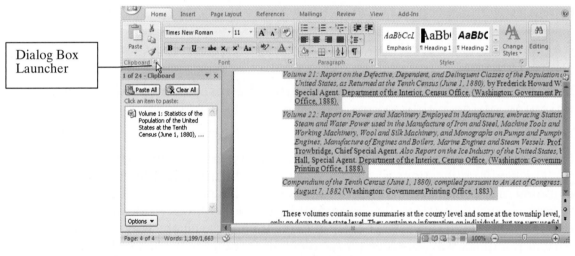

Dialog Box Launcher

FIGURE 2.28

7. **Display the Office menu and then click New. In the New Document dialog box, click Blank Document, and then in the lower right corner click Create.** A new blank document displays on your screen. The *Alcona Census* document is still open, but is not currently displayed on the screen.

8. **Type your name and then press** Enter ↵ **twice.** Notice that the Paste button in the Clipboard group is active. This indicates that there is something in the Clipboard available to be pasted.

9. **On the Clipboard task pane, click the Paste All button.** The publications list is pasted to a new document. The list also remains in the original document.

10. **Save this file in your folder as** Census Publications. **Display the Office menu and click Close.** The *Alcona Census* document displays on your screen.

11. Click anywhere in the document to clear the selection. Leave the *Alcona Census* document open to continue to the next lesson.

## LESSON 8: Moving Text and Using the Undo and Redo Commands

To move text, numbers, or graphics from one place to another, use the *cut* command. Cutting text removes it from its original location and stores it temporarily in the Office Clipboard. Position your mouse pointer in the location where you want to place the text and then use the Paste command to insert the text. Cut and paste can be used to move text within a file, between files, or between applications. This is different from deleting text, which removes it from the document and does not make it available to use in another location.

### To Use Cut and Paste

1. Scroll so you can see the *Non-population census schedules* paragraph on page 2, and then select the words *on microfilm* at the end of the last sentence in that paragraph.

2. On the Home tab, in the Clipboard group, click the Cut button. The selected text is removed from the screen and placed in the Clipboard

3. Place the insertion point after the word *available* in the same sentence, and then on the Home tab, in the Clipboard group, click the Paste button. The text is now placed at the insertion point location as shown in Figure 2.29.

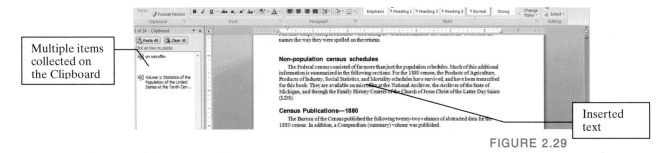

FIGURE 2.29

4. Scroll to the bottom of the document. The last census publication entry should be displayed on the screen.

5. Move the pointer to the left of the paragraph beginning with *Compendium*. When the mouse pointer turns into a white arrow drag down to select both lines of the paragraph.

6. **On the Home tab, in the Clipboard group, click the Cut button.** The paragraph is removed from the screen and placed in the Clipboard. Items that are cut or copied are added to the Clipboard task pane when it is displayed.

7. **Scroll to the beginning of the list of census publications, place the insertion point next to the first entry—*Volume 1*—and click the first item in the Clipboard task pane, which begins with *Compendium*.** The paragraph is moved to the insertion point location as shown in Figure 2.30. You can click an item listed in the Clipboard task pane to paste it in a new location. When you use the Paste button it pastes the last item that was cut or copied.

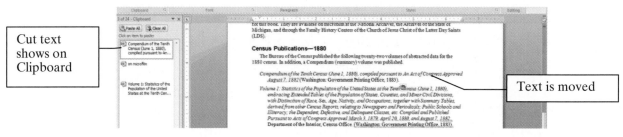

FIGURE 2.30

8. **Click the Close button on the Clipboard task pane. Do not save your changes until after you have completed the next section.**

---

## TO EXTEND YOUR KNOWLEDGE...

### ANOTHER TECHNIQUE FOR MOVING TEXT

***Drag-and-drop*** is another method that can be used to move text; however, when you use this process the text is not stored in the Office Clipboard. To use drag-and- drop, first select the text you want to move. Then point to the selected text, and, using the white mouse pointer, *drag* the text to a new location. When the pointer is positioned in the location where you want to place the text, release the mouse to *drop* the text in a new location. This method works in most applications, and once you have mastered the technique, it is a quick method for rearranging text

---

Sometimes you may accidentally delete text or paste something in the wrong location. You also, on occasion, may make several changes in a document and then decide that you would rather not use the changes you have made. Word gives you the option of undoing and redoing changes you have made with the *Undo* and *Redo commands* from the Quick Access Toolbar. This capability saves you from having to retype text. The Undo command undoes the most recent action, or a list of actions selected from the Undo button list. The Redo command reverses the action that was undone by the Undo command. The Redo button can also be used to repeat an action, in which case the button icon changes and the ScreenTip displays Repeat and the specific action that will be repeated.

## To Undo or Redo an Action

1. **On the Quick Access toolbar, click the Undo button.** The text you just pasted disappears, reversing the Paste step. The text is still in the Clipboard, but has not been replaced in its original location, which was another step.

2. **Click the Undo button again.** The Cut step is reversed, and the text is restored to its original location.

3. **Click the Undo button a third time.** The words *on microfilm* are removed from the location you pasted them.

4. **On the Quick Access toolbar, click the Redo button.** The Undo operation is reversed, and the text is reinserted.

5. **On the Quick Access toolbar, click the Save button. Display the Office menu and point to Print and then click Quick Print to print the document. Unless otherwise directed by your instructor; close the file and close Word.**

## TO EXTEND YOUR KNOWLEDGE...

### UNDOING OR REDOING MULTIPLE ACTIONS

Both the Undo and Redo buttons display arrows on the right of the button. If you click the arrow, a list of actions displays, with the most recent action listed first. If you want to undo several items on the list, move the pointer down the list until you have selected all of the items you want to reverse and then click. All of the selected items are undone. Similarly, you can reverse undo actions by using the arrow to the right of the Redo button, just in case you undid too many actions.

### USING KEYBOARD SHORTCUTS TO EDIT TEXT

Most of the commands you have used in this lesson are found on the Edit menu. Many of the commands also have keyboard shortcuts, which you might find quicker and easier to use. Table 2.3 lists the related shortcuts

| TO DO THIS | USE THIS KEYBOARD SHORTCUT |
|---|---|
| Cut text or graphic and place it in the Office Clipboard | Ctrl + X |
| Copy text or graphic and place it in the Office Clipboard | Ctrl + C |
| Paste the contents of the Office Clipboard | Ctrl + V |
| Undo an action | Ctrl + Z |
| Redo an action | Ctrl + Y |
| Find text | Ctrl + F |
| Find and replace text | Ctrl + H |

Table 2.3

## SUMMARY

In this project, you learned how to create files, enter data, make changes to existing files, and save files with a new name. First, you created an Excel Expense Report using a preformatted template, and then you created a simple Word document starting with a blank document.

You learned that opening a file from within Windows Explorer will start the related application and then display the selected file. Several problems that can prevent a file from opening were discussed.

You practiced editing techniques that are common to most applications. You navigated a short document using the scrollbar, scroll box, arrow keys, and navigation keys. You used the Go To and Find and Replace commands to move quickly through a longer document and locate specific phrases, or objects. ←Bksp and Delete were used to remove text, and then new text was inserted. You practiced several techniques for selecting text, and then you deleted or replaced the text. The Copy and Paste commands were used to repeat data in multiple locations and in a new document; and the Cut and Paste commands were used to move data from one place to another. Finally, you used the Undo command to reverse actions and the Redo command to reverse the undo action.

You can extend your learning by reviewing concepts and terms, and by practicing variations of skills presented in the lessons.

# KEY TERMS

arrow keys

backwardly compatible

Clipboard

copy

cut

desktop shortcut

drag-and-drop

field

Find command

global search

Go To command

insert mode

navigation keys

Office Clipboard

overtype mode

paste

recognizer

Redo command

Replace command

scrolling

select

selection bar

template

Undo command

word wrap

workbook

# CHECKING CONCEPTS AND TERMS

## SCREEN ID
Label each element of the screen shown in Figure 2.31.

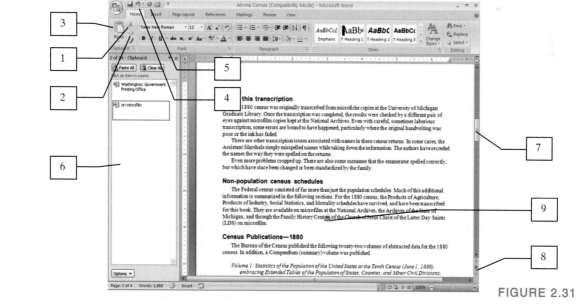

FIGURE 2.31

_____ A. Clipboard task pane

_____ B. Copy button

_____ C. Cut button

_____ D. Paste button

_____ E. Redo button

_____ F. Scroll box

_____ G. Select browse Object

_____ H. Paste Option button

_____ I. Undo button

## MULTIPLE CHOICE

Circle the letter of the correct answer for each of the following.

1. To locate and replace all occurrences of a word or phrase use this command. [L5]
a. Spelling and Grammar
b. Find and Replace
c. Go To
d. Copy and Paste

2. Use this key to remove characters to the left of the insertion point. [L4]
a. [←Bksp]
b. [Delete]
c. [→]
d. [←]

3. To select the entire document use this keyboard shortcut. [L6]
a. [Ctrl] + [Shift]
b. [Alt] + [Home]
c. [Ctrl] + [A]
d. [Alt] + [E]

4. When you cut or copy text, numbers, or graphics, it is temporarily stored in this location. [L7]
a. My Documents folder
b. Office Clipboard
c. Recycle bin
d. Template

5. This command reverses the previous action. [L8]
a. Undo
b. Redo
c. Remove
d. Recover

6. When this is active, existing text is replaced as you type. [L4]
a. Insert mode
b. Replace mode
c. Remove mode
d. Overtype mode

7. All of the following characteristics are true of templates except _____. [L1]
a. are preformatted
b. are available in most applications
c. provide the most flexibility for creating customized documents
d. can be used again and again

8. Which of the following is not a valid method for opening a file? [L2]
a. Desktop shortcut
b. Open button in an application
c. Find command
d. Double-click the file name in Windows Explorer

9. When text, numbers, graphics or other objects are cut or copied they can be pasted into another location in _____. [L7]
a. the same document
b. a different document
c. a different file in another application
d. All of the above are true

10. To select an entire paragraph, click in the paragraph and _____ [L6]
a. Triple-click
b. Double-click
c. Hold down [Ctrl] and press [P]
d. Hold down [Ctrl] and press [End]

# DISCUSSION

Creative Solution

1. New files can be created using a blank document, from an existing file, or from a template. In what circumstances would you use each of the three methods? What information would help you determine which method to use? [L1]

2. Provide examples of words that are not likely to be recognized by the spelling program. Would you expect the grammar program to be able to determine if *to*, *too*, or *two* are used correctly? If you remove all of the red and green wavy lines in your document, is it necessary to proofread it? Why? [L4]

3. If you have difficulty opening a file, what are the possible causes? What steps would you take to resolve the problem? [L2]

# SKILL DRILL

Skill Drill exercises reinforce project skills. Each skill reinforced is the same, or nearly the same, as a skill presented in the project. Detailed instructions are provided in a step-by-step format. All of these exercises can be completed with Microsoft Office XP or later versions. Instructions throughout the exercises are based on the Windows XP operating system, running Microsoft Office 2007.

## 1. Editing a Letter

You have been asked to make some changes to a letter addressed to members of a travel club.

1. Open **Windows Explorer** and navigate to the folder where the student files for this text are stored; locate *CE_0203* and double-click the file name to open the Word application and the file.

2. Display the Office menu and click **Save As**. Save the file with the name `Alaska_Letter` in the folder with your other files for this project.

3. Make sure the insertion point is at the beginning of the document and type `Dear Member`:

4. Click to the left of *right in* found in the third paragraph, first sentence; drag to the right to select both words and then type: `inside` to replace the selected words.

5. Double-click the word *absolutely* in the last sentence of the third paragraph; press Delete to remove the word.

6. Double-click the word *proposed* in the first sentence of the second paragraph; type: `tentative` to replace the selected word.

7. Double-click the word *tentative* that you just typed and on the **Home tab**, in the **Clipboard group**, click the **Cut** button.

8. Move the insertion point to the left of the word *dates* in the same sentence, and then on the **Home tab**, in the **Clipboard group**, click the **Paste** button.

9. Select the last sentence of the first paragraph that begins: *The more people...*; be careful to select only up to the period—do not select the space after the period. On the **Home tab**, in the **Clipboard group**, click the **Cut** button.

10. Click to the left of the previous sentence that begins *Please let us know...* and then in the **Clipboard** group click the **Paste** button to move the sentence.

11. On the Quick Access toolbar, click the **Undo** button to remove the paste that you just performed; click the **Undo** button again to place the sentence back in its original location.

12. On the Quick Access toolbar, click the **Redo** button twice to cancel the two undo actions and add a space between sentences, if necessary.

13. Right-click the status bar and click **Overtype** to add this button to the status bar. On the status bar, click the **Insert** button to turn on the overtype mode. Click to the left of *Member* in the greeting and type your name and delete any remaining characters.

14. Click **Overtype** on the status bar to return to the insert mode.

15. On the Quick Access toolbar, click the **Save** button to save your changes. From the Office menu, point to **Print** and then click **Quick Print** if necessary to provide a paper copy (optional). Close the Alaska Letter document and close Word.

## 2. Using Find and Replace

Your supervisor asked you to modify a summary of business organizations that will be used in a training seminar.

1. Open **Windows Explorer** and navigate to the folder that contains the files for this text; locate and double-click *CE_0204* to open the file, and then save it as **Business Organizations**.

2. On the Home tab, in the **Editing group** click **Find**; in the *Find what* box type: **Advantages**, and then press ⏎Enter. Pressing ⏎Enter activates the active button—Find Next—in the dialog box. The active button in a dialog box is outlined in blue.

3. Click the Replace tab in the Find and Replace dialog box; click in the *Replace with* box and type: **Benefits**.

4. Click the **More** button to display additional options.

5. Click the *Match case* check box, and the *Find whole words only* check box. This will ensure that only the word *Advantages* will be replaced and that the case will match those of the words typed in the dialog box.

6. Click **Find Next** and when *Advantages* is found—selected—click **Replace**. *Advantages* is replaced with *Benefits*.

7. Continue this process until all three occurrences of the word Advantages are replaced with Benefits.

8. Select the word *Advantages* in the *Find what* box and then type: `Dis-advantages`; select *Benefits* in the *Replace with* box and type: `Risks`.

9. Repeat the find and replace process to change all occurrences of *Disadvantages* to *Risks*, and then close the Find and Replace dialog box.

10. Click to the right of the title at the top of the document and press e. Type: `Edited by`: and then type your name.

11. **Save** your changes, print the file if required to do so, and then close the Business Organizations document and close Word.

### 3. Writing a Letter Starting with a Blank Document

You have been directed to write a thank you letter to the Local History Society.

1. Start **Microsoft Office Word**.

2. Type `December 10, 2008` at the insertion point. Press e twice to create a blank line between the date and the name and address lines.

3. Type the following name and address. Press [Enter ←] at the end of each line.

   ```
   Mary Louise Webster
   1835 Long Lake Road
   Ann Arbor, MI 48104
   ```

4. Press [Enter ←] twice after the postal code and type the salutation:

   ```
   Dear Ms. Webster
   ```

5. Press [Enter ←] twice and type the first full paragraph of the letter (include the misspellings):.

   ```
   Thank you for asking me to be the keynote
   speaker at next month's Local History Society
   meeting. As you suggested, I have included a few
   of my research findings for you to mention in
   your newsletter.
   ```

6. Press [Enter ←] twice and then type the next paragraph:.

   ```
   The average marriage age in the township around
   1900 were about 22.5 years for women and 27.8
   years for men. The average number of children
   per family was around eight. More than half of
   the township residents were born outside of the
   United States, nearly all from either Canada or
   the British Isles. Finally, the average life
   expectancy was far higher than expected. I'll
   let you know about that at the meeting!
   ```

7. Press [Enter ←] twice and then type the next paragraph:

   ```
   Once again, I am forever indebted to the society
   for the grant that has enabled me to pursue my
   research. I'm looking forward to seeing you
   again at the meeting.
   ```

8. Press ⌈Enter⏎⌉ twice, type: `Sincerely`, press e four times to make room for the signature and then type your name.

9. Right-click the word *metting* and choose *meeting* from the shortcut menu; right-click the word *newletter* and choose *newsletter* from the shortcut menu.

10. Right-click the long phrase that is underlined in green and select the appropriate suggestion.

11. Right-click *enable* and choose *enabled* from the shortcut menu.

12. Click the **Save** button on the Quick Access toolbar to display the Save As dialog box; type: `Local History Letter` in the File name box.

13. Click the **Save in** arrow, navigate to the folder where you are saving your files for this project, and then click the **Save** button

14. **Print** the document if you are required to do so, and then close the file and close Word.

## 4. Using Microsoft Help to Explore Keyboard Shortcuts

In this project you were introduced to a number of keyboard shortcuts that can help you navigate a window or edit a document. The keyboard shortcuts you used are common to most Microsoft Office applications, but their use may vary slightly from one application to another. In this Skill Drill you use Help to explore keyboard shortcuts that are available in other applications.

1. Open **Excel**; click the **Question Mark** on the right end of the Ribbon and type: `How do I use keyboard shortcuts?` (Note: The question mark is optional.)

2. Find a reference that promises to show you a list of keyboard shortcuts and click the reference; follow the instructions provided to examine a list of keyboard shortcuts.

3. Look for shortcut keys to select text, navigate a file, cut, copy, paste, undo, redo, find, replace, go to, and other commands you have practiced.

4. Open **PowerPoint**; press ⌈F1⌉: Type: `Keyboard shortcuts` and then press ⌈Enter⏎⌉.

5. Find a reference for keyboard shortcuts that will provide you a list and click that reference; examine the list of shortcuts. See if you can determine if it is the same list as displayed in Excel. (Hint: Use the taskbar to move between the two applications and their Help screens.)

6. Look for shortcut keys to select text, navigate a file, cut, copy, paste, undo, redo, find, replace, go to, and other commands you have practiced. Close Help and then close both applications.

## 5. Editing an Excel Worksheet

You have practiced navigating and editing a Word document. You decide you would like to practice these same skills in an Excel file to see if they work the same. In this Skill Drill, you open an Excel file, practice selecting cells, navigating the worksheet, editing entries, and copying and moving entries.

1. Open **Excel**; and locate and open the Excel file *CE_0205* in the student folder for this chapter; save the file in your folder as Inventory.
2. Click cell **A1** and drag down and to the right to cell **E21**. This selects the range of the entries in your worksheet.
3. Click cell **A4** and drag down to cell **A20**. This is the product list.
4. Click cell **A21** and drag to the right to cell **E21**. This is the total row in the inventory list.
5. Press Ctrl + Home to return to cell A1.
6. Click the **Review tab**, and in the **Proofing group** click **Spelling**. This launches the Spelling program and will check the spelling in the worksheet. The Spelling dialog box displays and *Tablecover* is listed in the *Not in Dictionary* box. *Table cover* displays in the *Suggestions* box.
7. Click the **Change** button to accept the suggestion and then click **OK** in the message box that informs you that spelling check is complete for the entire sheet. Cell B20 is the currently active cell because it is the cell that displays *Table cover*.
8. In cell **B20**, double-click to the left of *cover*. This places the insertion point in the cell so you can edit the contents of the cell.
9. Press Delete one time to remove *c*, and then type C
10. Press → four times, press Spacebar once, and then type: **(Paper)**. The entry in cell B20 now reads *Table Cover (Paper)*.
11. Press Tab. The active cell moves to the next column to cell *C20*. Type: **15**, and then press Tab. Cell D20 is now the active cell and the amount in cell E20 was recalculated to reflect the reduced quantity on hand. When you type in a cell in Excel it replaces the contents of the cell. To edit a cell, double-click the cell to position the insertion point in the cell, and then use the left- or right-arrow keys to position the insertion point at the exact location in the cell where you need to edit the text. Use Delete or ←Bksp to remove characters.
12. In cell **B14**, double-click just to the right of *Forks*. Type **, Knives**, and then press Enter←. The cell now reads *Forks, Knives, & Spoons*. The text you typed was inserted—the text to the right of the insertion point moved to the right as you typed. This works like a word processor. Notice that when you pressed Enter←, cell B15 became the active cell. Pressing Tab moves the active cell one cell to the right, while pressing Enter← moves the active cell down one cell in the same column.
13. Click cell **A21** and press Ctrl + X. This is the keyboard shortcut for the Cut command. Click cell **B22** and press Ctrl + V. This moves the contents of cell A21 to cell B22.
14. Repeat this process to move the contents of cell **E21** to cell **E22**.
15. Click cell **B20**, press Ctrl + C, press ↓ and then press Ctrl + V. This copies the contents of cell B20 to cell B21.
16. In cell **B21**, double-click to the right of *Cover*. Select *(Paper)* and then type **(Plastic)**. Press Tab and type **20**, press Tab and type: **2.79**

---

and then press Enter⏎. A value is calculated for this item because of a formula in cell E22, and the total value is recalculated. The revised total is *$8,678.87.*

17. Click cell **A21** and type: `42018` and press Enter; click cell **A24**, type your name, and press Enter⏎. Save the *Inventory* workbook and print it. Close the file and close Excel.

## CHALLENGE

Challenge exercises expand on or are somewhat related to skills presented in the lessons. Each exercise provides a brief narrative introduction, followed by instructions in a numbered-step format that are not as detailed as those in the Skill Drill section.

Each exercise is independent of the others, so you may complete the exercises in any order.

### 1. Using a Word Template to Create a Fax Cover

You have used an Excel template to create an expense report. Word also contains templates that can be used to create letters, faxes, memos, and other documents. They provide a basic layout—placement of information on the page—and style—choice of font, line spacing, graphics and design characteristics.

You have been asked to create a cover for a fax and decide to use one of the Word templates.

1. Start **Word**. From the Office menu, click **New**, and then under **Templates** click **Installed Templates**.
2. Click the **Median Fax**, and then click the **Create** button. The fax cover letter opens and displays placeholders for the recipient and sender information. There is also a place to enter comments at the end of the address information.
3. In the *Pick the date area*, click the arrow and then click today's date. Complete the fax cover with the information that follows. Use ↓ or click to place the insertion point next to each item before you type.

| | |
|---|---|
| Company Name: | `Your College Name` |
| To: | `Your Instructor's Name` |
| Phone Number: | `(999) 555—0220` |
| Company Name | `Your Class Name` |
| Fax Number: | `(999) 555—0022` |
| From: | `Your Name` |
| Phone Number: | `(212) 555—0110` |
| Fax Number: | `(212) 555—0011` |
| Action Requested: | `Itinerary for our upcoming trip` |

### 2. Using Drag-and-Drop to Move Text

You learned how to move text in a document using the cut-and-paste method.

You read about the drag-and-drop method to move text and decide to use this technique to edit a paper about the influence of computers.

1. Open Windows Explorer and then locate the file *CE_0206* in the student folder for this Project; double-click the file name to start Word and open the file.

2. Save the file in your folder with the name: `Computers Are Everywhere`.

3. In the first sentence, select the word *live*; point to the selected word. The mouse pointer turns into the white selection arrow—the same pointer that displays when you point to buttons on the toolbar.

4. In the same sentence, drag the selected word *live* to the left of *work*, and then release the mouse. As you drag the pointer, the outline of a box displays at the tail of the arrow and a vertical line displays at the point of the arrow. This is the move pointer.

5. Select *work* and then drag it so it is between the two commas—the place where *live* was positioned; adjust the spacing between the words and commas as needed.

6. In the same paragraph, select *cars we drive* at the end of the second line. Point to the selected phrase and drag it down one line, and to the left. Position the pointer to the left of *food we eat*, and then release the mouse.

7. Select *food we eat* and drag it up and to the right of *from the.* The two phrases are reversed in the sentence. Adjust the spacing between the words if necessary.

8. Use the drag-and-drop method to rearrange the words in the last line of the first paragraph to read: *computers are used to analyze, diagnose, record, and communicate.*

9. Click at the end of the title *Computers are Everywhere*, press [Enter ⏎], type `Edited by:`, and then type your name. Save the file and then print it if required.

## 3. Copying Information Between Applications

You learned how to copy text within a document and to copy text to a new document. You can also copy text and place it in another application. Here you copy information from a Word document and paste it into an Excel worksheet.

You have just been sent an itinerary for an upcoming trip with some friends. The information is in Word, but you want to put it in Excel so you can add information about where you will be staying to leave with your family and friends.

1. Open *CE_0207* in Word and select the entire itinerary starting with *City* and ending with *June 29*; press [Ctrl] + [C], which is the keyboard shortcut for the Copy command.

2. Open Excel. Press [Ctrl] + [V], which is the keyboard shortcut for the Paste command. The data is added to the worksheet starting in cell A1.

3. Click in cell **A14**, type your name, and then press [Enter ⏎].

4. Position your mouse pointer over the line between the column A and column B headings. A two-headed arrow displays.

5. Double-click the line between the column A and B headings to automatically adjust the width of column A.

6. Save the file as **My Itinerary**; click the **Print** button and then close the file and close Excel.

7. Close Word. If it prompts you to save changes to the open file, click **No**.

## 4. Opening a Document That Has a Different File Format

In this project, issues related to managing files were discussed. One reason that a file may not be found or opened with the application that is expected is a difference in file types. Word can open several different types of text files including text files that display a *.txt* file extension or Rich Text Format—*.rtf* file extensions.

You have received a file from a friend by e-mail. After saving it to your computer, you want to open it in Word.

1. Open Word. Display the Office menu, click **Open** and navigate to the folder that contains the files for this project.

2. Click the *Files of type* arrow at the bottom of the Open dialog box; scroll the list, and then click **Text Files.**

3. Select the *CE_0208.txt* file. Depending on the way your computer is set up, the *.txt* extension may not appear. You can tell the file is a text file by the notepad icon to the left of the file name.

4. Click the **Open** button in the Open dialog box. The file that opens is the file from the second Skill Drill exercise, saved in text format. Notice that nearly all of the formatting has been removed.

5. With the *CE_0208.txt* file open, display the Office menu, click **Save As**; navigate to another location on your computer, such as a USB drive, zip drive, or some other portable storage device.

6. Click the **Create New Folder** button in the *Save As* dialog box; type **Text Documents** in the New Folder dialog box.

7. Change the name of the document to **Text Doc** and then click **Save**. A File Conversion dialog box opens and warns that all the formatting may be lost if you save the file as a text file, which is the file type displayed in the Save As dialog box.

8. Accept the Windows (Default) setting and then click **OK.** The file is saved and the new file name displays in the title bar.

9. Add your name at the end of the first line and print the file if required; save your changes and close the file.

## DISCOVERY ZONE

Discovery Zone exercises require advanced knowledge of topics presented in *Essentials* lessons, application of skills from multiple lessons, or self-directed learning of new skills. Each exercise is independent of the others, so you may complete the exercises in any order.

## 1. Using Help to Discover More About Templates

In this project, you were introduced to templates. Each application comes installed with its own set of templates. Templates are also available online to help you create forms, reports, and letters. You can learn more about templates and explore the variety of templates available by using Help.

With Word open on your screen, in the Type a question for help box type: create a file using a template. Examine the topics that display in the Search Results task pane. If you are online, one of the topics that displays is Save time by using ready-made templates. This link will connect you to a Microsoft Web site where you can explore different templates that are available. Use this topic or others to examine some of the template options.

Locate a template you want to use. Open it or download it and then fill it out for practice. If requested, submit the completed file to your instructor. Be sure to include your name on the document

## 2. Creating and Envelope

When you write a letter, it is helpful to have an envelope printed at the same time. Open Word and type the name and address of your school, as if you are starting a letter. Address the letter to the Registrar and ask for a transcript of your grades. Add a closing to the letter and add your name. Use Help to learn how to make an envelope. Follow the instructions provided to create the envelope. Save the file and envelope as **Transcript Request**. Print the envelope and letter as specified in the Help topic (optional).

# UNIT 2: USING PRODUCTIVITY SOFTWARE

## Microsoft Office 2007   IC³

**Project 3:** Formatting Text and Performing Common Printing Functions

LESSON 1   Adding Emphasis to Characters
  2-1.3.8.1        2-1.3.8.3

LESSON 2   Changing Font and Font Size:
  2-1.3.8.1        2-1.3.8.2

LESSON 3   Changing Font Color
  2-1.3.8.1

LESSON 4   Applying Character Effects and Adding Symbols
  2-1.3.8.1        2-2.1.7.1
  2-1.3.8.4        2-2.1.7.2

LESSON 5   Changing Alignment
  2-1.3.8.5

LESSON 6   Previewing a Document before Printing
  2-1.4.1.1        2-1.4.2.1
  2-1.4.1.3        2-1.4.1.2

LESSON 7   Printing a Document
  2-1.4.3.1        2-1.4.3.3        2-1.4.5.2
  2-1.4.3.2        2-1.4.5.1

LESSON 8   Viewing the Print Queue and Changing the Default Printer
  2-1.4.3.1        2-1.4.3.2        2-1.4.3.3

# PROJECT 3

# FORMATTING TEXT AND PERFORMING COMMON PRINTING FUNCTIONS

## IN THIS PROJECT, YOU LEARN HOW TO:

- Add Emphasis to Characters
- Change Font and Font Size
- Change Font Color
- Apply Character Effects and Add Symbols
- Change Alignment
- Preview a Document before Printing
- Print a Document
- View the Print Queue and Change the Default Printer

# WHY WOULD I DO THIS?

Words, phrases, titles, and subtitles in documents need to be emphasized to help the reader follow the organization of the document and identify important information or ideas. In addition, the text should have a professional appearance that conveys information quickly and is aesthetically pleasing. Simple formatting tools enable you to change font, font size, and text alignment. You can emphasize text to make it stand out from the surrounding text by using bold, italics, underlines, color, and special character effects.

Documents are frequently printed for distribution. Several choices exist for printing documents, including page orientation, paper size, pages to print, number of copies, and several others. It is also helpful to understand how printers are set up and to have the ability to solve common printing problems.

In this project, you change character formatting in a document. You explore print options and learn how to solve common printing problems.

# VISUAL SUMMARY

In this project, you finish formatting a two-page document. You format titles and headlines, insert symbols, and use special character effects. You explore printing options and learn how to solve common printing problems. Figure 3.1 shows the formatted document.

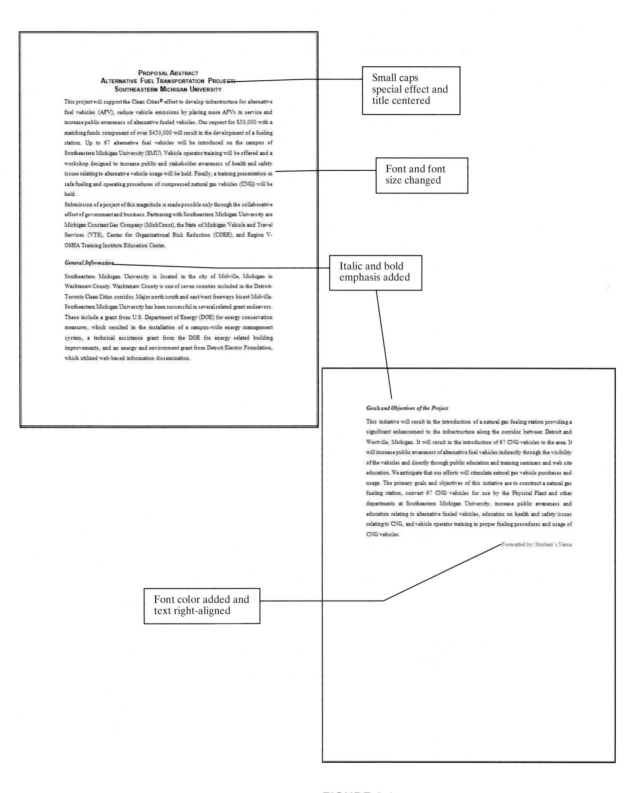

FIGURE 3.1

# LESSON 1: Adding Emphasis to Characters

Text formatting is used to emphasize important elements of a document. It helps you create effective, readable text, and draws the reader's attention to important concepts or facts. When you open the document used in this lesson, you will notice all of the text looks similar, even though it contains titles and subtitles. You emphasize text by applying bold, italic, or underline styles. These tools exist in many software programs and are common to most Microsoft Office applications.

In this lesson, you format titles and subtitles by applying bold and italic emphasis. You will work with a Microsoft Office Word document about an Alternative Fuel Proposal from a regional university.

All of these exercises can be completed with Microsoft Office 2007. Instructions throughout the lessons are based on the Windows XP operating system, running Microsoft Office 2007. Your screen may differ slightly from the figures shown, even if you are running Office 2007.

## To Add Emphasis to Characters

1. **Click the Office Button, click Open and open *CE_0301*, and then save it as a Word 97-2003 document named Alternative Fuel Proposal. Click the View tab, and in the Document Views group, click the Print Layout button and adjust the page width using the Zoom slider, if necessary.** The document that opens is very plain even though there are titles and headings in the document.

2. **Select the title *Proposal Abstract* on the first line of the document, click the Home tab, and in the Font group click the Bold button.** To make formatting changes, first select the text you want to affect. The first line of the title is now bold, which helps it stand out from the rest of the text.

3. **Select the next two title lines and then click the Bold button.** Bold is applied to all three title lines.

4. **Scroll down the document and select the *General Information* subtitle.**

5. **On the Home tab, in the Font group, click the Bold button and the Italic button.** You can apply multiple font characteristics at the same time. This emphasizes the subtitle and makes it stand out from the rest of the text as shown in Figure 3.2.

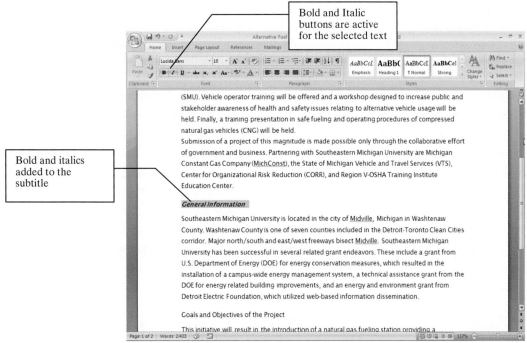

Bold and Italic buttons are active for the selected text

Bold and italics added to the subtitle

FIGURE 3.2

6. **Scroll down the document, Select the title** *Goals and Objectives of the Project,* **Right-click the selection and then click the Bold button and the Italic buttons on the Mini toolbar that displays.** The second subtitle in the document is formatted. When text is selected, the Mini toolbar displays the most common formatting tools.

7. **Click somewhere else in the document to deselect the text.** After applying formatting, click anywhere else in your document to clear the selection.

8. **Press** [Ctrl] + [Home] **to move the insertion point to the beginning of the document; save your changes to the** *Alternative Fuel Proposal* **document and leave the file open for the next lesson.**

---

TO EXTEND YOUR KNOWLEDGE...

## FORMATTING KEYBOARD SHORTCUTS

The emphasis buttons are *toggle* buttons. A toggle button is one that is turned on or off, usually by applying or removing the same command. Each of the emphasis buttons can also be applied or removed using keyboard shortcuts. This way, you do not have to reach for the mouse to emphasize text. To apply or remove bold, press [Ctrl] + [B]. The shortcut for italics is [Ctrl] + [I], and the shortcut for underline is [Ctrl] + [U].

---

# LESSON 2: Changing Font and Font Size

*Font* refers to the shape, weight, and design of a set of characters and numbers. There are two basic categories of fonts, *serif fonts* and *sans serif fonts*. Serif fonts have lines on the ends of characters that help lead the reader's eyes across a page. Serif fonts are generally used for a large amount of text such as reports and papers. Sans serif fonts do not have lines at the end of characters and are typically used for titles and other short phrases. *Font size* is the height of the characters measured in points. There are 72 points to an inch. The larger the font size the larger the font appears. A good choice for text paragraphs is 10 or 12 point font. Larger size fonts are used for titles and other places where you need to have the text stand out from the body of the document. The term *point* is abbreviated *pt*. Table 3.1 shows some examples of serif and sans serif fonts. The default font used in Microsoft Word 2007 is Calibri 11 point for normal text, and Cambria 13 pt for headings and titles.

| SERIF FONTS | SANS SERIF FONTS |
|---|---|
| Times New Roman | Arial |
| Bookman Old Style | Century Gothic |
| Century Schoolbook | Comic Sans MS |
| Courier New | Lucida Console |
| Cambria | Calibri |

TABLE 3.1

In this lesson, you change the font and font size of the title lines in the *Alternative Fuel Proposal* document.

## To Change Font and Font Size

1. **Select all three title lines at the top of the document, and then on the Home tab, in the Font group, click the Font arrow.** An alphabetical list of available fonts is displayed based on the current printer selected and the software that is installed on your computer. Each font name is displayed in its own font typeface. The most recently used fonts are shown at the top of the list, as shown in Figure 3.3, which makes it convenient to apply a font that you use frequently. Your list will probably look different from the one shown in the figure.

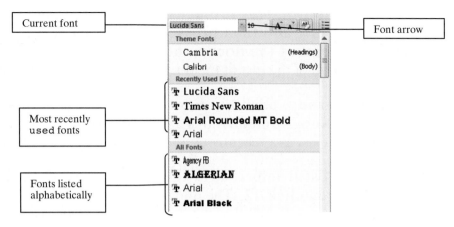

Current font

Font arrow

Most recently used fonts

Fonts listed alphabetically

FIGURE 3.3

2. **Scroll through the Font list and choose Arial. Note:** the text in the document changes as you scroll over the various fonts, which is the *Live Preview* feature of Word 2007. All three lines of text are changed to Arial.

3. **With the title lines still selected, in the Font group, click the Font Size arrow.** A list of font sizes, from 8 to 72, displays. The larger the font size, the larger the text looks when you print the document.

4. **Choose 14 from the Font Size list. As you scroll though the font sizes, notice that the Live Preview feature displays the different font sizes on the selected text.** The font size is now slightly larger as shown in Figure 3.4.

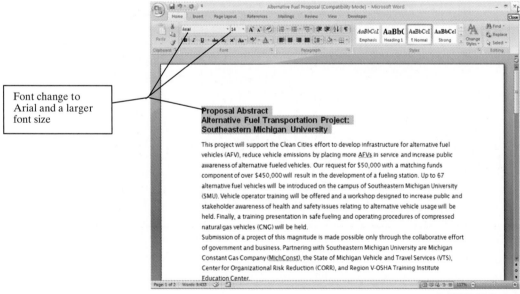

Font change to Arial and a larger font size

FIGURE 3.4

5. **Click to the left of *This project will* in the first paragraph; hold down Ctrl + Shift and then press End. The text from the insertion point to the end of the documen**t is selected. Now you can change the font and font size of the rest of the document.

6. **In the Font group, click the Font arrow, scroll the list, and then click Times New Roman.** If this font has been used recently, it will display at the top of the list as a recently used font.

7. **With the text still selected, in the Font group, click the Font Size arrow and then click 12.** The font size is increased from 10 pt to 12 pt as shown in Figure 3.5. Recall that the default font for Microsoft Office 2007 is Calibri.11 point font.

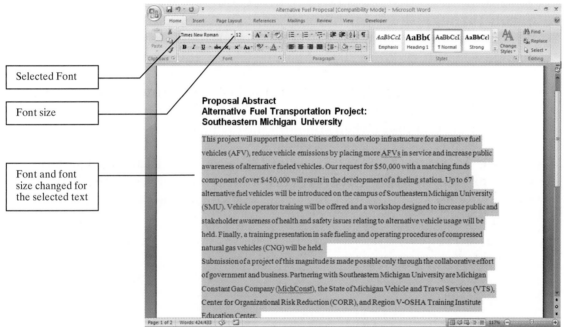

FIGURE 3.5

8. **Click anywhere in the document to clear the selection; save your changes to the *Alternative Fuel Proposal* document and leave the file open for the next lesson.**

## LESSON 3: Changing Font Color

Another formatting technique that will draw attention or differentiate text is font color. Font color should be used consistently and judiciously. For example, Microsoft Help uses blue font color for links to topics. You also need to consider how a document will be distributed before you decide to apply color to your font. If you distribute information online, font color can be very effective. If, however, you print a document and then make copies, unless you have a color copier, the color will show as a shade of gray.

1. With the *Alternative Fuel Proposal* document open, press Ctrl + End. The insertion point moves to the end of the document.

2. Press Enter↵ and type: Formatted by: and then type your name; select the line you just typed, and then on the Home tab, in the Font group, click the Font Color arrow. A gallery of colors displays. Here you can select a color to apply to the currently selected text. As you point to each color in the gallery, a ScreenTip displays the name of that color, as shown in Figure 3.6.

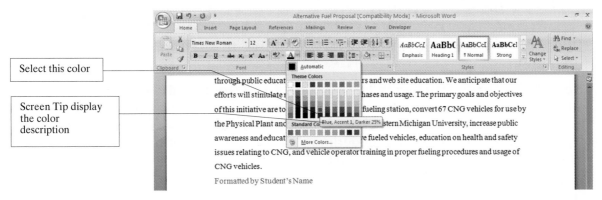

Select this color

Screen Tip display the color description

FIGURE 3.6

3. Point to the fifth column, fifth row. After the ScreenTip displays Blue, Accent 1, Darker 25%, click the color. Click at the end of the selected text to clear the selection. The color gallery closes and the font color of the selected text changes to blue.

4. Save your changes to the *Alternative Fuel Proposal* document and leave the file open for the next lesson.

---

## TO EXTEND YOUR KNOWLEDGE...

### APPLYING FONT COLORS

The default color for the Font Color button—when you open a new document—is red. After a different color has been selected, such as the blue you applied to your document, the Font Color button displays that color as the currently selected color. This makes it easier to apply the same color to different parts of a document. The selected color will continue to display on the button until the software application is closed or until a different color is selected.

---

## LESSON 4: Applying Character Effects and Adding Symbols

Character effects include such things as superscripts, subscripts, and strikethroughs. *Superscripts* are characters that are placed above the rest of the text in line, such as a number that represents a power in a formula ($e = mc^2$). ***Subscripts*** are characters that are placed below the rest of the text in line, such as the chemical formula for water ($H_2O$). Several text effects are available to enhance text in documents you create. ***Strikethroughs*** are letters with a line through them to indicate that they are to be deleted. They are often used when more than one person is working on the same document.

***Symbols*** are also characters that are not found on the keyboard. These include the copyright and trademark symbols, Greek letters, happy faces, and many others. In the next section, you will practice applying text effects and inserting symbols. Symbols and most character effects are available to use in most Microsoft Office applications.

### To Apply Text Effects and Add Symbols

1. **Press Ctrl + Home to move the insertion point to the top of the document.**

2. **Select the three title lines at the top of the document. On the Home tab, in the lower right corner of the Font group, click the Dialog Box Launcher button.** The Font dialog box opens. Here you can change the font, font style, font size, font color, underline style, or apply any of the special text effects that are listed in the Effects area.

3. **Click the Small caps check box in the Effects area.** The preview area displays the first line of selected text the effect is applied to the document so you can see how it will look as shown in Figure 3.7.

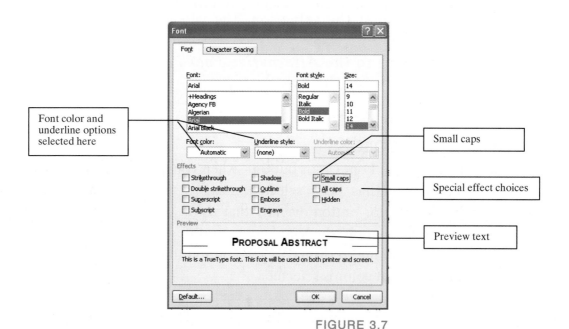

FIGURE 3.7

4. **Click OK, and then click anywhere in the document to clear the selection.** The three title lines are now displayed in *small caps*, which display the capital letters in a normal manner, but display the lowercase letters as capital letters that are approximately 3/4 height.

5. **Place the insertion point just to the right of *Cities* in the first sentence of the first full paragraph.** The organization, Clean Cities, has registered its name as a trademark, so you want to add a registered trademark symbol.

6. **Click the Insert tab, and in the Symbols group, click the Symbol button, and then from the displayed list click More Symbols.** The Symbol dialog box displays as shown in Figure 3.8.

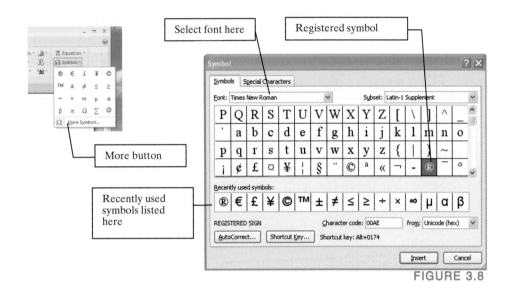

FIGURE 3.8

7. **Select Times New Roman from the Font box, if necessary; scroll through the list and locate the registered symbol ® and then click the symbol.** The registered symbol is selected—the background changes to blue to indicate it is selected to be inserted. Notice that the most recently used symbols are in a box near the bottom of the dialog box. This symbol may also be found there.

8. **Click the Insert button, and then close the Symbol dialog box.** The symbol is displayed at the insertion point location. This symbol needs to be displayed in super-script format.

9. **Select the registered symbol, and then click the Home tab and in the Font group, click the Superscript button. Click anywhere in the document to clear the selected text.** The Subscript and Superscript effects can be applied using the buttons in the Font group. The registered symbol is reduced in size and raised slightly above the line as shown in Figure 3.9.

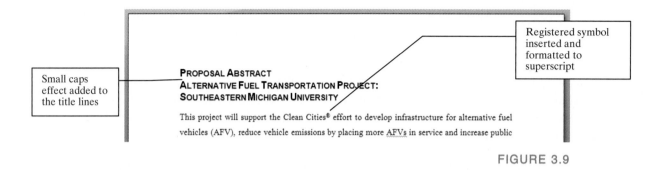

Small caps effect added to the title lines

Registered symbol inserted and formatted to superscript

**PROPOSAL ABSTRACT**
**ALTERNATIVE FUEL TRANSPORTATION PROJECT:**
**SOUTHEASTERN MICHIGAN UNIVERSITY**

This project will support the Clean Cities® effort to develop infrastructure for alternative fuel

vehicles (AFV), reduce vehicle emissions by placing more AFVs in service and increase public

FIGURE 3.9

10. Save your changes to the *Alternative Fuel Proposal* document and leave the file open for the next lesson.

# LESSON 5: Changing Alignment

*Alignment* is the horizontal placement of text, whether it is between the left and right margins in a Word document, in a cell on a Microsoft Office Excel worksheet, on a Microsoft Office PowerPoint slide, or in a graphic object. In documents, most text is arranged on the page so that there is a uniform white space between the left edge of the paper and the beginning of each line. Because the words in each line are of different lengths, the right edge of the paragraph is usually uneven. This type of alignment is called *left-aligned* because the words are evenly aligned on the left. The opposite alignment—with the right edge aligned and the left edge uneven— is called *right-aligned*. *Center* alignment places text in the center of an area. If text is aligned evenly on both sides—known as *justified*—the computer adjusts the size of the spaces between the words in each line to ensure that the text aligns evenly. In this lesson, you change the alignment of the title lines and the body of the text.

## To Change Text Alignment

1. **Select the three title lines at the top of the document. On the Home tab, in the Paragraph group, click the Center button.** All three lines are centered on the page.

2. **Click anywhere in the first full paragraph, and then in the Paragraph group click the Justify button.** Both the left and right margins are now evenly aligned. Notice that you do not have to select the entire paragraph to change paragraph formatting as long as the insertion point is somewhere in the paragraph you want to format (see Figure 3.10).

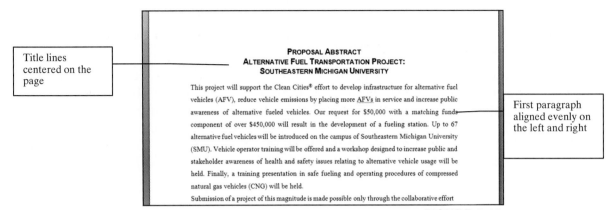

**Title lines centered on the page**

PROPOSAL ABSTRACT
ALTERNATIVE FUEL TRANSPORTATION PROJECT:
SOUTHEASTERN MICHIGAN UNIVERSITY

This project will support the Clean Cities® effort to develop infrastructure for alternative fuel vehicles (AFV), reduce vehicle emissions by placing more AFVs in service and increase public awareness of alternative fueled vehicles. Our request for $50,000 with a matching funds component of over $450,000 will result in the development of a fueling station. Up to 67 alternative fuel vehicles will be introduced on the campus of Southeastern Michigan University (SMU). Vehicle operator training will be offered and a workshop designed to increase public and stakeholder awareness of health and safety issues relating to alternative vehicle usage will be held. Finally, a training presentation in safe fueling and operating procedures of compressed natural gas vehicles (CNG) will be held.

Submission of a project of this magnitude is made possible only through the collaborative effort

**First paragraph aligned evenly on the left and right**

FIGURE 3.10

3. **Click in the next paragraph, Press F4 to repeat the previous format.** The next paragraph is aligned evenly on the left and right. Alternatively, on the Quick Access toolbar, click the Repeat button to repeat the previous action.

4. **On the Home tab, in the Clipboard group, double-click the Format Painter button.** When the pointer is on the document, it displays a paintbrush icon attached to the end of the pointer. This indicates that the Format Painter command has been activated. The Format Painter copies the format of the selected text and applies that format to the text that is selected next. The formatting that is copied—in this case an alignment format—can be applied to another paragraph simply by clicking somewhere in the paragraph.

5. **Scroll down the document and click in the next paragraph of body text.** The alignment on the left and right is applied to the third paragraph in the document as shown in Figure 3.11. The Format Painter icon is still attached to your pointer because you double-clicked the Format Painter button. It will remain active until you click the Format Painter button a second time to turn it off, or until you click another button.

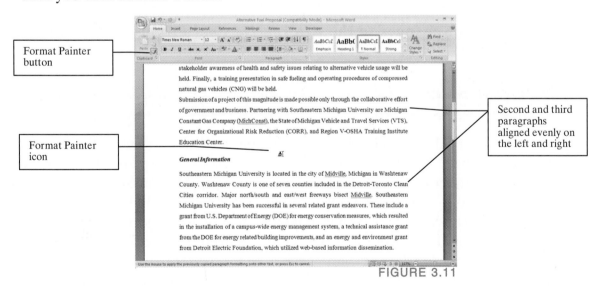

**Format Painter button**

**Format Painter icon**

**Second and third paragraphs aligned evenly on the left and right**

FIGURE 3.11

## If you have problems...

If the paintbrush icon is not attached to your pointer, it means you clicked the button with a single click rather than a double-click. A single click of the Format Painter but button attaches the paintbrush to your mouse for one use, after which it is turned off automatically. To apply the same format multiple times, double-click the Format Painter button, which keeps it attached to your pointer until you click the Format Painter button a second time to turn it off.

6. **With the Format Painter icon still attached to your pointer, scroll down and click the last full paragraph of body text to apply the justify alignment.**

7. **Click the Format Painter button to deactivate it.**

8. **Click in the *Formatted by:* line, and then in the Paragraph group, click the Align Right button.** The line with your name is aligned on the right side of the page as shown in Figure 3.12.

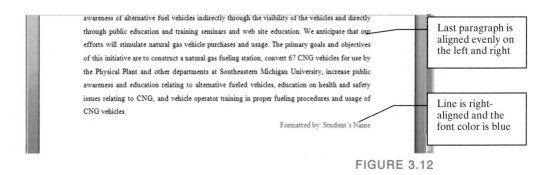

awareness of alternative fuel vehicles indirectly through the visibility of the vehicles and directly through public education and training seminars and web site education. We anticipate that our efforts will stimulate natural gas vehicle purchases and usage. The primary goals and objectives of this initiative are to construct a natural gas fueling station, convert 67 CNG vehicles for use by the Physical Plant and other departments at Southeastern Michigan University, increase public awareness and education relating to alternative fueled vehicles, education on health and safety issues relating to CNG, and vehicle operator training in proper fueling procedures and usage of CNG vehicles.

Formatted by: Student's Name

Last paragraph is aligned evenly on the left and right

Line is right-aligned and the font color is blue

FIGURE 3.12

9. **Save your changes to the *Alternative Fuel Proposal* document and leave the file open for the next lesson.**

## LESSON 6: Previewing a Document Before Printing

Documents, worksheets, and presentations often need to be printed for distribution on paper or to provide a paper copy of a file. Regardless of the type of file you are working with, many printing functions are common to most applications. For example, you can preview your work before you print it to see how it displays on the page. This provides the opportunity to view the overall layout of the text on the page and make adjustments if necessary. The orientation of the paper can be changed from *portrait*—the page is taller than it is wide—to *landscape*— the page is wider than it is tall. Previewing your work can help save paper by discovering and correcting layout problems before a document is printed.

Each application uses a set of defaults for common formatting controls such as font, font size, and *margins*—the white space between the edge of the paper and the text. Just as you changed font type and font size, you can also adjust the margins. Adjusting margins can some-times help you fit a document on one page rather than two.

In this lesson, you examine the Page Setup dialog box where you control the margins, page orientation, and paper size. You then examine the document using the Print Preview window and make an adjustment to the document.

### To Preview a Document Before Printing

1. **With the *Alternative Fuel Proposal* document open, from the Ribbon, click the Page Layout tab. In the Page Setup group, click the Margins button and then at the bottom of the list click Custom Margins.** The Page Setup dialog box displays. This dialog box is used to change several items that affect the setup of the page. The dialog box varies slightly between applications, but in all cases you can change margins, page orientation, and paper size using this dialog box. Other factors that are controlled here will be covered later in the individual applications.

2. **Select the value in the Left box under Margins and type: 1.25.** In a blank document in Word 2007, the default margins are 1" on all four sides.

3. **Press Tab. In the Right box, type: 1.25and then press Tab.** Pressing Tab moves the insertion point to the next text box. When changing margins you can use the spin arrows in the margin box to increase or decrease the value by .10 each time you click the arrow. It is not necessary to type the inch (") abbreviation because it is assumed.

4. **Click the Landscape button under Orientation.** If it is appropriate, you can change the orientation of your paper to landscape. Notice that the preview area has changed the orientation of the page and the margins also change.

5. **Click the Portrait button.** Most Word documents are printed in portrait layout, with individual pages printed in landscape when the information on the page warrants it. You will use landscape layout more frequently with Excel and PowerPoint files. Compare your screen with Figure 3.13.

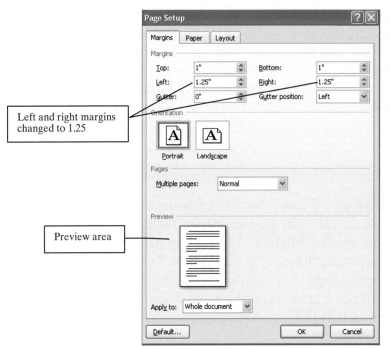

Left and right margins
changed to 1.25

Preview area

FIGURE 3.13

6. **Click the Paper tab and then click the Paper size arrow.** The default paper size is *Letter 8 1/2 x 11 in* (your Paper size box may only state *Letter;* this is controlled by the printer that is selected). In all applications, letter is the default paper size. If you need to use legal size, half size pages, or something else, change the paper size here (see Figure 3.14).

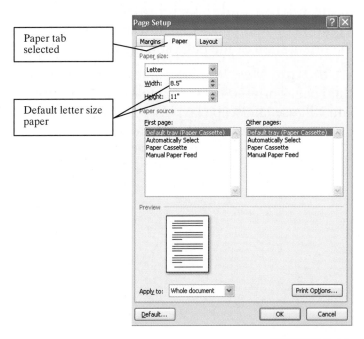

Paper tab
selected

Default letter size
paper

FIGURE 3.14

7. **Click the Paper Size arrow to close the list without changing the paper size. Click OK.** The dialog box closes and the left and right margins are increased to 1.25".

8. Click **the Office button, point to Print and then click Print Preview.** The second page of the document displays the way it will look when it is printed. The Print Preview toolbar displays at the top of the window. The pointer, as shown in Figure 3.15, is shaped like a magnifying glass with a plus in it. Clicking on the document will increase the magnification of the document on your screen

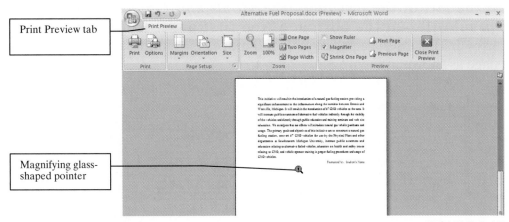

Print Preview tab

Magnifying glass-shaped pointer

FIGURE 3.15

9. **Scroll to the second page of the document, if necessary. Move the pointer to the top of the second page and click.** The top portion of page 2 displays in a larger view and you can now read the text. The magnifying pointer shows a minus sign. If you click again, the zoom will change to a smaller number and the whole page will display on the screen.

10. **On the Print Preview tab, in the Zoom group, click the Zoom button. In the displayed Zoom dialog box click the Many Pages button. Move the pointer to the right on the first row until 1 x 2 Pages displays as shown in Figure 3.16.** Here you select the number of pages you want to see at one time and whether the pages display horizontally or vertically on the screen.

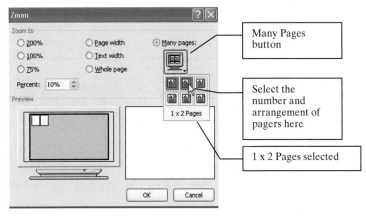

Many Pages button

Select the number and arrangement of pagers here

1 x 2 Pages selected

FIGURE 3.16

11. **Click to select the 1 x 2 Pages display, and then click OK.** Notice that a subtitle is shown at the bottom of page one. It would be better if that subtitle were at the top of the next page so it appears on the same page as the text that comes under it.

12. **On the Print Preview tab, in the Preview group, click Magnifier** to remove the check mark. The magnifier pointer is turned off. The pointer reverts to its normal characteristics for editing—it is an I- beam pointer on the document and a white arrow in the margins. Now you can make changes to your document in the Print Preview mode.

13. **Click to the left of the last line—the *Goals and Objectives of the Program* subtitle—at the bottom of the first page. Hold down** Ctrl **and press** Enter↵. This inserts a page break and moves the subtitle to the top of the second page as shown in Figure 3.17.

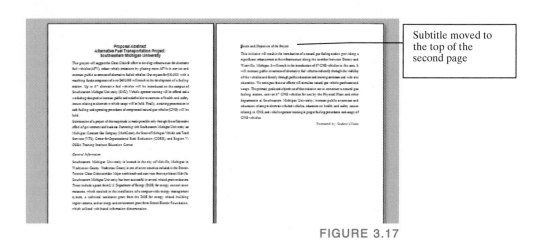

Subtitle moved to the top of the second page

FIGURE 3.17

14. **On the Print Preview tab, click the Close Print Preview button. Save your changes to the *Alternative Fuel Proposal* document and leave the file open for the next lesson.** The Print Preview window closes and the document returns to its previous view.

## LESSON 7: Printing a Document

You can print a file by selecting Print, or Quick Print from the Office menu, or by placing the Quick Print icon on the Quick Access toolbar. These methods are quick and easy and apply the preset defaults to the print output. In all cases, that means it will print all pages of the currently active file, or in the case of Excel, the currently active worksheet. Using the Print dialog box gives you more control over the print output. For example, you may want to select a different printer—a color printer—rather than using the default printer. The Print dialog box also enables you to print selected pages, or to print more than one copy.

In this lesson you examine the Print dialog box to see the printing options it controls and how to select a different printer.

To Print a Document

1. **From the Office menu, click Print and examine the Print dialog box. Locate each of the areas identified in Figure 3.18.** The printer listed for your computer may differ from the one that is shown in the figure. If you use the Print button on the Standard toolbar, the selections that show in the Print dialog box would be executed—one copy of all the pages in your document would be sent to the default printer.
   **Note:** Quick print will send the document to the default printer without selecting any options.

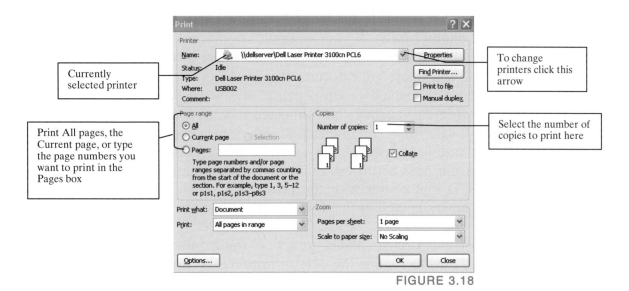

Currently selected printer

To change printers click this arrow

Print All pages, the Current page, or type the page numbers you want to print in the Pages box

Select the number of copies to print here

FIGURE 3.18

2. **Click the Name box arrow to see other printers that may be installed on your computer.** If you are using a computer lab you may see several printers installed both color printer and black and white.

3. **If a color printer is installed, select it.** If you have the option to use a color printer, select it to print this document so you can see how the colored font displays. If you do not have a color printer available, when you print your document notice how it handles the line that you changed to blue.

4. **Click OK in the lower-right corner of the Print dialog box.** The Print dialog box closes and the file is sent to the selected printer. Depending on your printer, a printer dialog box may display on your screen while the file is printing.

5. **Leave the *Alternative Fuel Proposal* document open and continue to the next lesson.**

### KEYBOARD SHORTCUTS

The keyboard shortcut to print your open document is [Ctrl] + [P]. Similarly, [Ctrl] + [S] is used to save a file and [Ctrl] + [O] is used to display the Open dialog box. Keyboard shortcuts are listed on the ScreenTip that displays when you point to a button or command.

## LESSON 8: Viewing the Print Queue and Changing the Default Printer

When you print a document it is sent to the default printer. The printer may be on your desk or down the hall in another room. If your computer is connected to a printer over a network, along with several computers, your file is sent to a *print queue* to wait its turn to be printed. If you want to see where your document is in the queue, you can look at the print queue. You can also use this window to stop, pause, or cancel a print job.

When you buy a new printer it needs to be connected to your computer and the *print driver*—the printer software that communicates with your computer—needs to be installed. With newer operating systems, this is usually a *plug-and-play* process where the computer recognizes the new hardware and searches automatically for the correct driver on the software CD that comes with the printer, or on the Internet. After the printer is installed it can be designated as the default printer or a shared printer if you are on a network.

In this lesson you use the Control Panel to access the printers available for your computer. You also learn how to change the default printer, and how to access the print queue window.

### To View the Print Queue and Change the Default Printer

1. **Click the Start button, and then click Control Panel from the Start menu.** The Control Panel window displays, as shown in Figure 3.19. Here you can view and control many aspects of your computer hardware and configuration, including the printer. This figure displays the Control Panel window in the Windows XP operating system. Your window may be configured differently than the one shown in the figure.

### If you have problems...

If your screen displays a vertical list, it is probably in the Control Panel Classics view. In the upper-left corner of the window, click the *Switch to Category View* option.

Click here to switch between Classic and Category views

Select Printer and Other Hardware option

Explorer Bar

FIGURE 3.19

2. **Select Printers and Other Hardware.** The Printers and Other Hardware window opens as shown in Figure 3.20. Here you can view the installed printers, add a printer, or look at other hardware installed on your computer, such as the mouse, keyboard, modem, or scanner.

 **If you have problems...**

The directions for this lesson are based upon the Windows XP operating system. If your computer uses another version of the Windows operating system, the directions for this lesson will not match exactly. For example, in Windows Vista, in the Control Panel click Hardware and Sound and then you would click Printers.

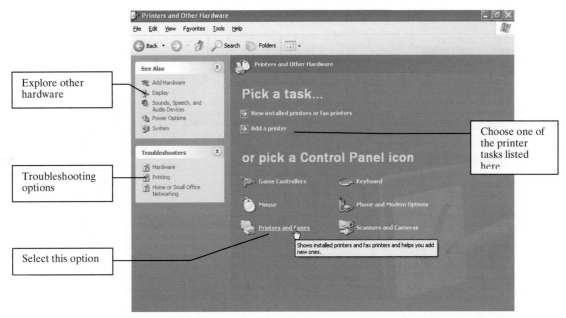

Explore other hardware

Troubleshooting options

Select this option

Choose one of the printer tasks listed here

FIGURE 3.20

## If you have problems...

The Explorer Bar on the left side of the window may be set to display folders, favorites, or to use for searching. If it does not match what is shown in the figure, click View, Explorer Bar on the menu bar. Click any item that is checked to clear the check marks. The Explorer Bar should now be set to display as shown in the figure.

3. **Select *Printers and Faxes* under *or pick a Control Panel icon.*** A list of available printers displays and the Printer Tasks display in the Explorer Bar. When you make a selection, the Explorer Bar changes to reflect the selection you have made.

4. **Click the printer that displays a check mark next to it.** The check mark indicates the default printer. A hand under the printer icon indicates that the printer is a shared printer—one that is available to more than one user on a network. Examine the Printer Tasks that are available in the Explorer Bar as shown in Figure 3.21. The printers that are shown on your screen may differ from those shown in the figure.

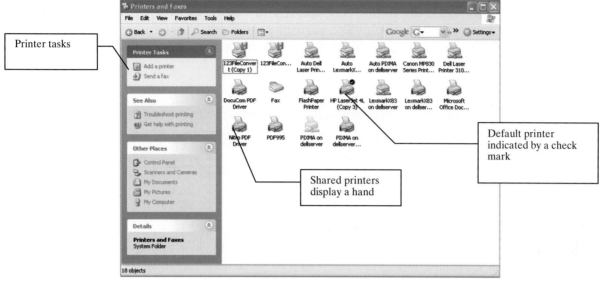

Printer tasks

Default printer indicated by a check mark

Shared printers display a hand

FIGURE 3.21

5. **Click the *See what's printing* option under Printer Tasks.** The print queue window opens and displays the name of the selected printer in the title bar. Here you view the documents that are currently in the queue to be printed as shown in Figure 3.22. Your print queue may be empty or it may display several documents that are waiting to be printed. If you right-click on a document listed, a shortcut menu appears, as shown in Figure 3.23, that gives you the option to pause, restart, or cancel the print job. If you pause, restart, or cancel a print job, the *Status* column changes to reflect the action you have taken.

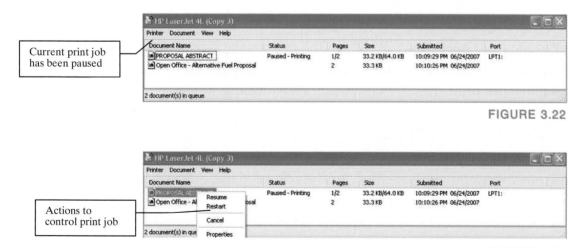

Current print job has been paused

FIGURE 3.22

Actions to control print job

FIGURE 3.23

6. **Close the print queue window; right-click on one of the printers listed in your Printer and Faxes window.** A shortcut menu, as shown in Figure 3.24, displays the actions that you can take with this printer. *Open* is displayed in bold and is the default choice. If you double-click the printer it opens the print queue window to display the current print jobs. You can use the shortcut menu to set a printer as the default printer, to share a printer, delete a printer, or perform the other actions listed.

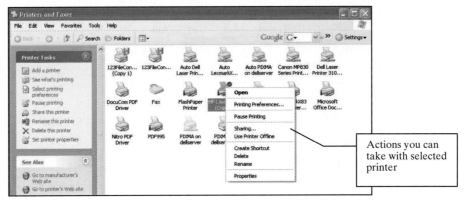

FIGURE 3.24

7. **Close the Printer and Faxes window without making any changes to your printer choices; close the** *Alternative Fuel Proposal* **document and close Word.**

---

## TO EXTEND YOUR KNOWLEDGE...

### SHORTCUT TO PRINT QUEUE WINDOW

A shortcut to the print queue may display in the tray on the right side of your taskbar after a document has been sent to the printer. Double-clicking the printer button shortcut displays the print queue window and provides quicker access to pausing or stopping a print action.

### RESOLVING PRINT PROBLEMS

When you click the Print button, a complex process takes place to transfer the document from your computer's memory to the printed page. Success depends on the proper functioning of each component in the process. If the document does not print, here is a list of possible reasons to check, from simple and most likely to more difficult and less likely.

**Document settings**—the document does not match the paper size or the printer's ability to print close to the edge.

♦ *Confirm that the document can be printed by the default printer*—look for error messages that appear on the screen when you try to print. If the message says that the document will not fit within the margins of the paper, you need to change the layout of the document. Click the Office Button, point to Print, and click on Print Preview to see if the document will fit. Click the Page Layout tab and use the Page Setup group to change the orientation or margins.

♦ *Confirm that the header and footer print correctly*—some printers can get closer to the edge of the paper than others. The footer may not print completely on some printers. If this problem occurs, click the Page Layout tab, choose Margins from the Page Setup group, and click Custom Margins. Check the size of the top and bottom margins. Click the Layout tab and check the distance of the header and footer from the edge. Increase these values until the header and footer print correctly.

**Printer hardware**—look for connection problems and consumable supplies problems.

♦ *Confirm that the printer is* receiving *power*—look for a power indicator light and check to see that the power cord is plugged into the wall and the back of the printer.

♦ *Confirm that the computer is connected to the printer*—check both ends of the cable that connects the computer and printer to be sure they are both seated properly.

♦ *Confirm that the printer is online*—this term means that the printer's own diagnostic program has determined that it is ready to print. The online status is usually indicated by an indicator lamp. If the printer is offline, the lamp may flash or a red light may display. If the printer is offline, check its display panel or indicator lights for a statement of the problem. The most common problems are paper jams and low ink or toner. Follow the directions in the printer's manual to clear paper jams or replace ink or toner cartridges.

**Printer software settings**—look for incorrect settings or problems with the print queue. Start each of the following items by opening the Control Panel. Choose Printers and Other Hardware and then select Printers and Faxes to open the Printers and Faxes window.

♦ *Confirm that the document was sent to the correct printer*—the default printer has a check box next to it. When you clicked the Print button, your document was sent to the default printer. If this is not the printer you expected, your document is probably in the out-tray of the default printer. To make a different printer the default printer for your computer, right-click on the desired printer and choose *Set as Default Printer.*

♦ *Confirm the* printer *is ready*—check the status of the default printer. If it says *Paused,* right-click the printer icon in the Printers and Faxes window and choose *Resume Printing.*

**Security**—you may not have permission to use this printer or in a work or lab setting during the evening or weekends. Start each of the following items by opening the Control Panel. Choose Printers and Other Hardware and then select Printers and Faxes to open the Printers and Faxes window. Right-click the printer icon and choose *Properties* to open the Properties dialog box for the printer.

♦ *Confirm that you have permission to use this printer*—if you share a printer over the network, the administrator may not have included your computer on the list of those that may use the printer. Click the Security tab. Confirm that you are a member of one of the groups that is allowed to use the printer. Click the Advanced button to see more details.

♦ *Confirm that the printer is available at the present time of day*—if you use a printer on a network, the network administrator may have blocked access to the printer at night to prevent unauthorized use. Click the Advanced tab and check to see that the printer is available.

**Printer installation**—if you recently upgraded the operating system or added the printer to your computer, look for installation problems with the drivers and assigned printer ports. Start each of the following items by opening the Control Panel. Choose Printers and Other Hardware and then select Printers and Faxes to open the Printers and Faxes window. Right-click the printer icon and choose *Properties* to open the Properties dialog box for the printer. If you find a problem in this list, it is usually better to install the printer again. This process is the last item on the list.

♦ *Confirm the printer is assigned to a port*—the computer should be programmed to send the document to a specific port for this computer. Click the Ports tab. Confirm that one of the Port boxes is checked for the printer. If the printer is plugged into the parallel port in the back of the system unit the port may be an LPT1. Printers may also use USB ports. If the printer is not listed, install the printer again.

♦ *Confirm the correct driver is installed*—click the Advanced tab. The printer name and model number listed in the Driver box should match your printer. If not, install the printer again.

♦ *Reinstall the printer*—in many cases you must run the installation program provided with the printer before you connect the printer to the system unit. If you upgrade to a new operating system you may need to download an upgraded version of the print driver to work with the new *operating* system. Download a new print driver or confirm that you have the installation disks that come with the printer and that they work with the operating system on your computer. Right-click the printer icon and choose Delete. Place the disc that comes with the printer in your computer and run the Setup program if it does not start automatically. Follow the directions. Connect the printer and turn it on after the software is installed. The installation program should assign the port correctly and install the correct driver.

If the document does not print after you have done these steps, make note of what you have tried and seek help from a qualified technician. Tell the technician what you have tried and the results. This is valuable information and the technician will be able to solve your problem more quickly if he or she does not have to check these items.

## SUMMARY

In this project, you used several formatting tools that are common in Microsoft Office applications and in many other software programs. Formatting makes a document easier to read because it identifies the document's organization and helps lead the readers' eyes across the page. You applied emphasis to text to make it stand out from the rest of the document and changed font, font size, and font color. You also applied special text effects and inserted a symbol.

You changed the alignment of text—the horizontal placement of text between the left and right margins in a document—within a cell or graphic object.

You used the Print Preview window to examine a document before it was printed and to adjust the layout of the document on the page. You changed margins in the Page Setup dialog box and explored the settings in the Print dialog box. Finally, you examined the print queue and learned how to change the default printer. A list of possible printer problems and how to correct those problems was presented.

You can extend your learning by reviewing concepts and terms, and by practicing variations of skills presented in the lessons.

## KEY TERMS

| | | |
|---|---|---|
| alignment | margins | serif fonts |
| center | plug and play | small caps |
| font | point (pt) | strikethroughs |
| font size | portrait | subscripts |
| justified | print driver | superscripts |
| landscape | print queue | symbols |
| left-aligned | right-aligned | toggle |
| Live Preview | sans serif fonts | |

## CHECKING CONCEPTS AND TERMS

### SCREEN ID
Label each element of the screen shown in Figure 3.25.

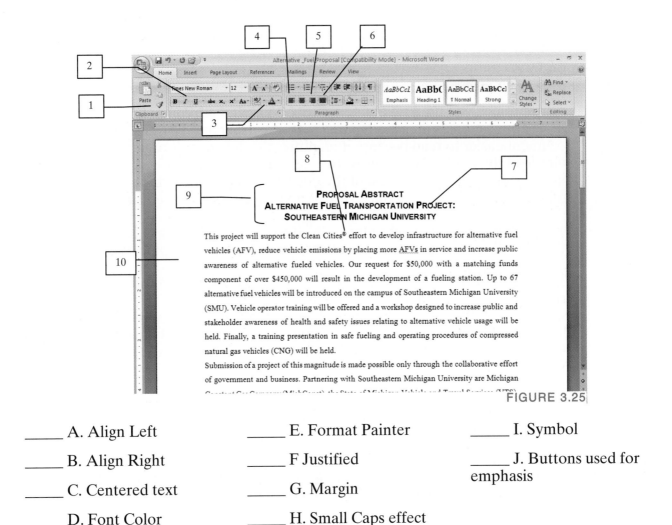

FIGURE 3.25

_____ A. Align Left  _____ E. Format Painter  _____ I. Symbol

_____ B. Align Right  _____ F Justified  _____ J. Buttons used for emphasis

_____ C. Centered text  _____ G. Margin

_____ D. Font Color  _____ H. Small Caps effect

## MULTIPLE CHOICE

### Circle the letter of the correct answer for each of the following.

1. Emphasis can be added to text by adding _____. [L1, L3]
a. color
b. bold
c. italics
d. All of the above

2. For the body of a document, it is generally better to use a_____ font because it helps lead the reader's eyes across the page. [L2]
a. serif
b. small caps
c. sans serif
d. Sanskrit

3. To add special characters to your document such as ®, © or ™ use the _____ dialog box. [L4]
a. Format
b. Symbol
c. Special Effect
d. Character Effect

4. The alignment that displays the text with the characters on the right side of the page uneven is _____. [L5]
a. justified
b. aligned-left
c. aligned-right
d. centered

5. The Print Preview window
_____. [L6]
a. displays the layout of the text on the page the way it will be printed
b. cannot be used to make changes to the document
c. shows only one page at a time
d. All of the above

6. To change the orientation of the document on the page, use the
_____. [L7]
a. Use the Orientation button on the Print Preview window
b. Use the Orientation button on the Page Layout tab
c. Use the Page Setup dialog box
d. All of the above will work

7. The print queue can be used to
_____. [L8]
a. change the default printer
b. select a different printer
c. cancel, pause, or restart a print job
d. share a printer with another computer on the network

8. If a document does not print you should check to be sure that
_____. [L8]
a. the printer is turned on
b. the printer has paper
c. your computer is connected to the printer
d. All of the above should be checked

9. A special character effect where the characters are placed below the rest of the text in a line is known as
_____. [L4]
a. small caps
b. subscript
c. superscript
d. strikethrough

10. Font size is measured in points and there
are 72 points to an inch, which means that a 12 point font size is _____ of an inch. [L2]
a. 1/3
b. 1/4
c. 1/6
d. 1/8

## DISCUSSION

1. Examine documents with different size fonts and that use a serif and a sans serif font for the body of the text. How does the choice of font affect your ability to read the document? What font size are you comfortable reading on the screen? On a printed document? Do you find it easier to read sans serf fonts or serif fonts? [L2]

2. When desktop computers were first used in offices, some claimed that offices would become paperless because everything could be stored on computers. That has not happened. Why do you think we continue to print documents? Do you print more using a computer or less? Why? Do you think using Print Preview to examine a document before it is printed will help reduce paper use? [L6]—[L8]

3. Examine two different examples of printed material such as a newsletter, magazine article, meeting minutes, or some other document that is distributed to a group. Compare the formatting in each and identify the font, font size, emphasis, color, or other special formatting techniques that has been used. Does it effectively draw your attention and help you understand the important ideas that are being conveyed? Could it be improved, and if so, what suggestions would you offer? [L1]—[L5]

# SKILL DRILL

Skill Drill exercises reinforce project skills. Each skill reinforced is the same, or nearly the same, as a skill presented in the project. Detailed instructions are provided in a step-by-step format. All of these exercises can be completed with Microsoft Office XP or later versions. Instructions throughout the exercises are based on the Windows XP operating system, running Microsoft Office 2007.

## 1. Changing Font, Font Size, Alignment, and Emphasis

Formatting is used to identify titles within a paper. In this Skill Drill, you format titles, author information, and subheadings so they stand out from the body of a document about distance education.

1. Start **Microsoft Office Word** and open the document *CE_0302* from the Student folder. Save it to your folder as a Word 97-2003 file named **Distance Education Technology.**

2. Select the first two lines of the document, which make up the title. On the **Home tab**, in the **Font Group**, click the **Font arrow**, and then click **Arial.** Click the **Font Size** button arrow, and then click **14.**

3. With the title still selected, in the **Font group**, click the **Bold** button. In the **Paragraph group**, click the **Center** button to align the title lines in the center of the page.

4. Select the two lines that identify the author and then in the **Paragraph group**, click the **Center** button.

5. On the line following the second author line, type **Edited by: Your Name** (use your own name), and then press the ⏎Enter key. Center this line.

6. Scroll down and locate the subheading *Interactive Technologies.* Move the pointer to the selection bar on the left and click to select the subtitle. Add bold emphasis and center the alignment.

7. With the subtitle still selected, double-click the **Home tab** and in the **Clipboard group**, click the **Format Painter** button. This copies the format to the Format Painter so it can be applied to other subheadings.

8. Scroll to the bottom of page two and select the next subheading, *Conclusion.* The subheading is bold and centered and the Format Painter remains attached to the pointer so you can use it again.

9. Scroll down and select the subheading *Reference List.* The bold and center formatting is applied; click the **Format Painter** button to deselect it, and then save your changes.

10. Click the **Office** button, point to **Print,** and then click **Print Preview.**

11. On the **Print Preview tab**, in the **Zoom group**, click the **Zoom** button. In the Zoom dialog box click the **Many pages** option button, and then click the **Many pages** button and choose **1 x 3** to view the three pages horizontally on the screen Click **OK.** Notice that the last two lines of the last paragraph under Interactive Technologies will print on the top of the second page.

12. On the **Print Preview tab**, in the **Page Setup group**, click the **Margins** button. Select **Custom Margins.** Change the **Top** and **Bottom** margins to

**0.8"** and then click **OK**. The page layout is adjusted and the two lines move to the bottom of the first page.

13. In the **Preview group**, click **Close Print Preview** to close the Print Preview window.

14. From the **Office** menu point to **Print** and then click **Print**. In the Print dialog box, click the **Pages** option button under **Page range** and then type **1**. Click **OK** to print the first page of the document.

15. Save your changes, close the document, and close Microsoft Office Word.

## 2. Formatting an Excel Worksheet

Now that you have practiced formatting a document, it would be helpful to practice these skills on an Excel worksheet.

1. Open **Microsoft Office Excel**. Locate and open the Excel file *CE_0303*. Save the file in your folder as an Excel 97-2003 file named **Inventory Formatted.**

2. Select cells **A4 through A20**, and then click the **Home tab**, and in the **Alignment group** click the **Center** button. The Product Numbers listed in this column are centered.

3. Select cells **A4 through E4**. On the **Home tab**, in the **Font group**, click the **Bold** button. The column headings listed in this row are now bold.

4. Click cell **A21**, and on the **Home tab**, in the **Clipboard group** click the **Cut** button. Click cell **B21** and in the **Clipboard group** click the **Paste** button. The cell contents are moved.

5. With cell **B21** still the active cell, on the **Home tab**, in the **Alignment group**, click the **Align Right** button to align this label on the right side of the cell, and then click the **Italic** button.

6. Press ⸤Tab⸥ three times to move to cell **E21** and then click the **Bold** button. The total value is now in bold.

7. Select cells **A1 through E1**. On the **Home tab**, in the **Alignment group**, click the **Merge and Center** button. It is common to center the title of a worksheet over the entire width of the columns that are used in the worksheet. When you do this with the Merge and Center button it merges the selected cells and then centers the text, after which the merged cells are treated as one cell.

8. With cell **A1** still the active cell, in the **Font group**, click the **Font arrow**, and then click **Comic Sans MS**; click the **Font Size arrow**, select **16**, and then click the **Font Color arrow** and under **Standard Colors** click **Green**—the sixth color.

9. Select cells **A2 through E2** and click the **Merge and Center** button. Change the Font to **Comic Sans MS**, the Font Size to **14**, and the Font Color to **Green**.

10. Click cell **B23** and type your name.

11. Save your changes, and then from the **Office** menu point to **Print** and then click **Print Preview**

12. On the **Print Preview tab**, click the **Page Setup** button. In the Page Setup dialog box, click the **Page tab**, if necessary. Click **Landscape** and then click **OK**. The file displays in landscape orientation.

13. On the **Print Preview tab**, click the **Print** button, and then in the Print dialog box click **OK**. Save your changes, close the file, and then close Microsoft Office Excel.

## 3. Using Special Character Effects

It is customary to use subscripts and superscripts in scientific papers and mathematical formulas. The Format, Font command enables you to select this type of format so you can properly represent scientific and mathematical notations. In this Skill Drill you will add scientific notations to a paper about Nuclear Energy.

1. Start **Microsoft Office Word**. Locate and open *CE_0304* and save it in your folder as a Word 97-2003 file with the name **Nuclear Energy**.

2. Scroll to the bottom of the first page. In the paragraph that starts *Chain Reaction* notice the subscript and superscript formats that have been used in the paragraph as notations identifying uranium and plutonium isotopes.

3. Scroll to the end of the document. In the last paragraph that begins *Breeder Reactors*, in the first line, select *92* in the first notation. On the **Home tab**, in the **Font group**, click the **Subscript** button. Select *238*, and in the **Font group** click the **Superscript** button. Now this notation for Uranium is properly displayed.

4. Repeat this process for the remaining five notations in this paragraph. To use the Format Painter, select the subscript *92*, double-click the **Format Painter** from the **Clipboard group**, and then select 92 or 94 in the remaining five notations. Click the **Format Painter** to clear the format from this tool. Select the superscript *238*, double-click the **Format Painter,** and then select the three digits that follow *U* in each of the remaining five notations. Click the **Format Painter** to deselect it. **Note:** Select the numbers only, if you click the notation, the format will be applied to the entire notation.

5. Click at the end of the last paragraph, press [Enter ↵] two times, and then type **Edited by**: and your name. Save your changes.

6. From the **Office** menu, point to **Print**, and click **Print Preview**. Click the **One Page** button if necessary. The second page of the document should be displayed. Click to magnify the page and confirm that all of the scientific notations in the last paragraph display properly—the first two digits as subscripts, and the last three digits as superscripts.

7. On the **Print Preview tab**, click the **Close Print Preview** button. From the **Office** menu click **Print**. Click the **Pages** option button in the *Page range* area, and then type 2. Click **OK** to print the second page of the document. Close the document and then close Microsoft Office Word.

## 4. Stopping a Print Job

You want to make sure you know how to pause, restart, or cancel a print job using your computer.

1. Start **Microsoft Office Word** and then open *CE_0301*. This is the *Alternative Fuel Proposal* file that was used in the project.

2. Display the **Office** menu, point to **Print** and then click **Quick Print**. Examine the shortcut tray on the right side of the taskbar. If you see a printer icon, double-click it to access the print queue window and continue to step 4.

3. If you do not see a printer icon, click **Start, Control Panel, Printers and Other Hardware,** and then click **Printers and Faxes.** Double-click the default printer (the one that displays a check mark) and then continue to the next step.

4. Right-click the *CE_0301.doc,* and then click **Pause** from the shortcut menu. After a moment the printer should stop.

5. In the print queue window, click **Document** on the menu bar and then click **Cancel.** Click **Yes** to confirm that you want to cancel the selected print job. Your print job for the *CE_0301.doc* should be removed from the print queue.

6. Close the print queue window. If necessary close the Printers and Faxes window and close the Control Panel window. Close the document and close Microsoft Office Word

## CHALLENGE

Challenge exercises expand on or are somewhat related to skills presented in the lessons. Each exercise provides a brief narrative introduction, followed by instructions in a numbered-step format that are not as detailed as those in the Skill Drill section.

Each exercise is independent of the others, so you may complete the exercises in any order.

### 1. Creating a Poster

You need a new roommate and decide to place some posters around campus. You started the poster earlier and now need to format it. The end results should look similar to Figure 3.26.

## ROOMMATE WANTED

FOR A GREAT APARTMENT
YOU GET:
✓YOUR OWN ROOM WITH A FABULOUS VIEW
✓3 NEW FRIENDS
✓TO BE CLOSE TO CAMPUS
✓REASONABLE RENT
CALL STUDENT'S NAME AT (212) 555-0323

FIGURE 3.26

1. Start **Microsoft Office Word** and open the file *CE_0305.* Save it in your folder as **Roommate.**

2. Display the Page Setup dialog box and then change the orientation to **Landscape.** Change the top and bottom margins to **1.5.**

3. Select all of the text. Center the text and then change the font to **Engravers MT, 20 point** and the Font Color to **Violet.** If you do not have this font choice, choose one that displays the text in all capital letters.

4. Select *Roommate Needed* and change the font size to **36 point**. Click at the end of *Roommate Needed* and press [Enter ↵] twice to place this on a separate line and insert a blank line.

5. Click to the left of *Your Own Room* and display the Symbol dialog box from the Insert tab. Click the **Font arrow**, scroll the list and select **Wingdings**. Locate a check mark of your choice, and then click **Insert**. Close the Symbol dialog box.

6. Copy the check mark you just inserted and paste it to the left of the next three lines.

7. View your poster in Print Preview. Click the Magnifier button to turn it off and then select *Student's Name* in the last line and type your name.

8. Save the poster and then print two copies. Close the file and close Word.

## 2. Creating a Invitation for a Dinner Party

You are having a few friends over for dinner and decide to send an invitation for this gourmet extravaganza. You want the invitation to be on a smaller size page similar to the one shown in Figure 3.27.

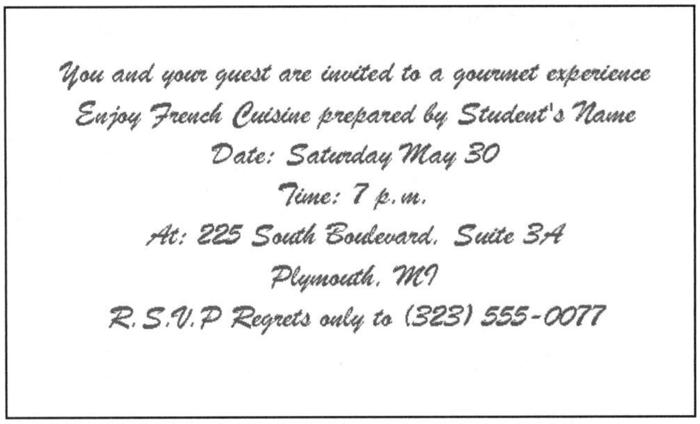

*You and your guest are invited to a gourmet experience*
*Enjoy French Cuisine prepared by Student's Name*
*Date: Saturday May 30*
*Time: 7 p.m.*
*At: 225 South Boulevard, Suite 3A*
*Plymouth, MI*
*R.S.V.P Regrets only to (323) 555-0077*

FIGURE 3.27

1. Open **Microsoft Office Word**. Create an invitation to a dinner party at your place. Include your name as host and the other vital information such as type of dinner party (barbeque, cookout, clam bake, etc.), the time, date, and location. Place each piece of information on a separate line similar to the example shown in Figure 3.27.

2. Display the Page Setup dialog box and change the paper size to a size that is smaller than 8 1/2 x 11 in. Select a size that is close to half a page—you may need to select a size and then see the dimensions that display in the Page Setup dialog box.

3. Format the text in your invitation by changing the font, font size, font color, and alignment. Make your choices match the type of dinner party you are planning.

4. View the invitation in the Print Preview window. Adjust the font size, margins, and layout (portrait or landscape) to ensure that your invitation would print on one page.

5. Save the file with the name **Invitation** and then print an example. Close Word.

# DISCOVERY ZONE

Discovery Zone exercises require advanced knowledge of topics presented in *Essentials* lessons, application of skills from multiple lessons, or self-directed learning of new skills. Each exercise is independent of the others, so you may complete the exercises in any order.

## 1. Creating a Vacation Flyer

*Creative Solution*

The formatting tools you learned about in this lesson can be used for a variety of tasks. They are particularly helpful when you are designing a poster or flyer, which could benefit from text formatting.

Create a flyer for a trip to a vacation spot (it should be a place you are interested in visiting or have already visited). Go online and find information about the vacation spot. If you cannot go online, do your research in a library. Include information about things to see in the area. Create an itinerary for the trip. Add any other information you think is appropriate. The flyer should be no more than one page long. Include in your poster the following formats:

- A font you have not used before in this text.
- Font size over 18 point.
- A font color of your choice.
- Text alignment other than align-left.
- One or more symbols from the Symbol dialog box. (Hint: Explore Webdings and Wingdings for a variety of symbols.)
- Make sure the content is balanced on the page, left to right and top to bottom.
- Remove any errors. Add your name at the bottom of the flyer.
- Save your file as **Vacation Flyer**.
- Preview the document and then print it.

## 2. Locating a Print Driver

If you change your operating system, you may need to upgrade the print driver for your printer so it will work with the new operating system. Often you can find the print driver that you need on the printer manufacturer's Web site. You may find that the printer you have is not supported if you upgrade to a new operating system.

Launch your Web browser. If you are familiar with using a search engine, and have one you like, use that search engine; otherwise, in the address box type **www.google.com** and then press (Enter←).

In the keyword search box, type the name of the manufacturer of your printer and print drivers (e.g., Epson print drivers). If you do not have a printer, type **HP print drivers** in the keyword search box and then press (Enter←).

Click on one of the links that provides support for that manufacturer and for print drivers.

Navigate the site to locate a print driver for Windows XP. If you need a sample printer to use on the HP Web site, type **Officejet v40** in the *Enter a product number box*.

Determine if a printer driver is available for your printer if you needed to upgrade your operating system to Windows XP. Close the browser without downloading the driver.

# UNIT 2: USING PRODUCTIVITY SOFTWARE

## Microsoft Office 2007

## Project 4: Using Graphic Tools

LESSON 1

Adding Borders and Shading Around Text

2-2.1.16.1    2-2.1.16.2    2-2.1.16.3

LESSON 2

Adding Clip Art

2-1.3.9.1    2-1.3.10.5    2-1.3.10.2

2-1.3.9.3    2-1.3.10.1

LESSON 3

Resizing and Moving Clip Art

LESSON 4

Adding and Formatting a Picture

2-1.3.9.2    2-1.3.10.4

LESSON 5

Using WordArt

LESSON 6

Adding Drawn Objects to a File

2-1.3.11.1

LESSON 7

Modifying Drawn Objects

2-1.3.11.2    2-1.3.11.3

# PROJECT 4

# USING GRAPHIC TOOLS

IN THIS PROJECT, YOU LEARN HOW TO:

- Add Borders and Shading Around Text
- Add Clip Art
- Resize and Move Clip Art
- Add and Format a Picture
- Use WordArt
- Insert Drawn Objects
- Modify Drawn Objects

# WHY WOULD I DO THIS?

Graphics can add visual components to your documents, spreadsheets, or presentations that help draw the reader's attention, or highlight an important idea or fact. You can add *clip art*—electronic images provided with your software—or insert pictures that you have in digital format. Graphic elements can be resized and repositioned. In Microsoft Office Word and Microsoft Office PowerPoint, text can be set to flow around the images. Images can be cropped and modified using several techniques. A wide variety of drawing tools are available to draw boxes, circles, lines, arrows, or more complex shapes. Borders and shading can be added to paragraphs or cells to make them stand out from the surrounding text. *WordArt* is a program that turns text into a decorative graphic that can be used for titles on newsletters or flyers. Adding graphics creates excitement and visual appeal.

In this project, you add graphic elements to a Microsoft Office Word document to create a flyer, and then add drawing objects to a Microsoft Office Excel worksheet.

# VISUAL SUMMARY

In this project, you use graphics to enhance a Microsoft Office Word document about a trip to Alaska. You add images, and then move, resize, and modify the images. You learn how to wrap text around an image, add a border and shading to text, and create a title using WordArt as shown in Figure 4.1a. Then you use drawing tools to highlight information on a Microsoft Office Excel worksheet as shown in Figure 4.1b.

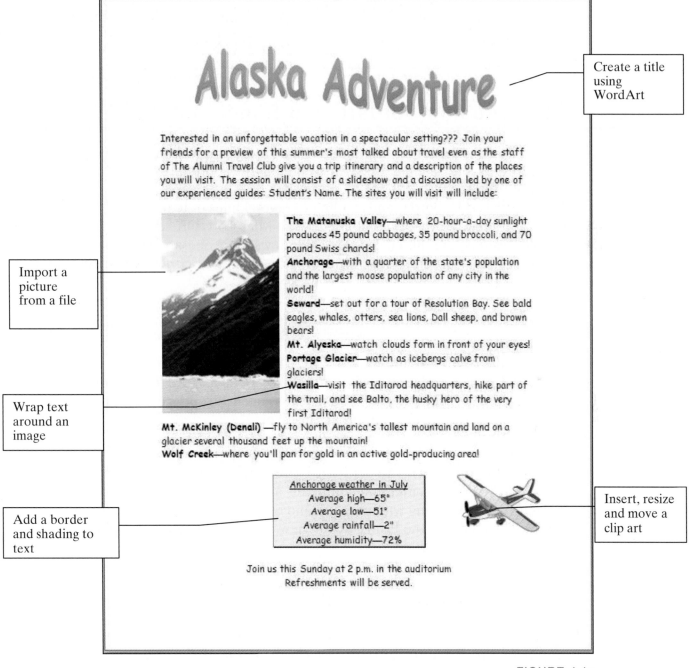

# Alaska Adventure

Create a title using WordArt

Interested in an unforgettable vacation in a spectacular setting??? Join your friends for a preview of this summer's most talked about travel even as the staff of The Alumni Travel Club give you a trip itinerary and a description of the places you will visit. The session will consist of a slideshow and a discussion led by one of our experienced guides: Student's Name. The sites you will visit will include:

**The Matanuska Valley**—where 20-hour-a-day sunlight produces 45 pound cabbages, 35 pound broccoli, and 70 pound Swiss chards!

**Anchorage**—with a quarter of the state's population and the largest moose population of any city in the world!

**Seward**—set out for a tour of Resolution Bay. See bald eagles, whales, otters, sea lions, Dall sheep, and brown bears!

**Mt. Alyeska**—watch clouds form in front of your eyes!

**Portage Glacier**—watch as icebergs calve from glaciers!

**Wasilla**—visit the Iditarod headquarters, hike part of the trail, and see Balto, the husky hero of the very first Iditarod!

**Mt. McKinley (Denali)** —fly to North America's tallest mountain and land on a glacier several thousand feet up the mountain!

**Wolf Creek**—where you'll pan for gold in an active gold-producing area!

Import a picture from a file

Wrap text around an image

Anchorage weather in July
Average high—65°
Average low—51°
Average rainfall—2"
Average humidity—72%

Add a border and shading to text

Insert, resize and move a clip art

Join us this Sunday at 2 p.m. in the auditorium
Refreshments will be served.

FIGURE 4.1a

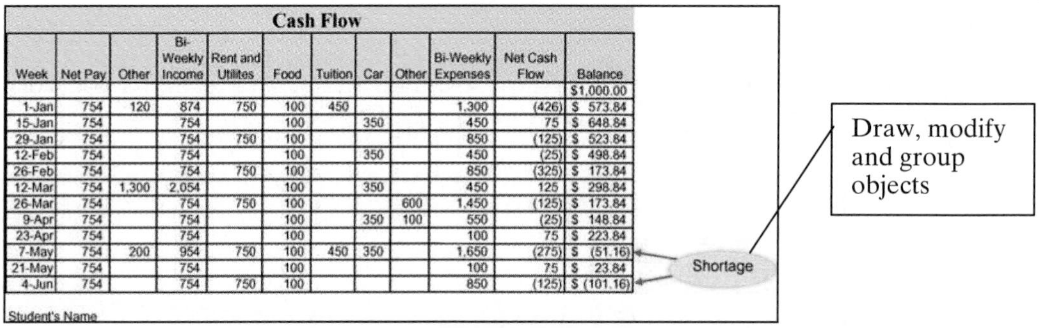

| | | | Bi-Weekly Income | Rent and Utilites | Food | Tuition | Car | Other | Bi-Weekly Expenses | Net Cash Flow | Balance |
|---|---|---|---|---|---|---|---|---|---|---|---|
| **Cash Flow** | | | | | | | | | | | |
| Week | Net Pay | Other | | | | | | | | | |
| | | | | | | | | | | | $1,000.00 |
| 1-Jan | 754 | 120 | 874 | 750 | 100 | 450 | | | 1,300 | (426) | $ 573.84 |
| 15-Jan | 754 | | 754 | | 100 | | 350 | | 450 | 75 | $ 648.84 |
| 29-Jan | 754 | | 754 | 750 | 100 | | | | 850 | (125) | $ 523.84 |
| 12-Feb | 754 | | 754 | | 100 | | 350 | | 450 | (25) | $ 498.84 |
| 26-Feb | 754 | | 754 | 750 | 100 | | | | 850 | (325) | $ 173.84 |
| 12-Mar | 754 | 1,300 | 2,054 | | 100 | | 350 | | 450 | 125 | $ 298.84 |
| 26-Mar | 754 | | 754 | 750 | 100 | | | 600 | 1,450 | (125) | $ 173.84 |
| 9-Apr | 754 | | 754 | | 100 | | 350 | 100 | 550 | (25) | $ 148.84 |
| 23-Apr | 754 | | 754 | | 100 | | | | 100 | 75 | $ 223.84 |
| 7-May | 754 | 200 | 954 | 750 | 100 | 450 | 350 | | 1,650 | (275) | $ (51.16) |
| 21-May | 754 | | 754 | | 100 | | | | 100 | 75 | $ 23.84 |
| 4-Jun | 754 | | 754 | 750 | 100 | | | | 850 | (125) | $ (101.16) |

Student's Name

Draw, modify and group objects

Shortage

FIGURE 4.1b

# LESSON 1: Adding Borders and Shading Around Text

Borders can be placed around text or graphics. They can be shown on one or on all sides of the object. Borders and shading are used to highlight important information that you want to stand out from the rest of the text.

In this lesson, you add a border and shading to several lines of text.

All of these exercises can be completed with Microsoft Office 2007. Instructions throughout the lessons are based on the Windows XP operating system, running Microsoft Office 2007. Your screen may differ slightly from the figures shown, even if you are running Office 2007.

## To Add Borders Around Text

1. **Start Microsoft Office Word 2007. From the Office menu click Open. Locate and open *CE_0401*. Save it as** a Word 97-2003 document named Alaska Flyer. You will add a picture, a clip art image, borders, and other non-text elements to improve this flyer.

2. **If necessary, change the view to Print Layout, and adjust the Zoom setting to fill the width of the screen.** In many documents, the view that you use to enter and edit text is a matter of personal preference. When you are working with graphics and other non-text elements, however, you will need to use the Print Layout view, because the graphics will not be displayed in the Draft view.

3. **Scroll to the bottom of the flyer and select the five lines pertaining to Anchorage weather.**

4. **On the Home tab, in the Paragraph group, click the arrow on the right of the Borders button. At the bottom of the menu, click Borders and Shading.** The Borders and Shading dialog box opens and the Borders tab displays.

5. **In the Setting area, click the Shadow button.** This option places a box around the selected text and gives the box a shadow effect. A preview of the shadow effect displays in the Preview area.

6. **Click the Color arrow and then in the fourth column, click the fourth color**—*Dark Blue, Text 2, Lighter 40%* as shown in Figure 4.2.

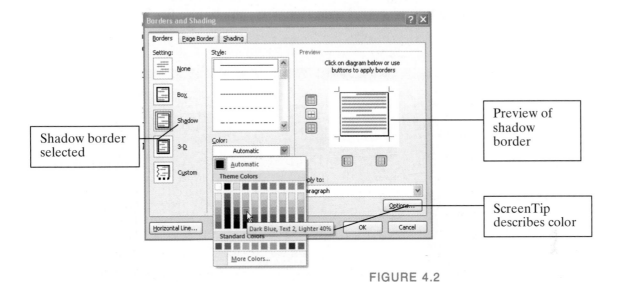

FIGURE 4.2

7. **Click the Width arrow and then click 1 pt from the displayed list.** The border will be blue with a 1-point width. The text color is unchanged.

8. **Click the Shading tab.** Here you can select a color to shade a paragraph.

9. **Click the Fill arrow, click More Colors and then select a pale yellow shade of color as shown in Figure 4.3 below. Click OK two times.**

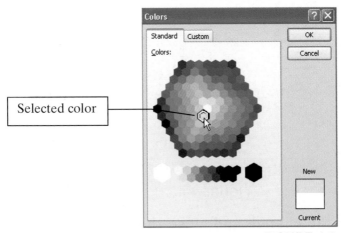

FIGURE 4.3

10. **On the Home tab, in the Paragraph group, click the Center button.** The border and shading is applied to the selected text and the lines are centered on the page, but the border box is wider than the text and needs to be adjusted (see Figure 4.4). To do this you can change the indents for this paragraph.

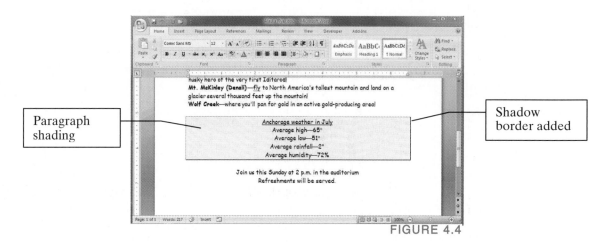

Paragraph shading

Shadow border added

FIGURE 4.4

11. On the **Home tab, in the Paragraph group, click the Dialog Box Launcher.** The Paragraph dialog box opens. Here you can change settings that affect paragraphs, such as line spacing and indents.

12. **On the Indents and Spacing tab, under Indentation, select the contents of the Left box and type: 2 press** Tab **and, in the Right box, type: 2 as shown in Figure 4.5.** This will leave a 2.5 inch space for the selected text, and reduce the size of the box that surrounds the text.

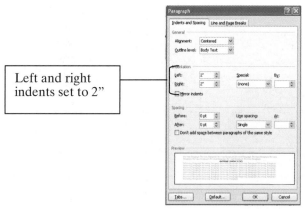

Left and right indents set to 2"

FIGURE 4.5

13. **Click OK to make the change and close the dialog box, and then click anywhere in the document to deselect the text.** The box is now the right size for the selected text. Notice how well the border and shading focus attention on the content of the box as shown in Figure 4.6.

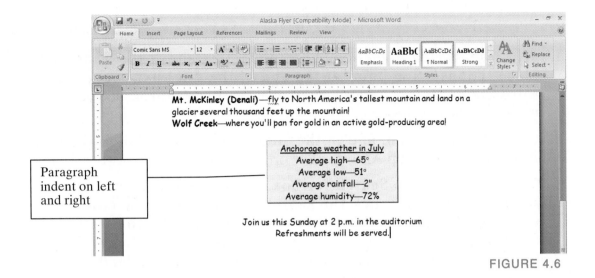

**Paragraph indent on left and right**

Mt. McKinley (Denali)—fly to North America's tallest mountain and land on a glacier several thousand feet up the mountain!
Wolf Creek—where you'll pan for gold in an active gold-producing area!

Anchorage weather in July
Average high—65°
Average low—51°
Average rainfall—2"
Average humidity—72%

Join us this Sunday at 2 p.m. in the auditorium
Refreshments will be served.

FIGURE 4.6

14. Save your changes to the *Alaska Flyer* document and leave the file open for the next lesson.

## TO EXTEND YOUR KNOWLEDGE...

### USING THE BORDER BUTTON

A Border button is located on the Home tab and on the Mini toolbar. It can be used to add simple borders to your documents or worksheets. This gallery of borders includes outside borders; inside borders; and top, bottom, left, and right borders. It is particularly useful in Microsoft Office Excel where borders are used frequently to format a worksheet and to provide traditional accounting formatting. To have a wider choice of border styles, however, you can use the Borders and Shading dialog box.

### ADDING A PAGE BORDER

Using the Borders and Shading dialog box, you can also add a border to a page by clicking the Page Border tab. To add a more decorative border, click the Horizontal Line button and scroll through the selection of decorative borders. This is another graphic element that can be added to create a theme or enhance your document.

## LESSON 2: Adding Clip Art

Quite a few clip art images are included with Microsoft Office. These images cover a wide range of topics and styles, from black-and-white stick art to detailed color drawings. When you need an illustration for a flyer, poster, or brochure, you can usually find one that is appropriate. If your computer is connected to the Internet, a larger selection of clip art images is accessible through Microsoft Online. Several software vendors also offer clip art that you can include in your documents. These are generally available as a purchased software program, or through a Web site.

In this lesson, you learn how to insert a clip art image into a document.

1. With the *Alaska Flyer* document open, just above the weather box, place the insertion point at the end of the line that begins with the words *Wolf Creek.* You will insert an image of an airplane here, and then move it in the next lesson.

2. **Click the Insert tab, and in the Illustrations group click the Clip Art button.** The Clip Art task pane opens on the right side of your window.

3. **Type** airplane **in the Search for box. Click the Search in arrow and select** *Everywhere;* **click the Search in arrow again to close the list. Click the** *Results should be* **arrow and be sure that only Clip Art is checked—click to remove other check marks.** The Search in list and the Results list are used to help restrict or broaden the search to the types of images and the locations where you want to search.

4. **Click the Go button.** All of the clip art images that have been identified by the key word *airplane* are displayed in the Tesults box as shown in Figure 4.7. The images that display on your screen may include several more images if your computer is connected to the Internet.

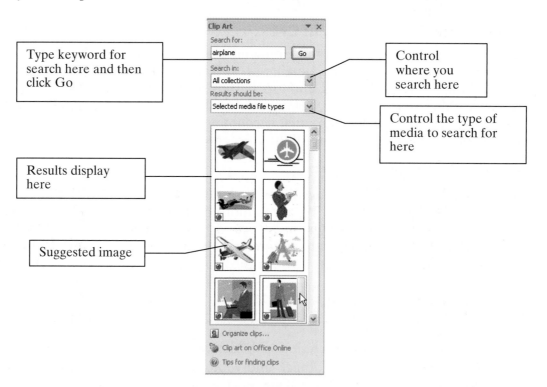

Type keyword for search here and then click Go

Control where you search here

Control the type of media to search for here

Results display here

Suggested image

**FIGURE 4.7**

5. **Move your mouse pointer over the first image in the Clip Art task pane.** A ScreenTip displays information about this image, including the keywords with which it is associated. It also lists the file size—both its physical dimensions, 260 (w) x 130 (h) pixels, and its file size, 6kb—and the type of file—WMF. The file size of images can vary greatly depending on the file type.

The file size can be an important factor if you have limited storage space or a slow Internet connection.

6. **If you have an Internet connection, scroll through the list of images to find the picture of a small private plane. Click the small plane image if you have it. If not, click the fighter plane image.** The image is inserted as shown Figure 4.8. This is a good example of the advantage of connecting to the Internet to expand your clip art choices. The image is much larger than it needs to be in this document. You will adjust the size and placement of the image in the next lesson.

Inserted image is larger than needed for this document

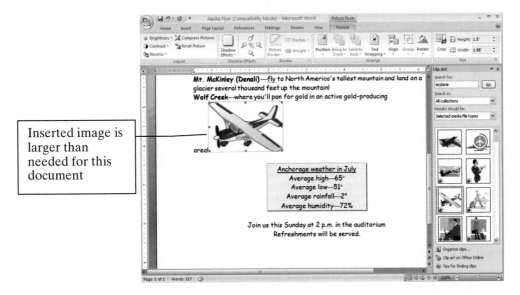

FIGURE 4.8

7. **Click at the end of the previous line of text to deselect the clip art image. Scroll to the top of the list of airplane images and right-click the second image in the Clip Art task pane.** The shortcut menu can be used to insert, copy, delete, add to your collection, and edit the keywords associated with the image, or find images that use a similar style.

8. **Click Insert from the displayed shortcut menu.** A second image is inserted. Multiple images can be inserted at the same time. You can change your search criteria and insert pictures related to a different topic.

9. **Click the second image that was inserted in the document.** *Sizing handles* display around the image, as shown in Figure 4.9 (see next page), which indicates that the image is selected. The sizing handles display as small circles and squares.

10. **Press** Delete **to remove the second image from the document.** If you add an image you don't want to use, it is easy to remove it. The original image remains inserted in the document.

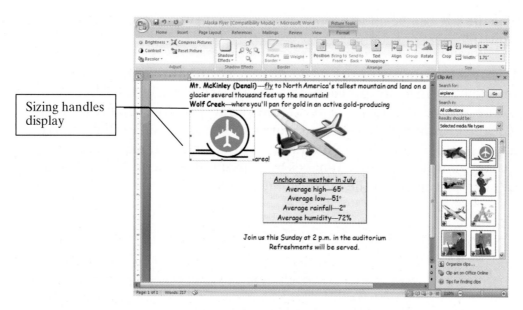

Sizing handles display

FIGURE 4.9

11. Close the Clip Art task pane. Save your changes to the *Alaska Flyer* document and leave the file open for the next lesson.

## TO EXTEND YOUR KNOWLEDGE...

### IMAGE FILE FORMATS AND FILE SIZE

Most images are saved in one of three formats—Bitmap, GIF, or JPEG—with the file extensions .bmp, .gif, or .jpg, respectively. Bitmap images assign three numbers to each picture element to represent over sixteen million colors. GIF is a compression technique that reduces the possible colors to only 256 and uses a program to determine which areas of the image are the same colors rather than save a number for each pixel. The JPEG compression method is similar to GIF except the number of colors to which the image is reduced is variable and may be selected when the file is compressed. The GIF method produces the smallest files when the image has a few colors and the objects have simple shapes and sharp edges. The JPEG method is better if the image has subtle variations in color and shading.

### TO COPY IMAGES

You can copy and paste images just like you would text. To make a copy of an image that is in a document, right-click the image and click Copy in the shortcut menu. Position the mouse pointer at the location where you wish to place the image, either in the same document or another one, and then on the Home tab, in the Clipboard group click Paste, or right-click and click Paste in the shortcut menu. In this manner you can make duplicates of images you want to use.

## LESSON 3: Resizing and Moving Clip Art

Clip art is almost never the exact size you want it when you insert it into your document, and it is seldom located exactly where you want it. To resize an image, drag the sizing handles that display around an image when it is selected. To move an image, drag the selected image to the location where you want to place it. When a graphic is inserted in a document it is treated as a character in a paragraph. To move the image freely, it is necessary to change the ***text wrapping*** setting, which controls how an image is treated and enables the text to flow around the image.

In this task, you learn to resize and move a clip art image in your document.

## To Resize and Move Clip Art

1. **Scroll, if necessary, so you can see the image you just inserted and the weather box you formatted in Lesson 1.** You need to be able to see the whole image on the screen.

2. **If necessary, display the ruler by clicking the View tab, and then in the Show/Hide group, click to place a check mark next to the Ruler. Click the airplane clip art image.** Sizing handles display at the corners and in the middle of the image's edges, which indicates that the image is selected. The Picture Tools Format tab shows on the Ribbon as shown in Figure 4.10. It is helpful to have the horizontal and vertical rulers displayed when you work with graphics so you can judge the size of the image.

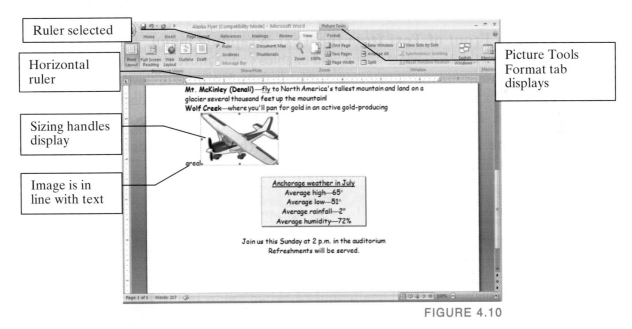

FIGURE 4.10

3. **Move the pointer onto the sizing handle in the lower-right corner of the image.** The pointer changes to a diagonal two-headed arrow. Using the corner sizing handles retains the original proportions of the image. Using the middle sizing handles will distort the image vertically or horizontally because the image is resized in only one direction.

4. **Drag the sizing handle up and to the left until the image is about 1.5 inches wide; release the mouse button. Use the horizontal ruler to determine the width of the image. For exact sizing on the Picture Tools Format tab, in the Size group, in the Width box type 1.5 as the dimension.**

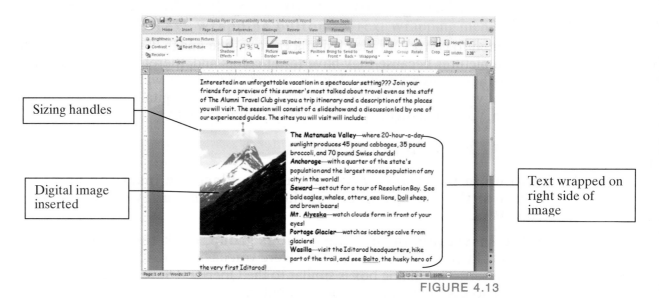

Sizing handles

Digital image inserted

Text wrapped on right side of image

FIGURE 4.13

7. **Scroll as necessary to see the text above and below the image; with the image still selected, on the Format tab, in the Size group, click the Crop button.** Crop marks display around the edge of the image and the crop icon is attached to the pointer arrow. When you *crop* an image you hide part of the image, similar to cutting away unnecessary parts of a picture. Cropping is generally used to focus attention on a particular part of an image. To do this, move the pointer, with the crop tool attached, to one of the crop marks.

8. **Position the crop pointer on the middle crop mark at the right edge of the image.** The crop tool attached to the pointer changes shape (see Figure 4.14). Now you can drag to crop that part of the image.

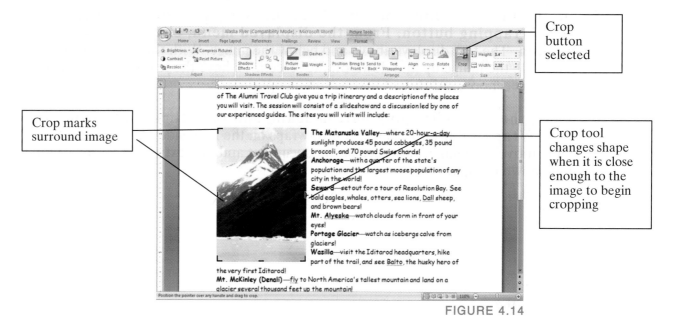

Crop button selected

Crop marks surround image

Crop tool changes shape when it is close enough to the image to begin cropping

FIGURE 4.14

9. **Hold down** [Alt] **and drag the middle right crop pointer to the left approximately 1/2 inch to the 2-inch mark on the horizontal ruler as shown in Figure 4.15; release the mouse button and then release** [Alt]. When you release the mouse button the line of text starting with *Mt. McKinley (Denali)* should be directly under the image. Using the [Alt] key while you drag enables you to drag the edge with greater precision.

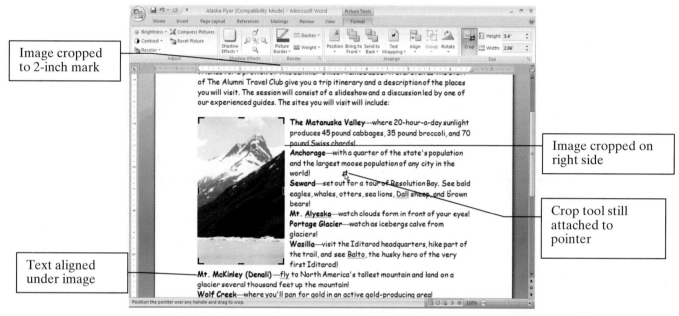

Image cropped to 2-inch mark

Image cropped on right side

Crop tool still attached to pointer

Text aligned under image

FIGURE 4.15

10. **Click the Crop button to deselect it.** The pointer returns to its normal icon and the crop marks are replaced by sizing handles around the image.

11. **Save your changes to the *Alaska Flyer* document and leave the file open for the next lesson.**

## TO EXTEND YOUR KNOWLEDGE...

### TO CROP IMAGES ON MULTIPLE SIDES

Cropping is often done to focus attention on a particular aspect of an image. To crop an image equally on both sides, hold down the [Ctrl] key and drag one of the middle crop handles inward. To crop an image in all four directions at once, hold down the [Ctrl] key and drag the corner crop handle toward the center of the image.

### TO REDUCE PICTURE FILE SIZE

When you crop an image, the portion that is cropped is actually hidden, but still stored as part of the image. To save room on your hard drive, or to reduce the file size of files that contain pictures, you can compress pictures. The Compress Pictures button is located on the Picture Tools Format tab in the Adjust group. This can be used to reduce the file size of selected images, or all images in a file. With a cropped picture, compressing it removes the hidden portion of the image.

# LESSON 5: Using WordArt

To make a title stand out from the rest of the text you can use emphasis (bold, italics, underline), a larger font size, or an unusual font, but you are limited to straight lines of text. WordArt is a program that turns text into graphics, to create a more decorative title. It gives you great flexibility in creating very artistic titles.

In this lesson, you add an artistic title to the Alaska Flyer using WordArt.

## To Use WordArt

1. **With the *Alaska Flyer* document open, press Ctrl + Home to move the insertion point to the top of the document.** The insertion point moves two lines above the first line of text. Empty lines were inserted in this document when it was created. The inserted image is no longer selected; therefore, the Picture Tools Format tab is no longer displayed.

2. **Click the Insert tab, and in the Text group click the WordArt button.** The WordArt Gallery displays. Here you select the design you want to use for your WordArt graphic.

3. **Point to the WordArt style in the fifth column, third row—WordArt style 17—as shown in Figure 4.16.** A border displays around the selected WordArt style.

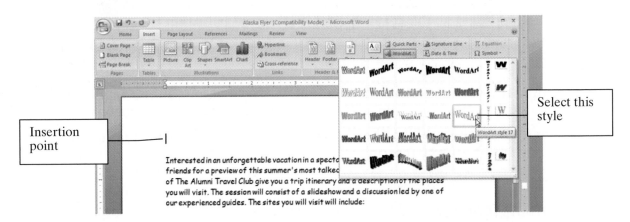

FIGURE 4.16

4. **Click to select WordArt Style 17.** The Edit WordArt Text dialog box displays. Here you enter the text you want to display as a WordArt graphic.

5. **Type: Alaska Adventure!** The default font, font size, and emphasis for the WordArt style you selected are indicated as shown in Figure 4.17. You can change these settings for this graphic here, or you can change it later after you have seen how it looks.

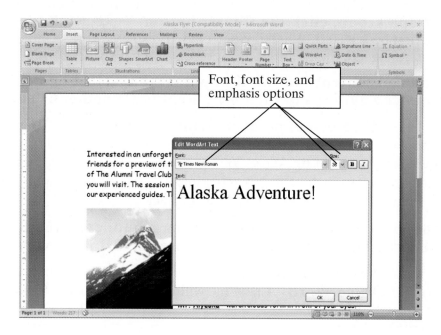

FIGURE 4.17

6. **In the Edit Word Art Text dialog box, click the Font arrow and then click Comic Sans MS.** This is the font used in the rest of the document.

7. **Click the Size arrow and then click 44 from the list. Click the Bold button, and then click OK.** The font and font size are changed, and bold emphasis is added. The WordArt displays at the top of the flyer as shown in Figure 4.18. It needs to be centered on the page.

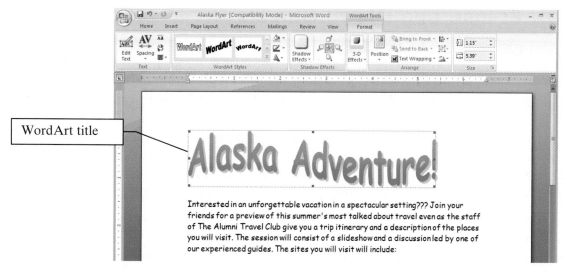

FIGURE 4.18

8. **If necessary, click the WordArt title. Click the Home tab, and in the Paragraph group, click the Center button.** To center the WordArt graphic it must first be selected. When it is selected, it displays sizing handles around its perimeter, just like the other graphic objects you have worked with.

9. **In the third sentence of the first paragraph, select *one of our experienced guides* and then type a colon (:) and your name.**

10. **From the Office menu, point to Print, and then click Print Preview to see the overall layout of the Flyer.** The flyer should fit on one page. Check the lower left corner of the Word 2007 window for page count. If it does not fit on one page, return to the document and adjust the size of the graphics as needed to match Figure 4.1 at the beginning of this Project.

11. **On the Print Preview tab, in the Print group, click the Print button. In the Print dialog box click OK. Close the Print Preview window.**

12. **Save your changes to the Alaska Flyer document. Close the file; close Microsoft Office Word.** A new file will be used for the next lesson.

---

## TO EXTEND YOUR KNOWLEDGE...

### USING THE WORDART TOOLS FORMAT TAB

You can change the color, shape, shading, font, size, and other aspects of a WordArt graphic. To do this use the buttons on the WordArt Tools Format tab Most of the tools display the effects using the Live Preview feature so that you can see the effect of changes before you apply them.

---

## LESSON 6: Inserting Drawn Objects

Lines, circles, squares, and other shapes can also be added as graphic objects to your documents, worksheets, or presentations using the Shapes button in the Illustrations group on the Insert tab. When a shape is selected, the Drawing Tools Format tab displays and gives you access to a wide variety of formatting tools. You can create a flowchart diagram using the flowchart shapes, use arrows to provide directions, or simple lines and boxes to create a map. Drawn objects can be resized, moved, and filled with color. Text may be added to most objects. Objects may be placed in layers where they appear in front or behind objects in other layers and they may be moved forward or backward in the layering. Grouping objects enables you to move the group of objects around as one graphic.

In this lesson, you will add shapes to a worksheet and use the Drawing Tools Format tab to format the objects that you draw using the shapes tools. .

1. **Start Microsoft Office Excel 2007. Display the Office menu, click Open, and then locate and open the** *CE_0403* **workbook. Save it as an Excel 97-2003 file named** Cash Flow. **Take a moment to examine the worksheet.** This workbook contains one worksheet that lists income and expenses for an individual as shown in Figure 4.19. The biweekly income displays in column D. The biweekly expenses display in column J. Column K lists the net cash flow on a biweekly basis—the difference between column D income and column J expenses. The cash balance is in column L.

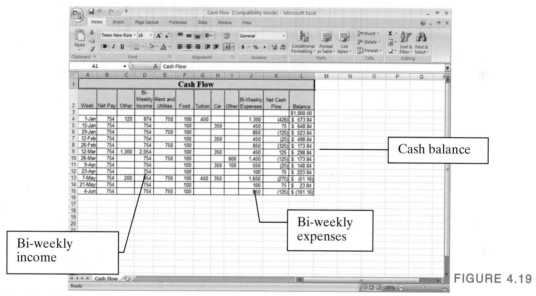

FIGURE 4.19

2. **Click the Insert tab, and in the Illustrations group, click the Shapes button. A gallery of shapes display as shown in Figure 4.20.**

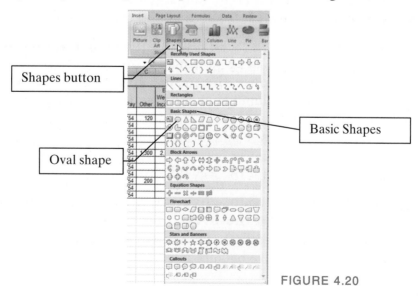

FIGURE 4.20

3. **Under Basic Shapes, in the first row, click the Oval tool.** Use the ScreenTip to help you identify the shape. Its location in the Basic Shapes group may differ from that shown in the figure. When you click a shape it activates the drawing tool so that you can draw an that shape. The mouse pointer changes to a plus shape. This is the precision select pointer that displays when a graphic tool has been selected.

4. **Position your pointer in the middle of cell M13 and drag down and to the right to the middle of cell N15 as shown in Figure 4.21; release the mouse button. Notice that the Drawing Tools Format tab displays. If the oval displays with a fill color, on the Drawing Tools Format tab, in the Shape Styles group, click the first button—Colored Outline Accent 6 button.**

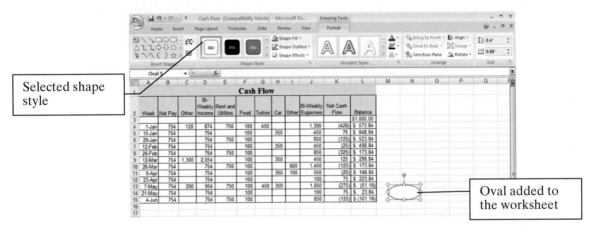

FIGURE 4.21

5. **On the Drawing Tools Format tab, in the Insert Shapes group, click the Arrow.** Note: if the oval is no longer selected, the Drawing Tools Format tab will not displays. To activate it again, click the oval.

6. **With the arrow selected, position the precision select pointer in the middle of the oval and drag up and to the left to point to cell L13— $(51.16)—and then release the mouse button.** An arrow is drawn to the first negative balance in column L. When you drag to create a shape, release the mouse button after you have reached the desired size and location for the image. You can always adjust the size and location of the image, or delete it if necessary and start over When drawing arrows, always drag in the direction you want the arrow to point because that is the way the arrowhead will be positioned.

7. **In the Insert Shapes Group, click the arrow again and position the pointer in the middle of the oval and drag down and to the left to point to cell L15—$(101.16)—as shown in Figure 4.22.** A second arrow points to the second negative balance in column L.

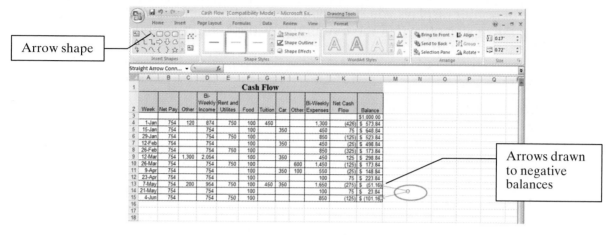

Arrow shape

Arrows drawn to negative balances

FIGURE 4.22

8. Save your changes to the *Cash Flow* workbook and leave the file open for the next lesson.

# LESSON 7: Modifying Drawn Objects

After you have added drawn objects you can change their line color, fill color, size, shape, or location. To move and resize objects, use the same techniques that you used to resize and move clip art and picture graphics. To change the fill color or line color, use the buttons on the Drawing Tools Format tab. In some circumstances you may want to add text to graphic objects. In the drawing you have created, the arrows display in front of or on top of the oval. This layering can be changed so the arrows appear to come from behind the oval. Finally, grouping objects is helpful so you can move and resize a group of objects as if it were one object. This maintains the proportion and relative position of the objects with each other pages, or to print more than one copy.

In this lesson, you add text to the oval and change the fill and line color of the oval. You also change the line color and weight of the arrows, and then send the arrows behind the oval. Finally, you group the objects and practice moving the group of objects.

## To Modify Drawn Objects

1. **With the *Cash Flow* worksheet displayed, right-click the oval object and click Edit Text from the displayed list.** An insertion point is placed in the oval so you can type. Notice that a hash-mark border displays around the oval. This indicates that the object is selected and can be edited.

2. **Type: Shortage and then click outside of the oval to deselect it.** Depending on the size of your oval, the text may not fit on one line, in which case it wraps to a second line. You will adjust the size of the oval later.

3. **Click the edge of the oval again to select it.** The border changes to a border that displays as a rectangle around the oval as shown in Figure 4.23. When this type of border displays you can change the font or font size of the text that was added to the oval. Notice that the font in the oval is Calibri 11 point, the default font for Microsoft Office 2007.

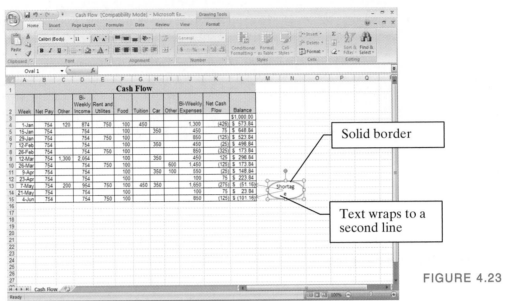

FIGURE 4.23

4. **On the Home tab, in the Font group, click the Font Size button arrow, and then click 12.** The font size is increased. You can change the font, font size, font color, and add emphasis to text in drawn objects.

5. **With the oval still selected, click the Drawing Tools Format tab, and in the Shape Styles group, click the Shape Fill button.** A gallery of colors displays that is similar to the Font Color gallery.

6. **Under Standard Colors, click *Yellow*.** The background of the oval is filled with yellow.

7. **On the Drawing Tools Format tab, in the Shape Styles group, click the Shape Outline button, and under Standard Colors click *Yellow*.** The line around the oval now blends with the yellow fill color used as shown in Figure 4.24.

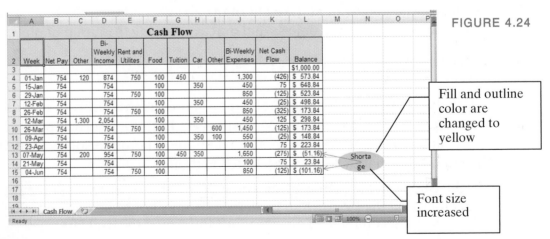

FIGURE 4.24

8. **Click one of the arrows. Hold down** Ctrl **and click the second arrow.** Holding down the Ctrl key enables you to select multiple objects. After the objects are selected, you can change the properties of the objects at the same time using the buttons on the Drawing Tools Format tab.

9. **On the Drawing Tools Format tab, in the Shape Styles group, click the Shape Outline button, and then under Standard Colors click Red.** The color of both arrows changes.

10. **On the Drawing Tools Format tab, in the Shape Styles group, click the Shape Outline button, and near the end of the list click Weight. In the displayed gallery click 1 1/2 pt.** The width of both arrows is increased as shown in Figure 4.25.

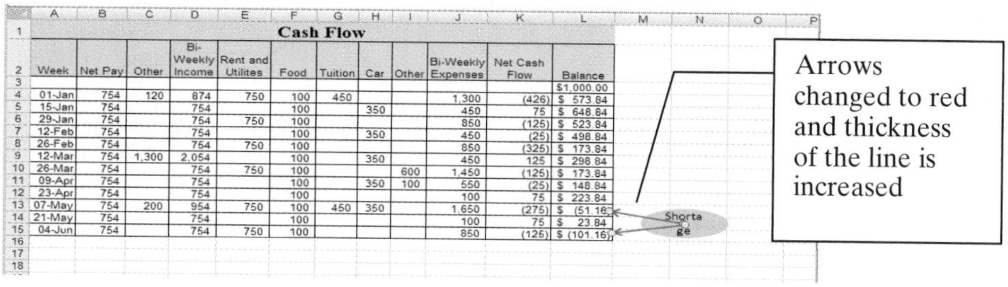

FIGURE 4.25

11. **Save your changes to the** *Cash Flow* **workbook and leave the file open for the next part of this lesson.**

Now that you have changed the appearance of the arrows and the oval, you can change the layering and group the objects together.

## To Layer and Group Objects

1. **If necessary, select both arrows.** Recall that holding down Ctrl enables you to select multiple objects.

2. **On the Drawing Tools Format tab, in the Arrange group, click the Send to Back button.** The arrows are placed behind the oval.

3. **With the arrows still selected, hold down** Ctrl **and then click the oval.** All three objects are selected. Be sure that sizing handles display at the ends of each of the three objects to indicate that they are selected.

4. **Right-click the selected objects and then on the displayed shortcut menu point to Group, and then from the submenu click Group.** The three objects are grouped and sizing handles display around the perimeter.

5. **Position the pointer over the right-middle sizing handle and drag to the right slightly to increase the size of the graphic and display the text on one line.** The arrows are resized with the oval. Compare your results with Figure 4.26

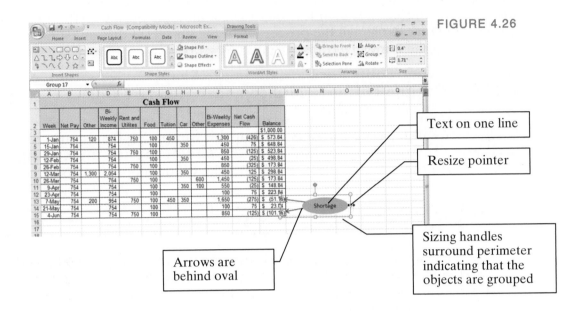

FIGURE 4.26

6. Click cell **A17**, type **your name** and then press Enter ⏎.

7. **Save your changes. From the Office menu, point to Print and then click Print Preview.** In Print Preview you can see that this document will not print on one page in its current orientation.

8. **On the Print Preview tab, click Next Page to see the second page.**

9. **On the Print Preview tab, in the Print group, click Page Setup.** The Page Setup dialog box displays. Here you can change the orientation of the page for printing.

10. **Be sure the Page tab is displayed, and then click Landscape. Click OK.** The orientation of the page is changed.

11. **On the Print Preview tab, in the Print group, click Print and then click OK to print the worksheet.**

12. **Save your changes and close the** *Cash Flow* **workbook, and then close Microsoft Office Excel.**

## TO EXTEND YOUR KNOWLEDGE...

### USING OTHER DRAWING TOOL BUTTONS

Knowing how to use drawing tools is particularly useful if you need to create a newsletter, or a presentation that describes a process. The Shapes button provides a wide variety of shapes and objects that can be added to your documents. There is also a Text Box tool that can be used to add text outside of paragraphs. Drawing objects are treated like other objects in that you can wrap paragraphs around drawn objects or move and resize them on your document or presentation.

## SUMMARY

In this project, you learned how to work with graphic elements that can be used to create interest, highlight an important point or idea, and improve the visual appeal of a document, presentation, or worksheet. You added a border and fill color to a group of paragraphs, and inserted clip art and pictures in a Microsoft Office Word document. You learned how to move, resize, delete, and crop images. The Picture Tools Format tab was used to change the text wrapping options so that text wrapped around the images. You inserted a WordArt image as a title. In Microsoft Office Excel, the Drawing Tools format was used to insert text in an oval shape and add arrows to highlight figures on the worksheet.

You can extend your learning by reviewing concepts and terms, and by practicing variations of skills presented in the lessons.

## KEY TERMS

clip art                    sizing handles              WordArt

crop                        text wrapping

## SCREEN ID
Label each element of the screen shown in Figure 4.27.

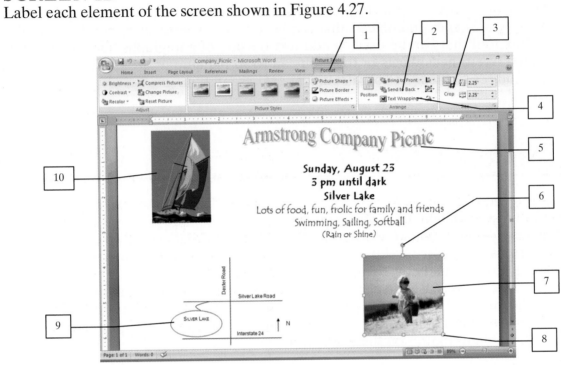

FIGURE 4.27

_____ A. Clip art

_____ B. Crop button

_____ C. Drawn objects

_____ D. Picture Format tab

_____ E. Inserted Picture

_____ F. Rotation handle

_____ G. Send to Back button

_____ H. Sizing handle

_____ I. Text Wrapping button

_____ J. WordArt

## MULTIPLE CHOICE

**Circle the letter of the correct answer for each of the following.**

1. You can do all of the following in the Borders and Shading dialog box except _____. [L1]

   a. choose a border style for a paragraph
   b. change the color of the border
   c. change the font in the paragraph
   d. preview the choices you have made

2. When a graphic image is selected _____ display(s) around its perimeter. [L2]−[L6]

   a. selection arrows
   b. bubbles
   c. sizing handles
   d. a dark border

3. To move a graphic anywhere on your document you need to change the _____. [L3]–[L4]

    a. image magnification
    b. text wrapping
    c. size of the image
    d. the format of the font

4. When you first place clip art or a picture in a document, it is treated like _____. [L2, L4]

    a. a character in the sentence
    b. an object
    c. a photograph
    d. a drawing

5. If you place a border around a paragraph, you can change the width of the box that surrounds the paragraph by changing the _____ found on the Paragraph dialog box. [L1]

    a. spacing
    b. box style
    c. width button
    d. indent settings

6. To control the layering of drawn objects use the _____ button on the Drawing Tools Format tab. [L7]

    a. Arrange group
    b. Order group
    c. Layer group
    d. Forward/Back group

7. To change text in a WordArt object use the _____ dialog box. [L5]

    a. WordArt Gallery
    b. Edit WordArt
    c. WordArt Style
    d. Create WordArt

8. To locate a clip art image enter a _____ in the Search for box. [L2]

    a. keyword
    b. description
    c. keycode
    d. name

9. When resizing an image or a drawing shape use a _____ to maintain the original proportion of the image. [L3]–[L4, L7]

    a. middle sizing handle
    b. corner sizing handle
    c. rotation handle
    d. center sizing handle

10. When you crop an image, you _____ part of the image. [L4]

    a. remove
    b. delete
    c. hide
    d. erase

## DISCUSSION

Creative Solution

1. In what circumstances are graphic elements most useful? Where would you be likely to use each of the graphic elements that have been introduced in this project? Give examples. [L1]—[L2], [L4]—[L6]

2. Examine your textbook and locate examples of different graphic elements that have been used. What role do these play in the overall design of the book? How do they help you learn? Provide examples. [L1, L2], [L4], [L6]

3. In a magazine, textbook, or other publication, find two examples that use graphics, one that provides a positive enhancement, and one that is inappropriate or distracting. What makes each one good or bad? What do you like or dislike about each one? How would

you change the graphics to improve the effect? What does the graphic convey to you? Does it support or distract from the words? [L1]—[L4], [L6]

## SKILL DRILL

Skill Drill exercises reinforce project skills. Each skill reinforced is the same, or nearly the same, as a skill presented in the project. Detailed instructions are provided in a step-by-step format. All of these exercises can be completed with Microsoft Office XP or later versions. Instructions throughout the exercises are based on the Windows XP operating system, running Microsoft Office 2007.

In these exercises, you add non-text elements to a poster created using Microsoft Word. The poster is for a staff benefits day for the Armstrong Pool, Spa, and Sauna Company. Work through exercise 1 first. The remaining Skill Drill exercises can be worked through in any order. Be sure to save your changes and close the document if you need more than one work session to complete the desired exercises. Continue working on the *Benefits_ Poster* instead of starting over with the original *CE_0404* file. After you have completed all of the exercises print a copy of the document (optional). Figure 4.28 shows the completed poster.

FIGURE 4.28

## 1. Adding Borders and Shading

You are an intern working in the corporate offices of Armstrong Pool, Spa, and Sauna Company. This week you are working in the personnel office. The benefits manager is planning a staff benefits meeting and has created a poster to announce the meeting. You offer to add some graphics to the poster to enhance its appearance.

1. Start **Microsoft Office Word**. Locate and open *CE_0404* and save it as a Word 97-2003 file named Benefits Poster. Select the last four lines of the poster.

2. Click the **Home tab**, and in the **Paragraph group**, click the **Borders button arrow**. At the end of the list click **Borders and Shading**. Click the **Box** button in the Setting area.

3. Click the **Color arrow**, and then choose **Blue Accent 1**; click the **Width arrow**, and then choose **2 1/4 pt**.

4. Click the **Shading** tab, click the **Fill arrow**, and then select **Aqua, Accent 5, Lighter 60%**. Click **OK**.

5. On the **Home tab**, in the **Paragraph group**, click the **Dialog Box Launcher**. Under **Indentation**, change the *Left* box to 2 and the *Right* box to 2. Click **OK**.

6. To the right of *Presenter:* press Spacebar and then type your name. Save the Benefits Poster document.

## 2. Using WordArt

Next you decide to add a vertical WordArt title along the left side of the poster.

1. In the *Benefits Poster* document, press Ctrl + Home to move the insertion point to the top of the document.

2. Click the **Insert tab**, and in the **Text group** click the **WordArt** button. In the displayed WordArt gallery, choose the last option in the fourth row— **WordArt style 24**. This is a vertical WordArt design.

3. Type: Staff Benefits Day in the Text area of the Edit WordArt Text dialog box. Change the font size to **48** points. Click **OK**. Notice that the WordArt image is considered the first character of the first paragraph.

4. Right-click the WordArt image to select it, and then from the shortcut menu click **Format WordArt**. Click the **Layout tab**, click **Square** and then click **OK**.

5. Move the pointer over one of the letters in the WordArt graphic until it changes to a four-way arrow, and then drag the image to the left side of the poster. Align the top of the WordArt with the first line in the poster.

6. Move to the bottom of the image and use the sizing handle on the bottom to adjust the image so that it is about 1/2" below the list of topics as shown in Figure 4.28.

7. Click in an open area on the document to deselect the WordArt image; save the *Benefits Poster* document.

### 3. Inserting, Resizing, and Moving Clip Art

You want to add an image to the poster that will invoke the idea of a meeting.

1. In the *Benefits Poster* document, place the insertion point to the right of *Retirement program*.

2. On the **Insert tab**, in the **Illustrations group** click the **Clip Art** button. In the Search for box type meeting and then click the **Go** button.

3. Click the meeting image shown in Figure 4.28 (or any other similar image). Close the Clip Art task pane.

4. Click on the meeting clip art image, and using the sizing handle in the upper-left corner, drag until the image is approximately 1" wide. If necessary, click **View, Ruler** to display the ruler to help you to determine the size of the image.

5. With the image selected, click the **Picture Tools Format tab**, and in the **Arrange group**, click the **Text Wrapping** button. From the Text Wrapping menu, click **Behind Text**. Notice that you can see the image behind the text.

6. Click the image and drag it to the left of the bordered text below the Word Art, as shown in Figure 4.28, and then save the *Benefits Poster* document.

### 4. Inserting and Modifying a Picture

You decide that the benefits idea would best be expressed by a picture and you happen to have pictures of your twin nieces when they were in the hospital.

1. In the *Benefits Poster*, place the insertion point to the right of the *Retirement program* line.

2. On the **Insert tab**, in the **Illustrations group**, click the **Picture** button. Locate and select the *CE_0405* jpeg file that is included with this book. Click the **Insert** button.

3. Select the picture. Drag the sizing handle in the lower-left corner and reduce the size of the image to about 2 1/2" in width.

4. With the picture selected, on the **Picture Tools Format tab**, in the **Arrange group**, click the **Text Wrapping** button, and then in the Text Wrapping list click **Square**.

5. On the **Picture Tools Format tab**, in the **Size group**, click the **Crop** button. Move the Crop pointer to the right-center crop mark, hold down Ctrl and drag inward to hide the portion of the picture just to the right of the head of the baby in the foreground. Holding down Ctrl while you drag enables you to crop both sides of the image at the same time. Click the **Crop** button to deselect it.

6. Move the picture up just to the right margin of the opening paragraph, as shown in Figure 4.28, and then save the *Benefits Poster* document.

### 5. Using Drawing Tools to Frame a Picture

As a final step you decide to put a frame around the picture you just added.

1. Click the picture that you just inserted to select it.

2. On the **Picture Tools Format tab**, in the Picture Styles group, click the Picture Border button, and then near the end of the list click Weight. In the displayed list, click the second line from the bottom of the list—**4 1/2 pt**. With the border selected, display the **Picture Border** menu, and in the fifth column select the first color—**Blue Accent 1**.

3. From the Office menu display Print Preview to see the overall layout of the poster. Adjust the size and location of the graphics as necessary to match Figure 4.28.

4. Save the *Benefits Poster* document. Print a copy of the document (optional).

## CHALLENGE

Challenge exercises expand on or are somewhat related to skills presented in the lessons. Each exercise provides a brief narrative introduction, followed by instructions in a numbered-step format that are not as detailed as those in the Skill Drill section.

Each exercise is independent of the others, so you may complete the exercises in any order.

### 1. Adding Graphics to a Memo

The Borders and Shading dialog box also gives you the option to add a decorative line to a document. This feature can be used to create a style for letterhead or memos. In this project, you learned how to insert a picture into a document. You have many options when working with pictures, one of which is to change the image to a *watermark*—a dim image or text background in a document. This fades the image and enables it to be used in the background with text in the foreground. You can also place text in the background as a watermark. This is particularly useful for indicating that the document is a draft copy or needs to be kept confidential.

The accounting manager at Armstrong Pool, Spa, and Sauna is sending a memo to the operations manager. She wants to mark the memo as confidential and has asked you to add a decorative line to the memo.

1. Start **Microsoft Office Word** and open the file *CE_406* and save it as a Word 97-2003 file named **Armstrong Memo**.

2. Press ⬇ two times to move the insertion point to the empty line between the company name and the To: line.

3. Display the Borders and Shading dialog box. On the Borders tab click the **Horizontal Line** button at the bottom of the dialog box. The Horizontal Line dialog box opens, displaying dozens of horizontal line options.

4. Select and insert a decorative line of your choice. You can work with this image as you would with any clip art image. Resize and reposition the line to a size and position you think enhances the memo.

5. On the **Page Layout tab**, in the **Page Background group**, click the **Watermark** button. Select **Custom Watermark**. Click **Text watermark** from the Printed Watermark dialog box, and then choose **CONFIDENTIAL** from the Text list box. Change the **Font** to **Arial Black**, which is a thick font and will display better. Notice that the Layout option selected is Diagonal. Click **OK**.

6. Move to the bottom of the document. Type your name where it says <*your name*>. Save the *Armstrong Memo* document. Print the document (optional) and then close Word.

## 2. Adding Graphics to a Microsoft Office Excel Worksheet

While you are interning in the Accounting Department at Armstrong Pool, Spa, and Sauna Company, you have a chance to look at some worksheets that have been previously created. You have some extra time on your hands and decide to add some graphic elements to the worksheets to enhance their visual appeal.

1. Open **Microsoft Office Excel**. Locate and open the *CE_0407* workbook file and save it as `Inventory`.

2. Select cells **A1:H2**. On the **Home tab**, in the Font group, click the **Fill Color** button and select **Aqua, Accent 5, Lighter 60%** from the displayed gallery.

3. With the cell still selected, click the **Borders button arrow** and then click the **Outside Borders** button. This places a border around the title lines. The Fill Color and Borders buttons are an alternative to using the Borders and Shading dialog box.

4. Select **B3:H3**, click the **Borders arrow** and then click the **Bottom Border** button.

5. Select **A4:A10**, click the **Borders arrow** and then click the **Right Border** button.

6. Select **B9:H9**, click the **Borders arrow** and then click the **Top and Bottom Border** button.

7. Select **A1:H10** and apply the **Outside Borders** option to surround the entire area with a border.

8. On the **Insert tab** click **Clip Art**. Make sure you are connected to the Internet and search for an image related to swimming or a spa. You will need to use the Clip art on Office Online option and search the Microsoft Office Clip Art and Media Web site. Follow their instructions to download the image you select.

9. Insert an image that you located. Resize the image and place it somewhere on the title rows where it enhances the worksheet. Compare your results with Figure 4.29.

### The Armstrong Pool, Spa, and Sauna Company

#### Swimming Pool Size

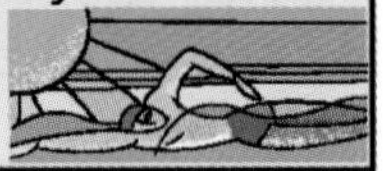

|  | 15' | 18' | 24' | 27' | 12'x24' | 15'x30' | 18'x33' |
|---|---|---|---|---|---|---|---|
| Q1 | 244 | 324 | 493 | 329 | 87 | 266 | 244 |
| Q2 | 251 | 334 | 499 | 340 | 95 | 266 | 248 |
| Q3 | 235 | 321 | 487 | 323 | 82 | 261 | 241 |
| Q4 | 187 | 253 | 389 | 256 | 63 | 207 | 187 |
| Total Sold | 917 | 1232 | 1868 | 1248 | 327 | 1000 | 920 |
| Shipped | 917 | 1232 | 1870 | 1248 | 327 | 1000 | 921 |
| Difference | 0 | 0 | -2 | 0 | 0 | 0 | -1 |

Student's
Name

FIGURE 4.29

10. Type your name in cell **A12.** Save the *Inventory* workbook and print the file (optional). Close the workbook and close Microsoft Office Excel

## 3. Adding Graphics to PowerPoint Slides

The personnel department is promoting computer classes they are offering through the local community college. They have created a presentation to show at the upcoming staff benefits meeting and have asked you to add some graphics to the presentation. You haven't worked in Microsoft Office PowerPoint yet, but understand that inserting graphics uses the same basic process in all of the applications, so you agree to give it a try.

1. Open **Microsoft Office PowerPoint.** Locate and open the *CE_0408* Microsoft Office PowerPoint file and save it as **Computer Training.** The file opens with the slide displayed on the right and the outline open on the left side of the screen. Close the outline pane; because you are working with graphics you will not be using the outline. This also helps you focus on the slide.

2. On the **Insert tab** click the **Clip Art** button. In the Search for box, type computer, and then click **Go**.

3. Locate and insert the image of a computer shown on the first slide in Figure 4.30. The image is inserted in the middle of the screen under the text. On the **View tab**, click **Ruler**, if necessary, to display the rulers.

4. Hold down [Ctrl] and drag the lower-right sizing handle down and to the right and increase the size of the image so it is approximately 6 inches wide. (Hint: The center of the ruler is 0, so you want the computer image to reach from the 3" mark on the left side of the ruler to the 3" mark on the right side.) Using [Ctrl] keeps the image centered on the screen. Move (drag) the image down so it does not cover the text.

5. Click the **Next Slide** arrow at the end of the vertical scrollbar. (In Microsoft Office Word, this button moves you to the next page in your document; in Microsoft Office PowerPoint it moves you to the next slide.)

6. On the **Insert tab**, click the **Picture** button. In the Insert Picture dialog box, locate and select the *CE_0409* picture file. Click **Insert**. The image needs to be cropped on the bottom edge of the picture.

7. With the image selected, on the **Format tab** click the **Crop** button. Drag the bottom middle cropping mark up approximately one-quarter of an inch until the writing is hidden. Deselect the Crop button.

8. Hold down [Ctrl] and drag one of the corner sizing handles to enlarge the picture until it is approximately five inches tall. Move the image down so it does not cover the text.

9. Click the **Next Slide** arrow. Add a clip art image of a computer user to the screen. Resize and center the image as needed.

10. With the image in slide 3 selected, on the **Format tab**, in the **Arrange group** click the **Rotate** button and the click **Flip Horizontal**.

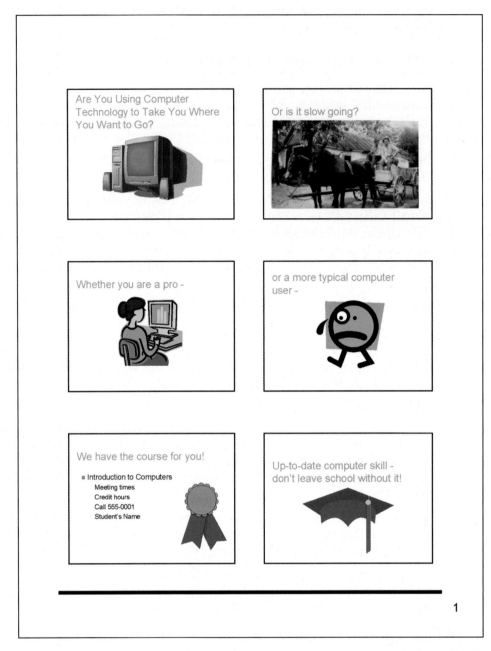

FIGURE 4.30

11. Click the **Next Slide** arrow and add a different clip art image that is appropriate to slide 4. Resize and center the image as needed.

12. Add your name under the phone number on the slide 5. Save the *Computer Training* presentation.

13. From the Office menu point to **Print** and then click **Print.** In the Print dialog box, click the **Print what** arrow on the lower left side of the dialog box, and then choose **Handouts.** Click **OK** to print a handout (optional). Close the *Computer Training* presentation file and close Microsoft Office PowerPoint.

Discovery Zone exercises require advanced knowledge of topics presented in *Essentials* lessons, application of skills from multiple lessons, or self-directed learning of new skills. Each exercise is independent of the others, so you may complete the exercises in any order.

### 1. Exploring Additional Graphic Features

▶Creative ▶
Solution

You have been introduced to the basics of graphic tools that are available with Microsoft Office software. It is time to explore these areas on your own. Using either the Drawing toolbar or the WordArt toolbar, create a single page that demonstrates additional features associated with these graphic elements. Keep a list of the features you try and the ones that you end up using.

For example, create a WordArt design using your name. Using the WordArt Tools Format tab, change the shape of the graphic, change the height of the letters, and use the other buttons on the WordArt Tools Format tab to see how they change the image. Alternatively, create a drawing using the shapes available from the Shapes gallery.. Create a message, using shapes. Modify the shapes using the buttons on the Drawing Tools Format tab.

With either the WordArt or drawn graphic, click the 3-D Style button on the related Format tab and change the 3-dimensional perspective of your graphic. Click the 3-D Effects and explore the options in the 3-D gallery. Examine the options available at the bottom of the gallery such as changing the lighting source.

On the same page as your graphic, make a list of the tools you have tried, and indicate the ones you used by applying a bold emphasis. Add your name to the document and save it as My Graphic. Print the document (optional) and then close it.

### 2. Creating a Flyer for an Event You Are Hosting

▶Creative ▶
Solution

You have had an opportunity to use a variety of different graphic tools. Now it is time for you to create something of your own using the skills you have practiced.

Create a flyer/poster of your own to describe an event you are hosting, or to advertise something. Consider your target audience for the event or topic. Use the application of your choice. In addition to text, include at least four of the following graphic elements: borders, shading, WordArt, drawing tools, clip art, or pictures as appropriate. Create a balanced, visually appealing poster, free of errors. Include your name somewhere on the poster. Make sure that the visual elements add to the poster and enhance the message you are trying to convey. Save the file as **My Poster** and print a copy (optional).

# UNIT 2: USING PRODUCTIVITY SOFTWARE

## Microsoft Office 2007

## Project 5: Formatting Paragraphs and Documents

LESSON 1 Changing Line and Paragraph Spacing and Adding Indents

| | | |
|---|---|---|
| 2-2.1.4.1 | 2-2.1.3.2 | 2-2.1.1.2 |
| 2-2.1.4.2 | 2-2.1.3.3 | 2-2.1.1.3 |
| 2-2.1.3.1 | 2-2.1.1.1 | |

LESSON 2 Creating, Applying, and Modifying Styles

| | |
|---|---|
| 2-2.1.17.1 | 2-2.1.17.3 |
| 2-2.1.17.2 | 2-2.1.17.4 |

LESSON 3 Creating a Numbered and a Bulleted List

| | |
|---|---|
| 2-2.1.5.1 | 2-2.1.5.3 |
| 2-2.1.5.2 | 2-2.1.5.4 |

LESSON 4 Working with Tab Stops

| | | |
|---|---|---|
| 2-2.1.1.3 | 2-2.1.10.2 | 2-2.1.11.2 |
| 2-2.1.10.1 | 2-2.1.11.1 | |

LESSON 5 Working with Headers and Footers

| | | |
|---|---|---|
| 2-2.1.8.1 | 2-2.1.13.2 | 2-2.1.14.2 |
| 2-2.1.8.2 | 2-2.1.13.3 | 2-2.1.14.3 |
| 2-2.1.13.1 | 2-2.1.14.1 | |

LESSON 6 Inserting Page and Section Breaks

| | | |
|---|---|---|
| 2-2.1.1.3 | 2-2.1.12.1 | 2-2.1.12.2 |

LESSON 7 Creating and Modifying Footnotes

| | |
|---|---|
| 2-2.1.15.1 | 2-2.1.15.2 |
| 2-2.1.15.2 | 2-2.1.15.4 |

# PROJECT 5

# FORMATTING PARAGRAPHS AND DOCUMENTS

IN THIS PROJECT, YOU LEARN HOW TO:

- Change Line and Paragraph Spacing and Add Indents
- Create, Apply, and Modify Styles
- Create a Numbered and a Bulleted List
- Work with Tab Stops
- Work with Headers and Footers
- Insert Page and Section Breaks
- Create and Modify Footnotes

# WHY WOULD I DO THIS?

In an earlier project, you used text formatting tools to make words and phrases stand out. Paragraphs and documents can also be formatted to make the text more readable, and to indicate the structure of the document.

Paragraphs can be single- or double-spaced, and the first line of each paragraph can be indented. Once you have formatted one paragraph, you can save the formatting and then use a shortcut called a style to quickly format other paragraphs. Lists can be created using numbers or bullets, and other special formatting can be added using tab stops.

Special document formats can also help you lay out your document more effectively. Page breaks can be used to manually end a page, and section breaks enable you to use different formatting in various parts of the document. Information, such as page numbers and the date and time, can be placed in areas reserved at the top and bottom of each page. Microsoft Office Word also enables you to place footnotes at the bottom of pages, or at the end of sections of the document.

In this project, you use paragraph and document formatting features to format an introductory section of a census book.

# VISUAL SUMMARY

In this project, you finish formatting a three-page document. You change line spacing and paragraph indents, and you create bulleted and numbered lists. You use tab stops to create a brief table of contents. You also add your name, the date, and the time to a document footer, and page numbers to the document header. You create an artificial page break, and a new section with a different document layout. You also add several footnotes. The finished document is shown in Figure 5.1.

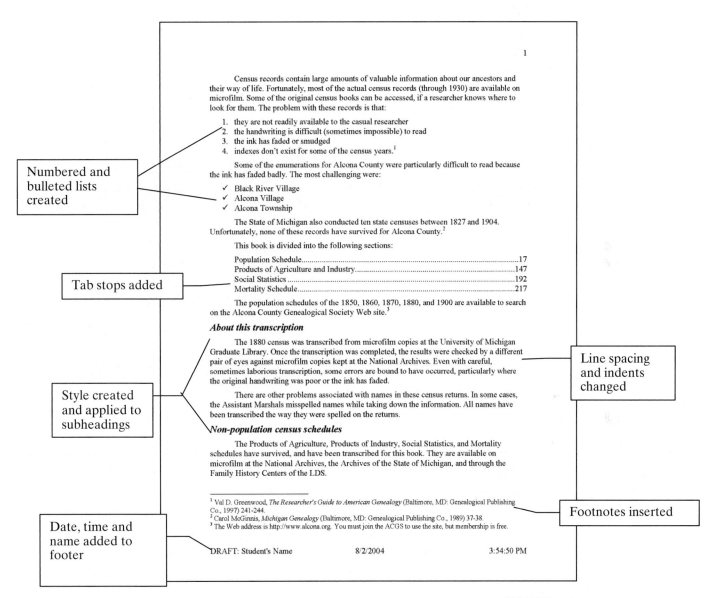

**Numbered and bulleted lists created**

**Tab stops added**

**Style created and applied to subheadings**

**Date, time and name added to footer**

**Line spacing and indents changed**

**Footnotes inserted**

1

Census records contain large amounts of valuable information about our ancestors and their way of life. Fortunately, most of the actual census records (through 1930) are available on microfilm. Some of the original census books can be accessed, if a researcher knows where to look for them. The problem with these records is that:

1. they are not readily available to the casual researcher
2. the handwriting is difficult (sometimes impossible) to read
3. the ink has faded or smudged
4. indexes don't exist for some of the census years.[1]

Some of the enumerations for Alcona County were particularly difficult to read because the ink has faded badly. The most challenging were:

✓ Black River Village
✓ Alcona Village
✓ Alcona Township

The State of Michigan also conducted ten state censuses between 1827 and 1904. Unfortunately, none of these records have survived for Alcona County.[2]

This book is divided into the following sections:

Population Schedule..................................................................................17
Products of Agriculture and Industry.........................................................147
Social Statistics.....................................................................................192
Mortality Schedule................................................................................217

The population schedules of the 1850, 1860, 1870, 1880, and 1900 are available to search on the Alcona County Genealogical Society Web site.[3]

### About this transcription

The 1880 census was transcribed from microfilm copies at the University of Michigan Graduate Library. Once the transcription was completed, the results were checked by a different pair of eyes against microfilm copies kept at the National Archives. Even with careful, sometimes laborious transcription, some errors are bound to have occurred, particularly where the original handwriting was poor or the ink has faded.

There are other problems associated with names in these census returns. In some cases, the Assistant Marshals misspelled names while taking down the information. All names have been transcribed the way they were spelled on the returns.

### Non-population census schedules

The Products of Agriculture, Products of Industry, Social Statistics, and Mortality schedules have survived, and have been transcribed for this book. They are available on microfilm at the National Archives, the Archives of the State of Michigan, and through the Family History Centers of the LDS.

---

[1] Val D. Greenwood, *The Researcher's Guide to American Genealogy* (Baltimore, MD: Genealogical Publishing Co., 1997) 241-244.
[2] Carol McGinnis, *Michigan Genealogy* (Baltimore, MD: Genealogical Publishing Co., 1989) 37-38.
[3] The Web address is http://www.alcona.org. You must join the ACGS to use the site, but membership is free.

DRAFT: Student's Name                    8/2/2004                    3:54:50 PM

FIGURE 5.1

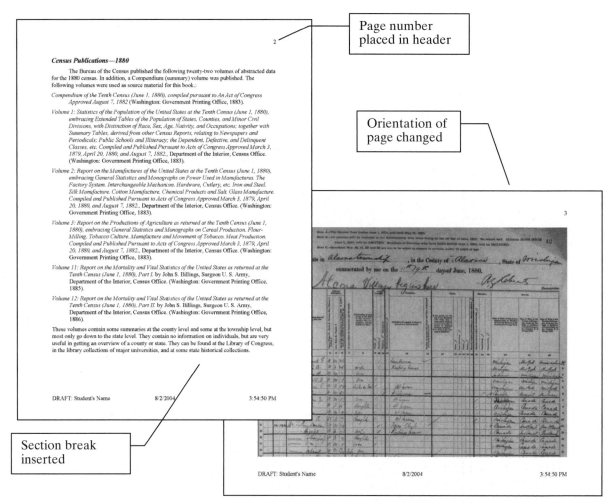

Page number placed in header

Orientation of page changed

Section break inserted

FIGURE 5.1 (CONTINUED)

# LESSON 1: Changing Line and Paragraph Spacing and Adding Indents

Double-spaced paragraphs—with the equivalent of a blank line between every line of text—are sometimes used during the drafting stage of document preparation for editing purposes. Once the text is edited, the document is often changed to single-spaced paragraphs, which result in shorter, easier to read documents. With single-spaced paragraphs, it may be difficult to determine where one paragraph begins and the other ends. To solve this problem, Word enables you to add spaces above or below paragraphs.

Another visual cue to indicate the beginning of a paragraph is an *indent*—extra space to the left of the first line of a paragraph. If there is extra space to the left of the first line of the paragraph, it is referred to as the *first line indent*. If the first line of the paragraph extends to the left of the rest of the paragraph, the remaining portion of the paragraph is referred to as a *hanging indent*.

In this lesson, you change line spacing, add space after each paragraph, and create indents and hanging indents. You also display hidden formatting marks

All of these exercises can be completed with Microsoft Office 2007. Instructions throughout the lessons are based on the Windows XP operating system, running Microsoft Office 2007.

Your screen may differ slightly from the figures shown, even if you are running Office 2007.

## To Change Line and Paragraph Spacing and Add Indents

1. **Start Word 2007. Open *WD_0501* and save it as a Word 97-2003 document named Census Introduction. Be sure you are in Print Layout View and adjust the page width from the Zoom box, if necessary. Scroll down and look through the document.** Notice that the document is hard to read because there are no visual cues to indicate which lines are lists (there are several), where paragraphs begin and end, and where the headings are.

2. **Press Ctrl + Home to move to the top of the document. On the Home tab, in the Paragraph group, click the Line Spacing button, and then from this list click 1.0.** The first paragraph is single-spaced.

3. **Press Ctrl + A to select the whole document. In the Paragraph group, click the Line Spacing button again, and then click 1.0.** The whole document is single-spaced, but it is still difficult to read.

4. **Press Ctrl + Home. On the Home tab, in the Paragraph group, click the Dialog Box Launcher to display the Paragraph dialog box. Click the Indents and Spacing tab if necessary.** To set paragraph formatting for a single paragraph, the insertion point must be in the paragraph, but it is not necessary to select the whole paragraph.

5. **Click the Spacing After up spin arrow once. Click the Special arrow in the Indentation area and click First line.** The After spacing should be set to 6 pt, and the First line indentation is set by default at 0.5" as shown in Figure 5.2. The up and down arrows at the end of some text boxes are referred to as ***spin arrows***. In this case, each time you click the spin arrow the spacing increases or decreases by 6 points.

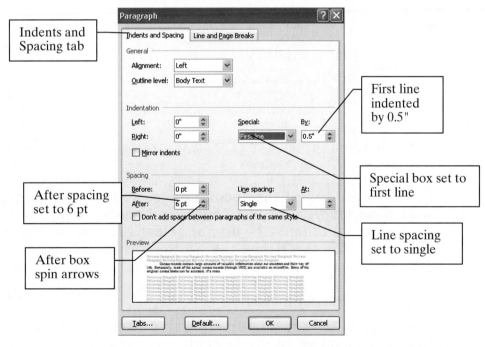

Figure 5.2

---

6. **Click OK.** A 6-point space is added after the first paragraph. The document uses a 12-point font, so a 6-point space is the equivalent of a half of a blank line of text. The first line of the paragraph is indented 1/2" inch.

7. **On the Home, in the Paragraph group, click the Show/Hide button.** The hidden formatting marks display, with paragraph marks indicating the end of paragraphs, and dots between words showing spaces created using the spacebar. Refer to Figure 5.3.

8. **Select the six paragraphs starting with *Some of the enumerations*, and ending with the one-line paragraph that begins *This book is divided*. Use the Format Paragraph dialog box, as you did in Steps 3-6 to add a 6-point space after each paragraph and indent the first line of each paragraph 0.5".**

9. **Select the eight paragraphs starting with *The population schedules*, and ending with the paragraph that begins *The Bureau of the Census*. Add a 6-point space after each paragraph and indent the first line of each paragraph 0.5".**

10. **Press** Ctrl **+** Home **to return to the top of the document.** Compare your document to Figure 5.3.

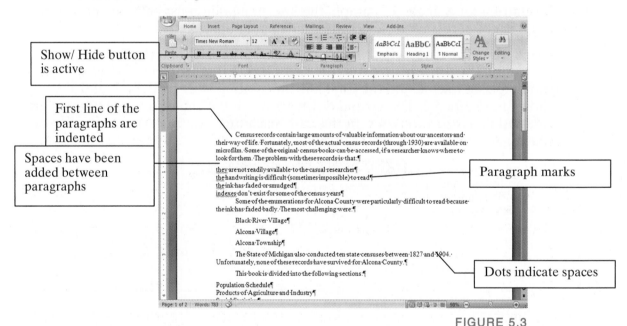

FIGURE 5.3

11. Scroll to the top of the second page. Select the paragraphs starting with *Compendium of the Tenth*, and ending with the paragraph that begins *Volume 12*—do not select the last paragraph in the document. On the Home tab, in the Paragraph group, click the Dialog Box Launcher button to display the Paragraph dialog box. These are book titles, which are often displayed using hanging indents because they are much easier to read.

12. Click the After spacing up spin arrow once to display 6 pt. Click the Special arrow in the Indentation area and then click Hanging.

**Click OK to accept the default hanging indent of 0.5". Click anywhere in the document to deselect the text.** Hanging indents are applied to the book titles. Notice how much easier they are to read as shown in Figure 5.4.

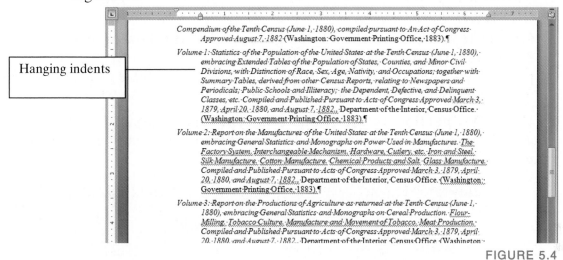

Hanging indents

FIGURE 5.4

13. **Save your changes to the *Census Introduction* document and leave the file open for the next lesson.**

## TO EXTEND YOUR KNOWLEDGE...

### PARAGRAPH INDENTS

In this lesson, you used first line indents and hanging indents on paragraphs. There is another type of indent called a paragraph indent. In the Paragraph dialog box, instead of using the Special box, you can use the Left or Right boxes under Indentation to move the edge of entire paragraph to the left or right of the document margins. The Increase Indent and Decrease Indent buttons on the Home tab in the Paragraph group are used for the same purpose. Each time you click one of these buttons, the indentation of an entire paragraph increases or decreases 1/2".

## LESSON 2: Creating, Applying, and Modifying Styles

*Styles* are combinations of formatting characteristics that are grouped together. Several styles—including four heading styles and a Normal paragraph style—are built into Word, and are available in all documents. The default *Normal style* for Word 2007 is 11-point Calibri font with 1.15" line spacing and 10-point spacing after. This is a change from earlier versions of Word which used 12-point Times New Roman and single-spacing. As you modify text, new styles are created in the background. You can create your own styles and use them to quickly format characters, paragraphs, tables, or lists.

In this lesson, you create a new paragraph style and apply it to subheadings in the document. You also modify the style.

1. **Press Ctrl + Home to return to the beginning of the document. Locate and select the *About this transcription* subheading on the first page.**

2. **On the Home tab, in the Styles group, click the Dialog Box Launcher. In the lower left corner of the displayed Styles task pane, click the New Style button.** The Create New Style from Formatting dialog box displays. The settings associated with the selected text are shown.

3. **Under Properties, in the Name box type Subheading.** Compare your screen to Figure 5.5. The Create New Style from Formatting dialog box is unusual because it has its own formatting tools.

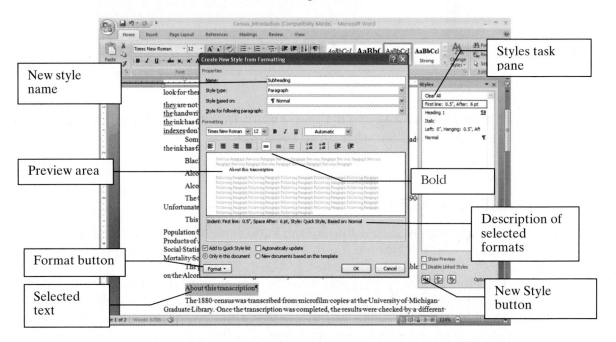

FIGURE 5.5

4. **Under Formatting, click the Bold button.** Notice that this change is represented in the preview area.

5. **At the bottom of the Create New Style from Formatting dialog box, click the Format button and then click Paragraph. The Paragraph dialog box displays.**

6. **In the Indentation area, click the Special arrow, and then click (none). Be sure the Spacing After is set to 6 pt. Click OK twice to close the two dialog boxes.** The style is recorded in the Styles task pane and has been applied to the selected text.

7. **Scroll down and select the *Non-population census schedules* subheading, and then in the Styles task pane click Subheading to apply the style to the selected text. Repeat this procedure to apply the Subheading style to *Census Publications—1880*.**

8. **On the Styles task pane, point to Subheading and then in the Subheading style box, click the arrow that displays on the right. From the menu, click Modify.** The Modify Style dialog box displays. After a style has been created, you can modify the style and update all text that uses that style.

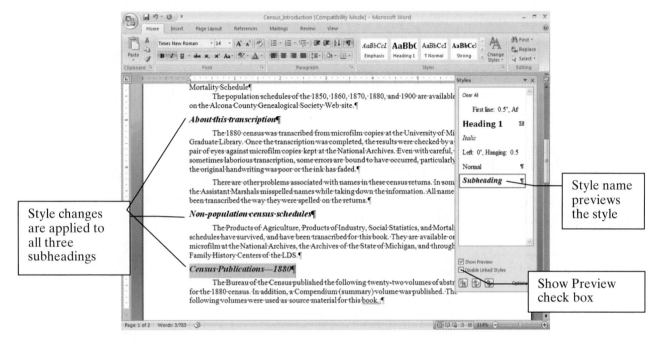

FIGURE 5.6

9. **Under Formatting, click the Italic button, then click the Font Size arrow and select 14. Click OK. At the bottom of the Styles task pane click to select the Preview check box.** Notice that all three subheadings reflect the changes you made to the style as shown in Figure 5.6. The Subheading name in the task pane previews the look of the style. In a long document, modifying styles instead of changing each paragraph to use that style saves a great deal of time.

10. **Close the Styles task pane. Save your changes and leave the** *Census Introduction* **document open for the next lesson.**

## LESSON 3: Creating a Numbered and a Bulleted List

Lists present data in an easy-to-read format, and draw the reader's attention to key points. Word enables you to quickly create two professional-looking list types. The first is a *bulleted list*, which is a list with each piece of information preceded by a small symbol—often a round black dot—called a *bullet*. Bulleted lists are generally used when there is no particular order to the items in the list. *Numbered list* items are preceded by numbers, and are usually used to display data that has some type of order—chronological, importance, or sequence.

In this lesson, you create a numbered list and a bulleted list, and then you modify the bulleted list.

1. Press Ctrl + Home to move to the top of the document. After the first paragraph, select the four lines beginning with *they are not readily* and ending with *indexes don't exist.* These lines paraphrase a reference source, and are listed in decreasing order of importance, making a numbered list appropriate.

2. **On the Home tab, in the Paragraph group, click the Numbering button.** The four lines are numbered and indented (refer to Figure 5.7). However, there is no extra space between the last item in the list and the following paragraph.

3. **Place the insertion point anywhere in the fourth line of the list. Right-click on the selected text. From the shortcut menu click Paragraph. In the displayed Paragraph dialog box. click the After spacing up spin arrow once, and then click OK.** A 6-point space is added after the fourth item in the list as shown in Figure 5.7.

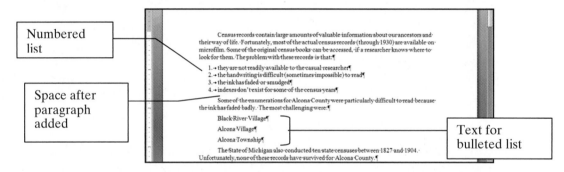

FIGURE 5.7

4. Place the insertion point in the *Black River Village* one-line paragraph. On the Home tab, in the Paragraph group, click the arrow on the right side of the Spacing button. From the displayed list click Remove Space After Paragraph. Repeat this procedure with the next line—*Alcona Village*.

5. Select the three location names—*Black River Village, Alcona Village*, and *Alcona Township*. On the Home tab, in the Paragraph group, click the Bullets button. Bullets are added to the three lines. The default bullet symbol is a round black dot, but if someone has used a different bullet icon, your bullets will be different. Bullet symbols can, however, be changed.

6. **With the bulleted list still selected, in the Paragraph group, click the arrow next to the Bullets button.** The Bullets dialog box displays, as shown in Figure 5.8

7. **Compare your dialog box with Figure 5.8.** Notice the Define New Bullet button. You can use this to choose any symbol, image or font you want for your bullets.

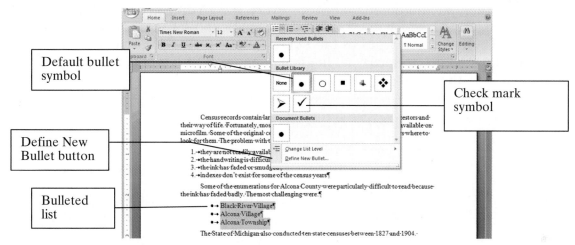

FIGURE 5.8

8. **Click the check mark symbol.** The three lines display check marks as bullets and are indented farther to the right than the numbered list.

9. On the Home tab, in the Paragraph group, click the Decrease Indent two times. This should move the bulleted list to the left margin. Click the Increase Indent button once to align the bulleted list with the numbered list. You can easily indent lists using the Increase Indent and Decrease Indent buttons. Compare your screen with Figure 5.9.

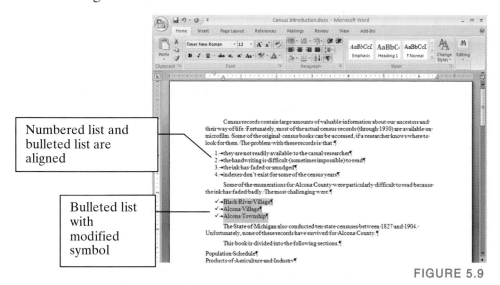

FIGURE 5.9

10. **Save your changes to the** *Census Introduction* **document and leave the file open for the next lesson.**

# LESSON 4: Working with Tab Stops

When you press Tab, the insertion point moves, horizontally, to the next tab stop. In the Normal style, there are automatic tab stops every 1/2". You can set the tab stops where you want them located, which overrides the automatic tab settings for that portion of the line of text.. There are five types of tab stops—left, center, right, decimal, and bar. The type of tab stop used determines what happens when you start typing (see Table 5.1).

| ALIGNMENT BUTTON NAME | BUTTON | DESCRIPTION |
|---|---|---|
| Left Tab | L | Text is left aligned at the tab stop and extends to the right. |
| Center Tab | ⊥ | Text is centered on each side of the tab stop. |
| Right Tab | ⌐ | Text is right aligned at the tab stop and extends to the left. |
| Decimal Tab | ⊥ | The decimal point aligns at the tab stop. |
| Bar Tab | I | A vertical bar is inserted in the document at the tab stop |

TABLE 5.1

To insert and work with tab stops, you will need to display the document ruler. Tab stops, and the Tab key on the keyboard, were once used extensively on typewriters. With word processors, their role has largely been supplanted by paragraph indents and tables.

## To Work with Tab Stops

1.  **Press Ctrl + Home. Check the top of the document window. If the ruler does not display, click the View tab, and in the Show/Hide group click the Ruler check box.** Rulers display across the top of the window, and on the left side of the window. The *ruler* displays inch markers by default, along with tick marks every tenth of an inch (it is possible to change the units to centimeters, points, or other units). On the horizontal ruler, there are several small alignment buttons that can be used to control paragraph margins and indents. The tab stop alignment buttons are all found in the same location; the Tab Alignment button on the far left end of the horizontal ruler. Clicking this button cycles through the five tab stop options. The Hanging Indent and First Line Indent paragraph alignment options are also included.

2.  **Select the four one-line paragraphs that begin with *Population Schedule* and end with *Mortality Schedule*.**

3.  **On the Home tab, in the Paragraph group, click the Dialog Box Launcher button. In the lower left corner of the displayed Paragraph dialog box, click the Tabs button.** The Tabs dialog box displays.

4.  **Type: 6 in the *Tab stop position* box. Click the Right option button in the Alignment area, and click 2 in the Leader area and then click Set.**

A right tab stop will be inserted at the 6"mark on the ruler. The space between the text and the tab stop will be filled with dots, called a leader. *Leaders* provide a visual connection between widely separated text. You can add several tab stops at the same time if you wish. Compare your dialog box to Figure 5.10.

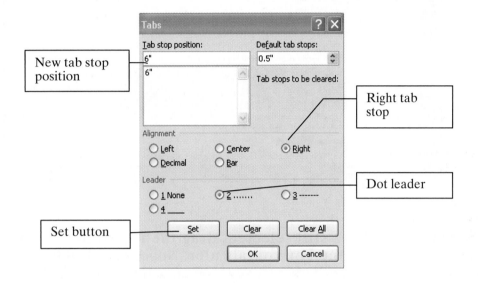

FIGURE 5.10

5. **Click OK. Position the insertion point at the end of the Population Schedule line, and then press** ⎡Tab⎤. The insertion point jumps to the 6"mark, and a series of dots are added.

6. **Type: 17.** This is the page number where the Population Schedule begins. Notice that the text moves to the left of the right tab stop as you type and dots display between the text and the number you typed. The right-pointing arrow is the tab formatting mark.

7. **Add page numbers to the other three lines as follows:**
   **Products of Agriculture and Industry       147**
   **Social Statistics                                        192**
   **Mortality Schedule                                 217**

8. **With the insertion point in the Mortality Schedule line, right-click, then select Paragraph from the menu. Under Spacing, click the After up spin arrow once to set the spacing to 6. Click OK.** A space is added between the last item in the list and the following paragraph.

9. **Select the four lines you just altered with dot leaders. Right-click the selection. From the displayed mini toolbar, click the Increase Indent button once.** The left margin of the four paragraphs is indented 0.5". Notice the left margin markers in the horizontal ruler as shown in Figure 5.11. The margin buttons in the horizontal ruler are discussed below. The Tab Alignment button on the left end of the horizontal ruler can be used to scroll through the tab options.

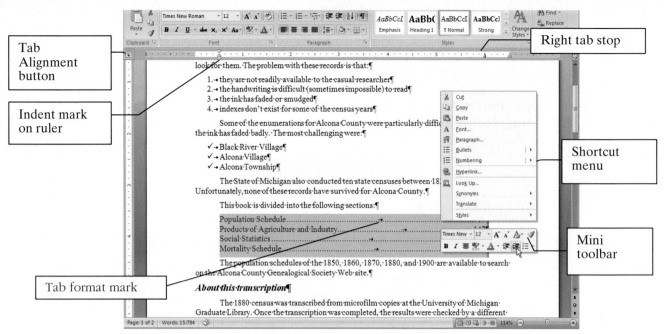

Tab Alignment button

Indent mark on ruler

Tab format mark

Right tab stop

Shortcut menu

Mini toolbar

FIGURE 5.11

10. **With the four lines still selected, drag the right tab stop marker to the 5.5" mark on the horizontal ruler.** Notice that all of the numbers associated with the tab marker move at the same time.

11. **With the four lines still selected, drag the right tab stop marker to the 6.5" mark on the horizontal ruler.** The right tab stop marker is at the same location as the right paragraph indent marker.

12. **Save your changes and leave the *Census Introduction* document open for the next lesson.**

## TO EXTEND YOUR KNOWLEDGE...

### PARAGRAPH INDENT MARKERS

Table 5.2 shows the paragraph indent markers on the horizontal ruler. The Left Indent and Hanging Indent buttons move together. When the Left Indent button is dragged, the First Line Indent also moves with the other two. When the Hanging Indent button is dragged the First Line Indent button does not move. The First Line Indent and the Right Indent buttons always move independently of the other buttons when they are dragged on the ruler.

| PARAGRAPH INDENT BUTTON | BUTTON | DESCRIPTION |
| --- | --- | --- |
| First Line Indent | ▽ | Indents only the first line of a paragraph. |
| Hanging and Left Indent | ⊔ | On the ruler, the top portion of this button is used to set a hanging indent, and the bottom portion is used to set a left indent for the entire paragraph. |
| Right Indent | ▽ | Indents the right margin of an entire paragraph. |

Table 5.2

## WORKING WITH TAB MARKERS ON THE RULER

In addition to changing the location of a tab stop by dragging it along the ruler, you can also set tabs directly on the ruler. First select the text that you want to affect. Click the Tab Alignment button until the type of tab you want to use is displayed. Click on the ruler at the position where you want to add a tab stop. Insert a tab in the text at the desired location. To remove a tab stop, drag the tab marker off of the ruler

---

# LESSON 5: Working with Headers and Footers

There are areas reserved at the top and bottom of each document page that are used to display the same information, or same type of information—such as page numbers, or the date or time—on multiple pages. The area reserved at the top of a page is called a *header*; the area at the bottom of a page is called a *footer.*

### To Work with Headers and Footers

1. **With the *Census Introduction* document open, press** Ctrl **+** Home **to move to the top of the document. Make sure the formatting marks are displayed.**

2. **Click the Insert tab, and in the Header & Footer group, click the Page Number button and then point to Top of Page. Observe the page number options.** The page number will be shown on all pages, including the first page. A small number in light gray displays the placement of the page number at the top of the page in each option as shown in Figure 5.12.

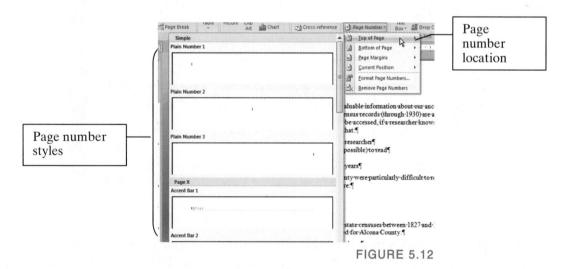

FIGURE 5.12

3. **Click Plain Number 3 to right align the number. The page number displays in the *Header* area on the right.** Text in the header and footer areas display in light gray. The Header & Footer Tools Design tab displays. The header and footer areas display in darker text when these areas are active, and the document text now displays in light gray.

---

4. **On the Header & Footer Tools Design tab, in the Navigation group, click Go to Footer.** The insertion point moves to the left side of the *Footer* area.

5. **Type: DRAFT: Student name, substituting your name for *Student name*.**

6. **Press ⎡Tab⎤, and then on the Design tab in the Insert group, click the Date & Time button. In the displayed Date and Time dialog box select the first format (mm/dd/yyyy) and then click OK.** The current date is inserted, and centered on the center tab stop. If you select Update automatically, every time you open this document, the current date will display. Consider if you want the date on your document to update every time it is opened. This may cause confusion about the date when the document was originally created.

7. **If necessary, on the horizontal ruler, drag the center tab stop to the 3.25" position.**

8. **Press ⎡Tab⎤. On the Design tab, in the Insert group, click the Date &Time button. Select the time format that is third from the bottom of the list (hh:mm:ss AM). Click OK. If necessary, drag the right tab stop marker to the 6.5" mark.** The time is now right aligned with the right margin of the document. Compare your footer to Figure 5.13. Notice the tab formatting marks in the footer.

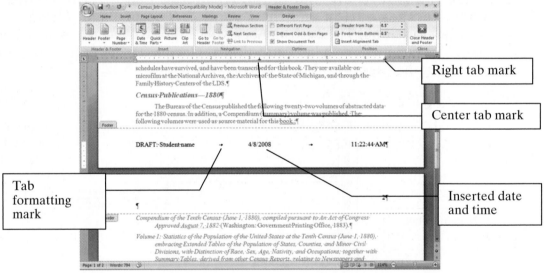

FIGURE 5. 13

9. **Double-click anywhere in the document return to the body of the document. Display the Office menu, point to Print and then click Print Preview. Scroll through the document and examine the header and footer areas.** Notice that the page numbers display on both pages, as do the three elements you added to the footer—your name, the date, and the time.

10. **On the Print Preview tab, click Close Print Preview. Save your changes and leave the *Census Introduction* document open for the next lesson.**

### OTHER HEADER AND FOOTER OPTIONS

On the Header& Footer Tools Design tab are several buttons which provide more header and footer features. The Header and Footer buttons enable you to select a style to use . From the Quick Parts button, if you select Fields, it displays a list of options such as File name that will display the name of your file in the header or footer. A variation of this is File name and path, which displays not only the file name, but also the location where the document is saved on your computer. When you insert page numbers one of the option is Page X of Y. This prints the page number on each page, and also displays the total number of pages in the document—for example, *Page 12 of 26.*

---

## LESSON 6: Inserting Page and Section Breaks

In multiple-page documents, you will often find that you want to move text from the bottom of one page to the top of the next page. Pressing Enter several times will move the text, but will cause a problem later on if you add or remove text earlier in the document. The solution is to insert a ***manual page break***—commonly referred to as a hard page break—to artificially end a page.

You can also insert a ***section break*** if you want to change the page layout format. A ***section*** is a portion of a document that can be formatted differently than the rest of the document. Sections are often used to change the page orientation of one or more pages in a document, or to display text in one part of the document in multiple-column format.

In this lesson, you insert a manual page break to place all of the book information on one page. You also insert a section break at the end of the document to change the orientation of the last page from portrait to landscape.

### To Insert Page and Section Breaks

1. **Scroll to the bottom of the first page. Position the insertion point to the left of the *Census Publications—1880* subheading.** The subheading and introductory paragraph should be included with the book information on the following page.

2. **Click the Page Layout tab, and in the Page Setup group, click the Breaks button.** A menu displays that describes various breaks that can be inserted, as shown in Figure 5.14. The first choice is Page which will create a break in the page at your insertion point.

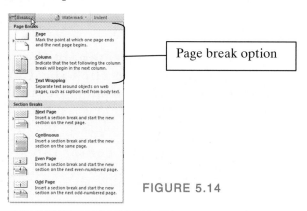

FIGURE 5.14

3.  **From the displayed list click Page.** The Census Publications subheading moves to the top of the following page. Notice the Page Break indicator, which only appears when formatting marks are displayed.

4.  **Press ⌈Ctrl⌉ + ⌈End⌉ to move the insertion point to the end of the document, and then press ⌈Enter ↵⌉.**

5.  **On the Page Layout tab, in the Page Setup group, click Breaks. Under *Section break types*, click Next page.** A new section is created, with the same formatting as the previous section.

6.  **In the Page Setup group, click the Orientation button and then click Landscape.** The formatting will be applied to the current section only.

7.  **Click the Insert tab, and in the Illustrations group click Picture. In the Insert Picture dialog box, locate and select *WD_0502.jpg*, and then click Insert.** The census image is inserted into the new section. Notice, however, that the footer tab stops are the same as they were in the previous section, and the page number in the header has reverted to page 1.

8.  **Double-click the Header on the newly inserted page 3. On the Header & Footer Tools Design Tab, in the Header & Footers group, click the Page Number button, and then click Format Page Numbers.** The Page Number Format dialog box displays, as shown in Figure 5.15.

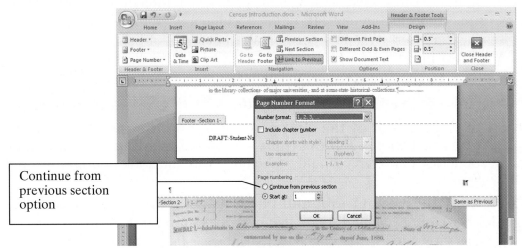

Continue from previous section option

FIGURE 5.15

9.  **Click the Continue from previous section option button, and then click OK.** The new page is now page 3.

10. **On the Header and Footer Design tab, in the Navigation group, click the Go to Footer button and then click the Link to Previous button to deselect this option.** The insertion point moves to the footer which is now displayed. The link to the previous section is removed. Any changes you make to the footer will not be reflected in the footers on the first two pages.

11. **On the horizontal ruler, drag the center tab stop marker to the 4.5"mark and then drag the right tab stop marker to the 9"mark.** The date is centered on the wider page, and the time extends to the right margin.

12. **Double-click anywhere in the document to leave the header and footer areas. Click the View tab, and in the Zoom group, click the Zoom button and then click Many Pages. Drag to select 1 x 3 Pages and then click OK.** Notice that the first two pages are in portrait orientation, while the new section is in landscape orientation. Also notice that changing the footer on the third page did not affect the layout of the footer on the first two pages as shown in Figure 5.16.

New section with different orientation

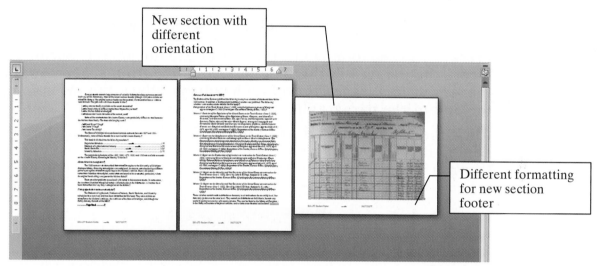

Different formatting for new section footer

FIGURE 5.16

13. **On the View tab, in the Zoom group, click the Zoom button. In the Zoom dialog box click Page Width, and then click OK. Save your changes and leave the *Census Introduction* document open for the next lesson.**

---

## TO EXTEND YOUR KNOWLEDGE...

### CREATING AUTOMATIC SECTION BREAKS

If you want to add columns to a document, there are several ways to proceed. You can place the insertion point at the beginning of the text and add a column section break. The columns will then extend to the end of the document, even if you do not want them to. You must then move to the end of the desired column text, insert another section break, and change the remaining text back to a single column. An easier way to create column text out of a portion of a document is to select the text that you want to make into columns, and then click the Columns button in the Page Setup group on the Page Layout tab. Word will automatically place a section break at the beginning and end of the selected text, and leave the formatting of the text before and after the columns the same.

### ANOTHER WAY TO INSERT A PAGE BREAK

To insert a page break using the keyboard, hold down Ctrl and then press Enter ↵.

---

# LESSON 7: Creating and Modifying Footnotes

Many scholarly and formal business documents require that information be properly referenced. Reference formats depend on the style guide used, but most notes are placed at the bottom of pages (***footnotes***), or at the end of sections or the end of the document (***endnotes***).

In this lesson, you add footnotes to the *Census Introduction* document.

## To Create and Modify Footnotes

1. **Press Ctrl + Home to move to the top of the document. Scroll down and locate the paragraph that begins *The population schedules* (just above the *About this transcription* subheading). Place the insertion point at the end of the paragraph.**

2. **Click the References tab, and in the Footnotes group, click the Dialog Box Launcher .** The Footnote and Endnote dialog box displays as shown in Figure 5.17. Take a moment to examine the available options.

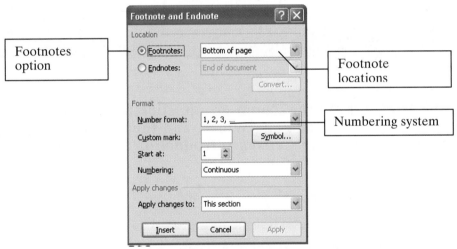

FIGURE 5.17

3. **Click Insert to accept the default footnote options.** A footnote box opens at the bottom of the page, with a line above the footnote area. A superscripted number 1 precedes the note, so you do not need to type a footnote number.

4. **Type: The Web address is www.alcona.org.** You must join the ACGS to use the site, but membership is free..

5. **Scroll to the top of the page and place the insertion point at the end of item 4 in the numbered list. On the References tab, in the Footnotes group, click the Insert Footnote button.** Notice that the new footnote is number 1, and the other footnote has been renumbered.

6. **Type: Val D. Greenwood, The Researcher's Guide to American Genealogy (Baltimore, MD: Genealogical Publishing Co.,1997) 241-244**

7. Under the bulleted list, locate the paragraph that begins *The State of Michigan* and place the insertion point at the end of the paragraph. In the Footnotes group, click Insert Footnote.

8. Type: Carol McGinnis, Michigan Genealogy (Baltimore, MD: Genealogical Publishing Co., 1989) 37-38. All of the footnotes have been entered, but they need to be modified—the book titles should be italicized.

9. In the first footnote, select the title of the book, point to the mini toolbar and then click the Italic button. Repeat this procedure to italicize the title of the book in the second footnote. Right-click the web address in the third footnote and on the displayed shortcut menu click Remove Hyperlink.

10. Scroll so you can see the bottom of the first page. Compare your footnotes with Figure 5.18.

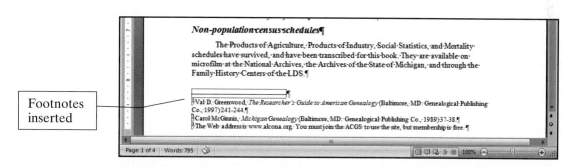

FIGURE 5.18

11. Save and print the *Census Introduction* document. Close the file; close Word.

## SUMMARY

In this project you learned how to apply paragraph and document formatting to make text more readable, and to indicate the structure of the document.

You changed a paragraph from double spacing to single and added a first line indent. After you formatted one paragraph, you saved the formatting as a style and applied that style to other paragraphs in your document. You also learned how to modify a style and update paragraphs that use that style.

You learned how to display information in bulleted and numbered lists. Bulleted lists are generally used when there is no particular order to the items in the list, whereas a numbered list is typically used to display data that has some type of order—chronological, importance, or sequence. You worked with tab stops to create horizontal lists of data. Individual tab stops enable you to align data on the right, center, left, or at a decimal.

You learned how to insert artificial page breaks and section breaks to control where information breaks across a page, or to display a page in a different orientation from the rest of the document. You added information to every page in a document by using the header and footer area. Typically page numbers, the date, filename, or file location are added to these areas. Finally, you learned how to add footnotes to cite references related to the document content.

## KEY TERMS

| | | |
|---|---|---|
| Bar Tab | footnote | numbered list |
| bullet | hanging indent | Right Tab |
| bulleted list | header | ruler |
| CenterTab | indent | section |
| Decimal Tab | leader | section break |
| endnote | Left Tab | spin arrows |
| first line indent | manual page break | style |
| footer | Normal style | |

## CHECKING CONCEPTS AND TERMS

### SCREEN ID
Label each element of the screen shown in Figure 5.19 on the next page.

_____ A. Bulleted list

_____ B. Bullets

_____ C. Centered tab stop

_____ D. Footer

_____ E. Footnotes

_____ F. Insert Date

_____ G. Numbered list

_____ H. Paragraph format mark

_____ I. Paragraph Indent indicator

_____ J. Show/Hide

_____ K. Go to Footer

_____ L. Tab format mark

_____ M. Tabbed list

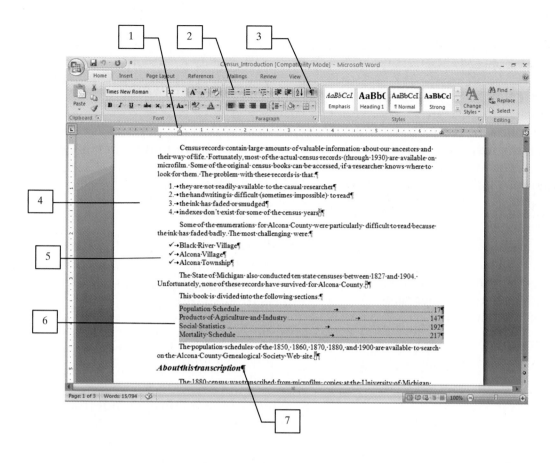

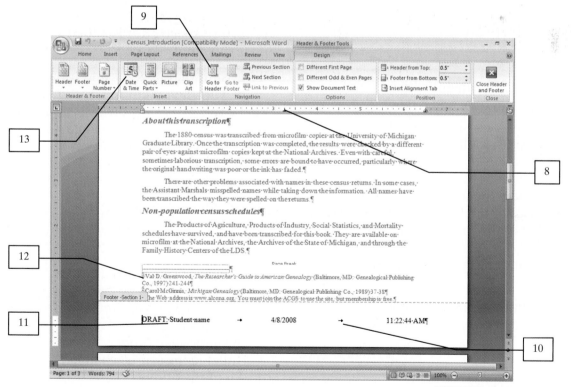

FIGURE 5.19

## MULTIPLE CHOICE

**Circle the letter of the correct answer for each of the following.**

1. Which of the following is a paragraph style in which the first line of a paragraph extends to the left of the rest of the paragraph? [L1]
   a. first line indent
   b. paragraph indent
   c. hanging indent
   d. right indent

2. A feature that fills the space between tab stops with a character such as a dash or a dot is know as a _____. [L4]
   a. leader
   b. follower
   c. filler
   d. spacer

3. The keyboard shortcut for creating a page break is _____. [L6]
   a. Shift + Enter
   b. Alt + Enter
   c. Ctrl + Enter
   d. Insert + Enter

4. If you have a document with several footnotes, and then add a new footnote, _____. [L7]
   a. you have to renumber the existing footnotes
   b. the program automatically renumbers the footnotes for you
   c. you have to tell the program to renumber the footnotes starting with the first one
   d. you cannot insert footnotes out of order

5. In addition to paragraphs styles, what other types of styles are available in Word?[L7]
   a. table styles
   b. character styles
   c. list styles
   d. all of the above

6. To display part of your text as columns, or change the orientation of a page in the document, insert a _____. [L6]
   a. page break
   b. section break
   c. new page
   d. format break

7. Which button displays hidden formatting marks?[L1]
   a. Show/Hide
   b. Show Formatting
   c. Format Painter
   d. Style

8. Which of the following is not true about the default Normal style in Word 2007? [L2]
   a. the font size is 11-point
   b. the font is Calibri
   c. a 10-pt space after is added
   d. text is single spaced

9. To ensure that headers and footers align with the text in the document, check the _____ indicators and adjust the _____ as needed. [L5]
   a. margin, tab stop
   b. footer, header
   c. border, alignment
   d. boundary, indent

10. Which of the following statements about lists is correct? [L3]
    a. Bulleted lists are usually used when the list data is in no particular order.
    b. Numbered lists are most often used for lists in sequential or chronological order.
    c. Bullet icons can be changed.
    d. All of the above.

# DISCUSSION

1. Which formatting tools demonstrated in this chapter will be most useful to you? When will you use them? Which formatting techniques are new to you? [L1–L7]

2. When is it useful to have the formatting marks displayed? How do they help you format your document? [L1–L7]

3. If you were responsible for establishing a letter or memo standard for your company, what would that standard be? How would you use styles to create the standard? Consider each of the formatting elements demonstrated in this project and any other formatting elements that you consider pertinent such as font and font size. [L1–L7]

## SKILL DRILL

Skill Drill exercises reinforce project skills. Each skill reinforced is the same, or nearly the same, as a skill presented in the project. Detailed instructions are provided in a step-by-step format.

Work through exercise 1 first. The rest of the Skill Drill exercises can be worked through in any order. Be sure to save your changes and close the document if you need more than one work session to complete the desired exercises. Continue working on *Alternative Fuel* rather than starting over with the original *WD_0503* file. After you complete all of the exercises, print a copy of the document (optional). All of these exercises can be completed using Microsoft Office XP or later versions. Instructions throughout the exercises are based on a Windows XP operating system, running Microsoft Office 2007.

### 1. Formatting Paragraphs and Creating and Applying Styles

You are on a committee that is working on a grant from the Clean Cities program to establish an alternative fuel vehicles test site. A proposal has been drafted and needs to be formatted. In this Skill Drill you format paragraphs by changing line spacing, adding indents, and then create styles to apply to titles and subtitles.

1. Start **Word** and open the document *WD_0503* from the Student folder. Save it to your folder as a Word 9702993 document named **Alternative Fuel.** On the Home tab, in the Paragraph group, click the **Show/Hide** button to display the formatting marks.

2. Select the first three lines of the document, which make up the title. Change the font to *Arial Rounded MT Bold*, the font size to *14*, and the alignment to *Center*.

3. Click in the paragraph that begins *This project will support...* On the **Home tab**, in the **Paragraph group**, click the **Dialog Box Launcher** button. Under **Indentation**, click the **Special** arrow and select **First line**. Under **Spacing**, click the **Line spacing** arrow and select **Double**. Click **OK**

4. On the **Home tab**, in the **Styles group**, click the **More** button and at the end of the list click **Save Selection as a New Quick Style**.

5. In the Create New Style from Formatting dialog box type: `Paragraph` in the Name box. Click **OK** to create a new Paragraph style.

6. Click in the paragraph that begins *Submission of a project...* On the **Home tab**, in the **Styles group**, click **Paragraph** to apply the style you created in step 5.

7. Apply the Paragraph style to the paragraph that begins *Southeastern Michigan University...* and to the paragraph that begins *This initiative will....*

8. Select the subtitle *General Information* and create a new style called Subheading. Change the style so that it is bold and italic. Apply the new Subheading style to the selected *General Information* subtitle, and to the subtitle *Goals and Objectives....*

9. Delete the empty paragraphs before and after the two subheadings that you just formatted. On the Styles and Formatting task pane, right-click the **Subheading** style and select **Modify**.

10. In the Modify Style dialog box, click **Format**, **Paragraph**. In the Paragraph dialog box, under Spacing, click the **After** up spin arrow one time to add a 6-point after format to this style. Click **OK** twice. The change in format is applied to both subheadings.

11. Save the *Alternative Fuel* document.

## 2. Adding Numbered and Bulleted Lists

There are a number of lists in this document that need to be formatted. You examine the document and decide a bulleted list would work best for the first and second lists, and that a numbered list is necessary for the third list.

1. With the *Alternative Fuel* document open, select the eight lines, beginning with *Development of a fueling station*, and ending with *natural gas vehicles (CNG)*.

2. On the **Home tab**, in the **Paragraph group**, click the **Bullets** button. On the Bullets button click the **arrow** and then select the right-pointing bullet.

3. Select the last paragraph in the bulleted list. Right-click the selected paragraph and then from the displayed submenu click **Paragraph**. In the Paragraph dialog box click the **After** up spin arrow one time to add a 6-point after space. Click **OK**.

4. Select the list at the end of the first page starting with *A grant from U.S.....* Do not select the *Goals and Objectives...* subheading. In the **Paragraph group**, click the **Bullets** button.

5. Select the last paragraph in the bulleted list. Right-click the selected text and then click **Paragraph**. Click the **After** up spin arrow one time to add a 6-point after space. Click **OK**.

6. Select the six lines on the second page starting with *Construction of . . .* and ending with *Vehicle operator.*

7. In the **Paragraph group**, click the **Numbering** to create a numbered list.

8. Save the *Alternative Fuel* document.

## 3. Creating a Tabbed List

At the last committee meeting, tentative dates were set for the completion of the project. You will add these dates to the bottom of the document by creating a tabbed list.

1. With the *Alternative Fuel* document open, select the last three lines in the document.

2. Click in the ruler at the 2.5" mark. This places a left tab stop at this location for each of the selected lines of text.

3. Click the **Tab Alignment** button on the left end of the horizontal ruler twice. The tab marker changes to a right tab. Click at the 6.25" mark on the ruler.

4. On the **Home tab**, in the **Paragraph group**, click the **Dialog Box Launcher** button. At the bottom of the Paragraph dialog box click the **Tabs** button. Select the 6.25" tab in the Tab stop position box. (Note: If the value is not 6.25, click the value, Click the Clear button and enter 6.25 in the Tab stop position.) In the **Leader** area click the **2** and in the **Alignment** area be sure that **Right** is selected. Click **OK**.

5. Click at the right end of the first line of text to which you added tabs. Press ⎹Tab⎸ and type: Phase I. Press ⎹Tab⎸ again and type: 7/05.

6. Finish the last two lines with the following information.

   Phase II    11/05

   Phase III   2/06

7. Save the *Alternative Fuel* document.

## 4. Inserting Page Breaks and Adding Headers and Footers

When you look over the document you see that the second subheading is separated from the text that follows it. A page break is needed to ensure this data displays with the text to which it relates. You also need to add some header and footer information.

1. With the Alternative Fuel document open, click to the left of the subheading *Goals and Objectives of the Project* at the bottom of page 1. Press ⎹Ctrl⎸ + ⎹Enter ↵⎸ to insert a page break.

2. Click the **Insert tab**, and in the **Headers & Footers group**, click the **Header** button. Select **Blank (Three Columns)**. Click in the *Type Text* place holder on the left side of the Header and type: `Southeastern Michigan University`.

3. Click in the right side of the Header and type `Alternative Fuel Vehicle Project`. Delete the middle text placeholder. Select the text in the header, point to the mini toolbar and then click the **Italic** button.

4. On the **Header & Footer Tools Design tab**, in the **Navigation group**,

click the **Go to Footer** button. On the left side of the Footer and using your name type: `Formatted by: Your Name`.

5. Press Tab. In the **Header & Footer group**, click the **Page Number** button, point to **Current Position** and then click **Plain Number**. Press Tab, and in the **Insert group** click the **Date & Time** button. Select Month, Day, Year and then click **OK**.

6. Double-click in the document to move out of the footer area. Save the *Alternative Fuel* document.

## 5. Inserting Footnotes

The Clean Cities program has its own Web site and you want to add that reference so people who read this proposal can view additional information about the program. You decide to add it as a footnote.

1. With the *Alternative-Fuel* document open, in the first line of the first paragraph, click to the right of the registered symbol next to Clean Cities.

2. Click the **References tab**, and in the **Footnotes group**, click the **Dialog Box Launcher** button. Click the **Endnotes** option. Be sure *End of document* displays in the location box and the Number format box displays *i, ii, iii . . . .*

3. Click **Insert**. Type: `To learn more about the Clean Cities Program go to their Web site at: www.eere.energy.gov/cleancities`.

   (If you happen to press the spacebar after the Web address, the Web address will change to a hyperlink and the text will display in blue with a blue underline. When you point to the Web address a ScreenTip displays that instructs you to press Ctrl and then click to follow the link.)

4. Save the *Alternative Fuel* document. Print a copy. Close the file and close Word.

## CHALLENGE

Challenge exercises expand on or are somewhat related to skills presented in the lessons. Each exercise provides a brief narrative introduction, followed by instructions in a numbered-step format that are not as detailed as those in the Skill Drill section.

Each exercise is independent of the others, so you may complete the exercises in any order.

### 1. Formatting a Distance Education Paper

In this Challenge exercise you will practice the skills you have learned by applying them to a paper about distance education

1. Open the file **WD_0504**. Save it in your folder as `Distance Education`.

2. On the Page Layout tab, click the Margins button and then click Customize. In the Page Setup dialog box and change the top margin to **1.5"**, and the bottom, left, and right margins to **1"**.

3. Click in the paragraph that begins *Distance Education is....*Create a style named `Text` that uses a first line indent and a 12-point after space. Apply the Text style to the first paragraph in the body of the document and to the paragraphs under Interactive Technologies, Computer Based Conferencing, and Conclusion. Close the Styles task pane.

4. Select the list of references at the end of the document. Display the Paragraph dialog box. Add a 12-point space after and a hanging indent to the selected text.

5. Select the four paragraphs under the *Conclusion* subheading starting with *Recently available....* The first and last paragraph in this section should not be selected. Click the **Bullets** button, and then click the **Decrease Indent** button twice, and the **Increase Indent** button once.

6. With the bulleted list still selected, click the **Bullets** button arrow and change the bullet symbol to the small square (the fourth choice under Bullet Library).

7. Insert a page break just before the *Conclusion* subheading to place it on the next page with the related text. Insert another page break just before the *Reference List* subheading to place the references on a different page.

8. Insert a page number in the center of the footer. Double-click at the right side of the footer and type your name. If necessary to align the footer with the document, on the horizontal ruler, drag the center tab to 3.25" and the right tab to 6.5".

9. On the Header & Footer Tools Design tab click the **Different First Page** checkbox. This enables you to create a different first page header and footer.

10. Go to the header and then in the Navigation group click the **Previous Section** button. With the insertion point on the left side of the header, display the Date and Time dialog box. Select the Month Day, Year format and insert the date on the left side of the First Page Header area.

11. Save the *Distance Education* file. Print a copy. Close the file.

## 2. Formatting a Lightning Paper

In this Challenge exercise you review a paper about lightning in Michigan and format the paper so it is more readable.

1. Open **WD_0505**. Save it in your folder with the name `Lightning Paper.`

2. Select the title at the top of the paper. Display the Styles task pane and click the *Heading 1* style. Modify the style to center the title on the page. and in the Name box type `Centered Title` to create a new style

3. Select the first paragraph of text. Use the **Line Spacing** button to double-space the paragraph. Display the Paragraph dialog box and set a first line indent.

4. With the paragraph still selected, in the Clipboard group, double-click the **Format Painter**. Recall that this button is used to paint a format from one

paragraph to others. Click each of the remaining paragraphs of text, excluding the tabbed list, to apply the format from the first paragraph. Click the **Format Painter** once to turn it off or press ⒠ⓈⒸ.

5. Display the formatting marks. Scroll through the document and remove the extra empty paragraph marks between each paragraph, except for the one after the title and the one that follows the tabbed list.

6. The tabbed list uses multiple tabs to try and align this data. Using right tabs would make the numbers align on the right as they should. Select the list and then set right tabs at 2.5", 4" and 5.5". Remove the extra tabs in each row as needed so the list aligns in four even columns of data with the numbers aligned on the right.

7. On the **Insert tab**, click the **Header** button and then click **Blank**. In the *Type text* box type Formatted by: and type your name. Go to the footer and on the left side of the footer, click the **Quick Parts** button and then click **Field**. In the Field dialog box, scroll the Field names and then select **File Name** and click **OK**. Your file name is inserted on the left side of the footer.

8. Tab to the right side of the footer. Click the **Page Number** button and then click **Current Position**. Scroll down the list and under *Page X of Y* click **Bold Numbers**. This inserts Page 1 of 2 in the footer. If necessary insert a right tab at the right margin to move the page number to the right on the same line as the file name.

9. Click at the end of the second sentence in the first paragraph following *...during that period*. On the Reference tab insert a Footnote. In the footnote area, type Lightning struck the Swedish Crucible Steel Co. of Hamtramck, causing $5 million in damages.

10. Click at the end of the first sentence in the second paragraph following *...boating, and swimming*. Insert another footnote and type: About 95% of lightning casualties occur outdoors.

11. Click at the end of the first sentence in the first paragraph; insert another footnote and in the footnote area type: Males account for nearly 80% of lightning casualties. The footnotes are renumbered. The last one you entered now is number 1.

12. Save the Lightning Paper document. Print a copy (optional). Close the file.

## 3. Formatting Columns

You need to create an index of the Alcona County Census information and have gathered all of the data together. The index is several pages long and you want to shorten it by displaying the data in columns. In this Challenge exercise you insert a section break and then display the data as columns.

1. Open **WD_0506**. Save it in your folder with the name **Census Index**. Display the formatting marks.

2. Click to the left of the large *A* below the title line. On the Page Layout tab,

click **Breaks**. Under *Section Break*, click **Continuous** and then click **OK**. A section break is added at the insertion point. Now you can format the rest of the document as columns.

3.  In the **Page Setup group**, click **Columns** and then click **Two**. The index displays as two columns and the number of pages is reduced from 21 to 11. You decide to try and reduce the number of pages by displaying three columns to a page.

4.  Click **Columns** again and then click **More Columns**. Click the **Three** box in the column *Presets* area and then select the **Line between** check box. Click **OK**. The line between helps define the columns and by changing to three columns the page count is reduced to seven.

5.  On the Insert tab, click **Page Number**. Set the page number to display in the center of the footer. Click Page Number again and then click the **Format Page Numbers**. In the Page Number Format dialog box, format the numbers to display as *i, ii, iii*. Click the **Start at** option button under Page numbering and be sure i displays in the text box. Click **OK**.

6.  On the **Insert tab**, click the **Footer** button and then click **Blank**. Delete the *Type text* box on the left side of the footer. In the **Insert group**, click the **Quick Parts** button and then click **Field**. In the Field dialog box, scroll the Field names and then select **File Name** and click **OK**. Your file name is inserted on the left side of the footer. Tab to the right side of the footer and type Formatted by: and type your name.

7.  Save the Census Index document. Print the first page only (optional). Close the file and close Word.

## DISCOVERY ZONE

Discovery Zone exercises require advanced knowledge of topics presented in *Essentials* lessons, application of skills from multiple lessons, or self-directed learning of new skills. Each exercise is independent of the others, so you may complete the exercises in any order.

### 1. Creating a Letterhead Template

Paragraph and document formatting are used to help guide the reader through a document. They can also be used to create a consistency of style within an organization. Many people in an organization may need to correspond with customers or suppliers. Most companies spend money to create a corporate identity which includes the logo, slogans, and colors used by the company and the way the company name is displayed. To ensure that everyone uses the company standards that have been established, letterhead and forms are designed and distributed along with a policy statement about how to display the company name, logo, and slogans. You can even distribute the letterhead and forms as an electronic file known as a template. The paragraph, font, margins, and other formatting are designed into the template. The template is available for repeated use. When you open a template, you create a new document that is then saved with a new name. The next time you need to send a letter, or complete a form, you start with the template file.

Create a letterhead template for the Alumni Travel Club. Open a blank document.

Use the tools that you have practiced to create a letterhead style for the organization. Include the following elements.

Enter the organization's name at the top of the document. Select a distinctive font, font size, and font color for the name. Align the name on the right.

Add a formatting line of your choice under the name using the Borders and Shading dialog box.

Under the formatting line add an address, phone number and e-mail address (use your own information for this or use your school's information). Align this information in a single line on the right. Use a smaller font size, and a font style that is similar to the font used for the organization's name.

Change the left and right margins to 1", and the top margin to 1.5".

Create a paragraph style that includes a first line indent and a space after format.

Add a footer that includes the file name and path.

Save the file with the name `Alumni Template`. In the Save As dialog box, change the *Save as type* box to *Word 97-2003 Template*. This saves the file in the Templates folder on your computer. If you are working in a lab, or on a public computer, navigate to your folder and save the template with your other files. Make sure it is saved as a **.dot** file.

Open the template and save it in your folder as `Alaska Letter`. Write a brief letter announcing a planning meeting for the upcoming Alaska trip. The meeting is scheduled for June 20, in the school library. Include your name somewhere in the letter. Print the letter (optional). Close the file and close Word.

## 2. Changing Text to Columns and Using a Mirror Margin Setting

Columns are used for newsletters and other documents to make them easier to read. Sometimes you will want text in the middle of the document to be in multiple columns and the rest to be in one column. When you highlight text in the middle of the document to change it to multiple columns, Word automatically puts section breaks at the beginning and end of the selected text. If you need to create a document that is going to be printed on both sides and bound in the middle, you should use the Mirror Margins feature. This ensures that the inside margin of each page is wide enough to accommodate the binding. When a document is formatted with different inside and outside margins, you will usually place the page number for the document on the outside edge. When Mirror Margins are used, this means that the location of the outside edge alternates every other page.

1. Open WD_0507. Save it with the name **Tornadoes**. Select the text beginning with the paragraph that begins *The southern half of Michigan . . .* and ending at the end of the paragraph just before the list of tornadoes. Change the alignment to left, rather than justified.

2. On the Page Layout tab, click the **Columns** button and then click **Two..** Notice the section breaks that are placed before and after the text that displays as two columns.

3. On the Page Setup tab click the **Margins** button and then click **Custom Margins**. In the Pages section, select **Mirror margins** from the Multiple pages text box.

4. Set the margins as follows: Top 1", Bottom 1", Inside 1.5", Outside 0.5". Change the Apply to box to **Whole document**.

5. Double-click Header area, and on the Design tab in the Options group, click the **Different Odd and Even Pages** check box. Without this step, you will not be able to place page numbers in different locations on odd and even pages.

6. On the first page, in the Odd Page Header area, tab over to the right edge of the header, and click the Insert Page Number button.

7. Move to the Even Page Header area and click then on the left side of the header use the **Insert Page Number** button to insert the page number. Go to the footer. From the **Quick Parts** button Field list, insert the **File Name** field on the left side of the footer and type your name on the right side. Go to the Odd Page Footer and insert the **FileName** field on the left and your name on the right. Return to the document.

8. Because the columns have now changed width, from the **Columns** button, click **More Columns** and then select the **Equal column width** check box.

9. Preview the document and look at both pages. Notice that the odd numbered page (the right page in a book) has the wide margin for binding on the left side. Just the opposite is true for the even numbered (left) page.

10. Save the Tornadoes document and print it (optional). Close the file, and then close Word.

# UNIT 2: USING PRODUCTIVITY SOFTWARE

## Microsoft Office 2007 C³

## Project 6: Working with Tables

LESSON 1 Inserting a Table into a Document

        2-2.2.1.1        2-2.2.1.2

LESSON 2 Entering Text in a Table

        2-2.2.2

LESSON 3 Adding Rows or Columns to a Table

        2-2.2.3.2        2-2.2.3.3

LESSON 4 Formatting Text in a Table

        2-2.2.3.1        2-2.2.4.2

LESSON 5 Formatting Borders and Shading a Table

        2-2.2.4.1        2-2.2.4.3        2-2.2.4.4

LESSON 6 Converting Text to a Table and Merging Cells

        2-2.2.1.3        2-2.2.3.4
        2-2.2.1.4        2.2.2.3.5

LESSON 7 Adjusting Column Width and Row Height

        2-2.2.3.6        2-2.2.3.8
        2-2.2.3.7        2-2.2.3.9

LESSON 8 Splitting and Sorting a Table

        2-2.2.3.10        2-2.2.2.5

LESSON 9 Using the Table Styles (AutoFormat) and AutoFit Tools

        2-2.2.4.5

# PROJECT 6

# WORKING WITH TABLES

IN THIS PROJECT, YOU LEARN HOW TO:

- Insert a Table Into a Document
- Enter Text in a Table
- Add Rows or Columns to a Table
- Format Text in a Table
- Format Borders and Shade a Table
- Convert Text to a Table and Merge Cells
- Adjust Column Width and Row Height
- Split and Sort a Table
- Use the Table Styles (AutoFormat) and AutoFit Tools

# WHY WOULD I DO THIS?

**T**ables are lists of information set up in a row and column format, similar to the layout of a spreadsheet. Each intersection of an individual row and column in a table is called a *cell*. The cells can contain text, numbers, or graphics. Tables are particularly useful when you need to create lists of parallel information, especially when the amount of information varies greatly from one column to the next. They are excellent for two-column tasks, such as résumés, in which the topic is on the left and the details are on the right.

The same formatting tools that are used throughout a document can be applied to a table. You can change font and font size, add bold, italic, or underline emphasis to text, add borders and shading to rows, columns, or individual cells. Data can be aligned both horizontally and vertically in a cell. Formatting can be applied to an individual cell, multiple cells, or an entire table at once.

Lists of information that are displayed as text can be converted to a table, and a table can also be converted to text. You can even draw a table with variable dimensions in different rows and columns. Cells can be merged or split, and column width and row height can be adjusted to your specification. In all, tables provide a very flexible method for displaying information in columns.

In this project, you create, edit, and format a table. You also learn how to convert text to a table, merge cells, and apply automatic formatting.

# VISUAL SUMMARY

In this project, you create a table to display data about tornadoes that have occurred in Michigan. You learn how to format the table using the formatting tools you worked with in the Common Elements section of this book. You then create a second table by converting a tabbed list, and apply formatting by using automatic formatting features. Figure 6.1 shows the finished document with the two tables.

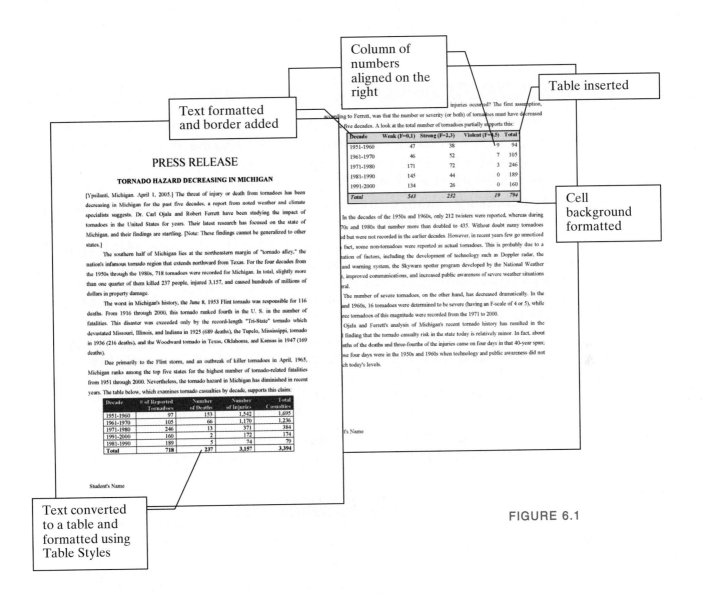

FIGURE 6.1

# LESSON 1: Inserting a Table into a Document

Adding a table to a document is just one method of displaying lists of information in columns and rows. You can use tabs for many of the same functions. Tables are much easier to use than tabs, however, and they are far more powerful and flexible. After you have mastered the use of tables, you will find that they save you a great deal of time and that you end up with a better-looking finished product. To add a table, on the Insert tab, use the Table button.

In this lesson, you learn to insert a table into a document.

All of these exercises can be completed with Microsoft Office 2007. Instructions throughout the lessons are based on the Windows XP operating system, running Microsoft Office 2007. Your screen may differ slightly from the figures shown, even if you are running Office 2007.

## To Insert a Table Into a Document

1. **Start Microsoft Office Word 2007 and locate and open** *WD_0601.* **Save it as a 97-2003 compatible file and name it Tornadoes.** This document is an article about the decline in the number of tornado related-deaths and injuries in Michigan

2. **If necessary, change the view to Print Layout, and adjust the page width with the Zoom slider.**

3. **Scroll down to the second page and locate the paragraph that begins with the words** *In the decades* **....Place the insertion point at the beginning of that paragraph. Press** [Enter◄┘] **to add a blank line, and then move the insertion point up to the blank line.** You are going to insert a table at the insertion point.

4. **Click the Insert tab, and in the Tables group, click the Table button, and then from the displayed list click Insert Table.** The Insert Table dialog box opens. Here you designate the number of rows and columns. You can also choose one of the *AutoFit* options, which controls how the data fits in the table and how the table displays on the page.

5. **Type: 5 in the Number of columns text box, press** [Tab] **and type 5 in the Number of rows text box as shown in Figure 6.2.**

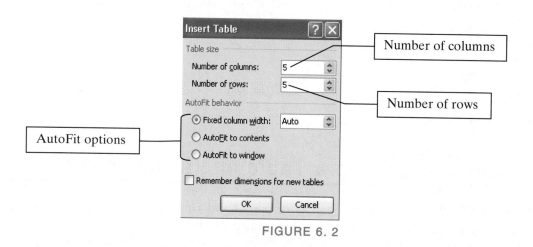

FIGURE 6. 2

6. **Click OK.** The outline of the table displays at the insertion point.

7. **Save the** *Tornadoes* **document and leave the file open to continue to the next lesson.**

### FORMATTING CHARACTERISTICS OF TABLES

A table inserted into a document takes on the characteristics of the paragraph where the insertion point was located when the table was created. That means that the font type and size of the table are the same as that of the paragraph. If the paragraph is double-spaced, the cells in the table are also double-spaced. To change these characteristics, use the same formatting buttons that you use to format other text.

### CREATING A TABLE USING THE TABLE BUTTON

Clicking the Table button on Insert tab displays a grid of columns and rows. As you move your pointer over the grid, the columns and rows are selected and the table dimension displays at the top of the grid. When you have selected the number of rows and columns you need, click on the grid to insert the table.

### CREATING A TABLE USING THE DRAW TABLE COMMAND

If you need a table of irregular dimensions with cells of different sizes in each row, you can use the Draw Table command on the Table button menu. When you choose this command, your window will change to Print Layout view (if necessary), and the pointer changes to a pencil icon. Drag the pencil tool to draw horizontal or vertical lines on your document, and as you do, the Tables Tools Design tab displays. When you finish drawing the table, press (Esc) to return the pointer to its default shape and function. In this manner, you can draw a table to your match your needs.

## LESSON 2: Entering Text in a Table

After you have set up the rows and columns of your table, the next step is to enter information into the table's cells. You can enter any kind of information you want. The most common table entries are text and numbers, but you can also insert graphics or an Internet address that is a *hyperlink*—a shortcut to a Web site.

In this lesson, you enter text and numbers into the table that you added to the *Tornadoes* document.

### To Enter Text in a Table

1. With the *Tornadoes* document open, and the table you just created on the screen, place the insertion point in the first cell, if necessary.

2. Type: Decade and then press (Tab). This is the column heading for the first column of the table. Notice that the text is left-aligned by default. Pressing (Tab) moves the insertion point to the second cell of the first row as shown in Figure 6.3.

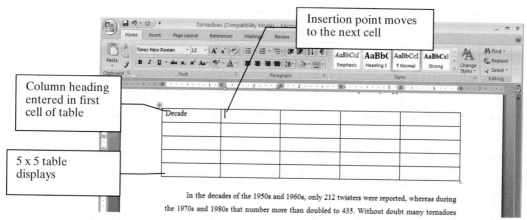

**Insertion point moves to the next cell**

**Column heading entered in first cell of table**

**5 x 5 table displays**

Decade

In the decades of the 1950s and 1960s, only 212 twisters were reported, whereas during the 1970s and 1980s that number more than doubled to 435. Without doubt many tornadoes

FIGURE 6. 3

## If you have problems...

Many people automatically press Enter ↵ when they finish typing a cell entry in a table. If you do so, the insertion point does not move to the next cell but instead creates a new line in the current cell. To recover from this error, press ←Bksp to remove the extra paragraph mark in the cell, then press Tab to move to the next cell.

3. Type: Weak (F=0, 1) in the second cell of the top row and then press Tab.

4. Type: Strong (F=2, 3) in the third cell of the top row and then press Tab.

5. Type: Violent (F=4, 5) in the fourth cell of the top row, press Tab, and then Type: Total in the last cell of the first row. The column headings are entered in the first row of the table as shown in Figure 6.4.

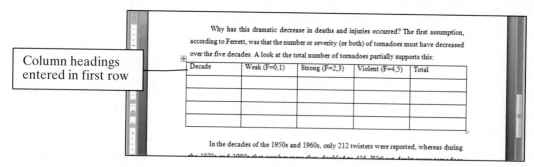

**Column headings entered in first row**

Why has this dramatic decrease in deaths and injuries occurred? The first assumption, according to Ferrett, was that the number or severity (or both) of tornadoes must have decreased over the five decades. A look at the total number of tornadoes partially supports this:

| Decade | Weak (F=0,1) | Strong (F=2,3) | Violent (F=4,5) | Total |
|--------|--------------|----------------|-----------------|-------|
|        |              |                |                 |       |
|        |              |                |                 |       |
|        |              |                |                 |       |
|        |              |                |                 |       |

In the decades of the 1950s and 1960s, only 212 twisters were reported, whereas during

FIGURE 6. 4

6. **Press** Tab. The insertion point moves to the first cell of the next row in the table. Use the Tab key to move forward one cell in a table

7. **Using the method you just practiced, enter the following information in the next four rows of the table:**

| 1961–1970 | 46 | 52 | 7 | 105 |
| 1971–1980 | 171 | 72 | 3 | 246 |
| 1981–1990 | 145 | 44 | 0 | 189 |
| 1991–2000 | 134 | 26 | 0 | 160 |

The year ranges in the first column are the row headings for the table as shown in Figure 6.5.

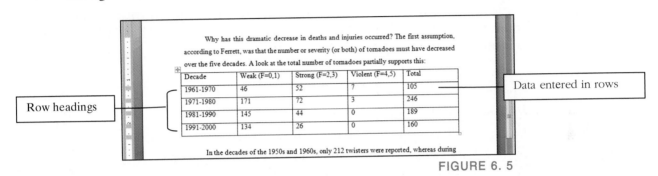

FIGURE 6. 5

8. **Save the *Tornadoes* document and leave the file open to continue to the next lesson.**

## TO EXTEND YOUR KNOWLEDGE...

### NAVIGATING A TABLE
If you need to change information in a cell, use the mouse to click in the desired cell, or use the arrow keys to move up, down, left, or right one cell at a time. To move back one cell, you can also press ⇧Shift + Tab.

### ACCESSING TABLE COMMANDS
When working with a table, the commands related to the table are available on the Table Tools contextual tabs. The Design tab contains commands related to the design of the table and the Layout tab contains the commands that affect the arrangement of the cells. You can also right-click the table to display the context-sensitive shortcut menu options. The Layout menu is used to create and modify the structure of a table, such as inserting rows or columns, merging cells, cell size, and text alignment and direction. The Design tab contains formatting commands that affect table borders and shading, and includes a wide variety of table styles. The shortcut menu offers quick access to many of the frequently used commands that affect how the table displays.

## LESSON 3: Adding Rows or Columns to a Table

When you create a table, you may not always know exactly how many rows or columns you need. After a table is created, it is simple to insert rows or columns into the middle of the table or at the end of the table.

In this lesson, you insert a row in the middle of the table. The process for inserting columns is just the same, except you choose columns, instead of rows, from the list of options. You will also add a new row at the bottom of the table using a convenient keyboard method.

## To Add Rows or Columns to a Table

1. **With the *Tornadoes* document open, place the insertion point anywhere in the second row of the table you created.** You need to add data for an earlier decade prior to the data you entered in Lesson 2.

2. **Right-click the table. From the displayed shortcut menu, click Insert.** A submenu displays a list of options, as shown in Figure 6.6. These are items that can be inserted at the current insertion point.

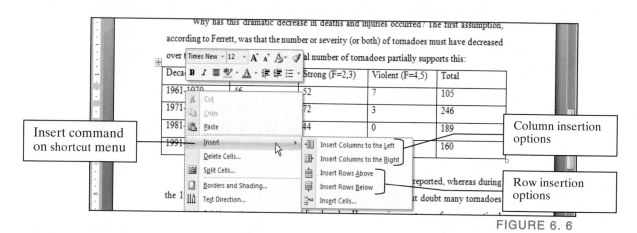

FIGURE 6. 6

3. **Select Insert Rows Above.** A new row is added to the table. The row that contained the insertion point moves down one row.

4. **Add the following information to the new row:**

   1951–1960        47        38        9        94

The data for the earlier decade is added to the table as shown in Figure 6.7.

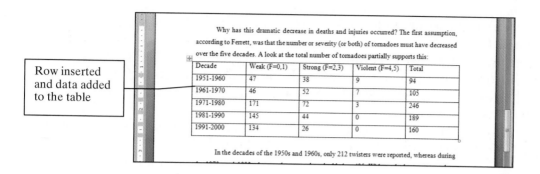

Row inserted and data added to the table

Why has this dramatic decrease in deaths and injuries occurred? The first assumption, according to Ferrett, was that the number or severity (or both) of tornadoes must have decreased over the five decades. A look at the total number of tornadoes partially supports this:

| Decade | Weak (F=0,1) | Strong (F=2,3) | Violent (F=4,5) | Total |
|---|---|---|---|---|
| 1951-1960 | 47 | 38 | 9 | 94 |
| 1961-1970 | 46 | 52 | 7 | 105 |
| 1971-1980 | 171 | 72 | 3 | 246 |
| 1981-1990 | 145 | 44 | 0 | 189 |
| 1991-2000 | 134 | 26 | 0 | 160 |

In the decades of the 1950s and 1960s, only 212 twisters were reported, whereas during

FIGURE 6. 7

5. **Click in the last cell in the table (160) and then press** [Tab]. A seventh row is added at the end of the table.

6. **Add the following data to the last row of the table:**

   Total      543      232      19      794

7. **Save the *Tornadoes* document and leave the file open to continue to the next lesson.**

## TO EXTEND YOUR KNOWLEDGE...

### INSERTING COLUMNS IN A TABLE

The procedure to insert a column in a table is similar to inserting rows. To add a column, place the cursor in a column to the right or left of where you want the new column to appear. Right-click the table, click Insert, and then click Columns to the Left (or Columns to the Right) from the shortcut menu.

### DELETING ROWS AND COLUMNS IN A TABLE

If you need to reduce the dimension of your table you can delete rows or columns from the Table Tools Layout tab. Click in a cell within the row or column you want to remove. On the Layout tab, in the Rows & Columns group, click the Delete button and from the displayed list click Delete Columns or Delete Rows. You can also select the row or column you want to remove, right-click on the selected area, and then choose Delete Rows or Delete Columns from the shortcut menu.

### USING THE LAYOUT TAB TO INSERT A ROW OR COLUMN

To insert a row in a table, with your insertion point in the table, on the Layout tab, in the Rows & Columns group, click the Insert Above or the Insert Below button. A row will be inserted above or below the insertion point. Likewise, if you click the Insert Left or Insert Right button, a column will be inserted to the left or right of the selected column.

## LESSON 4: Formatting Text in a Table

When you create a table, the text in the headings, the totals in the columns and rows, and the rest of the data all look the same. You can use standard formatting tools to emphasize important points, headings, and totals. This emphasis gives your table an easy-to-read, professional look.

Another way to make your table look more professional is to align the items in an attractive manner. Notice that your numbers do not line up on the right side in the table you just created. Generally, text in columns is aligned on the left and numbers are on the right. Column headings should generally be right-aligned or centered if they are above numbers. To improve the appearance of this table, the numbers and text need to be properly aligned.

In this lesson, you format text in the table you just created. In the process, you learn how to select a row or column of data, or several cells at once.

## To Format Text in a Table

1. **With the *Tornadoes* document open, select *Decade* in the first cell of the table, and then click the Home tab, and in the Font group click the Bold button.** The first column heading is now boldfaced.

2. **Place the insertion point to the left of the word *Weak* in the second cell of the first row and drag to the end of the row.** As you drag, the cells are selected as shown in Figure 6.8. In this manner you can select several cells at once. When the cells are selected, notice that the Mini toolbar displays.

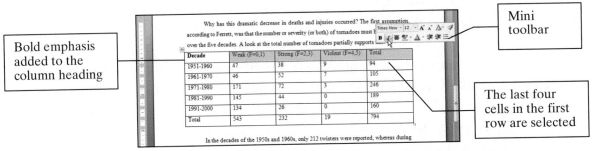

Bold emphasis added to the column heading

Mini toolbar

The last four cells in the first row are selected

FIGURE 6. 8

3. **Click the Bold button on the Mini toolbar.** The rest of the column headings in the first row now display in boldfaced font.

4. **Move the pointer to the left of the table, next to the last row. When the pointer displays as a white arrow, click once to select the entire row.** You can select a row of text in a table using the margin selection bar, just as you would to select one or more lines of text in a paragraph.

5. **On the Home tab, in the Font group, click the Bold button and then click the Italic button.** Bold and italic are applied to the entire row.

6. **Move the pointer to the top of the second column in the table. When the pointer changes to a downward pointing black selection arrow, as shown in Figure 6.9, click once to select the column.**

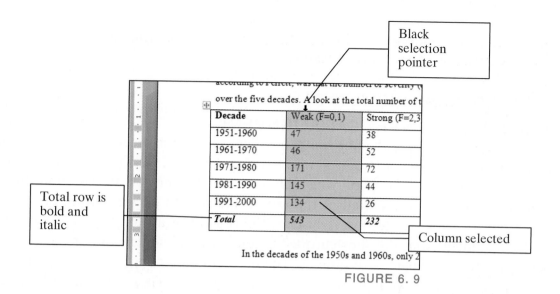

Black selection pointer

Total row is bold and italic

Column selected

| Decade | Weak (F=0,1) | Strong (F=2,3 |
|--------|--------------|---------------|
| 1951-1960 | 47 | 38 |
| 1961-1970 | 46 | 52 |
| 1971-1980 | 171 | 72 |
| 1981-1990 | 145 | 44 |
| 1991-2000 | 134 | 26 |
| *Total* | *543* | *232* |

over the five decades. A look at the total number of t

In the decades of the 1950s and 1960s, only 2

FIGURE 6. 9

## If you have problems...

If you have difficulty displaying the black selection pointer at the top of the column, you can also select a column by placing the insertion point to the left of the data in the top cell, clicking the left mouse button, and dragging down to the bottom of the column. You can also select a column by placing the insertion point anywhere in the column, and then on the Layout tab, in the Table group, click the Select button, and from the submenu click Select Column.

7. **Click the Home tab, and in the Paragraph group, click the Align Text Right button.** All of the numbers and the title at the top of the second column are now right-aligned.

8. **Move the pointer to the top of the third column until it turns into a black selection arrow. Drag to the right until the last three columns are selected.**

9. **On the Home tab, in the Paragraph group, click the Align Text Right button.** The items in the last four columns are now right-aligned as shown in Figure 6.10. Notice the table move handle, which can be clicked to select the entire table.

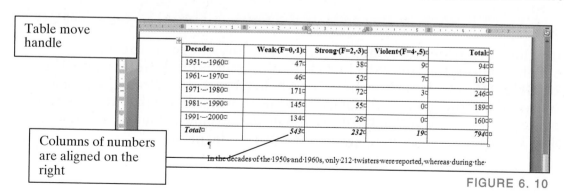

Table move handle

Columns of numbers are aligned on the right

| Decade | Weak (F=0, 1) | Strong (F=2, 3) | Violent (F=4, 5) | Total |
|--------|---------------|-----------------|------------------|-------|
| 1951 — 1960 | 47 | 38 | 9 | 94 |
| 1961 — 1970 | 46 | 52 | 7 | 105 |
| 1971 — 1980 | 171 | 72 | 3 | 246 |
| 1981 — 1990 | 145 | 55 | 0 | 189 |
| 1991 — 2000 | 134 | 26 | 0 | 160 |
| *Total* | *543* | *232* | *19* | *794* |

In the decades of the 1950s and 1960s, only 212 twisters were reported, whereas during the

FIGURE 6. 10

10. Save your changes to the *Tornadoes* document and leave the file open to continue to the next lesson.

### CHANGING THE VERTICAL ALIGNMENT

In addition to changing the horizontal alignment of text in a cell, you can also change the vertical alignment to control whether the text is placed at the top, middle, or bottom of a cell. This is useful when you have cell headings that take more than one line and you want to align all of the text in the row to be on the bottom or in the middle of the row. To do this, right-click the cell you want to affect and then choose Cell Alignment from the shortcut menu. Select the alignment option that you want from the displayed palette of options. This shortcut menu option can be used for both vertical and horizontal alignment of text in table cells. These alignment buttons are also available on the Tables Tools Layout tab in the Alignment group.

### CHANGING TEXT ORIENTATION

If necessary, text can be oriented vertically in a cell. This is useful when you want to minimize the space that is used by row headings. To do this, right-click the cell you want to affect and select Text Direction from the shortcut menu. In the Text Direction dialog box, select the orientation you want to use and then click OK, or us the Text Direction button on the Table Tools Layout tab.

# LESSON 5: Formatting Borders and Shading a Table

The sides of the cells in a table are called *borders*. These lines are usually the same thickness. You can visually highlight a group of cells by changing the thickness of the borders separating one group of cells from another. Another way to visually identify a group of cells is to use a color or a shade of gray as the background. Many other border and shading options are available to you, so that you can make the final table look exactly the way you want. The Borders and Shading buttons are located on the Table Tools Design tab.

In this lesson, you learn to change the borders of a table and to shade cells.

## To Format Borders and Shade a Table

1. With the *Tornadoes* document open, click anywhere in the table. On the Table Tools Layout tab, in the Table group, click Select and then click Select Table from the list. The whole table is now selected. You can also select the entire table by clicking the *table move handle* that displays at the upper-left boundary of your table when you move the mouse pointer onto the table. This handle enables you to move the table on the page.

2. **Click the Table Tools Design tab, and in the Table Styles group, click the Borders button arrow. Click the Borders and Shading option at the bottom of the menu, if necessary click the Borders tab .** The Borders and Shading dialog box displays the options for changing the table borders.

3. **Click Box in the Setting area, and then choose *1 1/2 pt* from the Width box.** This puts a 1 1/2-point border around the outside of the table. The *Preview* area displays a preview of your changes as shown in Figure 6.11

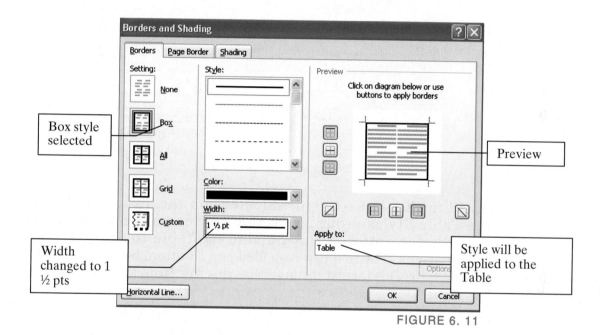

FIGURE 6. 11

4. **Click OK, and then click anywhere outside the table to deselect it.** A 1 1/2 pt border displays around the outside of the table, and the borders inside the table are gone. Light gray grid lines may still show, but they will not print. You can confirm this by viewing your document in Print Preview.

5. **Move the pointer to the left of the first row and click to select it.**

6. **Right-click the selected row and then click Borders and Shading from the shortcut menu.** The shortcut menu can also be used to access the Borders and Shading dialog box.

7. **Click the Shading tab, click the Fill arrow, and then in the first row click the third color—Tan, Background 2 as shown in Figure 6.12.**

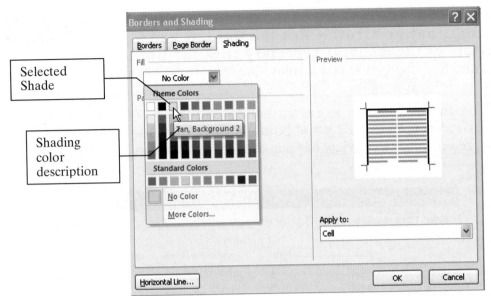

Selected Shade

Shading color description

FIGURE 6. 12

8. **Click OK. With the first row still selected, on the Table Tools Design tab, in the Table Styles group, click the Border button arrow choose the Bottom Border option. Click outside the table to look at your formatting changes.** The first row is shaded and a bottom border is added as shown in Figure 6.13. This format distinguishes this row from the rest of the table.

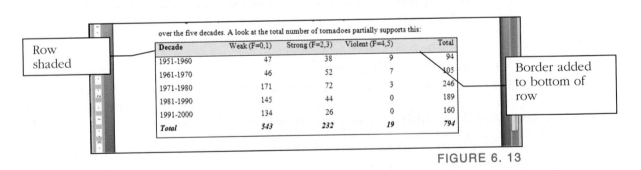

Row shaded

over the five decades. A look at the total number of tornadoes partially supports this:

| Decade | Weak (F=0,1) | Strong (F=2,3) | Violent (F=4,5) | Total |
|--------|--------------|----------------|-----------------|-------|
| 1951-1960 | 47 | 38 | 9 | 94 |
| 1961-1970 | 46 | 52 | 7 | 105 |
| 1971-1980 | 171 | 72 | 3 | 246 |
| 1981-1990 | 145 | 44 | 0 | 189 |
| 1991-2000 | 134 | 26 | 0 | 160 |
| *Total* | *543* | *232* | *19* | *794* |

Border added to bottom of row

FIGURE 6. 13

9. **Select the last row of the table. On the Table Tools Design tab, in the Table Styles, click the Shading button.**

10. **In the first row, click the third color—Tan, Background 2.** The same fill color as previously used is applied to the last row of the table

11. **On the Design tab, in the Table Styles group, click the Borders button arrow and then select the Top Border option. Click outside the table to view your formatting changes.** The last row of the table is formatted as shown in Figure 6.14. This makes the totals more distinct and helps the reader identify this as summary information.

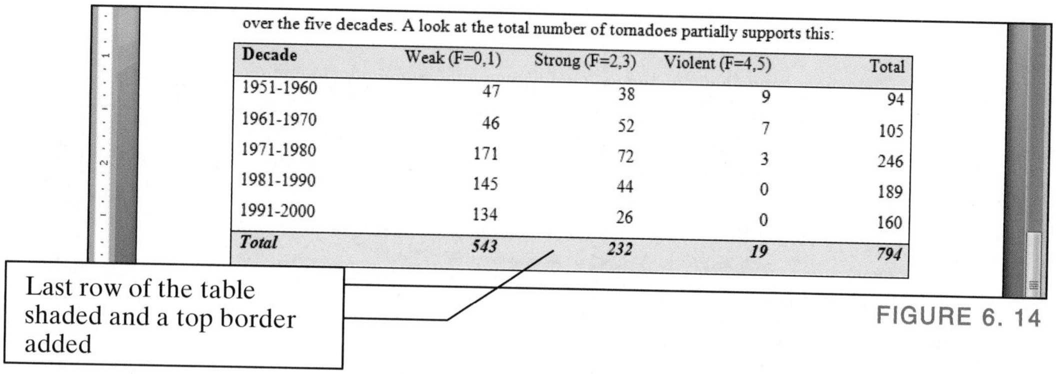

over the five decades. A look at the total number of tornadoes partially supports this:

| Decade | Weak (F=0,1) | Strong (F=2,3) | Violent (F=4,5) | Total |
|---|---|---|---|---|
| 1951-1960 | 47 | 38 | 9 | 94 |
| 1961-1970 | 46 | 52 | 7 | 105 |
| 1971-1980 | 171 | 72 | 3 | 246 |
| 1981-1990 | 145 | 44 | 0 | 189 |
| 1991-2000 | 134 | 26 | 0 | 160 |
| *Total* | *543* | *232* | *19* | *794* |

Last row of the table shaded and a top border added

FIGURE 6. 14

12. **Save your changes to the *Tornadoes* document and leave the file open to continue to the next lesson**

# LESSON 6: Converting Text to a Table and Merging Cells

Data that is in a tabbed list can be converted to a table, which makes it easier to format. If the data requires variable column widths it is easier to display it in a table. At other times you may need to convert a table of data to text. This flexibility helps you display your data in the best manner for the particular publication that you are creating. When you change data from text to a table, it is important that each column of data is separated by a tab, a paragraph mark, or a comma, rather than a series of spaces. Then the conversion process is fairly clean and simple. However, you may find that information that belongs in one cell is separated into two cells. In this situation, use the Merge Cells command to create one cell. If data is placed in the same cell but should be separated into two cells, use the Split Cells command.

In this lesson, you convert a tabbed list to a table and then merge two cells together.

## To Convert Text to a Table and Merge Cells

1. With the *Tornadoes* document open, click the Home tab, and in the Paragraph group click the Show/Hide button.

2. Scroll to the end of the first page and place the insertion point to the left of *Decade*—the beginning of the tabbed list at the end of the page. To convert text to a table, first check to ensure that the data is separated into columns and that a consistent method has been used to separate one column from the next. In this case, the Tab key was used between each piece of data as shown in Figure 6.15.

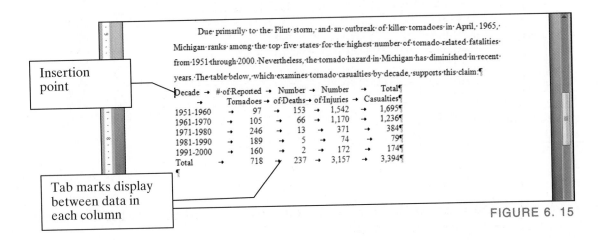

Due primarily to the Flint storm, and an outbreak of killer tornadoes in April, 1965, Michigan ranks among the top five states for the highest number of tornado-related fatalities from 1951 through 2000. Nevertheless, the tornado hazard in Michigan has diminished in recent years. The table below, which examines tornado casualties by decade, supports this claim.¶

| Decade → | # of Reported → | Number → | Number → | Total¶ |
| → | Tornadoes → | of Deaths → | of Injuries → | Casualties¶ |
| 1951-1960 → | 97 → | 153 → | 1,542 → | 1,695¶ |
| 1961-1970 → | 105 → | 66 → | 1,170 → | 1,236¶ |
| 1971-1980 → | 246 → | 13 → | 371 → | 384¶ |
| 1981-1990 → | 189 → | 5 → | 74 → | 79¶ |
| 1991-2000 → | 160 → | 2 → | 172 → | 174¶ |
| Total → | 718 → | 237 → | 3,157 → | 3,394¶ |

**Insertion point**

**Tab marks display between data in each column**

FIGURE 6. 15

3. **Select the list of data down through the last row, which displays the totals.** To convert the text to a table, first select the entire set of data.

4. **Click the Insert tab, and in the Tables group click the Table button and the from the displayed list, click Convert Text to table.** The Convert Text to Table dialog box displays. The program has assumed that *5* columns are needed as shown in the *Number of columns* box in Figure 6.16. If you count the columns in the selected table, you see that 5 is correct. It is always a good idea to verify that you agree with the number of columns that displays in this dialog box. If there is a discrepancy, check the table to ensure that the column separators—tabs—are not causing a problem.

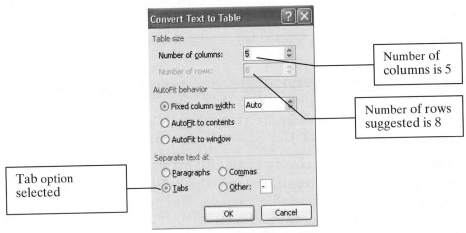

**Number of columns is 5**

**Number of rows suggested is 8**

**Tab option selected**

FIGURE 6. 16

5. **Verify that Fixed column widths is selected under *AutoFit behavior*, and Tabs is selected under the *Separate text at* section, and then click OK. Click outside the table to deselect it.** The text is converted to a table format. Notice that the column headings are separated into two cells as shown in Figure 6.17. This is because they had been placed on a separate row to make them align correctly over the data in the tabbed list.

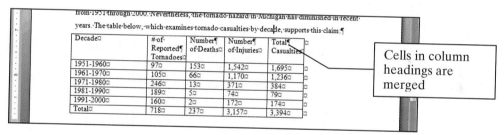

years. The table below, which examines tornado casualties by decade, supports this claim.

| Decade | #of Reported Tornadoes | Number of Deaths | Number of Injuries | Total Casualties |
|---|---|---|---|---|
| 1951-1960 | 97 | 153 | 1,542 | 1,695 |
| 1961-1970 | 105 | 66 | 1,170 | 1,236 |
| 1971-1980 | 246 | 13 | 371 | 384 |
| 1981-1990 | 189 | 5 | 74 | 79 |
| 1991-2000 | 160 | 2 | 172 | 174 |
| Total | 718 | 237 | 3,157 | 3,394 |

Column headings in two rows

FIGURE 6. 17

6. Select *Decade* in the first cell and the blank cell below it. To merge cells, first select the cells you want to merge.

7. **Right-click the selected cells, and then from the shortcut menu click Merge Cells.** The two cells are merged.

8. **Select the first two cells in the second column. Click the Layout tab, and in Merge group, click the Merge Cells button**

9. **Using one of the techniques you just practiced, merge the two cells that contain column headings for the next three columns. Compare your results with Figure 6.18.**

from 1951 through 2000. Nevertheless, the tornado hazard in Michigan has diminished in recent years. The table below, which examines tornado casualties by decade, supports this claim.

| Decade | #of Reported Tornadoes | Number of Deaths | Number of Injuries | Total Casualties |
|---|---|---|---|---|
| 1951-1960 | 97 | 153 | 1,542 | 1,695 |
| 1961-1970 | 105 | 66 | 1,170 | 1,236 |
| 1971-1980 | 246 | 13 | 371 | 384 |
| 1981-1990 | 189 | 5 | 74 | 79 |
| 1991-2000 | 160 | 2 | 172 | 174 |
| Total | 718 | 237 | 3,157 | 3,394 |

Cells in column headings are merged

FIGURE 6. 18

10. **Save your changes to the *Tornadoes* document and leave the file open to continue to the next lesson.**

## TO EXTEND YOUR KNOWLEDGE...

### SPLITTING CELLS IN A TABLE

The process of splitting cells in a table is similar to merging cells. Select the cell you want to split and then, on the Layout tab, in the Merge group, click Split Cells. You can also right-click the selected cell and choose Split Cells from the shortcut menu. In the Split Cells dialog box, enter the number of columns or rows into which the data should be split. Remember, if the results are not what you expected, you can always click Undo.

### CONVERTING A TABLE TO TEXT

If you need to convert a table to text, first select the table. On the Layout tab, in the Data group, click Convert to Text. In the Convert Table to Text dialog box, select whether you want to separate the text with paragraph marks, tabs, commas, or some other character, and then click OK.

# LESSON 7: Adjusting Column Width and Row Height

The column width or row height can be changed by moving the border between columns or rows or by setting the value to a specified measurement in the Table Properties dialog box. You can also adjust a column or row dimension by dragging the Move Table Column indicator on the horizontal ruler, or the Adjust Table Row indicator on the vertical ruler. To adjust a column width to the widest entry in the column, double-click the right border of the column.

In this lesson, you adjust the column width and row height in the table that you just created.

## To Adjust Column Width and Row Height

1. **With the *Tornadoes* document open, examine the heading in the second column of the table at the bottom of the first page. If necessary, click in an open area to deselect the cell.** Depending on your computer settings, the column heading may display the heading on three lines.

2. **Move the pointer to the right border of the second column until the pointer displays as a two-way arrow as shown in Figure 6.19.**

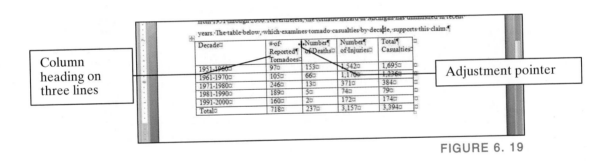

FIGURE 6. 19

3. **With the adjustment pointer displayed, double-click the right border of the column.** The column width changes to fit the widest entry in the second column. Make any other column adjustments necessary.

4. **Position the pointer on the bottom border of the first row until the adjustment pointer displays; drag up to move the row border until it is just below the text in the heading row.** The adjustment pointer displays horizontally along the row border. Even if you drag the row boundary into the text in the first row, it will adjust to the position needed to display all of the text in the first row.

5. **Right Click anywhere in the second column of the table; from the shortcut menu click Table Properties, and then click the Column tab.** The Table Properties dialog box is used to adjust size, horizontal alignment, and text wrapping of the table, row size, column width, and cell size and vertical alignment. On the Row tab you can also select whether text in a row is allowed to break across pages, and whether a header row should repeat at the top of each page in a table that breaks across pages. The width of *Column 2* is 1.14" as shown in Figure 6.20. (Yours might be different depending upon the columns in your table) The Previous Column and Next Column buttons enable you to see the width of the other columns in the table.

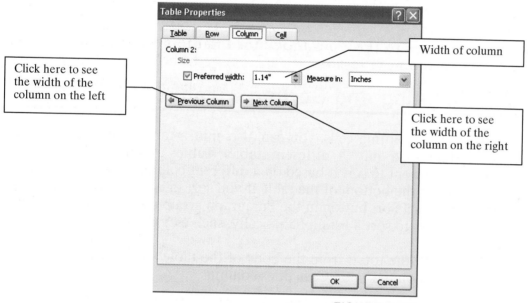

FIGURE 6. 20

6. **Click Previous Column to move to Column 1. Select the value in the Preferred width box and type: 1.00.** The width of the row heading column is changed.

7. **Click Next Column four times to see the width of the four columns of data.** Column 5 displays and its width is less than 1".

8. **Select the value in the Preferred width box and type: 1.20.** Column 5 is widened to the specified width.

9. **Click Previous Column. Select the value in the Preferred width box and type: 1.20.**

10. **Repeat step 9 to change the other two columns of data to a 1.20" width. Click OK.** Now, the four columns of data are the same width as shown in Figure 6.21.

---

from 1951 through 2000. Nevertheless, the tornado hazard in Michigan has diminished in recent years. The table below, which examines tornado casualties by decade, supports this claim:

| Decade | # of Reported Tornadoes | Number of Deaths | Number of Injuries | Total Casualties |
|---|---|---|---|---|
| 1951-1960 | 97 | 153 | 1,542 | 1,695 |
| 1961-1970 | 105 | 66 | 1,170 | 1,236 |
| 1971-1980 | 246 | 13 | 371 | 384 |
| 1981-1990 | 189 | 5 | 74 | 79 |
| 1991-2000 | 160 | 2 | 172 | 174 |
| Total | 718 | 237 | 3,157 | 3,394 |

Column widths are adjusted

FIGURE 6. 21

11. **Save your changes to the *Tornadoes* document and leave the file open to continue to the next lesson.**

# LESSON 8: Splitting and Sorting a Table

In addition to merging or splitting cells, you can also split a table. This is useful if you need to extract certain data into a different table. Tables often display numerical information and you may want to sort it based on a different column or you may not want to include the total row at the bottom of the table if you sort in descending order. To sort paragraphs of text, there is a Sort button in the Paragraph group on the Home tab. This is very useful when you need to sort a list alphabetically, such as a glossary list, an index, or a bibliography.

In this lesson, you split the totals from the body of the table so you can sort the table in descending order based on the Total Casualties column.

## To Split and Sort a Table

1. **With the *Tornadoes* document open, click in the *Total* cell at the bottom of the first column of the table on which you have been working.** To split a table, first position your pointer somewhere in the row where you want to split the table.

2. **On the Table Tools Layout tab, in the Merge group, click the Split Table button.** The *Total* row is separated from the rest of the table. Notice that there is a paragraph mark between the main part of the table and the Total row.

3. **Click in the Total Casualties cell in the last column of the main table.** To sort a table, click anywhere in the table to make the table active.

4. **On the Layout tab, in the Data group, click the Sort button.** The Sort dialog box displays as shown in Figure 6.22. Here you select the column you want to sort on, the direction of the sort— *ascending*—from A to Z, lowest to highest—or *descending*—Z to A, highest to lowest. In the Type box, specify if the values are numbers or text. You can also sort on more than one column of data.

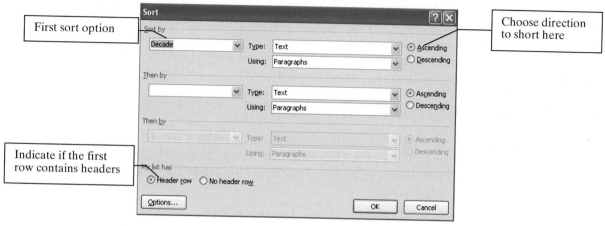

First sort option

Choose direction to short here

Indicate if the first row contains headers

FIGURE 6. 22

5. **Click the Sort by arrow, and then select** *Total* **from the list. Be sure that the Type box displays** *Number,* **and then click the Descending option button.** You only need to sort on the total casualties. Descending order is selected so it sorts from highest to lowest number. Notice that just the first word in the heading row displays in the Sort by list.

6. **At the bottom on the dialog box, under** *My list has,* **be sure** *Header* **row is selected, and then click OK. Click outside the table to see the results.** The data is sorted as shown in Figure 6.23. Notice that there were fewer total casualties in the '80s than in the '90s.

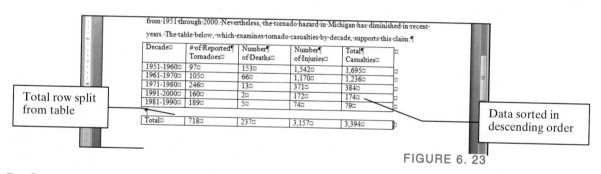

Total row split from table

Data sorted in descending order

from·1951·through·2000.·Nevertheless,·the·tornado·hazard·in·Michigan·has·diminished·in·recent· years.·The·table·below,·which·examines·tornado·casualties·by·decade,·supports·this·claim.¶

| Decade¤ | #·of·Reported¶ Tornadoes¤ | Number¶ of·Deaths¤ | Number¶ of·Injuries¤ | Total¶ Casualties¤ | ¤ |
|---|---|---|---|---|---|
| 1951-1960¤ | 97¤ | 153¤ | 1,542¤ | 1,695¤ | ¤ |
| 1961-1970¤ | 105¤ | 66¤ | 1,170¤ | 1,236¤ | ¤ |
| 1971-1980¤ | 246¤ | 13¤ | 371¤ | 384¤ | ¤ |
| 1991-2000¤ | 160¤ | 2¤ | 172¤ | 174¤ | ¤ |
| 1981-1990¤ | 189¤ | 5¤ | 74¤ | 79¤ | ¤ |
| Total¤ | 718¤ | 237¤ | 3,157¤ | 3,394¤ | ¤ |

FIGURE 6. 23

7. **Save your changes to the** *Tornadoes* **document and leave the file open to continue to the next lesson.**

## LESSON 9: Using the Table Styles (AutoFormat) and AutoFit Tools

The formatting tools you used in the earlier lessons give you complete control over the way your tables look. However, formatting a table can be time-consuming and there is a quicker and easier technique available to create a professional-looking table. *Table styles* in Word 2007 enable you to choose from many different table styles, which saves you a great deal of time if one of the styles fits your needs.

Sometimes tables are wider than necessary. When you insert a table, it stretches from the left margin to the right margin. Another tool, called AutoFit, changes the width of the columns to match the data that has been entered, or to match a specific column width. Then you can center the table on the screen, or wrap text around it, similar to wrapping text around a picture or other graphic.

In this lesson, you change the format of a table by applying one of the table styles and optimizing the column widths using the AutoFit tool.

## Use Table Styles (AutoFormat) and AutoFit Tools

1. **With the *Tornadoes* document displayed, click to the left of the paragraph mark between the table and total row at the bottom of the first page.** You will merge the two parts of this table back together, before you format it.

2. **Press Delete.** The total row is rejoined to the main body of the table. To merge tables, remove the empty space, or empty paragraphs, between the tables. If the column widths are not the same, you may need to make some adjustments so the table has uniform column widths.

3. **With your insertion point somewhere in the table, click the Table Tools Design tab, and in the Table Styles group, click the More button to expand the gallery.** The Table Style Gallery displays. A variety of table formats are available. When you select a format, keep in mind your printer's capabilities (can it print in color?) and the distribution requirements (are multiple copies required?).

4. **Move your pointer over the styles and notice that the Live Preview feature is active.** This format is different from the one you created for the new table. You can make changes to the look of the table choosing the Modify Table Style button at the bottom of the gallery.

5. **In row 4, column 4, point to *Table Grid 8*. Notice that the Live Preview feature displays the style on your table as shown in Figure 6.24 and then click *Table Grid 8* to select it.**

6. **In the Table Style Options group, click the Header Row and Total Row to select those formatting options, and clear the check mark from the First *Column check* box. Select the last four columns in the table. Click the Table Tools Layout tab, and in the Alignment group, click the Align Top Right button. Click outside the table.** This applies a bold format to the total row and aligns the numbers and headings on the right side of each cell. Notice how well this format fits the data, with the column headings using reverse text.

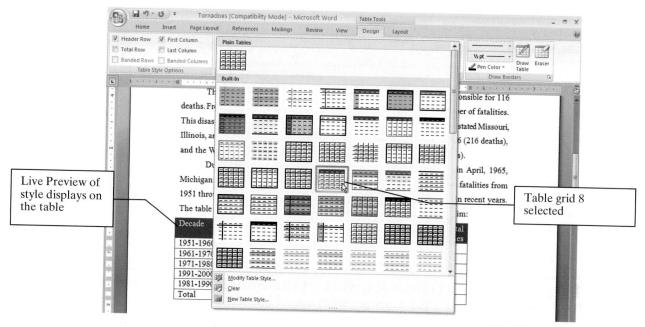

Live Preview of style displays on the table

Table grid 8 selected

FIGURE 6. 24

7. **Click the table move handle to select the table. Click the Home tab, and in the Paragraph group, click the Center button.** The table is centered between the left and right margins.

8. **Scroll down and select the table you created on the second page.**

9. **Click the Table Tools Layout tab, and in the Cell Size group, click AutoFit, and then click Auto Fit Contents.** The columns are resized to the width of the widest element in each column, usually the column header in this example.

10. **With the table still selected, click the Home tab and in the Paragraph click the Center button. Click somewhere else to deselect the table.** The table is centered horizontally on the page as shown in Figure 6.25. To center the table on the screen the entire table must first be selected.

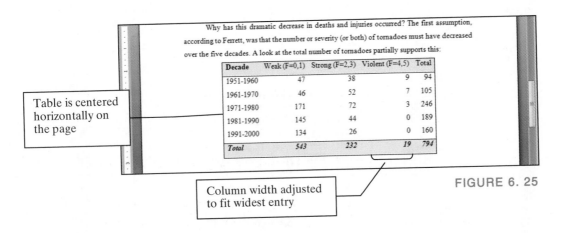

Table is centered horizontally on the page

Column width adjusted to fit widest entry

FIGURE 6. 25

11. **Click the Insert tab, and in the Header & Footer group, click Footer. Select Alphabet. On the left side of the Footer, type your name. Click the Close Header and Footer button.** Your name is added to the footer.

12. **Save the *Tornadoes* document. Preview the file and then print it. Close the file and close Word**

## SUMMARY

In this project, you learned how to work with tables. Tables provide a row and column format similar to a spreadsheet. Because a table keeps information aligned in a parallel format, it is easier to use than a tabbed list when the information in one column takes up more space than the information in another column. You learned how to create a table from scratch, enter data, and select cells, columns and rows. You used the Table Tools Layout and Design tabs to align columns and format headings to standout from the details. You learned how to insert rows and columns to expand the size of the table. You also converted a list to a table and used the Table Styles for formatting a table. Finally, you learned how to merge cells in a table, split a table, and sort data within a table.

You can extend your learning by reviewing concepts and terms, and by practicing variations of skills presented in the lessons. Use the following table as a guide to the numbered questions and exercises in the end-of-project learning opportunities.

## KEY TERMS

ascending

AutoFit

borders

cells

descending

hyperlink

Table move handle

Table Styles

# CHECKING CONCEPTS AND TERMS

## SCREEN ID

Label each element of the screen shown in Figure 6.26.

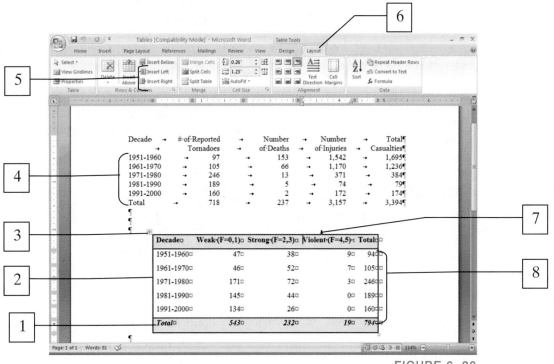

FIGURE 6. 26

_____ A. Outside border lines

_____ B. Formatted text

_____ C. Insert column buttons

_____ D. Right-aligned numbers

_____ E. Select column pointer

_____ F. Contains tools used to create and organize table cells

_____ G. Table move handle

_____ H. List that could be converted to a table

## MULTIPLE CHOICE

**Circle the letter of the correct answer for each of the following.**

1. All of the following are true except _____. [L8]

   a. you can split a table horizontally, but not vertically

   b. you can split a table vertically, but not horizontally

   c. you can sort a table on multiple columns

   d. to sort a table in alphabetic order choose ascending

2. To automatically adjust the column width to the widest entry in the column _____. [L7]]

   a. choose Table, Column width, Adjust from the Design tab
   b. double-click the left border of the column
   c. double-click the right border of the column
   d. choose Table Properties and then set the value in the Width box

3. To create a table you can _____. [L1]]

   a. convert a list of text to a table
   b. use the Table button
   c. draw a table
   d. do any of the above

4. To convert a list of data to a table, each column should be separated from the next with _____.[L6]

   a. spaces
   b. a tab
   c. a comma
   d. b and c but not a

5. To insert a row at the end of a table, click in the last cell in the table and _____ [L3]

   a. press [Tab]
   b. press [Enter ⏎]
   c. right-click and choose Insert Row
   d. from the Layout tab, click Row

6. To move forward from one cell to the next in a table press _____. [L2]

   a. [Enter ⏎]
   b. [Ctrl] + [⇧ Shift]
   c. [Tab]
   d. [↓]

7. To add shading to a table, first select the cells you want to shade, and then _____ [L5]

   a. right-click the selected area and choose Borders and Shading from the shortcut menu
   b. click the Home tab, and in the Paragraph group click the Shading button
   c. click the Design tab, and click the Shading button
   d. all of the above are will work

8. As you enter data in a table numbers are automatically aligned on the _____ and text is automatically aligned on the _____.[L2, L4]

   a. left, left
   b. right, right
   c. left, right
   d. right, left.

9. To delete a row in a table, select the row you want to delete, and _____. [L3]

   a. right-click the selected row and then click Delete Rows
   b. press [Delete]
   c. press [Enter ⏎]
   d. click Design tab and click the Delete button

10. The Table Styles gallery _____. [L9]

   a. displays 101 options for formatting a table
   b. offers a variety of preformatted table styles
   c. is inflexible because you cannot change the style after it is applied
   d. takes longer to apply than formatting a table using the Borders and Shading dialog box

# DISCUSSION

1. In papers you write for other classes, how can the use of tables help you present information? Give some examples of information that would be better presented in a table format. [L1-L2], [L6]

2. Examine a textbook from another class. Locate tables that have been used in the book. How do they help you as a student? Are they a good learning tool? Does the formatting help emphasize key elements in the table? Locate data in the text that would be better displayed in a table. [L1],[L4]-[L6]

3. Tables are often good tools for a résumé. If you had to prepare a résumé, how many columns would you include? What kinds of information would go in each column? Of the skills you have learned related to tables, which ones would be particularly useful if you created a résumé using a table format? What additional skills do you think you would need? [L1]-[L9]

## SKILL DRILL

Skill Drill exercises reinforce project skills. Each skill reinforced is the same, or nearly the same, as a skill presented in the project. Detailed instructions are provided in a step-by-step format.

In these exercises, you work with tables in a document, first by converting text to a table and using the Table Styles gallery to format the table, and then by creating a table, entering text, and formatting the table. To complete the Skill Drill exercises open the Word Document *WD_0602* and save it as 97-2003 compatible file named **Alaska Announcement**. Exercises 1 and 2 must be done in order. Exercise 3 must be done before you complete exercises 4 and 5. Be sure to save your changes and close the document if you need more than one work session to complete the desired exercises. Continue working on the *Alaska Announcement* document instead of starting over with the original file. After you have finished, print a copy of the document (optional). Figure 6.27 shows the *Alaska Announcement* after all of the exercises are complete.. All of these exercises can be completed using Microsoft Office XP or later versions. Instructions throughout the exercises are based on a Windows XP operating system, running Microsoft Office 2007.

### 1.Converting Text to a Table, Deleting a Column, and Adjusting Column Width

The Alumni Travel Club has a trip to Alaska planned for alumni, faculty, and students. You need to finish an announcement about the trip that will be mailed to people who have expressed an interest in the trip. You decide to use your new skills in creating tables to present some of the information in the announcement document. You already entered information in a tabbed list and decide to convert it to a table.

1. With the *Alaska Announcement* document open, select the six lines in the tabbed list, below the first full paragraph. Click the **Insert tab** and in the **Tables group**, click **Table** and then from the bottom of the list click **Convert Text to Table**.

2. In the Convert Text to Table dialog box, be sure *4* displays in the **Number of columns** box, and the **Tabs** option button is selected under *Separate text at*. Click **OK**. The table is converted, but there is an empty column on the left.

3. Move the pointer to just above the empty column on the left until a black downward pointing arrow displays. Click once to select the column.

4. Right-click the selected column and then click **Delete Columns** from the shortcut menu. Alternatively, on the Table Tools Layout tab, in the Rows & Columns group, click the Delete button, and then click Delete Column.

**Alumni Travel Club**
Announcement

Last month we sent you a letter about tentative plans for an upcoming trip to Alaska. We have finally gotten enough pieces of the puzzle in place to make an official announcement. Some of the activities we mentioned before did not pan out (especially the panning for gold). The dates for the trip are July 2 to July 13. We will fly into Seattle, spend the night there, and fly on to Anchorage on the July 3. The flight home will be non-stop. All of the activities listed below are included in the price of the trip. Attendance is not required, so if you want to plan ahead to do something else instead of one or more of these activities, please let us know so we can arrange transportation. The following are the dates and times of the excursions:

| Activity | Date | Length |
|---|---|---|
| Train trip to Seward | July 5 | all day |
| Trip to Portage Glacier | July 6 | afternoon |
| Flight to Denali from Talkeetna | July 8-9 | all day |
| Climb Mt. Alyeska. | July 10 | afternoon |
| Day in Fairbanks | July 11 | all day |

As we mentioned in the earlier letter, we have made arrangements with several places for lodging, including a couple of nights at the University of Alaska-Pacific, which is located right in the Anchorage city limits. According to our contact person, the moose family continues to wander through the parking lot several times a day.

There are three different plans available—single occupancy, double occupancy, and a special senior discount (double-occupancy only). Below are the costs for each plan, along with a minimum deposit, which is due on May 25.

| Package | Cost | Deposit |
|---|---|---|
| Seniors (double occupancy) | $1,300 | $600 |
| Double Occupancy | $1,500 | $750 |
| Single Occupancy | $1,800 | $900 |

Please let us know as soon as possible if you are seriously considering this trip. We need to make our travel reservations as soon as possible.

Student's Name

FIGURE 6. 27

5. Move the pointer to the right border of the last column. When the two-headed adjustment pointer displays, double-click to automatically adjust the width of the last column.

6. Move the pointer to the right border of the middle column, and double-click to automatically adjust the width of the middle column.

7. Save the Alaska *Announcement* document and leave it open to continue with the next exercise.

## 2. Using Table Styles and AutoFit Tools

You decide to use the Table Styles gallery to format the table you just created, and then adjust the table using the AutoFit tool.

1. With the *Alaska Announcement* open, click anywhere in the table you created in the previous exercise.

2. Click the **Table Tools Design tab**. In the **Table Styles group,** click the **More button** to display the gallery, and then in the first row, fourth column select **Table Classic 1.**

3. On the **Table Tools Design tab**, in the **Table Style Options group,** click the **Header Row** and **First Column** check boxes, if necessary, to select these options. Clear any check marks from the Last row and Last column check boxes.

4. Click the **Table Tools Layout tab**, in the **Cell Size group,** click **AutoFit** and then click **AutoFit Contents** from the list.

5. Click the move table handle just above the upper left corner of the table to select the table. Alternatively, in the Table group click Select, and then click Select Table from the list.

6. Click the **Home tab** and click the **Center** button to center the table between the left and right margins.

7. Save the *Alaska Announcement* document. Leave the file open if you plan to work on the next exercise.

## 3. Creating a Table, Entering Data, and Inserting a Row

Next, you decide to add a table listing the available rooms and pricing for each accommodation.

1. With the *Alaska Announcement* document open, scroll down to the last two paragraphs. Place the insertion point at the beginning of the second blank line between the last two paragraphs.

2. Click the **Insert tab**, and in the **Tables group** click the **Table** button. Move the pointer down and to the right until you have highlighted three rows and three columns. Click to insert a 3 x 3 table.

3. Type: `Package` in the first cell and press Tab, type: `Cost` in the second cell and press Tab, type: `Deposit` in the third cell and then press Tab to move to the second row.

4.  Finish filling the cells in the table by typing the following:

    ```
    Single Occupancy     $1,800     $900
    Double Occupancy     $1,500     $750
    ```

5.  Click in the second row and then click the **Table Tools Layout tab**, and in the **Rows & Columns group** click **Insert Rows Above**.

6.  Add the following information to the new row:

    ```
    Seniors (double occupancy)  $1,200    $600
    ```

7.  Save the *Alaska Announcement* document and leave it open to continue with the next exercise.

## 4. Formatting a Table

To make the table appear more professional, you decide to format the text and then add borders and shading using the techniques you just practiced.

1.  With the *Alaska Announcement* document open, click to the left of the first row of the table you created to select the row. Click the **Home tab**, and in the **Font group** click the **Bold** button.

2.  Select the last three cells in the first column, click **Bold**, and then click the **Italic** button.

3.  Move the pointer to the top of the middle column until the black downward pointer displays. Drag to the right to select the last two columns of the table and in the **Paragraph group** click the **Align Right** button.

4.  Place the insertion point anywhere in your new table. Click the table move button in the upper left corner of the table to select the table.

5.  On the **Home tab**, in the **Paragraph group**, click the **Border button arrow**. Select **Borders and Shading** and then select the **Borders tab** if it is not already displayed. Click **Grid** in the **Setting** area, click the **Width** arrow and choose **2 1/4 pt**, and then click **OK**. Click anywhere outside the table.

6.  Move the pointer to the left of the first row and click to select it. Right-click and then click **Borders and Shading** from the menu. Click the **Shading** tab.

7.  Click the **Fill arrow**, and in the first column, fourth row box select the color **White, Background 1, Darker 25%**.

8.  Click **OK**. Save your changes and leave the *Alaska Announcement* document open to continue with the next exercise.

## 5. Controlling Column Widths and Sorting a Table

To finish the table, the column widths need to be adjusted and the table would look better if it were centered on the page. You also decide to sort the table by cost, from the lowest to highest.

1.  With the *Alaska Announcement* open, click in the middle column of the second table.

2.  Right-click the table and click **Table Properties** from the shortcut menu. Click the **Column** tab. Notice the column width is at 2.22". Click the **Next Column** button and observe the column width.

3. Select the value in the *Preferred width* box for Column 3 and then type: 1.

4. Click the **Previous Column** button. Select the value in the Preferred width box for Column 2 and then type: 1.

5. Click the **Table tab**. Click the **Center** button under Alignment and then click **OK**. The width of the right two columns is reduced to 1" and the table is centered between the left and right margins.

6. Click anywhere in the table and then click the **Table Tools Layout tab**, and in the **Data group**, click the **Sort** button.

7. Click the **Sort by arrow** and then select **Cost**. Make sure the Type is set as Number and the **Ascending** option button is selected and **Header row** is selected under *My list has*. Click **OK**. The table is sorted by cost.

8. Click the **Insert tab**, and in the **Header & Footer group**, click the **Footer** button. Select **Blank Footer**. In the left side of the Footer, type **your name**. Close the Header and Footer toolbar.

9. Save the Alaska Announcement document. Print a copy of the document if required by your instructor. Close the file and close Word.

## CHALLENGE

Challenge exercises expand on or are somewhat related to skills presented in the lessons. Each exercise provides a brief narrative introduction, followed by instructions in a numbered-step format that are not as detailed as those in the Skill Drill section.

Each exercise is independent of the others, so you may complete the exercises in any order.

### 1. Merging Cells, Aligning Text Vertically, and Changing Text Direction

You need to consolidate some information about the different types of business entities for a presentation you are giving in your business management class. You have created a table with the necessary information and need to add the finishing touches.

1. Locate and Open the *WD_0603* document and save it as 97-2003 compatible file named **Business Entities**.

2. Click in the first row of the table Click the **Table Tools Layout tab**, and in the **Rows & Columns group** click **Insert Above**

3. Select the second, third, and fourth cell of the new empty row. Right-click the selected cells, and then select **Merge Cells** from the shortcut menu.

4. Repeat this process to merge the next three cells. Skip a cell, and then merge the last two cells. You should now have five cells in the first row.

5. Starting in the first merged cell—the second cell in the first row—and continuing across the row, type the following four headings: **Human Resources, Initial Funding, Government Regulations, Revenue.**

6. Select the four group headings in the first row, and then right-click the mouse. From the shortcut menu, point to **Cell Alignment** and select the option in the middle of the bottom row—**Align Bottom Center**. This will center the text horizontally and place the text on the bottom vertically.

7. With the four group headings still selected, change the font to **Bold 12-point**.

8. In the first column, select the three cells that contain text. On the **Layout tab**, in the **Alignment group** click **Text Direction**. The Text changes direction. Click the button again to cycle through the direction options. Select the vertical orientation that displayed the text on the left side of the cell.

9. On the **Layout tab**, click the **AutoFit** button and choose **AutoFit Contents**. Make any additional adjustments in the column widths or row height that may be necessary to ensure that the row headings are fully displayed, and the column headings display on two rows without words being divided.

10. At the end of the document, outside of the table type: Formatted by: `Your Name.`

11. Save the *Business Entities* document. Print the document and then close it

## 2. Sorting a Table on Multiple Columns, Converting a Table to Text

For a summer job, you are working as a teller for a local bank. The assistant manager has to keep track of sales made by the branch and product for their region. You offer to help her with the report. First the table needs to be sorted.

1. Locate and open the *WD_0604* document and save it as 97-2003 compatible file named `June Sales`.

2. Click in the table, and then on the Table Tools **Layout tab** click **Sort**.

3. In the Sort dialog box, in the **Sort by** box, choose **Product**. In the **Then by** box choose **Branch**, and in the second **Then by** box choose **Amount**. Sort the first two columns in ascending order, and the *Amount* column in descending order. Be sure the **Header row** option is selected and then click **OK**.

4. Select the table, and then on the Table Tools **Layout tab**, click the **Convert to Text**.

5. In the Convert Table to Text dialog box, be sure **Tabs** is selected and then click **OK**.

6. On the **Insert tab**, click **Footer** and choose **Blank Footer**. Add your name to the left side of the footer and then close the Header and Footer tab.

7. Save the *June Sales* document and print a copy (optional). Close the file and then close Word.

## 3. Using a Table to Write a Résumé

The table layout provides a convenient tool for writing a résumé. In this Challenge exercise, you will write your résumé using a table. An example is provided as a guide for how you can use a table to create a résumé (see Figure 6.28).

1. Open Word. In a blank document insert a three-column table, with at least five rows. Use the first column for topics, the middle column for dates if needed, and the third column for a description of your skills or other details.

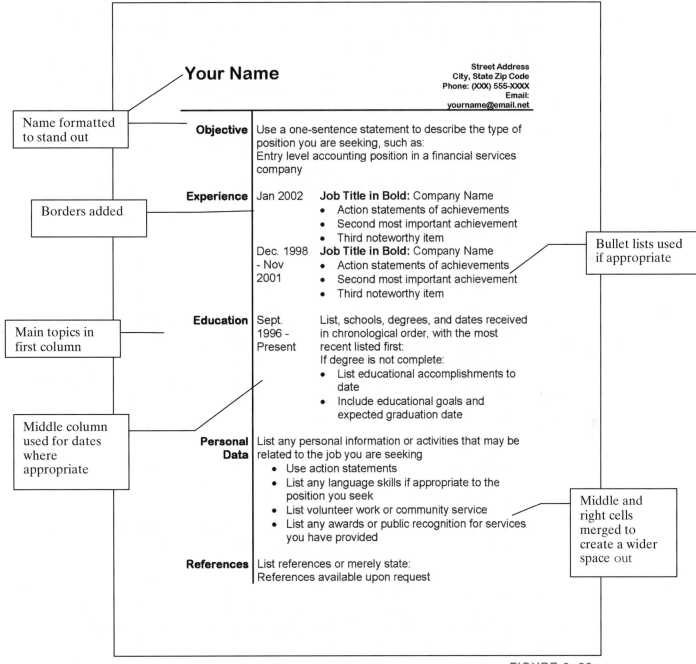

FIGURE 6. 28

2. Examine the example provided in Figure 6.28. The text of the sample resume provides instructions about the type of content to include. The callouts explain how the table format was used.

3. Enter your name and address in the first row of the table and format it appropriately. Enter a one-sentence statement of your objective for the job you are seeking.

4. To remove the gridlines from the table, select the table, and on the Table Tools **Design tab**, click the **Borders** drop-down arrow button and choose **No Border**.

5. Use the Borders and Shading dialog box to add borders at the bottom of the first row and to the right of the first column if you want. You do not have to match what is shown in the sample résumé.

6. Complete the résumé with your personal information as if you are applying for a position you already have, one you would like to have, or for one that you are aspiring to have.

7. As necessary, merge cells in the second and third column to accommodate your data. Add additional rows as needed, and adjust column width and row height to fit the data.

8. Proofread your résumé to make sure it does not contain any spelling, grammatical, or typographical errors. Select a font size and style for your table. Use bullet points, and paragraph formatting as needed to create a balanced and visually appealing résumé.

9. Save the file as **My Resume** and print a copy (optional).

10. Close the file and close Word

## DISCOVERY ZONE

Discovery Zone exercises require advanced knowledge of topics presented in *Essentials* lessons, application of skills from multiple lessons, or self-directed learning of new skills. Each exercise is independent of the others, so you may complete the exercises in any order.

### 1. Using a Formula in a Table

The assistant manager asks you to add totals to the June Sales table. You decide to use the Table, Formula command to calculate the totals rather than adding the figures separately on a calculator

In the *Search* box type: **formulas in a table**. Select the related topic that is displayed. Click the **Show All** button and read the instructions about adding a formula to a table.

Open the *WD_0604* file and save it as **June Totals**. Add a row to the end of the table. Click the empty cell at the bottom of the *Amount* column. Follow the instructions from the Help information to calculate a total for the amount column. Click the **Number format** arrow and select the format for dollars. A total of *$983,600* should display. Repeat this procedure to add a total at the bottom of the *Points* column and display it using a comma separator—1,000. The total should be *9,302*. Add shading to the totals row and type **Totals** in the first cell in the bottom row. Remove the middle border between cells in this row. Add your name in the left side of the footer. Save your changes, print the document (optional), and then close the file.

## 2. Drawing a Table and Inserting Graphics into a Table

In addition to using text and numbers in a table, you can also insert graphics. You are helping out for a week in the personnel department. They need to create a file that displays employee contact information including a picture of their immediate family members. You offer to come up with a design and decide to practice by using your own information and pictures of your family.

Use Help to learn about drawing a table and inserting pictures in a table. Decide what information should be included—such as name, address, home phone, other contact phones, e-mail address, and a photo—and how many columns you will need. Open a blank document and use the Draw Table button to create a table to display employee information. Put last name—family name—in the first column so the data can be sorted by last name. Make the family name cell larger to cover several family members. Add appropriate titles as column headings and then format the headings and family name column to make them stand out from the rest of the table. Complete the table with your information, inserting a picture of yourself in the photo column. Include information for two other family members. Format the table, adjusting column width and row height as needed.

Save the file and name it **My Personal Info**. Print a copy of the document (optional) and then close the file.

# UNIT 2: USING PRODUCTIVITY SOFTWARE

## Microsoft Office 2007

## Project 7: Using Outline, Track Changes, and Language Tools

LESSON 1

Creating an Outline

        2-2.1.6.1       2-2.1.6.2     2-2.1.6.3

LESSON 2

Tracking Changes and Adding Comments

        2-2.1.9.2       2-2.1.20.1   2-2.1.20.2

LESSON 3

Reviewing and Responding to Proposed Changes

        2-2.1.9.3       2-2.1.20.3

LESSON 4

Using Language Tools and Displaying Document Statistics

        2-2.1.19.1      2-2.1.19.3   2-2.1.21.1
        2-2.1.19.2      2-2.1.19.4   2-2.1.21.2

# PROJECT 7

# USING OUTLINE, TRACK CHANGES, AND LANGUAGE TOOLS

IN THIS PROJECT, YOU LEARN HOW TO:

- Create an Outline
- Track Changes and Add Comments
- Review and Respond to Proposed Changes
- Use Language Tools and Display Document Statistics

# WHY WOULD I DO THIS?

The process of writing often starts with an outline. An outline provides a framework for the content and helps you organize your thoughts and materials. After outlining your topic, write a first draft to flesh out the ideas. As you write, you may need to consult with other people in your department or organization. Collaboration tools enable you to easily gather input from various sources. *Track Changes* is a feature that records changes and comments made to a document by others. Once this feature is activated, each change is identified by the name of the person making the change and the date and time the change was made. If more than one person edits a document, the changes each person makes are displayed in a different color. The person doing the final edit can review the changes and accept or reject the changes that have been suggested.

When you proofread your document you may want to consult with the built-in thesaurus to search for *synonyms*—words that are similar in meaning. You may also want to change the grammar settings to check for certain types of styles or sentence structures. Finally, when you have finished writing, you can find out how many words are in your document and the general reading level.

In this project, you create an outline, and work with the Track Changes feature to record and review changes and comments. You use the thesaurus and the language tools to modify the grammar and count the words.

# VISUAL SUMMARY

In this project, you create an outline for a class paper. The topic you have chosen is computer ergonomics. You want to get input from your classmates, so you distribute a draft copy to a few friends and ask for some feedback. After reviewing their changes and comments, you finalize the paper by changing a few words, and checking the reading level and word count. Figure 7.1 shows the outline and the finished document.

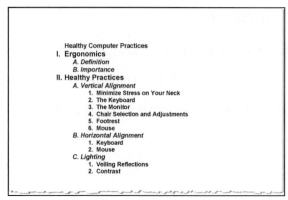

Outline created

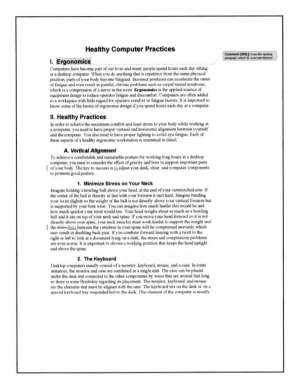

Document showing recorded changes

Document after changes have been accepted

FIGURE 7. 1

# LESSON 1: Creating an Outline

An *outline* is a list of topics for an oral or written report that visually indicates the order in which the information will be discussed and the relationship of the topics to each other and to the total report. Outlines are used in planning sessions to organize and rearrange information. The most basic outline is a numbered list, which has only one outline level. Microsoft Office Word provides up to nine levels in an outline. The first step in creating an outline is to set the format; then you enter the text using the Outline view.

In this lesson, you set the outline format, create an outline for a report on computer ergonomics for your computer class, and then manipulate the outline to reorganize the information.

All of these exercises can be completed with Microsoft Office 2007. Instructions throughout the lessons are based on the Windows XP or Microsoft Vista operating system, running Microsoft Office 2007. Your screen may differ slightly from the figures shown, even if you are running Office 2007.

## To Set the Outline Format

1. **Start Word 2007. From the Office menu, click New. In the New Document dialog box, be sure Blank Document is selected and then click Create. Click the Home tab, and in the Paragraph group click the Multilevel List button.** A list of outline formats displays. The first step in creating an outline is to define the outline format. This is done using the Multilevel list button.

2. **From the list that displays, under List Library, click the option shown in column 1, row 3.** The Roman numeral I displays on the page. On the Home tab, in the Font group the Font box displays Cambria (Headings), and the Font Size box displays 14. This is the format for the top level in the outline format you selected.

3. **On the Home tab, in the Paragraph group, click the Multilevel list button again. At the end of the list click Define new Multilevel List.** This is the traditional outline format. It has nine levels and uses Roman numerals for the highest level, capital letters for the second level, numbers for the third level, lower case letters for the fourth level and so forth. This outline format also applies heading styles to the outline. Compare the *Preview* area on your screen with the outline levels and heading styles shown in Figure 7.2.

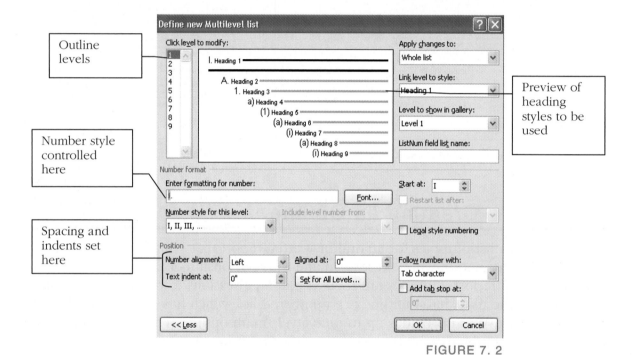

FIGURE 7. 2

4. **Click OK to accept the default settings for this outline format. On the Home tab, in the Paragraph group, be sure the Show/Hide button is active. Click the View tab, and in the Document Views group, click the Outline button.** Roman numeral I. displays on the document and the Outlining tab displays as shown in Figure 7.3. To use the Outline view, you must select one of the outline formats that use the built-in Heading styles. Working in the Outline view enables you to manipulate the data within the outline by changing its level or placement within the outline.

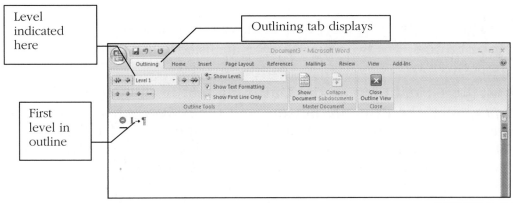

Level indicated here

Outlining tab displays

First level in outline

FIGURE 7. 3

Once you have chosen an outline format, you enter the text of your outline. The Outlining tab can be used to move topics up to a higher level of importance (**promote**) or to a lower level of importance (**demote**). In the Outline view, you can rearrange parts of the outline by dragging a topic up or down on the page. When you do this, all of the subtopics remain with the level as it is moved.

## To Create an Outline

1. **Type: Healthy Computer Practices.** A Roman numeral I displays to the left of the text you typed. This is the highest level in the outline.

2. **Press** [Enter ↵] **to move to the next line, press** [Tab] **to move to the next level and then type: Ergonomics.** The letter *A.* displays to the left of *Ergonomics* and the line is indented to *Level 2* to indicate it is a subtopic under *Healthy Computer Practices.* To demote a topic to the next level, you can use the [Tab] key or you can click the **Demote** button on the Outlining tab.

## If you have problems...

There can be many reasons why *Ergonomics* may not change to the next level heading. In Print Layout view, when you press [Enter ↵], Word changes from a Heading 1 style to Normal style. To make outlining easier you need to go into the Outline view first. In the Outline view, when you press [Enter ↵] the next line retains the same style level as the previous line. This means that if the line you are typing on is a Heading 1, then the next line will also be a Heading 1. Pressing [Tab] demotes the heading style to the next level.

If *Ergonomics* does not display in a heading style, click **Undo** and click the **Outline** button on the status bar. Position your pointer at the end of *Healthy Computer Practices* and repeat step 2.

3. Press ⌤Enter↵, press ⇥Tab, type: Definition press ⌤Enter↵ and type: Importance. The two main subtopics are listed under *Ergonomics* as 1. and 2. respectively.

4. Press ⌤Enter↵ and then on the Outlining tab, in the Outline Tools group, click the Promote button, and type: Healthy Practices. To move up a level you can click the Promote button on the Outlining tab, or you can press ⇧Shift + ⇥Tab. *B.* displays to the left of the text you typed. This is your second major topic for your paper and the topic that will have the most detail.

5. Press ⌤Enter↵, in the Outline Tools group, click the Demote button and then type: Vertical Alignment; press ⌤Enter↵, press ⇥Tab, and then type Minimize Stress on Your Neck. *Vertical Alignment* is the first *Level 3* topic under *B. Healthy Practices* and *Minimize Stress on Your Neck* is the first *Level 4* subtopic as shown in Figure 7.4.

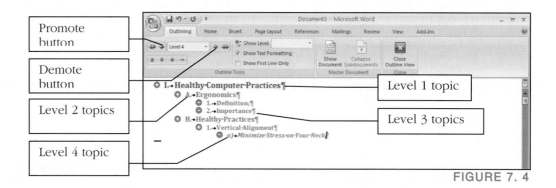

FIGURE 7. 4

6. Press ⌤Enter↵, type: The Keyboard, press ⌤Enter↵ and continue in this manner to type the remaining Level 4 subtopics pressing ⌤Enter↵ after each item to place it on a separate line:

The Monitor

Chair Selection and Adjustments

Footrest

Mouse

7. Press ⌤Enter↵ after the last entry and then press ⇧Shift + ⇥Tab to move up to *Level 3*.

8. Type: Lighting and then enter the next two items at *Level 4* under *Lighting:*, Veiling Reflections and Contrast as shown in Figure 7.5.

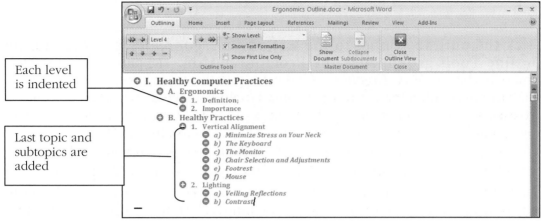

Each level is indented

Last topic and subtopics are added

FIGURE 7. 5

9. **Save the file in your folder as** Ergonomics Outline, **and leave it open for the next part of this lesson.**

As you examine your outline, you realize that there is only one Roman numeral level and you recall that a basic rule of outlining is to have more than one point at each level. Upon further consideration you recognize that *Healthy Computer Practices* is really the title of your paper and should not be part of the outline. Also a friend has suggested that you should discuss horizontal alignment as well as vertical alignment, so you want to add that to the outline. In this next part of the lesson, you learn how to manipulate the outline to move information around and to change levels.

## To Manipulate an Outline

1. **With the insertion point at the end of the outline, press** ⌷Enter↵⌷ **and then press** ⌷⇧Shift⌷ + ⌷Tab⌷, **and type:** Horizontal Alignment. A third topic is added at *Level 3.*

2. **Using the skills you have just learned, add two subtopics under** *Horizontal Alignment:* Keyboard, **and** Mouse. Two subtopics display at *Level 4.*

3. **Scroll to the top of your outline and click on the Roman numeral I.** This is the title for your paper and should not be included as part of the outline.

4. **In the Outline Tools group, click the Outline Level arrow (*Level 1*) and then choose Body Text from the displayed list.** The Roman numeral I is removed and the text is formatted as body text without a heading style.

5. **Select the title and using the Mini toolbar, change the font to Arial, 14 pt, Bold, and then center the line.** The title is formatted, but now you need to adjust the remaining outline up one level for each item listed. Note: Horizontal alignment, such as center and right-align do not display in the Outline view.

6. **Click the outline symbol to the left of *A. Ergonomics*, and then in the Outline Tools group, click the Promote button.** The plus-shaped outline symbol to the left of *A. Ergonomics* indicates that this topic has subtopics. When you click this symbol the entire *Ergonomics* topic is selected, and when you click the Promote button each item under this topic is promoted one level. *Ergonomics* is now Roman numeral I. Notice that *Healthy Practices* becomes C in the outline. *Healthy Practices* and its related subtopics all need to be promoted one level as well.

7. **Click the outline symbol next to *C. Healthy Practices* and then in the Outline Tools group, click the Promote button.** This section of the outline is promoted and now there are two Roman numerals in the outline as shown in Figure 7.6. As you examine the outline, you decide that horizontal alignment should follow vertical alignment, and precede the lighting topic.

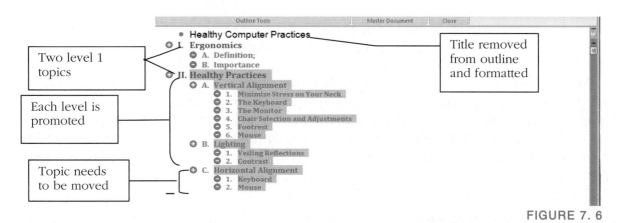

FIGURE 7. 6

8. **Click the outline symbol next to Horizontal Alignment and drag up until an insertion line displays above Lighting as shown in Figure 7.7, and then release the mouse button.** The outline is rearranged and *Horizontal Alignment* now precedes *Lighting* as a topic. The subtopics, *1. Keyboard* and *2. Mouse,* display a dash outline symbol to the left of each topic. This indicates that these two items do not contain any further subtopics.

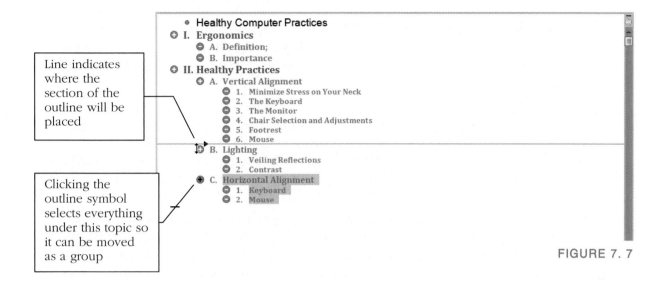

Line indicates where the section of the outline will be placed

Clicking the outline symbol selects everything under this topic so it can be moved as a group

FIGURE 7. 7

9. **Click somewhere on** *II. Healthy Practices,* **and then in the Outline Tools group click the Collapse button.** The Level 3 topics are collapsed and just the Level 2 topics display under *Healthy Practices.* The Expand and Collapse buttons on the Outlining tab expand or collapse the outline to display more or less detail. Each time you click one of these buttons, it expands or collapses the topics one more level.

10. **In the Outline Tools group, click the Expand button to redisplay all levels of the outline.**

11. **Click the Insert tab. In the Header & Footer group, click the Footer button and select the Blank (Three Columns) format. On the left side of the footer, select the** *Type text* **control and type your name. In the center of the footer, right-click the** *Type text* **control and then click Remove Content Control. On the right side of the footer, select the** *Type text* **control and type Ergonomics Outline.**

12. **Save the** *Ergonomics Outline* **document, print the outline (optional), and close the file.**

## LESSON 2: Tracking Changes and Adding Comments

The Track Changes feature records changes made to a document by others. Additions to the text are shown in a different color and deleted text is displayed in a different color with a line through it. ScreenTips display to show you the date, time and person who made the change. You can also add *comments* to a document, which is not a change to the text, but a suggestion, reminder, or note that is inserted into the document. Comments can be used as a way to communicate between reviewers and the author of the document.

You have written a draft of your *Healthy Computer Practices* paper and need to turn on the Track Changes feature; you will then add some comments to the document and make some changes before sending it out for review.

1. Open the *WD_0701* document and save it in your folder as Computer Ergonomics; if necessary change the Zoom to fit your screen. Make sure formatting marks are displayed. Text has been added to each heading in your outline from an earlier lesson.

2. Click the Office button and at the bottom of the list click the Word Options button. In the displayed Word Options dialog box, with the Popular list displayed, look at *Personalize your copy of Microsoft Office* area. This area lists the information about the person (or organization) to whom the computer software is registered. This information controls the name that displays when you make changes with the Track Changes feature.

3. If the name displayed is not your own, record the name and initials that display and then type your name in the User name box and your initials in the Initials box as shown in Figure 7.8. Click OK to accept the change in user information. After you have finished this lesson, you will change this information back to the previous name and initials, so be sure to keep track of the name and initials you have recorded. Now any changes or comments made will display your name and initials.

User name and initials changed in the Word Options dialog box

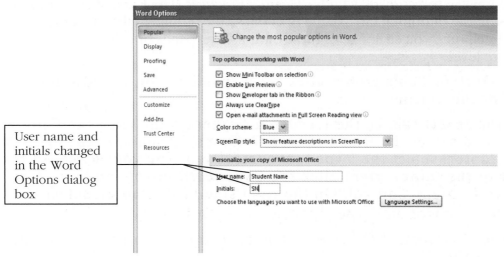

FIGURE 7. 8

4. Click the Review tab, and then in the Tracking group click the top portion of the Track Changes button. On the Review tab, in the Tracking group it shows *Final Showing Markup.*

5. On the Review tab, in the Tracking group, click the Show Markup button and be sure that a check mark displays next to Comments, Ink, Insertions and Deletions, Formatting, and Markup Area Highlight. A checkmark indicates that the selected item will be marked as a change in the change history record so it can be reviewed.

6. Click the Show Markup button a second time to close the list. In the Tracking group, click the Balloons button and be sure a check mark displays next to Show *Only Comments and Formatting in Balloons* as

**shown in Figure 7.9.** Changes and comments can display in balloons along the right side of the page with lines pointing back to the change on the screen. This is in addition to displaying the change on the document. You can choose to display all or none of the changes and comments in this manner, or to show only comments and formatting in balloons. It is a matter of personal preference how you set the balloons options.

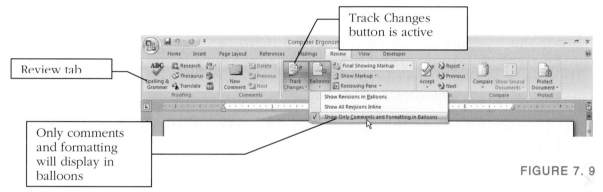

FIGURE 7. 9

7. **At the top of the document, select the *Ergonomics* heading. On the Review tab, in the Comments group, click the New Comment button.** A balloon displays at the right side of the text. When you type, your comment will display in this balloon. The color of the balloon that displays on your screen may not match what is shown in the figures.

8. **Type: Does this opening paragraph sound OK as an introduction?** As you type, the information is recorded in the comment balloon at the right side of the document as shown in Figure 7.10. Your initials display in brackets with *1* to designate this as the first comment.

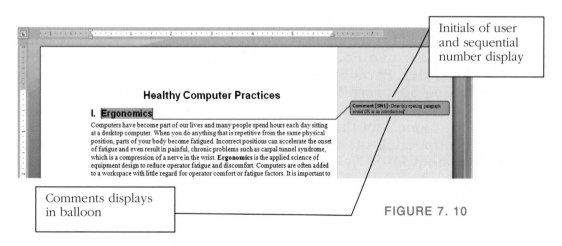

FIGURE 7. 10

9. **Click to the left of *adjust* in the last sentence in the *Vertical Alignment* paragraph.** A grammar line (squiggly green line) indicates that there is an error here.

---

10. **Type: to and press** Space. The word *to* is inserted and displays in a different color font with an underline. A bar displays to the left of the correction in the margin, which indicates that a change has been made.

11. **In the paragraph under the *Minimize Stress on Your Neck* heading, locate the word *disks* in the sixth sentence and replace it with:** discs. *Disks* displays with a line through it, indicating that it was removed; *discs* is inserted and displays with the same color font and underline as the previous change.

12. **Under the heading *The Monitor*, in the third sentence, type: (LCD) to the right of *liquid crystal display*; be sure there is one space on either side of the inserted text.** The inserted text displays with an underline and the same color font as used previously.

13. **Move the pointer over the last change you made until the ScreenTip displays as shown in Figure 7.11.** The ScreenTip lists the person's name, date and time of the changes, and describes what changes have been made.

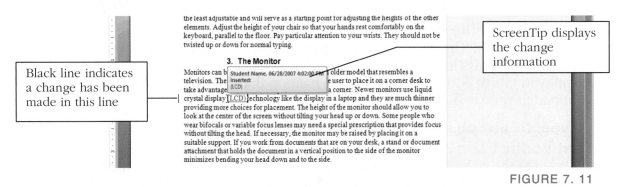

FIGURE 7. 11

14. **Click the Insert tab, and then in the Header & Footer group, click the Footer button. Insert a Blank Footer. Select the Type text control. On the Header and Footer Tools Design tab, in the Insert group, click the Quick Parts button and then click Field. In the displayed Field dialog box, scroll the Field names list, click File Name, and then click OK. Press** Tab **twice, and on the right side of the footer type your name. on the Header and Footer Tools Design tab, in the Close group, click the Close Header and Footer button to return to the document .**

15. **Display Office menu, click the Word Options button. Type the name and Initials you recorded in step 3 in the User Name and Initials areas. Click OK.** When using someone else's computer or one in a lab, it is proper etiquette to return the computer to its original settings.

16. **Save your document, print the first page of the document (optional), and then close the file. Leave Word open to continue to the next lesson.**

# LESSON 3: Reviewing and Responding to Proposed Changes

When a document is reviewed with Track Changes turned on, the changes or comments made by each reviewer display in a different color and the person is identified by name or initials in the ScreenTips, balloons, or the Reviewing Pane, which can be displayed at the bottom or side of the window. If you are the final editor of the document, you will review the changes and comments and decide whether to accept or reject the suggested changes and whether further action is needed.

In this lesson, you will open another version of the *Computer Ergonomics* paper that includes changes made by two other people in addition to the ones you were instructed to make. You will review the changes and decide which changes to accept and which ones to reject.

## To Review and Respond to Proposed Changes

1. **Open document *WD_0702* and save it in your folder with the name Computer Ergonomic Changes. Click the Review tab.** Changes you were directed to make display in one color under Student Name. Changes and comments made by Charity Hawkins display in a different color, and changes from Noah F. Armstrong display in a third color as shown in Figure 7.12. The colors you see may be different than the ones shown in the figures. Notice the black bar at the left of each line where a change has been made. This is another visual cue to indicate a change.

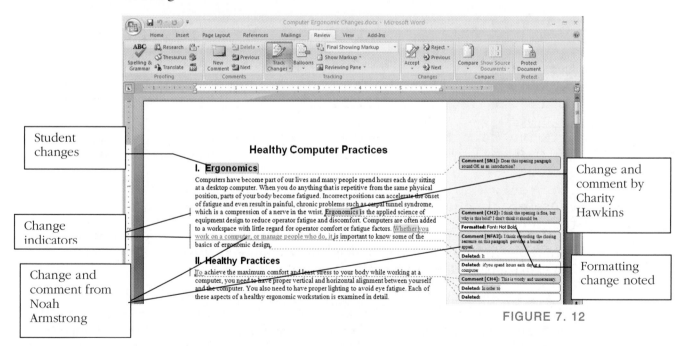

Student changes

Change indicators

Change and comment from Noah Armstrong

Change and comment by Charity Hawkins

Formatting change noted

FIGURE 7. 12

2. **On the Review tab, in the Tracking group, click the Reviewing Pane button arrow and then click Reviewing Pane Horizontal ; scroll through the Reviewing Pane until you can see the first comment made**

by **Charity Hawkins, labeled CH2.** The Reviewing Pane at the bottom of the window displays the name of each reviewer, the date and time of each change, what was changed, and what type of change was made. This is a third way to look at the changes that were made. In Word 2007, the reviewing pane can also be displayed vertically to the left of the document.

3.  **Scroll through the changes, using the scroll bar in the Reviewing Pane.** Notice that the comments are numbered sequentially regardless of the person making the comment. If you click on a comment in the Reviewing Pane, the insertion point moves to that location in the document.

4.  **On the Review tab, in the Tracking group, click the Reviewing Pane button to close the Reviewing Pane; press** Ctrl + Home **to ensure that your insertion point is at the top of the document.**

5.  **On the Review tab, in the Changes group, click the Next button.** The first change or comment is selected. In this case, it selects the first comment that was inserted by the student. Since this is your comment and it does not require further action, you can delete it to remove it from the document.

6.  **On the Review in the Changes group, click the Reject button.** The comment is removed from the document and remaining comments are renumbered as shown in Figure 7.13.

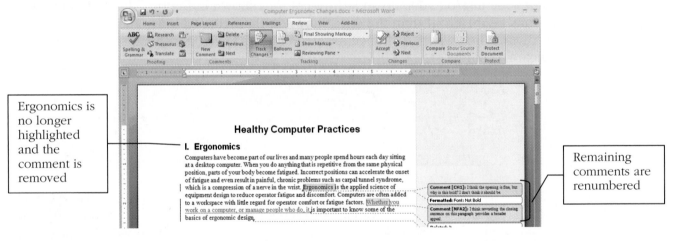

Ergonomics is no longer highlighted and the comment is removed

Remaining comments are renumbered

FIGURE 7. 13

7.  **In the Changes group, click the Next button.** *Ergonomics* is selected. The formatting for this word was changed and a comment was inserted by Charity Hawkins, labeled *CH*, asking why the word was bold.

8.  **In the Changes group click the Accept button, and then in the Changes group click the Reject button.** When you click the Accept button, the change that removed the bold formatting is accepted and the next change or comment is selected because it is attached to the same word.. In this case, the next change is the comment from Charity regarding the bold formatting, which you then removed by clicking the Reject button.

9. **In the Changes group click the Next button.** A change made by Noah F. Armstrong to the last sentence in the paragraph is selected. The change to this sentence includes deleting the clause at the end of the sentence. After reading the sentence with all the changes, you decide to accept the changes.

10. **Select the last three lines in the Ergonomics paragraph, which include all of the changes made by Noah, and then click the Accept button.** Changes often include several parts and you can accept all of the changes as a group by selecting the portion of your document that includes the changes and then clicking the Accept button. This is quicker than moving from one change to the next with the Next button and accepting each change one at a time.

11. **Click the Next button to highlight the comment made by Noah, which is still displayed, and then click the Reject button.** The change made was accepted and the comment from Noah is removed. There are several more changes and one comment left to review.

12. **Following the same procedure, accept the next changes made by Charity Hawkins and then remove the comment.** *In order to* is removed and is replaced by *To*. In this manner, you can review each change that has been suggested and accept or reject the changes and remove the comments.

13. **Click the Accept button arrow, and then click *Accept All Changes in Document* from the displayed list.** All of the remaining changes in the document are accepted and the change formatting is removed.

14. **Click the Track Changes button to turn off Track Changes.**

15. **Save your changes and leave the *Computer Ergonomic Changes* document open for the next lesson.**

---

## TO EXTEND YOUR KNOWLEDGE...

### REVIEWING CHANGES BY TYPE OR BY REVIEWER
You can control the review process by displaying only certain types of changes—formatting, or insertions and deletions—or by displaying the changes from specific reviewers. On the Show Markup list, point to Reviewers and then clear the check mark next to the reviewers you want to hide. You can also clear the check marks next to the different types of changes such as formatting or comments, and review only the selected changes. The other changes remain in the document but will not be displayed until you select them again.

### ANOTHER WAY TO REVIEW CHANGES
A quick way to review changes is to right-click on the change and respond to it by using the shortcut menu that displays.

---

# LESSON 4: Using Language Tools and Displaying Document Statistics

There are several other tools that can help you with the writing process. One of them is the built-in thesaurus. If you want to use a different word to provide more variety to your writing, a thesaurus can help you explore other word choices. You can control the level of grammar that is used in a document by changing the grammar settings to look for contractions, slang, jargon, gender specific words, passive voice, and other style-related issues. You can also check the read-ability level of the content and the number of words contained in your paper.

In this lesson you will use the thesaurus to change a few words, check the grammar setting and then check the word count and readability level of the *Computer Ergonomics Changes* paper.

## To Use Language Tools

1. **With the *Computer Ergonomic Changes* document open, locate the word *achieve* in the first sentence in the paragraph under *Vertical Alignment*; right-click *achieve* and then point to Synonyms in the displayed shortcut menu.** A list of possible synonyms for *achieve* displays as shown in Figure 7.14. If none of the words are acceptable, you can click *Thesaurus* at the bottom of the list.

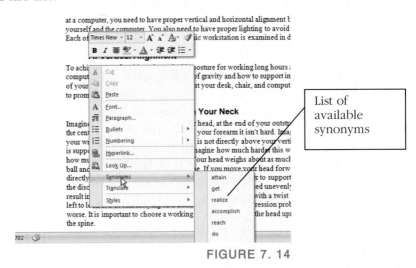

FIGURE 7. 14

2. **Click *attain* from the displayed list.** *Achieve* is replaced with *attain*

3. **Right-click the word *important* in the last sentence of the paragraph under *Minimize Stress on Your Neck*, point to Synonyms, and then click *essential*.** *Important* is replaced with *essential*. In this manner you can look for synonyms for other words in your paper.

4. **On the Review tab, in the Proofing group, click the Spelling & Grammar button. In the displayed Spelling and Grammar dialog box, click the Options button. In the displayed Word Options dialog box under *When correcting spelling and grammar in Word*, click the Show readability statistics check box, if it is not already selected.** The Proofing section on the Word Options dialog box displays the options for when and how spelling and grammar are checked as shown in Figure 7.15. The default is to check the spelling and grammar as you type, enabling you to correct your mistakes as you go. You can also change the level of grammar by changing the *Writing style* setting and by selecting from the list of options displayed when you click the Settings button.

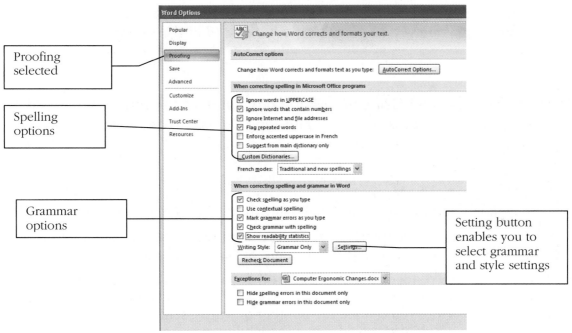

FIGURE 7. 15

5. **Click the Settings button.** The Grammar Settings dialog box displays. Here you control what is checked. Items are classified either as grammar or as style.

6. **Scroll and read the list of items that can be checked, and then under *Style*, click *Contractions* to select this check box.** You can review your document for contractions and remove them if you want.

7. **Click OK in the Grammar Settings dialog box and then click Recheck Document in the Word Options dialog box.** A message box displays to inform you that this will reset the spelling and grammar checker, including those things you chose to ignore.

8. **Click Yes to continue, and then click OK to close the Word Options dialog box.** The Spelling and Grammar dialog box displays the first grammatical error, identified as *Subject-Verb Agreement*. Two suggestions are made as shown in Figure 7.16, and neither suggestion is correct. The grammar tool does not always

correctly identify the grammatical error that may exist and a different solution from the one suggested by the program may be necessary. It is important to examine and critically evaluate the suggestions before accepting a change.

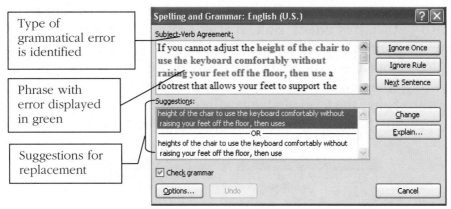

FIGURE 7. 16

9. **In the Spelling and Grammar dialog box, click to the left of the green *to* in the sentence that is selected, and type in order and then click Change.** The error is corrected and the green underline is removed. The next error that is displayed in the dialog box is the use of the contraction *isn't.* In formal papers, it is usually best to avoid using contractions. The suggested replacement—*is not*—displays in the Suggestions box. **Note:** If the contraction *isn't* does not show in the Spelling and Grammar box, return to step 6 and make sure the contraction option is checked.

10. **Click Change to accept the suggested replacement.** The contraction *isn't* is replaced with *is not*, and another incident of *isn't* is located.

11. **Click Change to accept the suggested replacement.** Because this is the last change in the document the Readability Statistics dialog box displays as shown in Figure 7.17. Here you can see the number of words, sentences, and paragraphs in your document. It also provides two readability scores and the average number of sentences and words per paragraph.

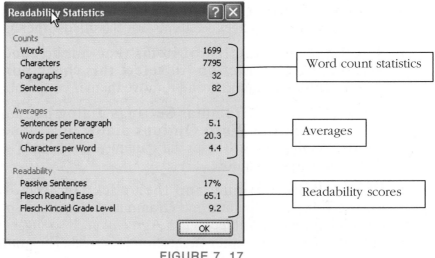

FIGURE 7. 17

12. Write down the number of words in the document and then click OK to close the Readability Statistics dialog box.

13. Click the Insert tab. In the Header & Footer group click the Header button and select Blank format. On the left side of the header type the number of words you wrote down in the previous step.

14. On the Header & Footer Tools Design tab, in the Navigation Group click the Go to Footer button. Press [Tab] two times and on the right side of the footer type your name, and then in the Close group click the Close the Header and Footer button.

15. Save your changes and then print the first page of the *Computer Ergonomic Changes* document (optional). Close the file but leave Word open.

---

## TO EXTEND YOUR KNOWLEDGE...

### WHAT DO READABILITY SCORES MEAN?

The Flesch Reading Ease score tells you how easy it is to read a document. The higher the score, the easier it is to read. Most standard documents should be in the range of 60 to 70. The Flesch-Kincaid Grade Level score equates the document to a U.S. school grade level; a score of 9 would be equivalent to a 9th grade reading level.

---

### To Return the Computer to Its Previous Settings

1. Display the Office menu and click the Word Options button.

2. On the left click Proofing to display the Proofing tools. Under *When correcting spelling and grammar in Word*, click to remove the Show readability statistics check mark.

3. Click the Settings button, and then in the Grammar Settings dialog box, under Style, click to remove the check mark next to *Contractions*.

4. Click OK in the Grammar Settings dialog box and then click OK in the Word Options dialog box. Close Word

---

## SUMMARY

In this project, you worked with several tools that help with the writing process. You learned how to use the Outline feature to organize ideas and content and define the relationship of one topic to another. You created an outline by setting the formatting style and entering topics. You learned how to manipulate the outline by using the Promote and Demote buttons to display the key points at different levels in the outline. You also rearranged the outline by dragging topics from one location to another.

Working in a different document you learned how to use the Track Changes feature to seek feedback from others. You entered changes and comments in a document and then reviewed changes and comments, accepting some and rejecting others.

Finally, in a third document, you used the thesaurus to locate synonyms, and the grammar tool to examine the document for contractions, slang, jargon, or other style related issues, as well as basic grammar. To determine the reading level of the document, you opened the Readability Statistics dialog box, which displays the number of words, sentences, paragraphs, averages, and a reading level evaluation.

## KEY TERMS

| | | |
|---|---|---|
| comments | outline | synonyms |
| demote | promote | Track changes |

## CHECKING CONCEPTS AND TERMS

### SCREEN ID
Label each element of the screen shown in Figure 7.18.

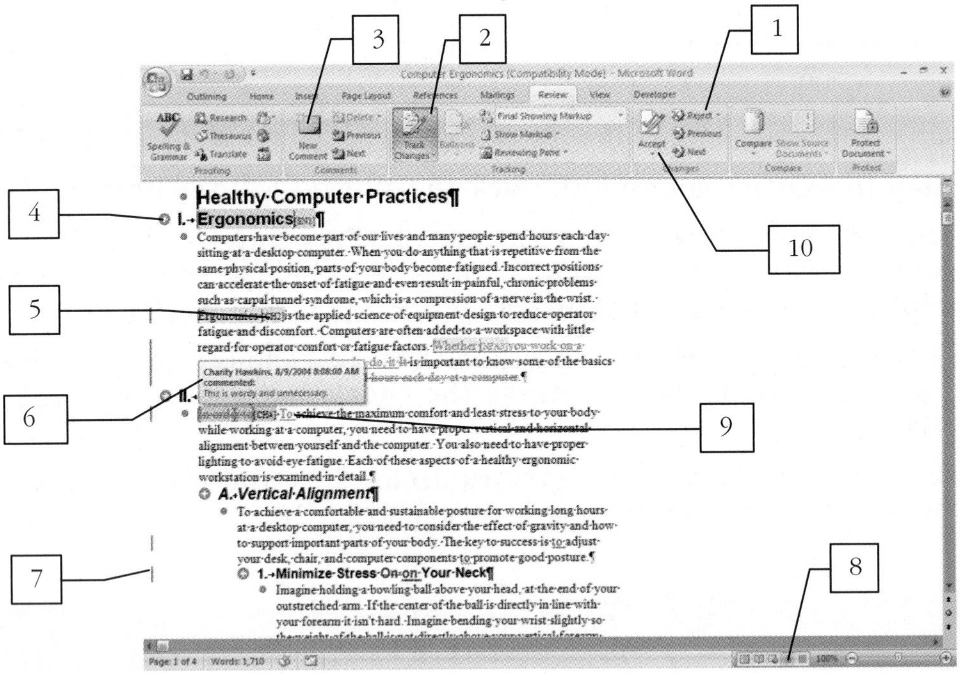

FIGURE 7. 18

_____ A. Accept changes

_____ B. Change indicator

_____ C. Comment ScreenTip

_____ D. Expand button

_____ E. Initials of person making a comment

_____ F. Insert Comment

_____ G. Insertion

_____ H. Outline button

_____ I. Reject changes

_____ J. Track Changes

# MULTIPLE CHOICE

**Circle the letter of the correct answer for each of the following.**

1. The style used for an outline is set in the _____ gallery? [L1]
   a. Bullets and Numbering
   b. Multilevel List
   c. Format
   d. Style

2. To accept a group of changes, first _____ and then click the Accept button. [L3]
   a. select the text containing the changes
   b. click the Next button
   c. move to the end of the document
   d. you have to accept each change separately

3. When Track Changes is enabled, it records changes made to _____. [L2]
   a. formatting
   b. text that is added
   c. text that is deleted
   d. all of the above

4. To look at all levels in your outline, click the _____ button on the Outlining toolbar. [L1]
   a. Display
   b. Show All
   c. Expand
   d. Exhibit

5. Spelling & Grammar is set to check _____ by default. [L4]
   a. styles
   b. grammar errors
   c. contractions
   d. all of the above

6. The Readability Statistics dialog box displays _____. [L4]
   a. number of misspelled words
   b. number of grammar errors
   c. reading errors
   d. average number of words per sentence

7. Outlines can assist you with all of the following except _____. [L1]
   a. writing the details of your paper
   b. organizing topics into groups
   c. visually displaying the relationship between topics
   d. rearranging topics

8. Tracked changes are displayed on the screen in _____. [L2]–[L3]
   a. balloons along the right side of the page
   b. the Reviewing Pane at the bottom of the window
   c. ScreenTips on the page
   d. all of the above are methods for displaying tracked changes

9. Changes that are tracked in a document are identified by _____. [L2]−L3]
   a. computer, person, method
   b. date, serial number, quotations
   c. person, date, and time
   d. initials, sound, length of time to make the change

10. A thesaurus is helpful for locating _____. [L4]
    a. translations
    b. definitions
    c. synonyms
    d. all of the above

## DISCUSSION

1. When collaborating on a document with many people, under what circumstances would inserted comments be more appropriate than tracking changes and vice versa? What should you consider before using the Accept All or Reject All options? [L2]—[3]

2. In what circumstances do you use an outline? In what careers do you think outlining would be particularly useful? If you were a journalist, what outline topics do you think you would use for most every story that you wrote? How would an outline format ensure that you have gathered all of the relevant material? [L1]

3. When you write, how do you ensure that your papers are without errors? Which tools that you have learned about do you think you would utilize? How can you use these tools to improve your writing? [L1]—[L4]

## SKILL DRILL

Skill Drill exercises reinforce project skills. Each skill reinforced is the same, or nearly the same, as a skill presented in the project. Detailed instructions are provided in a step-by-step format.

Each of the Skill Drill exercises is independent and can be completed in any order. All of these exercises can be completed using Microsoft Office XP or later versions. Instructions throughout the exercises are based on a Windows XP operating system, running Microsoft Office 2007.

### 1. Inserting and Printing Comments in a Prospectus

You are reviewing a prospectus and want to insert comments for another colleague to review before you distribute it at the next board meeting. First you will change the user information and insert comments; then you will change the name of the user back to its original setting and review the comments and make changes.

1. Open **WD_0703** from the Student folder. Save it to your folder as **Prospectus**.
2. From the Office menu, click the Word Options button. Write down information in the **User Name** and **Initials** text boxes, and then type your name in the **User Name** box and your initials in the **Initials** box. Click **OK**.
3. Select *August 1, 1983* in the paragraph next to the heading *The Fund*. Click the **Review tab**, and in the **Comments group**, click **New Comment** to display a comment balloon in the right margin.
4. Type: `I think the date was July 1, 1984 in the balloon`.
5. Scroll to the end of the document and select *$1,000* in the paragraph next to the *Minimum Purchase* heading. In the Comments group, click the **New Comment** button and type: `I think it is $1,500 in the balloon that displays`.
6. Select *$1.00* in the paragraph next to the *Public Offering Price* heading and click the **New Comment** button. Type: `I think it is $10.00 a share`. Save the document.

7. Display the Office men, click the **Word Options** button and change the **User Name** box back to the name you recorded in step 2 and then change the **Initials** box back to the initials you recorded in step 2. Click **OK**.

8. Select *August 1, 1983* in the paragraph next to the heading *The Fund*. On the **Review tab**, click the **New Comment** button and type: `You are` `correct`. In the Tracking group, click the **Reviewing Pane** button. The comment displays in the Reviewing Pane with the current user name and initials and in a new balloon.

9. Scroll through the Reviewing Pane to display the comment that displays *$1,500*. Click in the comment in the Reviewing Pane to the right of *$1,500* and type: `but Mark Carson thinks it will be increased to` `$2,000 at the board meeting next week`. Notice that the author of this response to the comment is not identified, and the response also shows in the original balloon.

10. Click in the last comment, and then on the Review tab, in the Changes group click the Reject button, because the share price is still $1.00.

11. Save the *Prospectus* document and display the Print dialog box. In the **Print what** box, be sure *Document showing markup* is displayed, and then click **OK** to print the document including the comments. Close the *Prospectus* document and close Word.

## 2. Formatting, Creating, and Manipulating an Outline for a Proposal

You work for a company that is making a proposal to add a multimedia component to a local automobile historical museum. You decide to use the outlining feature in Word to organize the notes you took when you met with the museum staff so you can discuss and present the information to your colleagues.

1. . Open **WD_0704** and save it as **Museum Proposal**. Select the first line and format the font to Arial Rounded MT Bold, 14-point. If you do not have this font, choose a similar font style.

2. Click to the left of *Purpose* and then click the **View tab**. In the **Document Views group**, click the **Outline** button.

3. On the **Home tab**, in the **Paragraph group**, click the **Multilevel List** arrow. Click the first option in the third row. *I.* should display next to Purpose.

4. Click the **Outlining tab**, and in the **Outline Tools group** click the **Promote to Heading** 1 button at the left end of the group. The Heading 1 style is applied.

5. Select *Audience* and then in the **Outline Tools group** click the **Promote** button. This becomes Roman numeral II—the Level 1 format with a Heading 1 style.

6. Follow the same procedure to apply a Level 1 format to *What to include*; *Format (How)*; *When*; and *Content*. The six main topics are formatted at Level 1 with a Heading 1 style. (The text will not line up because of the different width in the Roman numeral. headings.)

7. Select the four points under *Purpose* and then in the Outline Tools group click the **Demote** button. These become subtopics *A.* through *D.* In a similar manner, select the items listed under each of the major topics and demote them to *Level 2*.

8. Under topic *III. What to include*, select *B.* and *C.* and demote them to *Level 3*.

9. Under *I. Purpose*, select *A. Multimedia module.* Point to the outlining symbol to the left of the selected text and drag this item down to be the first point under *Format (How)*.

10. On the **Insert tab**, in the **Headers & Footers group**, click **Footer**. Select the **Blank Footer** format. In the **Insert group**, click **Quick Parts** and then click **Field**. Scroll the **Field Names** list and select **File Name**. Click **OK**. Tab to the right side of the footer and type your name. In the **Close group**, click the **Close the Header and Footer** button.

11. Save the *Museum Proposal* document and print the document (optional). Close the file and then close Word.

## 3. Reviewing Changes and Using Grammar, Thesaurus, and Readability Tools

A friend has reviewed a paper that you wrote for a class. You need to review the changes and apply finishing touches to it before turning it in.

1. Open *WD_0705* and save it as **Precipitation**.

2. On the **Review tab**, in the **Comments group**, click the **Next** button to examine the first comment. Read the comment and take the appropriate action to correct all spelling errors as suggested by the comment.

3. On the **Review tab**, in the **Changes group** click the **Next** button to move to the next change *(average)* and then click the **Accept** button. Move to and accept the next change (a comma is deleted).

4. Notice the balloon informing you of a change in formatting. Accept this change. **Note:** Click the arrow on the Accept button and see that the default is to Accept and Move to the Next change.

5. The next change is a deleted sentence. Reject this change, and reject the sentence that was inserted to replace the deleted sentence.

6. Review the rest of the document and accept the remaining changes. Select the comment at the top of the document and click in the **Comments group** click the **Delete** button.

7. On the **Review tab**, in the **Proofing group**, click the **Spelling & Grammar** button. In the Spelling and Grammar dialog box click the **Options** button. Under *When correcting spelling and grammar in Word* select the **Show readability statistics** check box.

8. Click the **Settings** button, and then under *Style* click to select the first two items. Click **OK** and then click **Recheck Document**. Click **Yes** to continue and then click **OK** to close the Word Options dialog box.

9. Using the **Spelling and Grammar** dialog box, locate and change three contractions found in the text. Examine the readability statistics that display and write down the Flesch Kincaid Grade Level. Close the Readability Statistics dialog box.

10. In the introductory paragraph at the top of the document, right-click *zilch* in the second line of the first sentence. Point to **Synonyms** and then select **nothing** from the displayed list.

11. In the last line of the paragraph under the table in Page 1, right-click the word *plainly*, point to **Synonyms** and then select **clearly**.

12. Click the **Insert tab**, and in the **Header & Footer group** click **Header**. Select the **Blank (Three Columns)** format. On the left side of the Header, enter the Quick Parts Field for the file name. Delete the middle text box. Tab to the right side of the header, type your name and then type the Flesch-Kincaid Grade level that you recorded in step 9. Adjust the right tab stop so it aligns with the right margin. Close the Header and Footer toolbar.

13. Display the Word Options dialog box and in the Proofing list deselect the *Show readability statistics* check box. Click the **Settings** button and clear the check mark next to the first two items under Style. Click **OK** twice.

14. Save the *Precipitation* document and print the first page (optional). Close the file. Close Word

## CHALLENGE

Challenge exercises expand on or are somewhat related to skills presented in the lessons. Each exercise provides a brief narrative introduction, followed by instructions in a numbered-step format that are not as detailed as those in the Skill Drill section.

### 1. Formatting, Creating, and Manipulating an Outline and Adding Comments

You have been assigned the task of creating a policy manual for the employment practices and policies of the company for which you work. You decide to start with an outline to make sure you cover all the main points and get the information properly organized.

1. Start with a blank document. Display the Multilevel list and select the traditional outline format that starts with a Roman numeral. Change to the Outline view.

2. Using the skills you have learned create the outline as shown in Figure 7.19.

I. Employment Policies
    A. Terms of Employment
        1. Conditions for Employment
        2. Cause for Termination
        3. Job Classifications
    B. Benefits
        1. Medical
        2. Dental
        3. Paid Days-Off
        4. Holidays
        5. Retirement Benefits
    C. Salary and Wages
        1. Salary Scale
        2. Commission Scale
    D. Evaluations
        1. Review Periods
           a) Initial review after six months
           b) Annual reviews of performance and salary
        2. Performance Based Evaluations
II. Work Policies
    A. Job Descriptions
    B. Supervisor Responsibilities
    C. Employee Rights and Responsibilities
        1. Rights
        2. Responsibilities

FIGURE 7. 19

3. After showing this outline to a few people you need to make some changes. Under *B. Benefits*, demote *Holidays* to *Level 4* and then add: `Vacation days` and `Sick days` as two more sub-points at *Level 4*.

4. Under *A. Terms of Employment* add a new point 1. `Employer Responsibilities`, and change *Cause for Termination* to `Termination Process` with two sub-points: `Cause, Procedures`.

5. Select *A. Job Descriptions* under *II. Work Policies* and move it to be *a Level 4* sub-point under *4. Job Classification*s at the top of the outline. Change *Descriptions* to `descriptions` to match the format for Level 4 sub-points. Add a second sub-point to *Job Classifications*: `Job ranking`.

6. Save the file as `Employment Outline`.

7. From the Office menu, click the Word Options button and record the name and initials that display, and then change this information to your name and initials. Click **OK**.

8. Select *Employment Policies* at the top of the page and then insert a comment: `Jeff, what other topics do you want included here?`

9. Select *Benefits* and insert a note to Samantha, the benefits manager, asking about other benefits that need to be included. Similarly, select *Work* near the end of the document, and ask Joe, the union representative, what other items he thinks should be included.

10. On the **Insert tab**, in the **Header & Footer group** insert a blank Footer. and use the Quick Parts to add the file name on the left side of the footer, and your name on the right side.

11. Save the Employment Outline document. Print a copy with the comments (optional). Close the file. Change the user information in the Word Options dialog box back to the name and initials you recorded in step 7. Close Word.

## 2. Inserting Changes and Entering Comments; Changing the Outline Format

In this Challenge exercise, you review an outline of a presentation about a computer implementation that failed. You will add the changes and corrections as noted in Figure 7.20.

1. Open **WD_0706**. Save it in your folder with the name `Computer Implementation.`

2. Display the Word Options dialog box. Record the name and initials of the User and then change this information to your name and initials.

3. Change the view to Print Layout. On the Review tab click **Track Changes** and then make the changes that are shown in Figure 7.20.

4. In the title, use the thesaurus to look for an alternative to the phrase *Gone Wrong* and insert a comment making a recommendation for another way to word this.

5. Turn off the Track Changes. Click to the left of *What's the Problem?* Display the Home tab, in the Paragraph group, display the Mutilevel List dialog box, choose the second alternative in the first row. This is another style for formatting an outline.

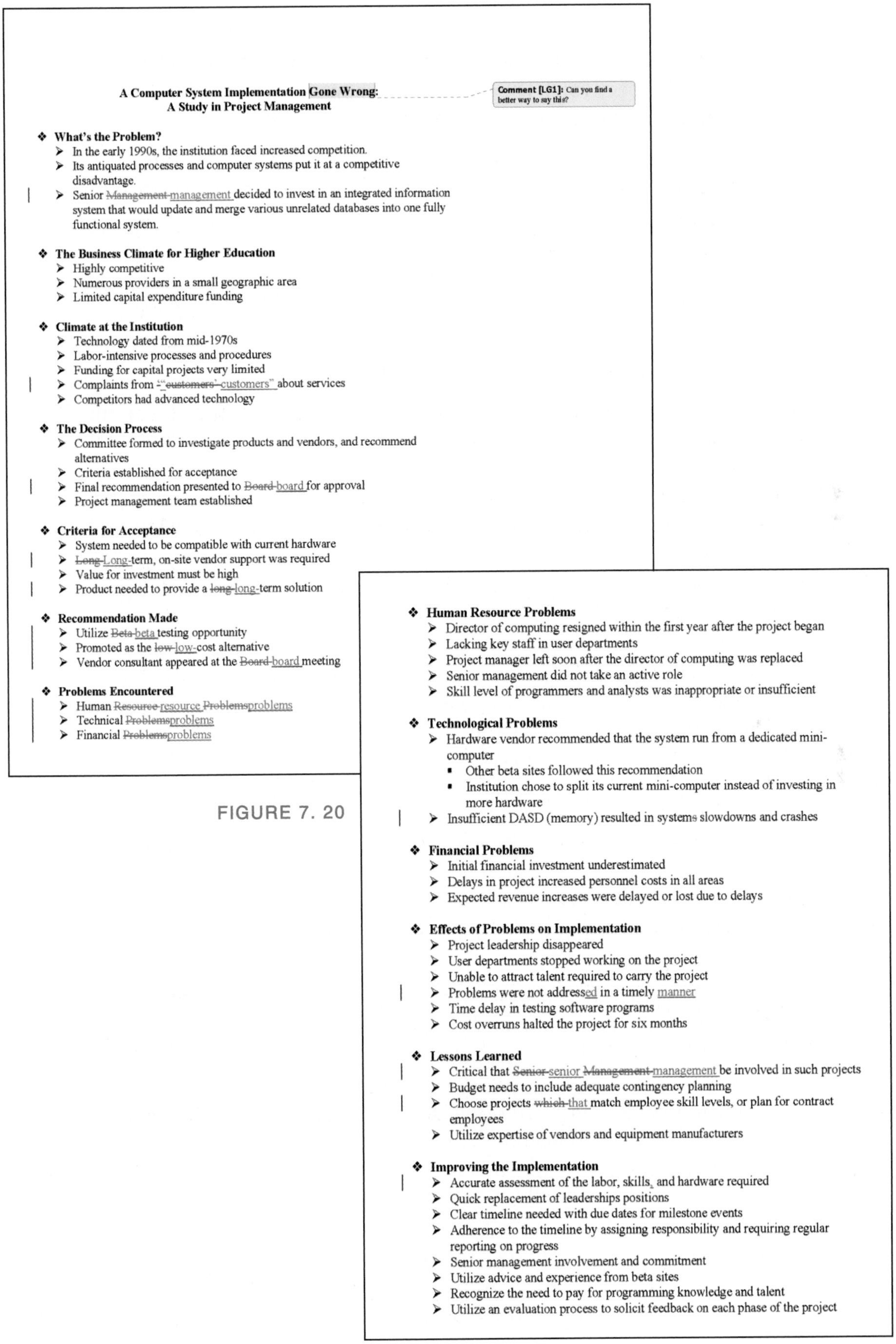

**A Computer System Implementation Gone Wrong:**
**A Study in Project Management**

Comment [LG1]: Can you find a better way to say this?

❖ **What's the Problem?**
  ➢ In the early 1990s, the institution faced increased competition.
  ➢ Its antiquated processes and computer systems put it at a competitive disadvantage.
  ➢ Senior ~~Management~~ management decided to invest in an integrated information system that would update and merge various unrelated databases into one fully functional system.

❖ **The Business Climate for Higher Education**
  ➢ Highly competitive
  ➢ Numerous providers in a small geographic area
  ➢ Limited capital expenditure funding

❖ **Climate at the Institution**
  ➢ Technology dated from mid-1970s
  ➢ Labor-intensive processes and procedures
  ➢ Funding for capital projects very limited
  ➢ Complaints from ~~'customers'~~ "customers" about services
  ➢ Competitors had advanced technology

❖ **The Decision Process**
  ➢ Committee formed to investigate products and vendors, and recommend alternatives
  ➢ Criteria established for acceptance
  ➢ Final recommendation presented to ~~Board~~ board for approval
  ➢ Project management team established

❖ **Criteria for Acceptance**
  ➢ System needed to be compatible with current hardware
  ➢ ~~Long~~ Long-term, on-site vendor support was required
  ➢ Value for investment must be high
  ➢ Product needed to provide a ~~long~~ long-term solution

❖ **Recommendation Made**
  ➢ Utilize ~~Beta~~ beta testing opportunity
  ➢ Promoted as the ~~low~~ low-cost alternative
  ➢ Vendor consultant appeared at the ~~Board~~ board meeting

❖ **Problems Encountered**
  ➢ Human ~~Resource~~ resource ~~Problems~~ problems
  ➢ Technical ~~Problems~~ problems
  ➢ Financial ~~Problems~~ problems

❖ **Human Resource Problems**
  ➢ Director of computing resigned within the first year after the project began
  ➢ Lacking key staff in user departments
  ➢ Project manager left soon after the director of computing was replaced
  ➢ Senior management did not take an active role
  ➢ Skill level of programmers and analysts was inappropriate or insufficient

❖ **Technological Problems**
  ➢ Hardware vendor recommended that the system run from a dedicated mini-computer
    ▪ Other beta sites followed this recommendation
    ▪ Institution chose to split its current mini-computer instead of investing in more hardware
  ➢ Insufficient DASD (memory) resulted in system~~s~~ slowdowns and crashes

❖ **Financial Problems**
  ➢ Initial financial investment underestimated
  ➢ Delays in project increased personnel costs in all areas
  ➢ Expected revenue increases were delayed or lost due to delays

❖ **Effects of Problems on Implementation**
  ➢ Project leadership disappeared
  ➢ User departments stopped working on the project
  ➢ Unable to attract talent required to carry the project
  ➢ Problems were not address~~ed~~ in a timely manner
  ➢ Time delay in testing software programs
  ➢ Cost overruns halted the project for six months

❖ **Lessons Learned**
  ➢ Critical that ~~Senior~~ senior ~~Management~~ management be involved in such projects
  ➢ Budget needs to include adequate contingency planning
  ➢ Choose projects ~~which~~ that match employee skill levels, or plan for contract employees
  ➢ Utilize expertise of vendors and equipment manufacturers

❖ **Improving the Implementation**
  ➢ Accurate assessment of the labor, skills, and hardware required
  ➢ Quick replacement of leaderships positions
  ➢ Clear timeline needed with due dates for milestone events
  ➢ Adherence to the timeline by assigning responsibility and requiring regular reporting on progress
  ➢ Senior management involvement and commitment
  ➢ Utilize advice and experience from beta sites
  ➢ Recognize the need to pay for programming knowledge and talent
  ➢ Utilize an evaluation process to solicit feedback on each phase of the project

**FIGURE 7. 20**

6. Turn Track Changes back on. Under *Technological Problems* demote *b)* and *c)* to *i)* and *ii)* respectively. The formatting change is noted with a balloon at the right side of the page.

7. On the Insert tab insert a **Blank (Three Columns)** footer. On the left side of the footer, insert the Quick Parts File Name field; on the right side type your name.

8. Save the *Computer Implementation* document. Print a copy (optional). Close the file.

9. Open the Word Options dialog box, change the User Name and initials back to the original information you recorded in step 2. Close Word.

## 3. Responding to Comments and Changes

A colleague has reviewed your draft of the multimedia proposal for the Ypsilanti Historical Automobile Museum. You need to review and respond to the changes and comments.

1. Open **WD_0707**. Save it in your folder with the name `Automobile Multimedia`. On the Review tab, be sure the Track Changes button is not selected.

2. Click **Next** to move to the first change — a deleted word. Accept the change. Then accept the second change.

3. In the third change, you decide that you do not like the word *flashy*. Select *flashy*, and then on the **Review tab**, in the **Proofing group** click Thesaurus. (Because this word is marked as a change, you cannot use the shortcut menu to look for synonyms.)

4. The Research task pane displays on the right and a list of possible replacements is displayed. Click on one of the words to see another list of words that are possible synonyms for the word you selected. Click the **Back** button to return to the previous list and try another word. Continue in this manner to explore the selection of words. When you find one you think is appropriate, right-click the word and then click **Insert**. *Flashy* will be replaced with the word you selected.

5. Continue to review and accept each of the changes.

6. Based on the comment at the end of the document, replace the sentence next to *Content:* with a sentence or two that recommends the two vehicles that are mentioned in the comment, and then delete the comment.

7. If you want to gather more information, try using the Research task pane. Type `Stanley Steamer` in the *Search for* box. Click the arrow next to *All Reference Books*, select *All Other Services* and then click the green Start searching arrow. (You need to be connected to the Internet.) Follow a few of the links that are provided and use some of the information that you locate to augment what you write in the content area.

8. Right-click *basically* in the first sentence of the *User* paragraph, point to **Synonyms** and select *chiefly* from the list.

9. On the Insert tab, insert a Footer using the Alphabet Footer format. In the footer [Type Text] type your name.

10. Save the *Automobile Multimedia* document. Print a copy (optional). Close the file and close Word.

## DISCOVERY ZONE

Discovery Zone exercises require advanced knowledge of topics presented in *Essentials* lessons, application of skills from multiple lessons, or self-directed learning of new skills. Each exercise is independent of the others, so you may complete the exercises in any order.

### 1. Reviewing and Outlining a Document

When changes are made to a document the reviewer may introduce new errors and they may not correct all of the errors in the original document. In this Discovery Zone exercise, you open a document, review the suggested changes, and then review the document again to correct any other errors. You will then create an outline based on this document. This outline is part of a larger document and therefore has only one Level 1 heading.

Open the file **WD_0708** and save it as **Digital Divide**. In the Word Options dialog box on the Proofing list, click the Recheck Document button so you can review the grammar. Review the changes that have been made and decide whether to accept or reject the changes. Use the spelling and grammar tool to correct any other changes that may be in the document. In the paragraph under

United States, use the thesaurus to replace the word important with a less commonly used word. Switch to Outline view, and select an outline style from the Multilevel list. The text displays as Body text in the Outline Level box. Use the buttons on the Outlining tab to promote the topics in this paper to an appropriate heading level. The paragraphs should be left as body text, but change the bullet points to a Level 3. Collapse the outline to Level 3.

Add the file name and your name to the footer and adjust the right-tab stop in the footer to align with the right margin. Save the file and print a copy (optional). The full document will print even when you have collapsed it to Level 3 in the Outline view.

### 2. Accepting and Rejecting Changes to an Invitation and Inserting Voice Comments

The grand opening of your new restaurant is in three weeks and you need to edit the invitation. Mary Milford and Theresa Reilly have already added comments for your review. Open **WD_0709** and save it as **Invitation**.

Turn on Track Changes and incorporate all of the suggestions made by Mary Milford and reject the suggestions made by Theresa Reilly. This requires you to make the changes because the reviewers have made comments, but have not changed the content. When finished, delete the comments. Add the file name and your name to the footer. Adjust the spacing as needed to ensure that the invitation prints on one page. Save the file and print a copy (optional).

Save the Invitation document and then close it.

# UNIT 2: USING PRODUCTIVITY SOFTWARE

## Microsoft Office 2007 IC³

## Project 8: Working with Text and Numbers in a Spreadsheet

LESSON 1 Entering Text and Numbers in a Worksheet

| | | |
|---|---|---|
| 2-3.1.1 | 2-3.1.2.2 | 2-3.1.3.2 |
| 2-3.1.2.1 | 2-3.1.3.1 | 2-3.1.4.6 |

LESSON 2 Editing Tables

| | | |
|---|---|---|
| 2-3.1.2.3 | 2-3.1.4.3 | 2-3.1.4.5 |
| 2-3.1.4.1 | 2-3.1.4.4 | 2-3.2.7 |
| 2-3.1.4.2 | | |

LESSON 3 Formatting Numbers

| | |
|---|---|
| 2-3.1.2.3 | 2-3.1.5 |

LESSON 4 Resizing and Emphasizing Table Elements

| | |
|---|---|
| 2-3.1.4.9 | 2-3.1.6 |
| 2-3.1.4.10 | 2-3.1.7 |

LESSON 5 Printing a Worksheet


LESSON 6 Copying Worksheets and Using Cell Styles (AutoFormat)

| | | |
|---|---|---|
| 2-3.1.4.6 | 2-3.1.4.8 | 2-3.1.4.11 |
| 2-3.1.4.7 | 2-3.1.2.4 | 2-3.1.8 |

LESSON 7 Sorting Tables

2-3.2.1

# PROJECT 8

# WORKING WITH TEXT AND NUMBERS IN A SPREADSHEET

IN THIS PROJECT, YOU LEARN HOW TO:

- Enter Text and Numbers in a Worksheet
- Edit Tables
- Format Numbers
- Resize and Emphasize Table Elements
- Print a Worksheet
- Copy Worksheets and Use Cell Styles (AutoFormat)
- Sort Tables

# WHY WOULD I DO THIS?

Word processing programs, such as Microsoft Office Word, can display tables. They are not, however, designed to work with tables of data where the values in some cells are calculated using the values in other cells. Tables that organize and calculate financial data are called *spreadsheets* and they are an important tool of any business or organization. They are used to manage expenses, budgets, and sales projections. If you work with money at home or on the job, you will probably use a spreadsheet program, such as Microsoft Office Excel, to manage it. Therefore, you need to be familiar with how numbers and text are entered, edited, formatted, and printed.

# VISUAL SUMMARY

In this project, you create a table of data that shows the sales figures for a chain of stores that sell saunas, spas, and pools. You learn how to enter the data and edit it by adding cells, rows, and columns. You also learn how to display the numbers in several different formats and how to align text as shown in Figure 8.1. You will learn how to copy the data and paste it into another worksheet. You will remove its formatting and then format the whole table at once by selecting a set of table formats from a gallery as shown in Figure 8.2. Finally, you will create a third copy of the table and sort it based on the values in two of the columns to determine which store in the chain did the best in two sales categories. See Figure 8.3.

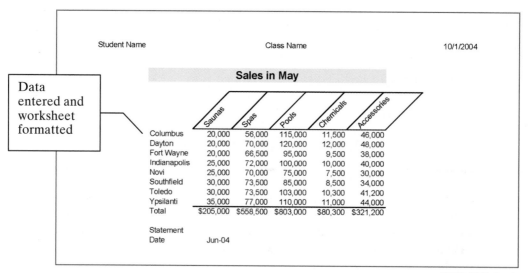

FIGURE 8. 1

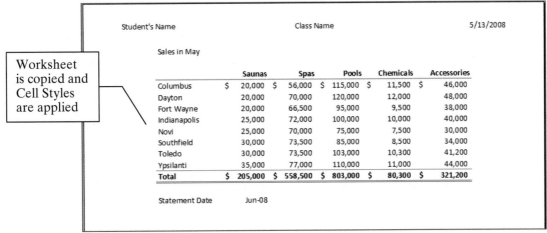

Worksheet is copied and Cell Styles are applied

| Student's Name | | | | Class Name | | | | | 5/13/2008 |
|---|---|---|---|---|---|---|---|---|---|

Sales in May

| | Saunas | Spas | Pools | Chemicals | Accessories |
|---|---|---|---|---|---|
| Columbus | $ 20,000 | $ 56,000 | $ 115,000 | $ 11,500 | $ 46,000 |
| Dayton | 20,000 | 70,000 | 120,000 | 12,000 | 48,000 |
| Fort Wayne | 20,000 | 66,500 | 95,000 | 9,500 | 38,000 |
| Indianapolis | 25,000 | 72,000 | 100,000 | 10,000 | 40,000 |
| Novi | 25,000 | 70,000 | 75,000 | 7,500 | 30,000 |
| Southfield | 30,000 | 73,500 | 85,000 | 8,500 | 34,000 |
| Toledo | 30,000 | 73,500 | 103,000 | 10,300 | 41,200 |
| Ypsilanti | 35,000 | 77,000 | 110,000 | 11,000 | 44,000 |
| Total | $ 205,000 | $ 558,500 | $ 803,000 | $ 80,300 | $ 321,200 |

Statement Date        Jun-08

FIGURE 8. 2

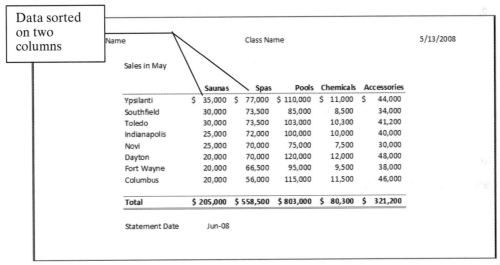

Data sorted on two columns

| Name | | | | Class Name | | | | | 5/13/2008 |
|---|---|---|---|---|---|---|---|---|---|

Sales in May

| | Saunas | Spas | Pools | Chemicals | Accessories |
|---|---|---|---|---|---|
| Ypsilanti | $ 35,000 | $ 77,000 | $ 110,000 | $ 11,000 | $ 44,000 |
| Southfield | 30,000 | 73,500 | 85,000 | 8,500 | 34,000 |
| Toledo | 30,000 | 73,500 | 103,000 | 10,300 | 41,200 |
| Indianapolis | 25,000 | 72,000 | 100,000 | 10,000 | 40,000 |
| Novi | 25,000 | 70,000 | 75,000 | 7,500 | 30,000 |
| Dayton | 20,000 | 70,000 | 120,000 | 12,000 | 48,000 |
| Fort Wayne | 20,000 | 66,500 | 95,000 | 9,500 | 38,000 |
| Columbus | 20,000 | 56,000 | 115,000 | 11,500 | 46,000 |
| Total | $ 205,000 | $ 558,500 | $ 803,000 | $ 80,300 | $ 321,200 |

Statement Date        Jun-08

FIGURE 8. 3

# LESSON 1: Entering Text and Numbers in a Worksheet

To understand how to use Excel, you first need to have a basic understanding of how Excel is structured. As explained in previous projects, an Excel file is a workbook that consists of several worksheets identified by tabs at the bottom of the window. Each worksheet is divided into rows and columns; their intersections form cells

You must select a cell before you can enter text, numbers, or formulas. If a cell is selected it is the active cell, and displays a dark border around its perimeter. Selecting cells is one of the most commonly used procedures in Excel and there are several ways to do this. Text is entered into cells to provide labels and other information for users of the worksheet. Numbers are used in calculations and formulas. Both are necessary and you need to know how to place them on the worksheet to maximize the usefulness of the data.

In this lesson, you learn to navigate between worksheets in a workbook and enter text and numbers to make a functional worksheet.

All of these exercises can be completed with Microsoft Office 2007. Instructions throughout the lessons are based on the Windows XP, running Microsoft Office 2007. Your screen may differ slightly from the figures shown, even if you are running Office 2007.

## To Use Worksheets in a Workbook

1. **Start Excel 2007. Take a moment to identify the items shown in Figure 8.4 in your window.** A blank workbook opens that includes three blank worksheets. The column headings are letters and the row headings are numbers. An individual cell is identified by the combination of the column letter and row number, known as the cell address. The bar at the top of the worksheet is the *formula bar*; the contents of the active cell display here, as well as in the cell.

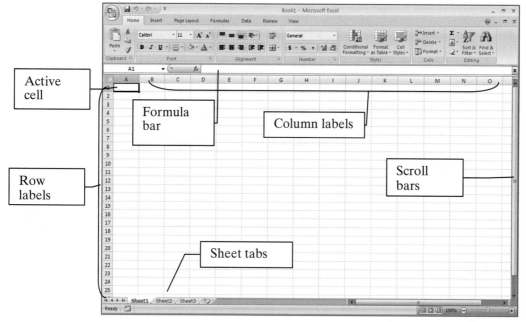

FIGURE 8. 4

2. **At the bottom of the window click the Sheet2 tab.** The second empty worksheet is displayed. Several related worksheets may be saved together in a single workbook. Additional worksheets may be added. For example, you could track annual expenses in a workbook that had a worksheet for each month of the year.

3. **Click the Sheet1 tab.** The first empty worksheet is displayed.

4. **Double-click the Sheet1 tab to select it, type:** `May Sales` **and then press** [Enter ↵]. The name on the tab is changed from Sheet1 to *May Sales* as shown in Figure 8.5.

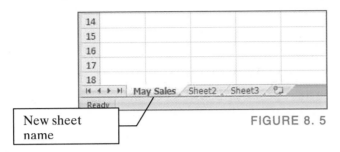

New sheet name

FIGURE 8.5

5. **Click the Sheet 2 tab, and then double-click it to select the sheet name, type:** `AutoFormat` **and then press** [Enter ↵]

6. **Right-click the Sheet3 tab, and from the displayed shortcut menu click Rename. Type:** `Sorted` **and then press** [Enter ↵]. The three worksheets are named *May Sales*, *AutoFormat*, and *Sorted*.

7. **Save the workbook in your work folder. Name it** `Spring Sales` **and leave the file open to continue to the next lesson.**

To enter data in a cell it must first be selected. You select a cell by clicking it, or by using the arrow keys, Tab key, or Enter key to navigate to a cell. You can also drag to select a *cell range*—a group of contiguous cells. Cells are identified by an address which consists of the column letter and row number. For example, if you are told to select cell B3, you could do so by clicking the cell where the second column and the third row intersect. To enter a row or column of numbers or text, you usually start by clicking on the first cell in the upper left corner of the worksheet to select it. You then type the number or text. If you want to enter a row of numbers or text, you press [Tab] to move the selection to the right. If you want to enter a column of numbers or text, you press [Enter ↵] to move the selection downward.

Before you start to enter words and numbers into a worksheet, it is a good idea to plan for the future. It is easier to copy formulas, chart data, and transfer tables of data into Word or Microsoft Office Access if the data and its labels are organized correctly. If you plan to gather the same data each week, month, or quarter, consider using a separate, identical worksheet for each time period. Place labels in cells at the top of a column or at the left of a row of data. Do not use empty cells or cells with dashes to separate sections of a table. Visual cues such as these should be signaled with borders or shading. Summaries are most useful if they are presented on their own sheet the same way that year-end summaries of quarterly data are treated.

A cell may contain text or numbers. If a cell has a mix of text and numbers, all data in that cell is treated as text and the number is not available for use in calculations. If only numbers have been entered into the cells, you can manipulate the numbers, perform calculations, and use the numbers to visually portray a trend by creating a chart.

If you wish to enter text as a title, leave a blank row between the title and the first row of the table. This will prevent confusion later when some of the automated features try to determine which row of the table contains the column labels.

In this project, you will create a table that shows the *May sales* figures for the Armstrong Company, which has a chain of stores that sells saunas, spas, and pools in several cities throughout the Midwest.

## To Enter a Table of Data into a Worksheet

1. Click the *May Sales* sheet tab in the *Spring Sales* workbook.

2. Click cell A1 and then type: `Sales Figures for the Month of May.` This text will serve as a title for the worksheet.

3. Press [Enter↵] three times to move the selection to cell A4. Type: `Columbus` and press [Enter↵]. The first row label is entered into cell A4 and cell A5 becomes the active cell. Do not be concerned if the text overlaps the cell to the right. You will adjust the column widths in the next lesson.

4. Use this method to enter the following city names: `Dayton, Fort Wayne, Indianapolis, Novi, Toledo, Ypsilanti`, and `Total` into cells A5, A6, A7, A8, A9, A10, and A11. The city names are entered in the first column of the worksheet where they are row labels as shown in Figure 8.6.

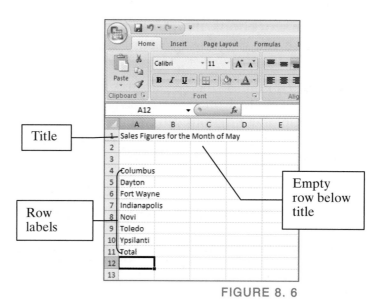

FIGURE 8. 6

## If you have problems...

If you make a typing mistake, click the cell to select it and type the name again. Press [Enter↵] or click another cell to finish. What you type will replace the incorrect contents.

5. Click cell B3 to select it and then type: `Saunas.` When you enter data in a cell it displays in the cell and in the formula bar at the top of the worksheet.

6. Press Tab to move to the next cell to the right and then type: Spas. The next column label is entered in cell C3.

7. **Repeat this process to enter** Pools **and** Accessories **in cells D3 and E3. If necessary, click cell E3 to make it the active cell.** The column labels are entered for the table as shown in Figure 8.7. Notice that *Accessories* displays both in cell E3 and in the formula bar. Do not be concerned if the cells are not wide enough to display the entire contents of the cell.

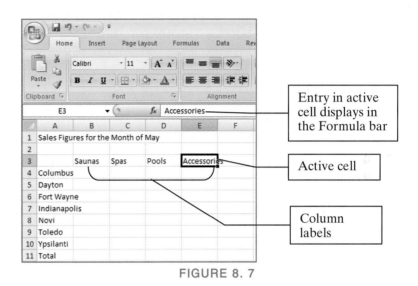

FIGURE 8. 7

8. **Click B4, type** 20000 **and then press** Tab **to move to cell C4.**

9. **Enter the remaining data, as follows. Use the** Tab **key to move across the row and at the end of the row press** Enter↵. When you use the Tab key to move across and press Enter↵ at the end of the row, the active cell moves to the beginning of the next row to cell B5. Now you are ready to continue entering data in row 5 for the Dayton store. Notice that a cell is left empty intentionally in the *Spas* column. Compare your screen to Figure 8.8.

|  | Saunas | Spas | Pools | Accessories |
|---|---|---|---|---|
| Columbus | 20000 | 56000 | 115000 | 46000 |
| Dayton | 20000 | 70000 | 120000 | 48000 |
| Fort Wayne | 20000 | 66500 | 95000 | 38000 |
| Indianapolis | 25000 | 70000 | 100000 | 40000 |
| Novi | 25000 | 73500 | 75000 | 30000 |
| Toledo | 30000 | 77000 | 103000 | 41200 |
| Ypsilanti | 35000 |  | 110000 | 44000 |

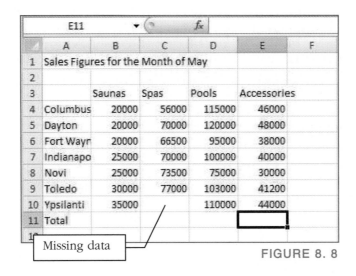

| | A | B | C | D | E | F |
|---|---|---|---|---|---|---|
| 1 | Sales Figures for the Month of May | | | | | |
| 2 | | | | | | |
| 3 | | Saunas | Spas | Pools | Accessories | |
| 4 | Columbus | 20000 | 56000 | 115000 | 46000 | |
| 5 | Dayton | 20000 | 70000 | 120000 | 48000 | |
| 6 | Fort Wayr | 20000 | 66500 | 95000 | 38000 | |
| 7 | Indianapo | 25000 | 70000 | 100000 | 40000 | |
| 8 | Novi | 25000 | 73500 | 75000 | 30000 | |
| 9 | Toledo | 30000 | 77000 | 103000 | 41200 | |
| 10 | Ypsilanti | 35000 | | 110000 | 44000 | |
| 11 | Total | | | | | |

Missing data

FIGURE 8. 8

10. Save the *Spring Sales* workbook and leave the file open for use in the next lesson.

## TO EXTEND YOUR KNOWLEDGE...

### CORRECTING DATA ENTRY ERRORS

If you make a mistake entering data you can edit the data directly in the cell or in the formula bar that displays at the top of the worksheet. To edit contents in the cell, double-click the cell, or click the cell and then press F2 . This places the insertion point in the cell. Use the left and right arrow keys to move the insertion point within the cell, or the Delete and ←Bksp keys to remove data. If you click the cell and type, the contents will be replaced by the new data you type. To edit contents in the formula bar, click the cell and then click in the formula bar at the desired location to edit the contents.

# LESSON 2: Editing Tables

It is possible to make mistakes when entering data. Also, information may change and need to be adjusted. The power of using an electronic spreadsheet is in the ability to easily change information and have formulas recalculate automatically.

In this lesson, you modify the title, insert missing data, add a row, and add a column into the table in the *May Sales* sheet of the *Spring Sales* workbook. You also use a *function*—a predefined formula—that sums the numbers in a column.

1. **With the *Spring Sales* workbook open and the *May Sales* sheet selected, click on cell C7 to select it.** This column is missing one of its numbers. To simulate a common error, the sales figure for spas in Indianapolis was not included, as if you skipped it when typing in this column of data.

2. **Click the Home tab, and in the Cells group click the Insert arrow and then click Insert Cells.** The Insert dialog box displays. In this case you want to move the values down one cell each to make room for the missing data but you do not want to affect the other columns (see Figure 8.9).

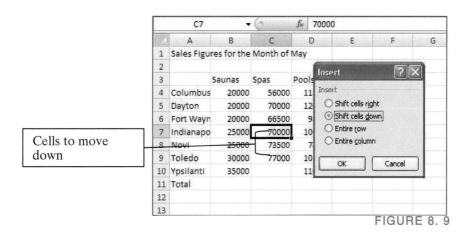

FIGURE 8. 9

3. **Confirm that *Shift cells down* is selected and click OK.**

4. **Type: 72000 and then press** [Enter ↵]. Sales figures for the Southfield store were left out. To keep the listing of cities in alphabetical order, it should appear in row 9.

5. **Click row heading 9 to select the entire ninth row.** Clicking a row or column heading will select the entire row or column as shown in Figure 8.10.

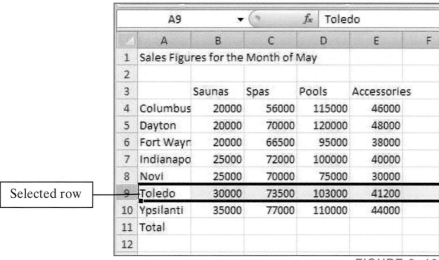

FIGURE 8. 10

6. **On the Home tab, in the Cells group click the Insert arrow and then click Insert Sheet Rows** A new row is inserted and the rest of the rows are moved downward

7. **Click A9. Using the method you just practiced, enter the following information in the newly inserted row:**

   `Southfield 30000 73500 85000 34000`

   The sales figures for the store in Southfield are added. Another category of sales may be added by inserting a column.

8. **Click column heading E. On the Home tab, in the Cells group, click the Insert arrow and then click Insert Sheet Columns.** A new column is inserted to the left of the selected column.

9. **Click E3. Using the method you just practiced, enter the following information in column E of the table:**

   `Chemicals`
   
   `11500`
   
   `12000`
   
   `9500`
   
   `10000`
   
   `7500`
   
   `8500`
   
   `10300`
   
   `11000`

   The sales figures for chemicals at all the stores are added as shown in Figure 8.11.

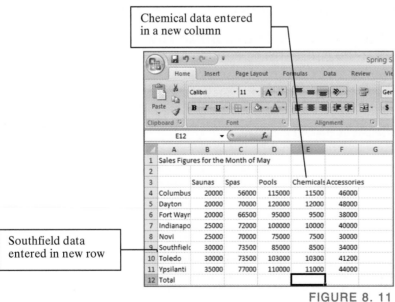

Chemical data entered in a new column

Southfield data entered in new row

FIGURE 8. 11

10. **Save the *Spring Sales* workbook and leave the file open to continue to the next lesson.**

### INSERTING ROWS AND COLUMNS

In addition to using the menu commands to insert a row or a column, you can also right-click a cell and choose Insert from the shortcut menu. In the Insert dialog box, choose the Entire row option, to insert a row above the location of the active cell, or choose the Entire column option to insert a new column to the left of the current cell.

The purpose of most tables is to make calculations based on the data you enter. The simplest and most commonly used calculation is the sum calculation. It is used so often, in fact, that Excel includes a *Sum* button on the Home tab and on the Formulas tab. When you select a cell and then click the Sum button, the program checks the cells nearby to see which ones contain numbers and outlines the cells that are the most likely choice. To accept this choice, press Enter↵ (or click the Sum button again). To choose a different range of cells, drag the mouse pointer across the cells to select them and then press Enter↵. You will learn more about other built-in functions in the next project. The Sum function is especially easy to use and it is part of almost every worksheet table.

#### To Sum Numbers in a Table

1. **With the *Spring Sales* workbook open and the *May Sales* sheet selected, click cell B12 to select it.** This cell will contain the sum of the numbers in the *Saunas* column.

2. **On the Home tab in the Editing group, click the Sum button.** The SUM function is inserted in B12 and the numbers in the column above are enclosed with a moving dotted line as shown in Figure 8.12. The program has selected the correct set of numbers to sum.

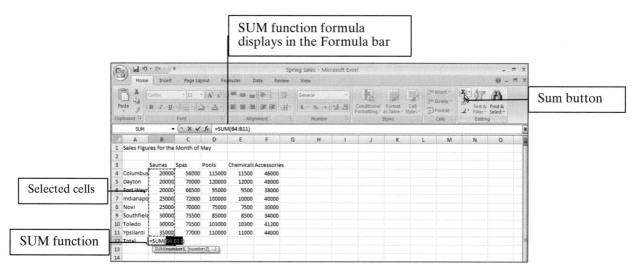

FIGURE 8. 12

3. **Press** [Enter ↵]. Pressing [Enter ↵] locked in the selection choice that was automatically made. The sauna sales figures are summed to provide a total of column B in row 12.

4. **Repeat the process you just practiced to sum the remaining columns.** Each of the columns has a calculated total as shown in Figure 8.13

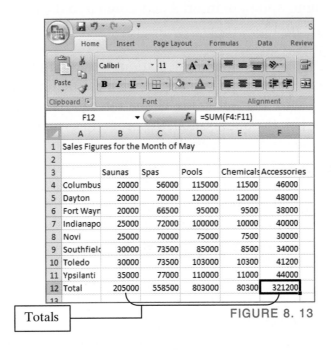

Totals

FIGURE 8. 13

5. **Save the** *Spring Sales* **workbook and leave the file open to continue to the next lesson.**

## LESSON 3: Formatting Numbers

A variety of formatting techniques can be used to improve the appearance of a worksheet. Formatting your worksheet also makes it easier to read. This is especially important for worksheets that are used by others.

To apply a format to a cell, it must first be selected. It is usually much faster to select a group of cells that will have the same format and apply the format to the selected cells at the same time. To select a group of cells that form a continuous block, you can use the mouse to drag the group of cells, or you can select the first cell at one corner of the group, hold down the [⇧ Shift] key and use the arrow keys on the keyboard to select the remaining cells in the group.

Excel has a variety of formats that may be used to display different types of numbers such as currency, percentage, and comma separated values.

In this lesson, you work with the current worksheet and learn how to improve its appearance, make the numbers easier to read, and give it a professional look.

## To Format Numbers in a Table

1. **With the *Spring Sales* workbook open to the *May Sales* sheet, select cell B4. Hold down [⬆ Shift] and use the [↓] and [→] arrow keys to expand the selection to F11.** The range of cells from B4 in the upper-left corner to F11 in the lower-right corner is selected. The selected range displays with a shaded background, and a dark border displays around the group of cells. The first cell in the range—B4—displays with a white background.

2. **On the Home tab in the Cells group, click the Format button. At the end of the displayed menu, click Format Cells.** The Format Cells dialog box opens. The Format Cells dialog box is used to apply formats to numbers or text, change font characteristics or alignment options, or add a border or background color to cells.

3. **Click the Number tab, if necessary. In the Category box, select Number.**

4. **Click the check box next to *Use 1000 Separator (,)*. Change the *Decimal places* box to 0.** The selected cells will be formatted as simple numbers with no decimal places and commas to separate the larger numbers into groups of three. See Figure 8.14.

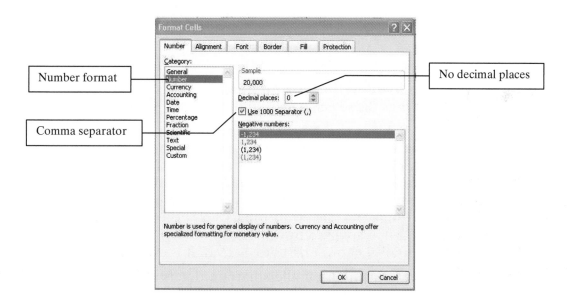

FIGURE 8. 14

5. **Click OK.** The selected cells display numbers with commas that separate the thousands.

6. **Drag across the bottom row of cells from B12 through F12.** The cells in the *Total* row are selected. This is another way to select a range of cells.

7. **On the Home tab in the Number group, click Number Format arrow, and point to Currency as shown in Figure 8.15.** This format applies a currency symbol to the left of the numbers and displays two decimals.

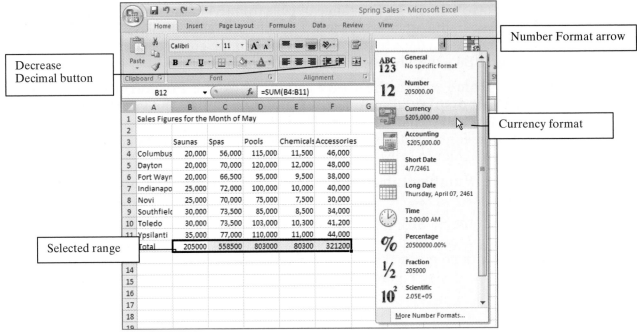

FIGURE 8. 15

8. **From the displayed gallery of number formats click Currency.** Currency displays as the selected style in the Number Format box.

9. **On the Home tab, in the Number group, click the Decrease Decimal button two times to remove both of the numbers displayed to the right of the decimal.** The selected cells are formatted with dollar signs, commas to separate the larger numbers into groups of three, and no decimals.

10. **Save the *Spring Sales* workbook and leave the file open to continue to the next lesson.**

Dates and times are sequential numbersthat are determined from the artificial date 1/0/1900, which is given the value of zero. Dates may be displayed in traditional formats, but they may also be used in calculations. When you display dates as a series of numbers separated by dashes or slashes, you assume the reader knows which number is the month, day, and year. In the United States, it is common practice to use the month/day/year sequence. In many other countries, the day/month/year format is used, and some computer software groups are promoting use of year/month/day. You can avoid this confusion by using a format that displays the name of the month instead of a number

1. With the *Spring Sales* workbook open to the *May Sales* sheet, click cell B14. Type: June  1 and then press ⏎Enter . Click cell B14 again. The text is recognized as a date and displays with the default date format.

2. On the Home tab, in the Number group, click Dialog Box Launcher to open the Format Cells dialog box.

3. On the Number tab, in the Category box, click Date.

4. **Scroll down the Type box and click Mar-01.** The selected cell will display the date by showing the name of the month followed by the 2-digit value for the year as shown in Figure 8.16. The year that displays on your screen may be different from the one in the figure.

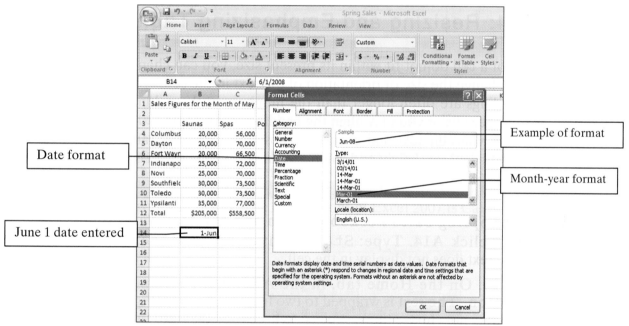

FIGURE 8. 16

5. Click OK.

6. Save your changes to the *Spring Sales* workbook and leave the file open to continue to the next lesson.

4. **Release the mouse button.** The text wraps between the two words, however the first column is still not wide enough to display all of the city names.

5. **Click cell A7, and on the Home tab, in the Cells group, click the Format button. From the displayed menu click AutoFit Column Width to widen column A so that Indianapolis is fully displayed.**

6. **Double-click cell A1.** The insertion point is placed in the text within the cell. In this mode, you can edit the text, numbers, or formulas in a cell.

7. **Edit the text in cell A1 to shorten the title to *Sales in May*. Press** `Enter ⏎`. The title is shortened and fits into column A. However, titles are often centered over tables.

8. **Drag across cells A1 through F1.** The cells above the table are selected.

9. **On the Home tab, in the Alignment group, click the Merge and Center button.** The cells are merged into one long cell and the text is centered within the new cell as shown in Figure 8.19.

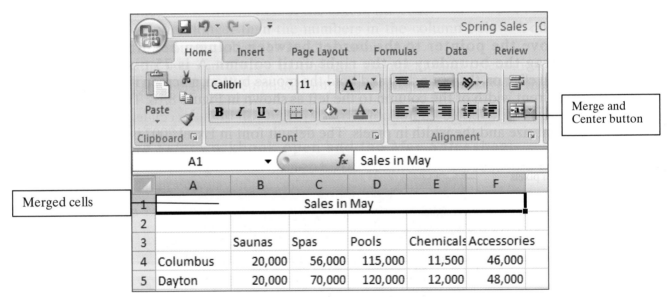

FIGURE 8. 19

10. **Select cells B3 through F3. On the Home in the Alignment group click the Dialog Box Launcher.**

11. **In the Orientation section, drag the red box up to the 45-degree position in the as shown in Figure 8.20.** The text in the selected cells will be oriented at an angle to the columns below.

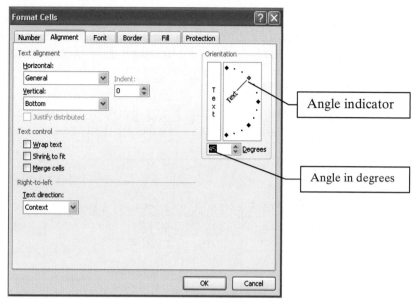

Angle indicator

Angle in degrees

FIGURE 8. 20

12. **Click OK.** The cell height is increased, and the column labels are oriented at a 45-degree angle to the columns below.

13. **Save your changes to the *Spring Sales* workbook and leave the file open to continue with the next portion of this lesson.**

## TO EXTEND YOUR KNOWLEDGE...

### ADJUSTING ROW HEIGHT

You can adjust column width to automatically fit to the widest entry in a column by double-clicking the right border of the column heading. To adjust row height, you can drag the lower border of a row heading to increase the height of a row, or in the Cells group, you can click Format button and then click AutoFit Row Height. To set a row to a specific height, in the Cells group, click Format and then click Row Height and type the desired height in the Row Height dialog box.

Cell borders and shading identify special sections of the table and make the table more visually interesting.

1. **With the *Spring Sales* workbook open and the *May Sales* sheet selected, select cells B3 through F3, if necessary.** Labels that are oriented at an angle may overhang adjacent cells. It helps to associate the label with a particular cell if the cells have borders.

2. **On the Home tab in the Font group, click the Borders button arrow.** The Borders gallery displays border options as shown in Figure 8.21.

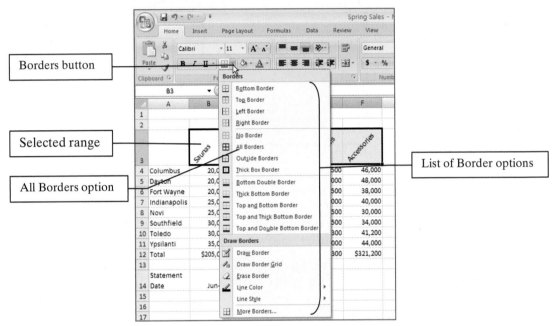

FIGURE 8. 21

3. **Click the All Borders option.** Borders are added to all sides of the selected cells.

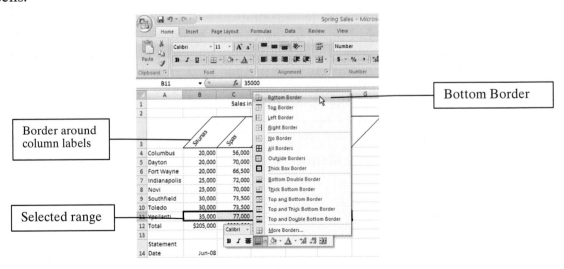

FIGURE 8. 22

4. **Select cells B11 through F11 and right-click the selected cells. On the displayed Mini toolbar, click the Border button arrow and then point to the Bottom Borders option.** The Mini toolbar is another way to access the Border options. Totals at the bottom of a table may be distinguished from other numbers in the table by using a border that places a line between the totals and the rest of the table (see Figure 8.22).

5. **Click the Bottom Border option. Click another cell in the table so you can see the border.** A line is placed along the bottom border of the selected cells, which is the end of the numbers that were summed in row 12. Shading is another technique used to identify special elements of the table.

6. **Click cell A1 to select the title in the merged cells. On the Home tab, in the Font group, click the Fill Color arrow. Point to the ninth column the third color.** The Fill Color palette displays color choices as shown in Figure 8.23. When you point to a color on the Fill Color menu, a ScreenTip displays the name of the color.

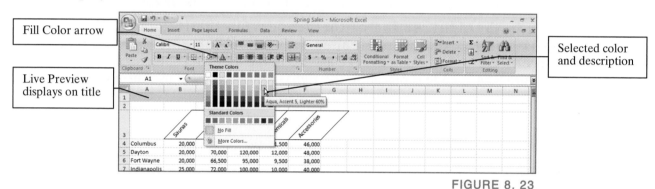

FIGURE 8. 23

7. **Click the Aqua, Accent 5 Lighter 60% color—the ninth color in the third row.** The background color in the selected cells is changed.

8. **With cell A1 still selected, in the Font group, click Bold button, and increase the font size to 14.** The text of the title is bold and enlarged to 14-point size.

9. **Save your changes to the *Spring Sales* workbook and leave the file open to continue to the next lesson.**

---

## TO EXTEND YOUR KNOWLEDGE...

### USING THE FORMAT CELLS DIALOG BOX
You have practiced formatting areas of a worksheet using the Home tab and the Mini toolbar. You can also use the Format Cells dialog box to change font, font size, apply emphasis, change font color, apply borders, or add shading to cells.

---

## LESSON 5: Printing a Worksheet

Printing worksheets is similar to printing other documents but there are some differences. The header and footer do not normally appear on the screen but you can view them using print preview. You can choose to print a single worksheet, which is the default choice, or you can print all the worksheets in a workbook. You can also choose to center the table horizontally or vertically on the sheet.

In this lesson, you add your name, class, and date to the header and print the *May Sales* worksheet.

## To Add Your Name, Class, and Date to the Header

1. **With the *Spring Sales* workbook open and the *May Sales* sheet selected, click the Insert tab, and in the Text group click Header & Footer.** The Header & Footer Tools Design tab displays and the worksheet changes to the Page Layout view.

2. **Click in the left side of the Header area and type your name in the left section of the header.**

3. **Press** Tab **and type the name of your class in the center section of the header.** This step is optional at the preference of the instructor.

4. **Click in the right section of the header. On the Header & Footer Tools Design tab, in the Header & Footer Elements group, click Current Date.** Your name and class are in the left and center sections. As shown in Figure 8.24, a code is placed in the right section that will use the computer's system clock to print the current date.

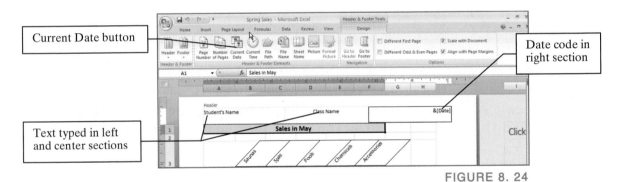

FIGURE 8. 24

5. **Click anywhere in the spreadsheet.** The Header & Footer Tools Design tab is no longer displayed. The changes in the Header are displayed.

6. **Click the Page Layout tab, and in the Page Setup group, click Margins. From the bottom of the menu click Custom Margins.** Here you can change the margins or position the table as desired on the page.

7. **Click the check box next to Horizontally in the *Center on page* section.**

8. **Click Print Preview. Click Zoom, if necessary, to show the full width of the page.** A preview of the worksheet with a header is displayed as shown in Figure 8.25. If you are using a printer that does not have color printing capabilities, the shading behind the title is gray.

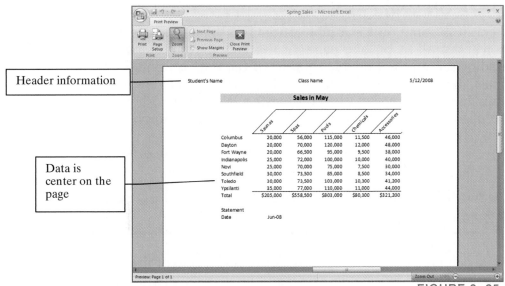

Header information

Data is center on the page

FIGURE 8. 25

9. **On the Print Preview tab, in the Print group, click Print. In the Print dialog box, click OK.** The worksheet is printed and the worksheet displays in Page Layout view.

10. **On the status bar click the Normal button.** A dotted line is displayed on the screen, as shown in Figure 8.26. This is where a page break would occur if the worksheet included more columns.

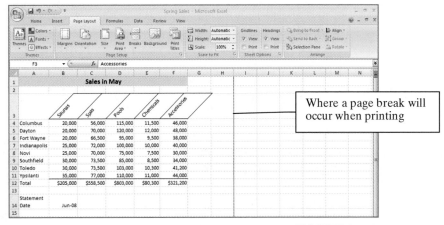

Where a page break will occur when printing

FIGURE 8. 26

11. **Close Print Preview. Save your changes to the *Spring Sales* workbook and leave the file open to continue to the next lesson.**

### FITTING DATA ON ONE PAGE

In a worksheet, it is common for a table of data to extend across many columns and rows, which will not all fit on one page. In the Page Setup dialog box, the Page tab includes a scaling section that enables you to fit the data on one or more pages. You can also adjust the page breaks using the Page Break Preview window. The Page Break Preview button is on the View tab, in the Workbook Views group. Here you can drag the page break lines to a location that is more suitable to the data that is being printed.

## LESSON 6: Copying Worksheets and Using Cell Styles (AutoFormat)

Formatting a table can take time. It is often faster to apply one of the standard cell styles and modify it if necessary. In this lesson, you copy the worksheet you created and paste it into another sheet in the workbook where you apply cell styles. The cell styles used provide a selection of preformatted number formats, borders, and shading.

### To Copy a Worksheet and Apply Cell Styles

1. **With the *Spring Sales* workbook open and the *May Sales* sheet selected, click the Select All button in the upper-left corner of the worksheet where the column and row headers intersect.** The entire worksheet is selected as shown in Figure 8.27.

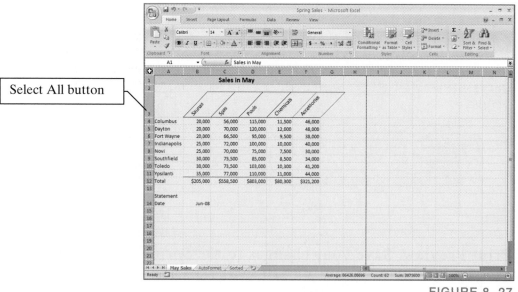

FIGURE 8. 27

**On the Home tab, in the Clipboard group click Copy.** To copy the table of data, you could also select just the range that contains the data—cells A1 through F14—and then click the Copy button.

2. **Click the _AutoFormat_ sheet tab at the bottom of the worksheet.** The blank _AutoFormat_ worksheet is displayed.

3. **Be sure cell A1 is the active cell, and then on the Home tab, in the Clipboard group click Paste.** The contents of the _May Sales_ worksheet, including all formatting, are pasted into the _AutoFormat_ worksheet.

4. **With all of the cells still selected, on the Home tab, in the Editing group, click the Clear button, and then click Clear Formats. Click any cell in the worksheet to clear the selection.** The formatting is removed from the numbers and text. Notice the date is shown as a number as shown in Figure 8.28. Dates are stored as the number of days since January 1, 1900, which in this case is over 39,000 days.

|  | A | B | C | D | E | F | G |
|---|---|---|---|---|---|---|---|
| 1 | Sales in May |  |  |  |  |  |  |
| 2 |  |  |  |  |  |  |  |
| 3 |  | Saunas | Spas | Pools | Chemicals | Accessories |  |
| 4 | Columbus | 20000 | 56000 | 115000 | 11500 | 46000 |  |
| 5 | Dayton | 20000 | 70000 | 120000 | 12000 | 48000 |  |
| 6 | Fort Wayne | 20000 | 66500 | 95000 | 9500 | 38000 |  |
| 7 | Indianapolis | 25000 | 72000 | 100000 | 10000 | 40000 |  |
| 8 | Novi | 25000 | 70000 | 75000 | 7500 | 30000 |  |
| 9 | Southfield | 30000 | 73500 | 85000 | 8500 | 34000 |  |
| 10 | Toledo | 30000 | 73500 | 103000 | 10300 | 41200 |  |
| 11 | Ypsilanti | 35000 | 77000 | 110000 | 11000 | 44000 |  |
| 12 | Total | 205000 | 558500 | 803000 | 80300 | 321200 |  |
| 13 |  |  |  |  |  |  |  |
| 14 | Statement Da | 39600 |  |  |  |  |  |
| 15 |  |  |  |  |  |  |  |

Date without formatting

FIGURE 8. 28

5. **Select cells A3 to F3 On the Home tab, in the Styles group, click Cells Styles to display the Cells Style gallery as shown in Figure 8.29.** Before you apply a format, the range of cells in the table must be selected.. As you move your pointer across the cell styles a Live Preview of the style displays on the selected cells.

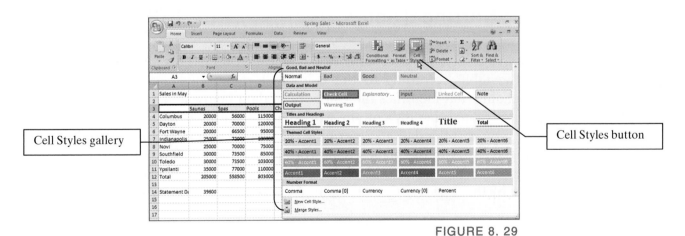

Cell Styles gallery

Cell Styles button

FIGURE 8. 29

6. Under Titles and Headings click **Heading 3**, and then on the Home tab, in the Alignment group, click the **Align Text Right** button. The Heading 3 format is applied to the column headings and the column titles are aligned on the right side of the cell.

7. Select cells **B4** through **F4**, hold down Ctrl and select cells **B12** through **F12** to select these two non-adjacent ranges. On the Home tab, in the Styles group, click the **Cell Styles** button and then under Number Format click **Currency [0]**. This adds the currency symbol to the left side of the selected cells , and displays the number as a whole number with nothing to the right of the decimal point.

8. Select the range from cell **B5** through **F11** and in the Styles group, click the **Cell Styles** button, and then apply the **Comma [0]** style. which displays the numbers as whole numbers with nothing to the right of the decimal point.

9. Select cells **A12** through **F12**, display the Cells Styles gallery and then under Titles and Headings, click the **Totals** style. A single line is added at the end of the entered numbers and a double line is added under the sums.

10. Click the column **A** heading. On the Home tab, in the Cells group click **Format** and then click **AutoFit Column Width**. The first column is automatically widened to fit the longest text in the column; in this case, the text in A14—*Statement Date*.

11. Right-click **B14** and then click **Format Cells** from the shortcut menu. Click the **Number** tab, under Category click **Date** and then choose the same date format you used in the *May Sales* sheet—Mar-01. Click **OK**. Compare your results with Figure 8.30 (see next page).

12. Click the Insert tab, and in the Text group click **Header & Footer**. In the left side of the Header area type your name, in the center section type the name of your class. In the right section of the header, on the Header & Footer Tools Design tab, in the Header & Footer Elements group, click **Current Date**.

13. Save your changes to the *Spring Sales* workbook and leave the file open to continue to the next lesson.

## LESSON 7: Sorting Tables

Tables of data may be sorted in ascending or descending order. This feature works if you have designed the table according to the guidelines mentioned earlier. Each column should have a heading that identifies the category of data below it. The data to be sorted should be separated from other data on the worksheet by empty rows.

In this lesson, you sort the data to determine the winner of a sales contest. The winner of the contest is the city with the highest sales for Spas. If there is a tie, the store with the most Sauna sales wins. You insert a blank row above the totals row and sort the table in descending order by the Spas and Saunas columns to bring the winning store to the top of the table.

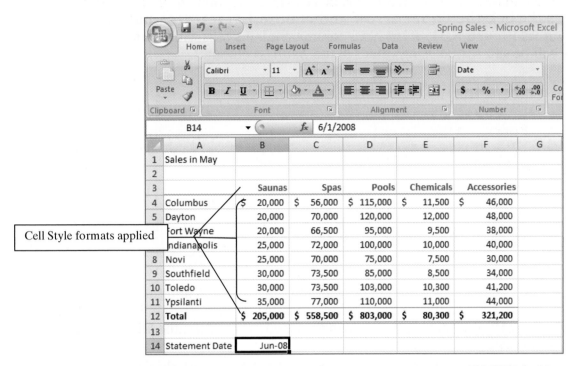

Cell Style formats applied

FIGURE 8. 30

## To Sort a Table on Two Criteria

1. **Select cell A1 and drag down to F14, right-click the selected data and then click the Copy from the shortcut menu. Click the *Sorted* sheet tab, right-click cell A1 and then click Paste from the shortcut menu.** The range of cells A1 through F14 is selected, copied, and pasted into the *Sorted* worksheet. The ### symbols display in some of the total cells because the columns are not wide enough to display the totals.

2. **Click the column A heading, and then drag to the right to select the columns through column F. On the Home tab, in the Cells group, click the Format button and then click AutoFit Column Width to widen all of the selected columns.**

3. **Insert a row above the Total row.** The title and the totals are separated from the rest of the table by empty rows. This prevents them from being included in the sorting process. Alternatively, select the range of cells to be used in the sort, and exclude the total row.

4. **Click in one of the cells in the table of data. Click the Data tab, and in the Sort & Filter group, click Sort to display the Sort dialog box.**

5. **To the right of the buttons, confirm that the *My data has headers* option is selected.** The labels in the top row of the table will be used as category labels for each column.

6. **Click the Sort by arrow and choose *Spas*. Click the Order arrow and choose Largest to Smallest to sort the data in descending order based on the values in the *Spas* column. Confirm that the *Sort On* is set to Values.**

7. **Click the Add Level button. Click the Then by arrow and choose** *Saunas.* **Click the Order arrow and choose Largest to Smallest as shown in Figure 8.31.** If the *Spas* column contains cells with equal values, those rows will be sub-sorted using values in the *Saunas* column.

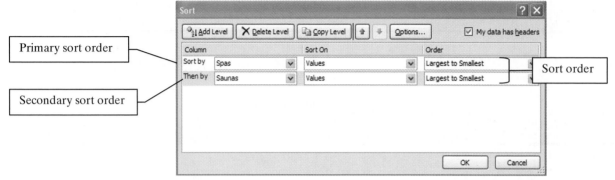

FIGURE 8. 31

8. **Click OK.** The table is sorted in descending order by *Spas* and then by *Saunas.* This brings the Ypsilanti store to the top of the list. It also lists the Novi store ahead of the Dayton store; even though they tied in spa sales, the Novi store had more sauna sales.

9. **Add your name, class, and the date to the header of this worksheet. Center the worksheet horizontally.**

10. **Print the worksheet (optional). Save the workbook. Close the workbook and close Excel.**

## SUMMARY

In this project, you entered data in a worksheet by entering a title, column and row labels, and numerical data. You learned how to insert a cell, column, and row to expand the data area so that you could enter additional data. You learned the importance of worksheet design and arrangement of data. You summed the columns of data using the Sum function.

You worked with formats to make the data more readable. The Merge and Center button was used to center the title over the data. The column labels were aligned at an angle so they fit better over the numbers. The comma style was applied to the data and the currency format was applied to the *Total* row. You also inserted a date and learned how to change the date format using the Format Cells dialog box.

The sheet names in the workbook were renamed and you copied the original data and pasted it into two other worksheets. On the AutoFormat sheet you removed the manual formats that had been applied to the data, and then applied several cell styles.

In the Sorted sheet, you inserted an empty row so that you could sort the data on two columns. The importance of proper worksheet design was emphasized, such as the use of column and row labels and, using empty rows or columns to separate the data from other text or data, which mark its boundaries so automated functions like sorting can be performed.

You can extend your learning by reviewing concepts and terms, and by practicing variations of skills presented in the lessons. Use the following table as a guide to the numbered questions and exercises in the end-of-project learning opportunities.

## KEY TERMS

| AutoSum | formula bar | spreadsheet |
|---|---|---|
| cell range | function | |

## CHECKING CONCEPTS AND TERMS

### SCREEN ID
Label each element of the screen shown in Figure 8.32.

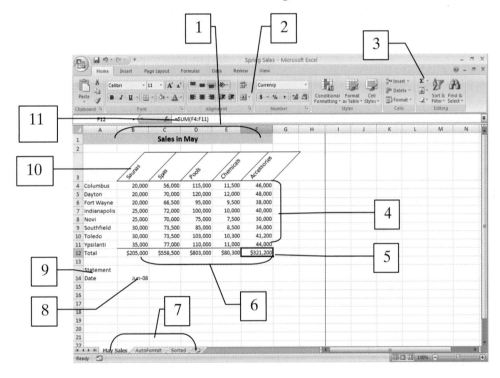

Figure 8.32

_____ A. Active cell

_____ B. Angle alignment

_____ C. AutoSum button

_____ D. Comma separated formatting

_____ E. Currency formatting

_____ F. Date format applied

_____ G. Merge and Center button

_____ H. Merged cells

_____ I. Sheet tabs

_____ J. Sum function formula

_____ K. Wrapped formatting

# MULTIPLE CHOICE

## Circle the letter of the correct answer for each of the following.

1. All of the following are methods of selecting a cell except _____. [L1]

    a. moving the selection to the desired cell with arrow keys on the keyboard
    b. right clicking on the cell and choosing Select from the shortcut menu
    c. left clicking on the cell
    d. pressing [Tab] if the selection is currently in the cell to the left

2. All of the following are false about entering text into a cell except _____. [L1]

    a. the text must be short enough to fit within the width of the cell, otherwise you will get an error message
    b. only uppercase letters are allowed in titles
    c. you must press [Enter ↵] when you are finished. It is the only way to leave the cell and record what you typed
    d. you can mix letters and numbers in the same cell. If you do, the entry is formatted as text

3. To insert a new row in a worksheet, you start by _____. [L2]

    a. clicking the row heading at the intended location of the new row
    b. clicking the column heading above the intended location of the new row
    c. dragging the column headings that span the existing table
    d. deleting the data in the row that currently occupies the intended location of the new row

4. The formatting style that places dollar signs at the left of the number and separates large numbers with commas is called _____. [L3]

    a. the euro
    b. comma separated
    c. currency
    d. numismatic

5. A date is really a number that may be formatted several different ways. The number used to identify a particular date in Excel is the number of days since _____. [L3]

    a. January 1, 2000
    b. January 1, 1900
    c. January 1, 1975
    d. July 4, 1776

6. If the text of a column label is too long for the current column width, you would not_____ to solve the problem. [L4]

    a. use a shorter label
    b. widen the column
    c. align the column headings at an angle
    d. add zeros to the numbers under the label to make them as wide as the label

7. If you use color to shade a range of cells and then print the table on a printer that only uses black ink or toner, the colored background is normally printed as _____. [L5]

    a. white if the text is black
    b. black if the text is a color
    c. a shade of gray
    d. white, regardless of the color of the text

8. If you clear the format from a cell that contains a date, the date will be displayed as _____ by default[L3]

    a. Month-Day, Year
    b. Year-Month-Day
    c. Day/Month/Year
    d. a simple number

9. If you sort a column in descending order, the _____ number is at the top. [L7]

    a. smallest
    b. largest
    c. longest
    d. shortest

10. If you sort a table by two different columns at the same time, what happens if the first column you sort by contains duplicate values? _____[L7]

a. The rows with duplicates have little green rectangles in the corners to indicate a problem.

b. A dialog box displays and you get to choose the order in which to display the rows with duplicate values.

c. An error message displays that suggests you try sorting on a different column.

d. The rows with duplicate values are sub-sorted based on the values in the second column chosen for sorting.

## DISCUSSION

1. When you enter a table of numbers into a worksheet, do you prefer to enter them by row or by column? Explain why you think one method is better than another for you. [L1]

2. Discuss the pros and cons of formatting a worksheet manually versus using the cell styles. Which do you prefer and why? Do you think that spending time formatting a table that will be shared with other people at work is worth the time it takes to do it manually? Do you think the cell style choices are adequate for your needs? [L6]

3. Do you use the numeric keypad to enter numbers in worksheets or other tables? Explain why you do or do not. [L1]

## SKILL DRILL

Skill Drill exercises reinforce project skills. Each skill reinforced is the same, or nearly the same, as a skill presented in the project. Detailed instructions are provided in a step-by-step format. All of these exercises can be completed using Microsoft Office XP or later versions. Instructions throughout the exercises are based on a Windows XP operating system, running Microsoft Office 2007.

In these exercises, you work with the utility expenses for a chain of stores that sell pools, spas, and saunas. To complete the Skill Drill exercises, open the Excel workbook *EX_0801* and save it as a 97-2003 compatible file named **Store Utilities**. Exercise 1 uses the SD#1 sheet. Exercises 2 and 3 use the SD#2 and 3 sheet and must be done together. Exercises 4 and 5 use the SD#4 and 5 sheet and must be done together. Be sure to save your changes and close the workbook if you need more than one work session to complete the desired exercises. Continue working on the *Store Utilities* workbook instead of starting over with the original file. Print copies of the worksheets if your instructor requires it.

### 1. Inserting Numbers, Editing Tables, and Printing a Worksheet

The stores in the Armstrong Pool, Spa, and Sauna Company report their monthly utility expenses to headquarters. You start with a worksheet that is partially filled-in and you add a piece of missing data, add a column for electricity expenses, and a row for the Southfield store.

1. With the *Store Utilities* workbook open click the **SD#1** sheet tab, if necessary. Click cell **C8**. The water bill for the Columbus store was skipped when the data was entered by another employee.

2. Click the **Home tab**, and in the **Cells group**, click **Insert**. Notice that the cells below shift downward.

3. Type **75** and press Enter↵. The water bill for the Columbus store is added. The electricity expenses were also omitted and a column needs to be added.

4. Click column heading D to select the column. On the **Home tab**, in the **Cells group** click **Insert**. A new column is added between the columns for Water and Phone.

5. Click cell **D3** and type: **Electric**. Press Enter↵. Type: **250** and press Enter↵. Use this procedure to enter the following column of numbers:

   225

   215

   185

   170

   285

   156

6. Click row heading 8. On the **Home tab**, in the **Cells group** click **Insert** to insert a new row at this location. The utility expenses for the Southfield store were also omitted.

7. Click cell **A8**. Type: **Southfield** and then press Tab. Use this procedure to enter a row of utility expenses for the store in Southfield (do not type the commas): **118, 55, 125**, and **110**.

8. Position your mouse pointer over the right border of column A and double-click to automatically adjust the column width to display all the data.

9. Click the **Insert tab** and in the **Text group**, click **Header & Footer**. Press ⇧ Shift + Tab to move to the left section. Type your name in the left section. Press Tab to move to the center section, type your class name in the Center section. Press Tab to the right section, and then in the **Header and Footer Elements group**, click **Current Date**.

10. Click cell **A1**. Click the **View tab**, and in the **Workbook Views group** click **Normal**. Click the **Page Layout tab**, and in the **Page Setup group**, click **Margins**, and then at the end of the menu click **Custom Margins**. On the Margins tab, under Center on page, click the **Horizontally** check box and then click **OK**. Print the page (optional).

11. Save the *Store Utilities* workbook, and leave it open to continue with the next exercise.


## 2. Using the Sum Function and Formatting Numbers

The SD#2 and 3 sheet in the *Store Utilities* workbook shows all the utility data, but also includes a row and column for totals and a place for the date. You may enter the sum function in each of the cells or do them all at once.

1. With the *Store Utilities* workbook open, click the **SD#2 and 3** sheet tab.

2. Select cells **B4** through **F12** to highlight the cells with the expenses plus the empty cells in the *City Total* column and *Utility Total* row.

3. Click the **Home tab**, and in the **Editing group** click the **Sum** button. Summation functions are added to the end of each row and at the bottom of each column. Cell F12, at the bottom right, is a grand total of all the selected cells.

4. Select cells **B12** through **F12**; right-click the selected cells and then click **Format_Cells** from the shortcut menu.

5. Click the **Number** tab, if necessary. Click **Currency** in the *Category* box. Change *Decimal places* to **0** and then click **OK**.

6. Repeat this procedure to format the numbers in column F as currency with 0 decimal places.

7. Click **B14** and type **06/13** and press [Enter ↵] to display the date.

8. Select **B14** again. On the **Home tab**, in the **Number group** click the **Dialog Box Launcher**. On the Number tab click **Date** in the Category box.

9. In the *Type* box, click **\*Wednesday, March 14, 2001**, which is an option that displays the written day of the week, month, and year. Click **OK**. This action widens column B excessively, which will be fixed in the next exercise.

10. Save the *Store Utilities* workbook, and leave it open if you plan to work on the next exercise.

## 3. Resizing and Emphasizing Table Elements and Formatting Numbers

To make the worksheet easier to read, formatting needs to be applied and column widths adjusted.

1. With the *Store Utilities* workbook open, click the **SD#2 and 3** sheet tab. Drag the boundary line between columns B and C to the left to make the column 64 pixels wide to match the width of the other columns. The column width is too narrow to display the long date in cell B14.

2. Select **B14** through **D14**. On the **Home tab**, in the **Alignment group** click the **Merge and Center** button.

3. Double-click **A1**. Edit this title to read: **Utility Expenses for May**.

4. Select the range **A1** through **F1** and then on the **Home tab**, in the **Alignment group** click the **Merge and Center** button.

5. Click the column A heading. On the **Home tab**, in the **Cells group** click **Format**, and then click **AutoFit Column Width**.

6. Select cells **B11** through **F11**. On the **Home tab**, in the **Font group**, click the **Borders button** and then click **Bottom Border**.

7. Click the title in row 1. In the **Font group**, click the **Fill Color arrow** and in the fifth column click **Blue, Accent 1, Lighter 80%**.

8. Click the **Insert tab**, and in the **Text group**, click **Header & Footer**.

9. Press ⌂Shift + Tab and type your name in the left section. Press Tab and type your class name in the center section. Tab to the right section and then click the **Current Date** button. Click a cell in the worksheet.

10. Click the **Page Layout tab**, and in the **Page Setup group**, click **Margins** and then click **Custom Margins**. Select Horizontally from the Center on the page area. Print the page (optional).

11. Save the *Store Utilities* workbook and leave the document open to continue with the next exercise.

## 4. Using Cell Styles

Another method for formatting the table is to use Cell Styles.

1. With the *Store Utilities* workbook open, click the **SD#4 and 5** sheet tab.

2. Select **B3** through **F3**. Click the **Home tab**, and in the **Styles group**, click **Cell Styles** and then under **Titles and Headings** click **Heading 2**. With the cells still selected, in the **Alignment Group** click the **Center** button.

3. Select cells **B12** through **F12**. Display the **Styles Cell** gallery and under **Number Format** click **Currency**. With the cells still selected, display the **Cell Styles gallery**, and under **Titles and Headings** click **Total**

4. Select cells **B4** through **F11**, display the **Cell Styles** gallery and click **Comma**. Double-click the column A border to adjust the width of the column

5. Save your changes and leave the *Store Utilities* workbook open to continue with the next exercise.

## 5. Sorting a Table

To finish the table, sort the table by *City Total*, from the highest to lowest.

1. With the *Store Utilities* workbook open, make sure the **SD#4 and 5** sheet tab is displayed.

2. Select cells **A3** through **F11**—everything except the title and the total row.

3. Click the **Data tab**, and in the **Sort & Filter group** click **Sort** to display the Sort dialog box.

4. Click the **Sort by** arrow and click **City Total**. Select the **Largest to Smallest** option next to *Sort by*.

5. If you were you add a sort field you would use the Add Level button. Confirm that **Header row** is selected and then click **OK**. The rows are sorted by *City Total*.

6. Select **B4** through **F4**. Click the **Home tab**, and in the **Styles group**, click the **Cell Styles** button. Under **Number Format** click **Currency**. This finishes the formatting of the data.

7. Click the **Insert** tab, and in the **Text** group click **Header & Footer**.

8. Type your name in the left section and your class name in the center section. Click in the right section and then click the **Current Date** button. Click in a cell in the worksheet.

9. Click the **Page Layout tab**, and in the **Page Setup group**, click **Margins** and then click **Custom Margins**. Click the **Horizontally** check box and click **OK**. Print the page (optional).

10. Save the *Store Utilities* workbook. Close the workbook and close Excel.

---

## CHALLENGE

Challenge exercises expand on or are somewhat related to skills presented in the lessons. Each exercise provides a brief narrative introduction, followed by instructions in a numbered-step format that are not as detailed as those in the Skill Drill section.

To complete the Challenge exercises, open the Excel workbook *EX_0802* and save it as a 97-2003 Compatible workbook named **Summer Sales**. Each Challenge exercise uses a different sheet in this workbook. Make sure to save your changes and close the workbook if you need more than one work session to complete the desired exercises. Continue working on the *Summer Sales* workbook instead of starting over with the original file. Print copies of the worksheets if your instructor requires it. Each exercise is independent of the others, so you may complete the exercises in any order.

### 1. Transposing Tables for Sorting

Tables may be sorted by columns but not by rows. If you need to sort a table by its row values, you can transpose the rows and columns and then sort it.

1. Open the *Summer Sales* workbook. Make sure the **CH#1** sheet tab is selected.

2. Select cells **A16** through **J24**, and then on the **Home tab**, in the **Clipboard group** click the **Copy** button.

3. Right-click cell **A3** and from the displayed shortcut menu click **Paste Special** to display the Paste Special dialog box.

4. Click the **Transpose** check box and then click **OK**. The columns and rows are transposed. Some of the numbers are too wide for the columns and pound signs display in those cells.

5. Press Esc to clear the selection marquee displayed around the copied text.

6. On the **Home tab**, click **Format**, and **AutoFit Column Width**. Left-align the row labels in cells A4 through A11. Adjust the width of column F so the total displays at the bottom of the original table.

7. Insert an empty row in row 12 and then sort the data at the top of the worksheet in descending order (largest to smallest) by column I.

8. On the **Page Layout tab**, in the **Page Setup group** click **Orientation** and then click **Landscape**. On the **Custom Margins** select **Horizontally**. On the **Header/Footer** tab, add your name, class, and the date to the footer. Print the worksheet (optional).

---

9. Save the ***Summer Sales*** workbook. Leave the workbook open if you plan to do another Challenge exercise.

### 2. Adding Patterns and Boarders Using the Format Cells Dialog Box

Most of the commonly used options for adding color to cells are available from the Fill Color button on the Home tab. Similarly, the Borders button provides options for adding borders to cells. However, the Format Cells dialog box provides a full set of options that gives you more control over the borders used in the table. Here you can also apply patterns to cells. This is useful when printing in black and white, because patterns are easier to distinguish from each other than colors which print in shades of gray.

1. Open the ***Summer Sales*** workbook. Click the **CH#2** sheet tab.

2. Select **A2** through **J2**. Right-click the selected cells and click **Format Cells**. Click the **Fill** tab.

3. Click the **Pattern Style** arrow and then choose the fifth pattern in the second row, *Diagonal Crosshatch*. Click **OK**.

4. Select **B11** through **I11**; right-click the selected cells and then click **Format Cells**.

5. Click the **Border** tab. Click the thick black horizontal line in the *Style* box that is in the second column, sixth from the top.

6. Click at the top of the example box in the *Border* section as shown in Figure 8.33. Click **OK**.

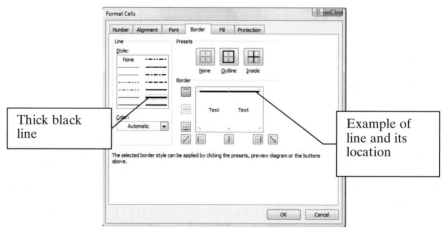

FIGURE 8. 33

7. Repeat this process to add a thick black line to the left side of cells **J4** through **J10**.

8. On the **Page Layout tab**, click **Orientation** and then click **Landscape**. Display the Page Setup dialog box and set the centering to **Horizontally**. In the **Header**, add your name, class, and the date to the header. Print the worksheet (optional).

9. Save the *Summer Sales* workbook. Leave the workbook open if you plan to do another Challenge exercise.

### 3. Copying Worksheet Data and Applying Formats

The sales figures in the *Summer Sales* workbook include all sales that are considered part of the summer season, which is longer than the traditional summer months of June, July, and August. The accounting department needs to report figures for the third quarter sales report as of the end of September. In this Challenge exercise, you will copy the necessary figures to a new worksheet, apply formatting, and then sum the figures.

1. Open the *Summer Sales* workbook. Click the **CH#1** sheet tab.

2. From original table of data at the bottom of this worksheet, select the data containing the names of the cities. This may be in row 17 (A17 through I17), or it may be in row 16, depending on whether or not you completed Challenge 1.

3. Hold down Ctrl and select the months and figures for July through September. Do not select the totals. Using Ctrl enables you to select two non-contiguous cell ranges. Make sure both ranges are the same length—the same number of cells.

4. Copy and paste this data to the **CH#3** sheet starting in cell **A14**.

5. Select the data you just copied to sheet CH#3, click **Copy**. Right-click cell **A3**, and from the shortcut menu click **Paste Special** and then click the **Transpose** check box. Click **OK**. The numbers are now in columns by months.

6. Select the table of data starting in cell **A14** and press Delete.

7. Type **Totals** in cell **E3** and **A12**. Use the **Sum** button to sum the columns and rows for the months and cities.

8. Left-align the row labels, and right-align the column labels. In cell **A1** type: 3$^{rd}$ **Quarter Sales**, and merge and center this title over the data. Format the title to Arial Black, 14-point font, and add a Light Green fill color.

9. Select the figures in column E and display the **Number Format** list and click **Accounting**. Click the **Decrease Decimal** button twice. Use the same buttons to format the figures in row 12. Adjust column widths, if necessary, to display all of the data.

10. Add a **Bottom Border** under the column labels, and apply the **Top and Double Bottom Border** to the column totals.

11. Center the worksheet horizontally. Add your name, class, and the date to the footer. Print the worksheet (optional).

12. Save the *Summer Sales* workbook. Close the file and then close Excel.

Discovery Zone exercises require advanced knowledge of topics presented in *Essentials* lessons, application of skills from multiple lessons, or self-directed learning of new skills. Each exercise is independent of the others, so you may complete the exercises in any order.

### 1. Using the Numeric Keypad for Data Entry

Some tasks require that you enter numbers in many cells. Most keyboards have a numeric keypad located on the right side of the keyboard to assist in this type of task. People who are not already proficient in using the numeric keypad may be hesitant to practice while entering important financial data on the job. If you are not familiar with the keypad, this is a good time to learn more about it by practicing with numbers that do not really matter.

Open Excel and select cell **A1**. Make sure the [N][U][M] [L][O][C][K] key in the upper-left corner of the numeric key pad is enabled. A green light may display somewhere on your keyboard to indicate that this key is active. It functions like a [Caps Lock] key, which ensures that the letters you type display as uppercase letters. The [Num Lock] ensures that the numeric keypad will display numbers. If you type a number and the active cell moves to another cell, click cell A1 again, and then press [Num Lock].

Place your right hand on the keypad. The number five usually has a raised dot or bar to help you identify it by feel. Use the keypad to enter the number 456 and then use the smallest finger on your right hand to press the [Enter ←] key that is part of the keypad. The selection will move to the cell below.

Look at one of the printouts from this project and practice entering columns of numbers with the keypad.

Click the **Office** button, click **Excel Options**, and then click **Advanced**. Under Editing options, under *After pressing Enter, move selection* section, change the Direction box from Down to **Right**. Click **OK**.

Use the numeric keypad and the [Enter ←] key on the keypad to enter a row of numbers.

Display the Excel Options dialog box and on the Advanced page, in the *After pressing Enter, move selection* section, change the Direction box from Right back to **Down**. Click **OK**.

You may use this method to rapidly enter data with the numeric keypad in columns or rows.

### 2. Confirming Data Entry with the Speak Cells on Enter Feature

Entering data while looking at a sheet of paper can be very slow if you stop to confirm each number by looking back and forth between the paper and the screen. If you try to speed up by not looking back and forth, you run the risk of making a mistake that you do not catch. This is a barrier to fast data entry and to learning new data entry techniques like using the numeric keypad.

One option to reduce input errors is to have the program say the number or text each time you enter a number or text in a cell. The speech feature must be installed on the computer you are using. If it is not already installed, you will be asked to supply the installation disk. This feature does not require a training period because you are not using the speech recognition feature. You need speakers or headphones to use do this exercise.

To the right of the Quick Access Toolbar, click **Customize Quick Action Toolbar arrow** and then click **More Commands**. In the Excel Options dialog box, in the *Choose commands from* box, click the arrow and then click **Commands Not in the Ribbon**. Scroll the displayed list and then click **Speak Cells** and click the **Add** button. Click **OK**. Click the Speak Cells button on the Quick Access toolbar and enter some numbers in a worksheet. It will speak the cells as you enter numbers. To remove the button from your toolbar, right-click the **Speak Cells** button and then click **Remove from Quick Access Toolbar**.

# UNIT 2: USING PRODUCTIVITY SOFTWARE

## Microsoft Office 2007 IC³

## Project 9: Using Formulas, Functions, and Charts

LESSON 1

Writing Formulas

        2-3.1.3.3       2-3.2.2       2-3.2.3

LESSON 2

Using Formulas

        2-3.2.6

LESSON 3

Using Functions to Analyze Data

        2-3.2.4       2-3.2.8
        2-3.2.5       2-3.2.9

LESSON 4

Charting Data

        2-3.2.10.1     2-3.2.10.3     2-3.2.10.5
        2-3.2.10.2     2-3.2.10.4     2-3.2.10.6

LESSON 5

Analyzing Data with Charts

        2-3.2.10.7     2-3.2.11

# PROJECT 9

# USING FORMULAS, FUNCTIONS AND CHARTS

IN THIS PROJECT, YOU LEARN HOW TO:

- Write Formulas
- Use Formulas
- Use Functions to Analyze Data
- Chart Data
- Analyze Data with Charts

# WHY WOULD I DO THIS?

**S**preadsheets were created to manage money. No matter what type of organization you manage or belong to, it probably has expenses and a budget that can be managed, reported, and analyzed faster and more accurately with a spreadsheet. If numbers are a major part of your job and you need to analyze them or communicate what they mean to others, a spreadsheet with built-in analysis and charting functions is a powerful tool that makes you more effective.

# VISUAL SUMMARY

In this project, you practice creating formulas in Microsoft Office Excel 2007, as shown in Figure 9.1. Then you apply them to a worksheet used to calculate total cost, retail value, and percent of contribution to total sales, as shown Figure 9.2. You will use the average, median, minimum, and maximum functions to analyze rainfall in Seattle and Buffalo to learn skills for analyzing data in a table. Finally, you chart the data to see how charting is used to analyze data and communicate your analysis more effectively to others, as shown in Figure 9.3.

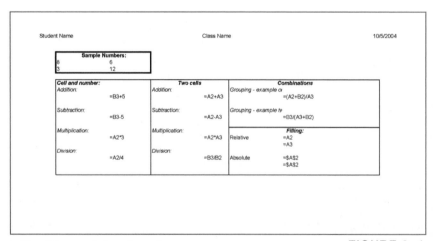

Practicing worksheet formulas        FIGURE 9. 1

### Patio Furniture Division

| Inventory | Quantity | Average Cost | Total Cost | Retail Price | Retail Value | Percent Mark Up | Percent Contribution |
|---|---|---|---|---|---|---|---|
| Patio Chairs | 5000 | $35.00 | $175,000 | $65.00 | $325,000 | 86% | 37% |
| Grills | 1500 | $38.50 | $57,750 | $89.00 | $133,500 | 131% | 15% |
| Patio Tables | 1000 | $48.00 | $48,000 | $120.00 | $120,000 | 150% | 14% |
| Table Umbrellas | 2000 | $22.70 | $45,400 | $45.00 | $90,000 | 98% | 10% |
| Lounge Chairs | 3450 | $5.00 | $17,250 | $22.00 | $75,900 | 340% | 9% |
| Side Tables | 2000 | $19.25 | $38,500 | $33.00 | $66,000 | 71% | 8% |
| Citronella Torches | 5000 | $2.50 | $12,500 | $12.50 | $62,500 | 400% | 7% |
| | | | $394,400 | | $872,900 | | 100% |

Formulas used to calculate Total Cost, Value, Percent Mark-Up and Percent Contribution columns

FIGURE 9. 2

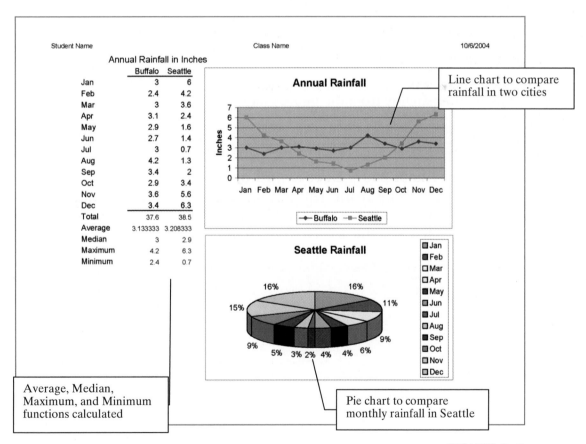

Line chart to compare rainfall in two cities

Average, Median, Maximum, and Minimum functions calculated

Pie chart to compare monthly rainfall in Seattle

FIGURE 9. 3

# LESSON 1: Writing Formulas

Worksheets have been used in paper form for years as a means of keeping track of financial data. The value of using an electronic worksheet program, such as Excel, is its ability to quickly make mathematical calculations. Before the era of computers, people were employed to calculate rows and columns of numbers for use in navigational charts or other types of computational charts. The job title for those who performed these calculations was Computer. In today's world, electronic computers keep track of financial data and perform mathematical computations. Computers are faster and more accurate than people for these kinds of tasks.

When you use Excel to perform a mathematical operation, it needs to be done in a way that is similar to ordinary math, but with a few special rules. For example, all formulas must begin with an equal sign (=), and you use cell references or names in the formulas instead of single letters. The order of mathematical operations is the same as in ordinary math, where parentheses are always done first and exponents are done before multiplication and division, which are done before addition and subtraction. All operations proceed from left to right across the equation unless parentheses dictate otherwise..

If you are challenged by math, you can still do this. Take your time and work through Lesson 1 carefully. It proceeds step-by-step and provides a good foundation for the other lessons. The program does the work of calculating—you do the work of designing the worksheet.

In this lesson, you practice applying the basic Excel formula rules. The sheet you produce serves as a convenient reference for later use.

All of these exercises can be completed with Microsoft Office 2007. Instructions throughout the lessons are based on Windows XP, running Microsoft Office 2007. Your screen may differ slightly from the figures shown, even if you are running Office 2007.

## To Use Formulas for Addition, Subtraction, Multiplication and Division

1. **Start Excel 2007. Locate and open** *EX_0901* **and save it as an Excel 97-2003 compatible file named** `Worksheet Formulas`. You will fill in this worksheet, as shown in Figure 9.4, with each type of formula. After it is completed, you can use it as a reference.

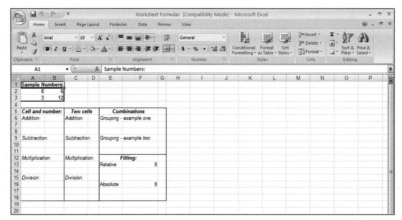

FIGURE 9. 4

2. **Select B7 and type: =B3+5 in the cell, as shown in Figure 9.5.** This formula adds the contents of cell B3 and the number 5. Before you go to the next step, look at the contents of cell B3 and determine what the answer should be if you add 5 to it.

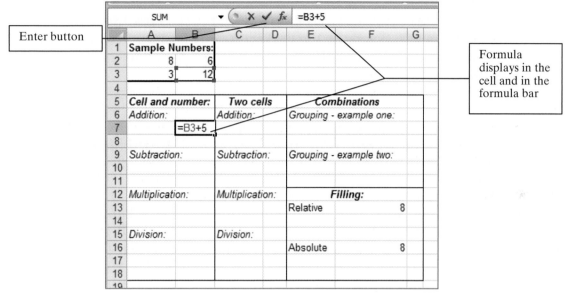

FIGURE 9. 5

3. **Click the check mark (Enter button) on the formula bar. Confirm that the result of the formula is 17 as you expected.** The calculation will occur as soon as you move the selection to another cell. The advantage of using the Enter button on the formula bar instead of the [Enter ↵] button on your keyboard is that the cell containing the formula remains active. You can see the results of the calculation in the cell and the formula itself in the formula bar.

## If you have problems...

If you do not see the formula bar, click the View tab, and in the Show/Hide group, click to place a check mark next to the Formula Bar.

4. **Select cell B10 and type: =B3–5. Determine what you think the answer should be before you proceed. In this case, you subtract 5 from the contents of cell B3.**

5. **Click Enter on the formula bar.** Confirm that the answer you expected is displayed. If you anticipated a different answer, take the time to figure out why. In the next step, you use the asterisk key, *, to indicate multiplication.

6. **Select cell B13 and type: =A2*3. Determine what you think the answer should be if you multiply the contents of A2 by 3. Click Enter on the formula bar.** Confirm that the answer you expected is displayed. In the next step, you use the forward slash key, /, to indicate division.

7. Select cell B16 and type: =A2/4. Determine what the answer should be if you divide the contents of cell A2 by 4, and then click Enter on the formula bar.

## If you have problems...

There are two slash keys. The forward slash, /, is used to indicate division in Excel formulas. If you use the backslash, \, by mistake, Excel displays *#NAME?* to indicate that it does not recognize your entry as a formula, but thinks it is a misspelled cell reference.

8. Save your changes to the *Worksheet Formulas* workbook and leave the file open to continue to the next part of this lesson.

When writing a formula, it is common to refer to numbers entered in more than one cell on your worksheet. For example, if you want to know the profit for your business, you subtract expenses from income. If you want to know the percent increase in sales, you use numbers entered for two different sales periods to make that calculation.

You may want to add the contents of several cells together and then multiply or divide by the contents of another cell. To do this, use parentheses to group operations together to control which calculation is done first. Excel performs calculations within parentheses first.

In this exercise, you learn to use numbers from more than one cell to make calculations

### To Use Two or More Cell References in the Same Formula

1. Select cell D7 and type: =A2+A3. Estimate the answer and then click Enter ↵. This formula tells the program to take the number in cell A2 and add it to the number in cell A3.

2. Select cell D10 and type: =A2−A3. Estimate the answer and then click Enter ↵. This formula tells the program to take the number in cell A2 and subtract the number in cell A3.

3. Select cell D13 and type: =A2*A3. Estimate the answer and then click Enter ↵. This formula tells the program to take the number in cell A2 and multiply by the number in cell A3.

4. Select cell D16 and type: =B3/B2. Estimate the answer and then click Enter ↵. This formula tells the program to take the contents of cell B3 and divide by the contents of cell B2, as shown in Figure 9.6.

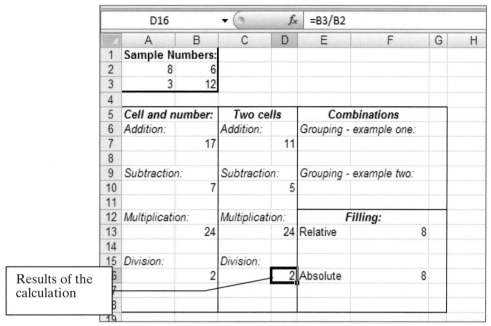

| | A | B | C | D | E | F | G | H |
|---|---|---|---|---|---|---|---|---|
| 1 | **Sample Numbers:** | | | | | | | |
| 2 | 8 | 6 | | | | | | |
| 3 | 3 | 12 | | | | | | |
| 4 | | | | | | | | |
| 5 | *Cell and number:* | | *Two cells* | | *Combinations* | | | |
| 6 | *Addition:* | | *Addition:* | | *Grouping - example one:* | | | |
| 7 | | 17 | | 11 | | | | |
| 8 | | | | | | | | |
| 9 | *Subtraction:* | | *Subtraction:* | | *Grouping - example two:* | | | |
| 10 | | 7 | | 5 | | | | |
| 11 | | | | | | | | |
| 12 | *Multiplication:* | | *Multiplication:* | | *Filling:* | | | |
| 13 | | 24 | | 24 | Relative | | 8 | |
| 14 | | | | | | | | |
| 15 | *Division:* | | *Division:* | | | | | |
| 16 | | 2 | | 2 | Absolute | | 8 | |

Results of the calculation

FIGURE 9. 6

---

The formula bar shows D16 and =B3/B2

---

## If you have problems...

If any of your answers differ from those in the figure, review the exercises again. If you still get the wrong answer, ask your instructor for help. Do not stop now—you are close to mastery of this skill. If you type a formula incorrectly, double-click the cell and edit the formula or select the cell and type it in again.

---

5. **Select cell F7, and then type: =(A2+B2)/A3. Estimate the result if you add the contents of cells A2 and B2, and then divide by the number in cell A3 (the answer is not a whole number).**

6. **Click Enter on the formula bar to confirm your estimate.** Notice that the numbers in cells A2 and B2 (8 and 6) are added first and then divided by the number in cell A3 (3). The answer is 4 2/3, which is represented in decimal form as 4.666666667.

7. **Select cell F10 and then type: =B3/(A3+B2). Estimate the answer if you add A3 and B2 together and then divide B3 by the sum of A3 and B2. Click Enter to confirm your estimate, as shown in Figure 9.7.**

---

Project 9   Using Formulas, Functions and Charts

UNIT 2: 531

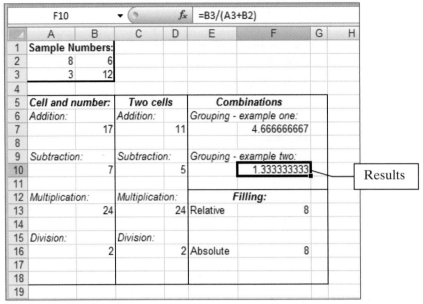

FIGURE 9. 7

8. **Save your changes to the *Worksheet Formulas* file and leave it open for use in the next part of this lesson.**

If the same formula is used in several cells, it may be filled into those cells using the ***fill handle***. The fill handle is a small box at the lower-right corner of a selected cell that can be used to fill in a series of cells. Sometimes you want cell references to change to adapt to the new position in which they are placed; for example, you may have a formula that totals the cells above it and wish to copy this formula across several columns to perform the same function in each column. In each case, you want the formula to add up the column of cells directly above the formula. This is called a ***relative reference***. In other cases, you want the cell reference to always refer to a specific cell. A cell reference that does not change when you copy or fill it into other cells is called an ***absolute reference***.

In this exercise, you learn how to fill cells with formulas that use relative and absolute cell references.

### To Fill Formulas with Relative and Absolute References

1. **With the *Worksheet Formulas* workbook open, select cell F13.** Look at the formula in the formula bar. It shows that the formula—*=A2*—simply equals the value of cell A2.

2. **Point to the fill handle in the lower-right corner of cell F13. When the mouse pointer changes to a black cross, drag the fill handle down to cell F14. Release the mouse button.** Notice that cell F14 displays the number 3, which is the value in cell A3. The Auto Fill Options button (refer to Figure 9.8) that appears next to the fill handle may be used to choose options for how to fill a selection. For example, you could choose to fill the formatting rather than the numbers or text.

3. **Select cell F14.** Notice that the formula is =A3. The formulas in cells F13 and F14 both refer to a cell that is eleven rows up and five columns to the left.

4. **Select cell F16. Look at the formula in the formula bar.** In this case, a $ has been placed to the left of the column and row identifiers, as shown in Figure 9.8, to indicate that the cell reference will not change when it is copied. The dollar signs do not indicate currency format when used for this purpose.

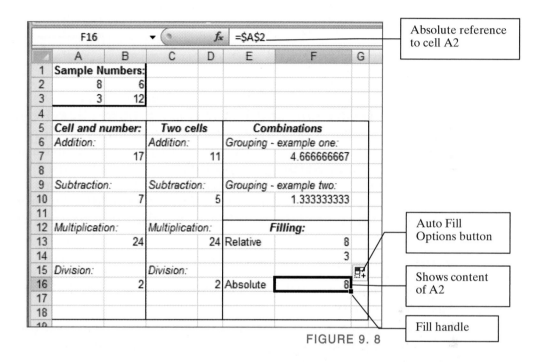

FIGURE 9. 8

5. **Use the fill handle to fill this formula into cell F17.** Notice that cell F17 also displays the contents of cell A2.

6. **Select cell F17. Look at the formula in the formula bar.** Notice that it did not change when the formula was filled into the cell. This type of cell reference (with the $ sign) is called an absolute reference. Use an absolute reference when you want to ensure that the formula always refers to a specific cell.

7. **Press Ctrl + the accent grave mark (`). (On a standard keyboard, the accent grave mark is found on the number row, to the left of the 1 key; if you are using a laptop, the accent grave mark may be in a different location on your keyboard.)** Using Ctrl and `displays the formulas for each cell as shown in Figure 9.9. This gives you the opportunity to examine the underlying formulas in a worksheet.

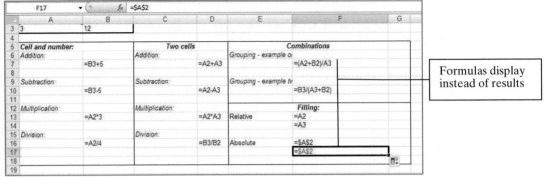

FIGURE 9. 9

8. Click the Insert tab, and in the Text group, click Header & Footer. Add your name, class name, and date to the Header. Click in the Spreadsheet to close Header & Footer. Click the Page Layout tab, and in the Page Setup group click the Orientation button and then click Landscape. In the Page Setup group, click the Dialog Box Launcher, and in the displayed Page Setup dialog box click the Margins tab. Under Center on page click Horizontally and then click OK.

9. Print the formula view of the worksheet (optional).

10. Press Ctrl + ⎄ to return the worksheet to the Normal view, showing the formula results.

11. Save the *Worksheets Formulas* workbook. Close the workbook, but leave Excel open to continue with the next lesson.

---

## TO EXTEND YOUR KNOWLEDGE...

### USING THE FILL HANDLE

The fill handle can be used to complete a series of values, such as the months of the year, days of the week, calendar quarters, or a series of dates. This *AutoFill* feature helps save time when entering a logical series of values. Table 9.1 below lists some of the series that Excel can automatically produce.

---

| START WITH: | AUTOFILL GENERATES THIS SERIES: |
| --- | --- |
| Jan | Feb, Mar, Apr... |
| January | February, March, April... |
| Mon | Tue, Wed, Thu... |
| Monday | Tuesday, Wednesday, Thursday... |
| Qtr 1 | Qtr 2, Qtr 3, Qtr 4... |
| Quarter 1 | Quarter 2, Quarter 3, Quarter 4... |
| Oct-04 | Nov-04, Dec-04, Jan-05... |
| 18-Jan | 19-Jan, 20-Jan, 21-Jan... |
| 1st Period | 2nd Period, 3rd Period, 4th Period... |
| Product 1 | Product 2, Product 3, Product 4... |
| 10:00 AM | 11:00 AM, 12:00 PM, 1:00 PM... |

TABLE 9. 1

# LESSON 2: Using Formulas

When you use formulas in a worksheet, you usually design the formula with relative and absolute references so that it may be filled into adjacent cells. This ability to fill formulas enables you to perform the same type of calculation on several different rows or columns of data.

The Armstrong Pool, Spa, and Sauna Company added a line of patio furniture to supplement its sales. In this lesson, you use relative and absolute formulas to fill in a table that is used to compare sales of each type of furniture item.

### To Use Formulas with Relative References

1. Locate and open *EX_0902* and save it as a 97-2003 Compatible file, and name it Patio Furniture.

2. Select cell D3 and type: =B3*C3. This formula multiplies the quantity of items sold in B3 by the average cost per item in C3 to determine the total cost. The cell references in the formula in cell D3 are displayed in different colors that match the outline color used to identify the cells used in the formula, as shown in Figure 9.10.

| | A | B | C | D | E | F | G | H |
|---|---|---|---|---|---|---|---|---|
| | | | | | | SUM | ▾ | X ✓ ƒx =B3*C3 |
| 1 | | | Patio Furniture Division | | | | | |
| 2 | Inventory | Quantity | Average Cost | Total Cost | Retail Price | Retail Value | Percent Mark Up | Percent Contribution |
| 3 | Table Umbrellas | 2000 | $22.70 | =B3*C3 | $45.00 | | | |
| 4 | Patio Chairs | 5000 | $35.00 | | $65.00 | | | |
| 5 | Patio Tables | 1000 | $48.00 | | $120.00 | | | |
| 6 | Side Tables | 2000 | $19.25 | | $33.00 | | | |
| 7 | Grills | 1500 | $38.50 | | $89.00 | | | |
| 8 | Citronella Torches | 5000 | $2.50 | | $12.50 | | | |
| 9 | Lounge Chairs | 3450 | $5.00 | | $22.00 | | | |
| 10 | | | | | | | | |
| 11 | | | | | | | | |

Colors help identify cells used in formula

FIGURE 9. 10

3. **Click** [Enter ↵]. The total cost of buying this item is calculated and the currency style format is applied. Cell C3 is formatted as currency, therefore, currency style is applied to formulas that use this cell. This same calculation needs to be performed for each of the items in the table. Because the formula uses relative cell references that multiply together the two cells to the left of the current cell, it may be filled into the cells below using the fill handle.

4. **Drag the fill handle on D3 down to D9 and release the mouse button.** The formula is filled into the cells below. The number in cell D4 may be too wide for the column, which will cause the cell to display ### signs.

5. **Click one of the new formulas in column D to view how the relative references changed when they were filled.**

6. **Select D3 through D9. Click the Home tab, and in the Number group, click the Decrease Decimal button two times. If necessary, adjust the width of the column.** The Decrease Decimal button decreases the decimals by one place each time it is clicked. The new column of calculations is complete without entering each formula individually, as shown in Figure 9.11.

| | A | B | C | D | E | F | G | H |
|---|---|---|---|---|---|---|---|---|
| 1 | | | Patio Furniture Division | | | | | |
| 2 | Inventory | Quantity | Average Cost | Total Cost | Retail Price | Retail Value | Percent Mark Up | Percent Contribution |
| 3 | Table Umbrellas | 2000 | $22.70 | $45,400 | $45.00 | | | |
| 4 | Patio Chairs | 5000 | $35.00 | $175,000 | $65.00 | | | |
| 5 | Patio Tables | 1000 | $48.00 | $48,000 | $120.00 | | | |
| 6 | Side Tables | 2000 | $19.25 | $38,500 | $33.00 | | | |
| 7 | Grills | 1500 | $38.50 | $57,750 | $89.00 | | | |
| 8 | Citronella Torches | 5000 | $2.50 | $12,500 | $12.50 | | | |
| 9 | Lounge Chairs | 3450 | $5.00 | $17,250 | $22.00 | | | |
| 10 | | | | | | | | |

Formula copied to the remaining cells in column D

FIGURE 9. 11

7. **Select cell F3 and type: =b3*e3 to calculate the retail values. Press** [Enter ↵]. In this example, you use lowercase letters in the cell references. Capitalization of a cell reference does not matter in Excel. This formula multiplies

the quantity in column B by the retail price in column E. It also uses relative cell references and may be filled into the cells below.

8. **Use the fill handle to copy this formula into cells F4 through F9. Decrease the Decimal two spaces.**

9. **Select D10. On the Home tab, in the Editing group click the Sum button. Click the Sum button a second time.** The total cost of items in the Total Cost column is summed.

10. **Drag the fill handle on D10 to the right to cell H10 and release the mouse button.** The SUM function uses relative cell references and may be copied. It serves no useful purpose to sum the retail price or percent markup columns, but it is often faster to fill a range of cells and then delete the formulas you do not want.

11. **Delete the formulas in cells E10 and G10.** The unnecessary formulas are deleted.

12. Widen column F, (if necessary), to accommodate the total in F10 and then compare your results with Figure 9.12.

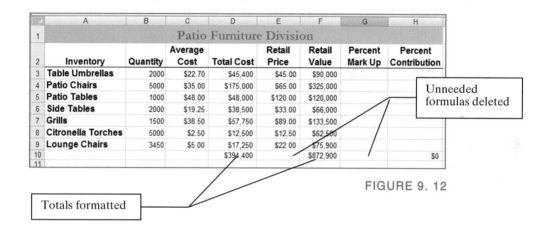

FIGURE 9. 12

13. **Save your changes to the *Patio Furniture* workbook and leave the file open to continue to the next part of this lesson.**

---

## TO EXTEND YOUR KNOWLEDGE...

### AUTOMATICALLY FILLING A COLUMN

If you double-click the fill handle in a cell, it will automatically copy the contents of that cell down the column to match the length of the column to the left. For example, if column B contains values in cells B3 through B14 and you enter a formula in cell C3, double-clicking the fill handle on cell C3 will copy the formula in C3 down to C14. This is a quicker method for copying cell contents down a column of data and is especially useful if the columns are extremely long.

---

The percent markup on an item is calculated by first subtracting the cost from the retail value and then dividing by the cost. To write this formula, you need to use parentheses to ensure that the subtraction takes place before the division.

An absolute cell reference may be used in the same formula with relative cell references. In this exercise, you enter a formula that determines what percent contribution each type of furniture makes to the entire retail value. To do this, you divide the retail value of that item by the total retail value. To write a formula that may be filled, you need a relative reference to the retail value that will change as you fill the formula and an absolute reference to the cell that contains the total.

## To Use Formulas with Parentheses and Absolute References

1. **With the *Patio Furniture* workbook open, click on cell G3 and type: =(E3–C3)/C3. Click Enter on the formula bar. On the Home tab, in the Number group click the Percent Style button.** The markup for this item is 98%. Markup is the percent of the product cost that is added to the cost to arrive at a selling price.

2. **Fill this formula into cells G4 through G9.** The percent markup is calculated for each item, as shown in Figure 9.13.

G3 =(E3-C3)/C3

| | A | B | C | D | E | F | G | H |
|---|---|---|---|---|---|---|---|---|
| 1 | Patio Furniture Division | | | | | | | |
| 2 | Inventory | Quantity | Average Cost | Total Cost | Retail Price | Retail Value | Percent Mark Up | Percent Contribution |
| 3 | Table Umbrellas | 2000 | $22.70 | $45,400 | $45.00 | $90,000 | 98% | |
| 4 | Patio Chairs | 5000 | $35.00 | $175,000 | $65.00 | $325,000 | 86% | |
| 5 | Patio Tables | 1000 | $48.00 | $48,000 | $120.00 | $120,000 | 150% | |
| 6 | Side Tables | 2000 | $19.25 | $38,500 | $33.00 | $66,000 | 71% | |
| 7 | Grills | 1500 | $38.50 | $57,750 | $89.00 | $133,500 | 131% | |
| 8 | Citronella Torches | 5000 | $2.50 | $12,500 | $12.50 | $62,500 | 400% | |
| 9 | Lounge Chairs | 3450 | $5.00 | $17,250 | $22.00 | $75,900 | 340% | |
| 10 | | | | $394,400 | | $872,900 | | $0 |



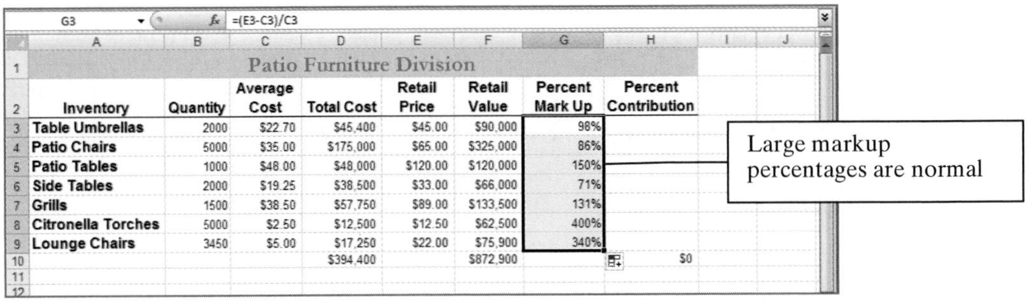

FIGURE 9. 13

3. **Click H3. Type: =F3/$F$10 and then press** Enter. The retail value of the table umbrellas is displayed as a decimal—.1031...which is approximately 10% of the total retail value of all the items.

4. **Fill this formula down to cells H4 through H9. Select cells H3 through H10 and then in the Number group click the Percent Style button.** The percentage that each item makes to the total retail value is calculated for each inventory item. *100%* displays as the total in cell H10.

5. **Select cells A2 through H9.** You can select the range of cells you want to sort and exclude the total row.

6. **Click the Data tab, and in the Sort & Filter group click the Sort button. In the Sort by box select Percent Contribution and change the Order box to Largest to Smallest. Be sure the *My data has headers* check box is selected, and then click OK.** The items are sorted with those that make the most contribution to the total retail value at the top.

7. **Select D9. Press and hold** [Ctrl] **while you click cells F9 and H9.** You may use the [Ctrl] key to select cells that are not next to each other.

8. **Click the Home tab, and in the Font group click the Bottom Border button to add a border under the selected cells. Click in an empty cell.** The table is completed, as shown in Figure 9.14.

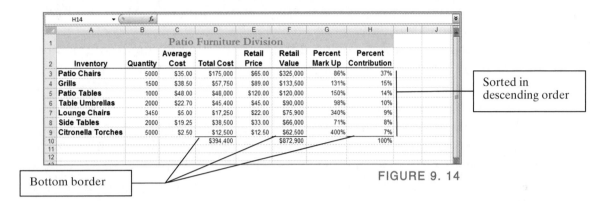

FIGURE 9. 14

9. **Click the Insert tab, and in the Text group click Header & Footer. Add your name, class name, and date to the Header. Change the orientation to Landscape and center the worksheet horizontally. Print the worksheet (optional).**

10. **Press** [Ctrl] + [ `] **to display the formulas. Click the Page Layout tab, and in the Scale to Fit group click the Dialog Box Launcher. On the Page tab under** *Scaling,* **click the Fit to option 1 page wide by 1 tall. Print the formulas (optional).** The Scaling option shrinks the font so all of the formulas print on one page.

11. **Press** [Ctrl] + [ `] **again to display the results. Save the** *Patio Furniture* **workbook and close it. Leave Excel open for the next lesson.**

---

## TO EXTEND YOUR KNOWLEDGE...

### USING MIXED CELL REFERENCES

You already know that you can mix relative and absolute cell references in a formula. For example, in step 3, you wrote the formula =F3/$F$10 and then copied it to other cells. In that formula, the reference to cell F3 is relative and the reference to cell F10 is absolute. You can also mix relative and absolute settings within a single cell reference, if needed, to produce the desired copy results. For example, $F10 would always use the value in column F when the formula was copied, and F$10 would always use the value in row 10 when the formula was copied.

### USING F4 TO MAKE CELL REFERENCES ABSOLUTE

Excel can enter the dollar sign(s) to make one or more parts of a cell reference absolute. When you create or edit a formula, click within a cell reference and press F4 until you get the desired result.

---

# LESSON 3: Using Functions to Analyze Data

A table of data may contain a pattern that you can recognize by looking at the numbers, but many patterns or trends are not readily apparent. Many different methods are available for analyzing data.

In the previous project, you used the Sum function to sum a column of numbers. Some of the more commonly used functions—predefined formulas—are used to analyze data such as the AVERAGE, MINIMUM, MAXIMUM, and COUNT functions.

When you use a function, you specify the cells that contain the values to be used by the function. These input values are called *arguments*. For example, in the SUM function, the argument is simply a range of adjacent cells. The formula to calculate the monthly payment needed to repay a loan is fairly complex, but it only requires three pieces of data. These values or arguments are the number of payments, the interest rate, and the amount of the loan.

Functions may be included in formulas individually or in combination with other functions or mathematical operations. If the arguments for a function are a range of cells, the range is identified by references to two cells in opposite corners or either end of the range, separated by a colon. For example =SUM(A3:A7) is the SUM function to add the values in cells A3 through A7. Arguments are contained within parentheses with a comma between each argument. This example only contained one argument so a comma isn't needed.

In addition to financial data, a worksheet can be used to analyze scientific data. In this lesson, you learn how to use the SUM, AVERAGE, MIN, and MAX to analyze and compare the monthly rainfall in the cities of Seattle and Buffalo. You also fix a common error that occurs when the program selects a range of cells.

## To Use Sum, Average, and Median Functions to Analyze Data

1. **Locate and open *EX_0903* and save it as an Excel 97-2003 compatible file named Rainfall.** This table shows the rainfall in two cities that are in different parts of the country.

2. **Click B15 and then on the Home tab, in the Editing group click the Sum button.** The SUM function displays in cell B15. Notice that the equal sign makes it part of a formula and the argument is a range of cells (B3:B14), as shown in Figure 9.15.

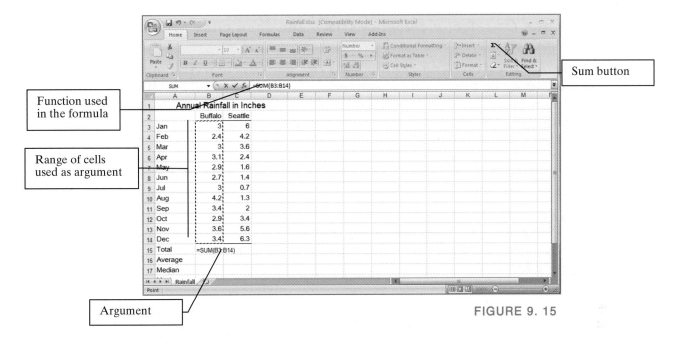

FIGURE 9. 15

3. **Click Sum button again.** The results of the function are displayed in B15, showing the total annual rainfall in Buffalo.

4. **Click C15. Double-click the Sum button.** The total rainfall for Seattle is displayed. Notice that both cities receive almost the same total amount of rain.

5. **Click B16. Click the Insert Function button on the formula bar.** The Insert Function dialog box opens and displays a list of the most recently used functions on your computer. Your list will differ from those shown in Figure 9.16. Here you select the function you want to use. A description of the currently selected function displays at the bottom of the dialog box. An equal sign displays in the formula bar and in cell B16 where the function will be placed. This is the beginning of any formula or function.

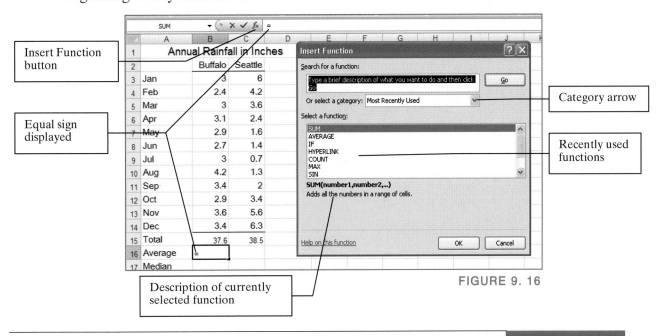

FIGURE 9. 16

6. **Click the *Or select a category* arrow and then click Statistical.** A list of statistical functions is displayed.

7. **Click AVERAGE and then click OK.** The Function Arguments dialog box opens. Notice that the function assumes that the range should be B3:B15. However, you want to find the average of the rainfall from B3 through B14. Do not automatically accept the range that the program suggests. The suggested range is not always correct, and it is a common error to automatically accept the suggestion without examining it. The *Formula result* displays in the dialog box. The range B3:B15 produces an average of 5.78 which is larger than any single figure. An average is always between the highest and lowest values.

8. **On the worksheet, drag across cells B3 through B14. If necessary, move the Function Arguments dialog box out of the way.** The range of cells to be used as arguments is corrected in the dialog box, as shown in Figure 9.17.

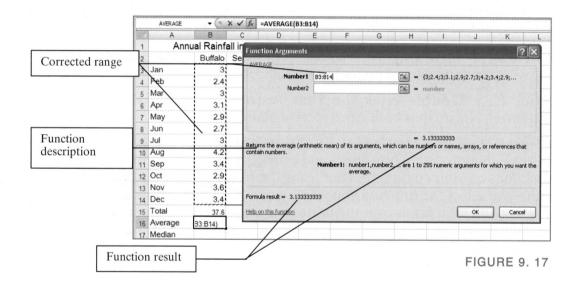

FIGURE 9. 17

9. **Click OK.** The average rainfall in Buffalo is slightly more than 3 inches per month.

10. **Drag the fill handle on B16 to C16.** Notice that the average rainfall per month is almost the same in both cities. The Error Checking smart tag displays and a green triangle appears in the upper-left corner of the two cells that contain the average formula. Whenever Excel thinks an error may have occurred, the Error Checking smart tag displays to provide help. If you clicked this button, it would give you a list of options. In this case, Excel recognizes that this cell contains a formula and the cell is not protected from being inadvertently changed. The message that displays depends on what the program perceives to be a potential problem. If the green triangle does not display in the cell, it means that the settings on your computer have been changed in the Excel Options dialog box.

11. **Click C16.** Notice that the cell references in the functions are relative by default and that they change when you fill the formula into adjacent cells.

12. **Select cell B17. Follow the same procedure to calculate the MEDIAN function of cells B3:B14 and fill the function formula into C17.** The median is the value in the list of arguments that has as many values in the list that are greater or smaller. If you sort the column, the median value would be in the middle. Notice that the median rainfall values for both cities are almost the same.

13. **Save your changes to the *Rainfall* workbook and leave the file open for use in the next part of this lesson.**

---

## TO EXTEND YOUR KNOWLEDGE...

### USING THE SUM BUTTON FOR OTHER FUNCTIONS

The Sum button is available on both the Home tab and on the Formulas tab, where it is named AutoSum. Both buttons include other commonly used functions such as average, minimum, and maximum. Click the AutoSum arrow and then choose one of the functions displayed, or choose More Functions to display the Insert Functions dialog box. The Formulas tab includes a Function Library group in addition to a large Insert Function button.

---

The rainfall in both cities has three similarities. The total is almost the same, plus the average is almost the same and so is the median. One would be tempted to say that both cities have the same rainfall. It is important to recognize the value and limitations of these common functions. You would get the same results if almost all the rainfall in one of the cities occurred in one month. You need to use other functions to see whether there are hidden differences between the two.

In this exercise, you use the MIN and MAX functions to compare extremes of rainfall. You also observe another common error that people make when they select a range of cells to serve as arguments for functions and include the cell that contains the function itself. This is known as a ***circular reference***. If you ever see an Excel spreadsheet with the phrase *circular:* in the status bar, then the cell listed after it contains a circular reference.

1. **Click cell B18. Type =MAX(B3:B14) and press** Enter↵. If you know the function arguments, you can type the function directly in the cell. The maximum rainfall for one month in Buffalo is 4.2 inches.

2. **Click C18. Use the Insert Function dialog box to insert the MAX statistical function except, this time, make an intentional error and select C3 through C18.** A warning box displays to tell you that you have created a circular reference. A circular reference error occurred because the function cell—*C18*— was included in the function argument. A cell where the function is to display cannot be included as part of the argument A Excel Help dialog box may also display.

3. **Click Cancel.** *Circular References: C18* displays in the status bar to let you know that a circular reference error exists in that cell. To correct the error, you need to re-enter the formula.

4. **Use the fill handle to copy the MAX formula from B18 into C18.** A correct version of the MAX function is filled into C18.

5. **Click B19. Use one of the two methods you have practiced to insert the MIN statistical function. Select B3:B14 as the range of cells for the argument.**

6. **Fill the MIN function from B19 to C19. Click an empty cell.** The MIN and MAX functions are significantly different for rainfall in the two cities, as shown in Figure 9.18. Unlike the SUM, AVERAGE, and MEDIAN functions, the MIN and MAX functions have identified significant differences between rainfall patterns in the two cities. By comparing these two functions, you can conclude that the rainfall in Seattle has a wider range of variation in its monthly rainfall. The

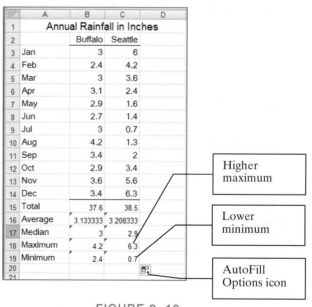

FIGURE 9. 18

AutoFill Options button that displays can be used to change the fill options. The default is to copy the cell. If you click this button, you can choose to fill just the formatting or fill the contents without the formatting.

7. **Save the *Rainfall* workbook and leave the file open to continue to the next lesson.**

---

### USING OTHER FUNCTIONS

Another commonly used function is the COUNT function, which counts the number of values in a list: =COUNT(A3:A14). This is useful if you need to know the number of records that are included. The COUNTA function counts only alphabetic values in a list. More complex functions, that use more than one argument, use commas to separate one argument from the next. For example, the payment function is PMT (rate, nper, pv) where *rate* is the monthly interest rate, *nper* is the number of monthly payments over the length of the loan, and *pv* is the present value of the amount that is being borrowed. This function is used to calculate the monthly payment needed to pay back a specified amount of money borrowed for a stated period of time at a fixed interest rate. The Function Arguments dialog box prompts you for each piece of data to complete the function formula.

---

# LESSON 4: Charting Data

People process information in several different ways. Most of us recognize trends more readily if a line or a series of columns of differing heights is used to represent the numbers. We also recognize how one member of a group compares to the others if they are represented by slices of a pie chart. If you select rows or columns of data in a table, the spreadsheet program can display that data as a ***chart***—a graphical representation of numbers.

If you set up your table of data correctly, the program can chart it conveniently. Select either rows or columns, not both at the same time. Select a row or column of labels that will be used as chart labels and one or more rows or columns of the table. The rows or columns selected should be the same length.

In this exercise, you chart the rainfall in both cities as lines on the same chart so you can visually compare them and observe patterns.

#### To Chart Rainfall Data with a Line Chart

1. **With the *Rainfall* workbook open, select the range of cells from A2 through C14.** You are selecting three columns of data, as shown in Figure 9.19. Cell A2 is included in the first column so all three columns are the same length. Do not include the totals in row 15. You typically do not chart the totals on the same chart as the data.

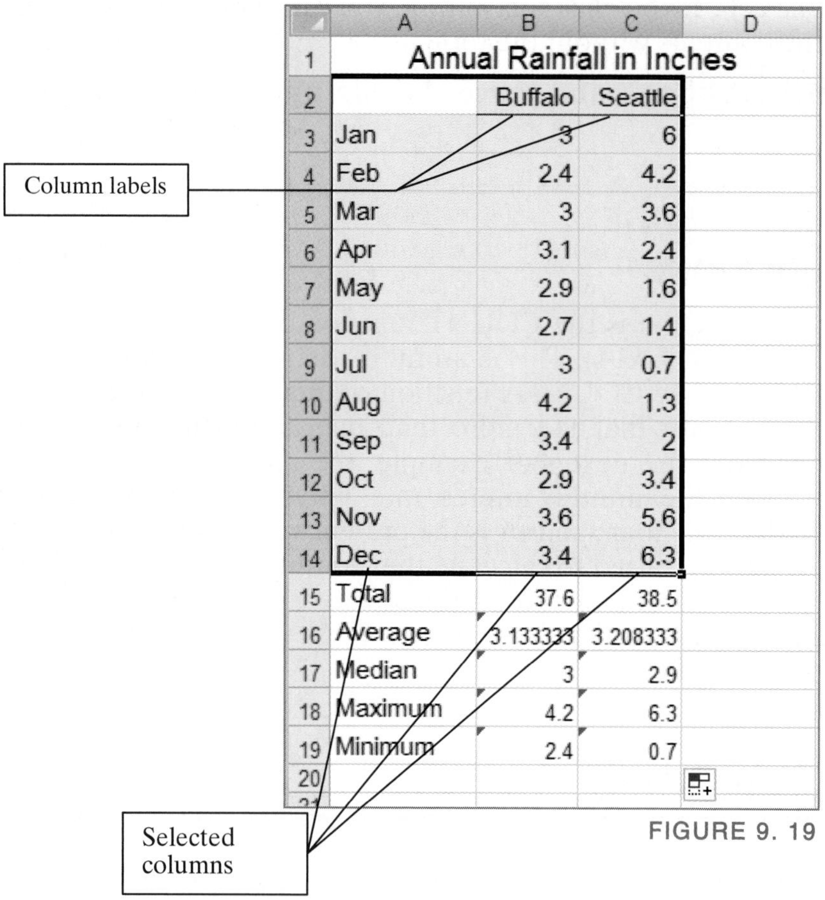

| ▲ | A | B | C | D |
|---|---|---|---|---|
| 1 | Annual Rainfall in Inches | | | |
| 2 | | Buffalo | Seattle | |
| 3 | Jan | 3 | 6 | |
| 4 | Feb | 2.4 | 4.2 | |
| 5 | Mar | 3 | 3.6 | |
| 6 | Apr | 3.1 | 2.4 | |
| 7 | May | 2.9 | 1.6 | |
| 8 | Jun | 2.7 | 1.4 | |
| 9 | Jul | 3 | 0.7 | |
| 10 | Aug | 4.2 | 1.3 | |
| 11 | Sep | 3.4 | 2 | |
| 12 | Oct | 2.9 | 3.4 | |
| 13 | Nov | 3.6 | 5.6 | |
| 14 | Dec | 3.4 | 6.3 | |
| 15 | Total | 37.6 | 38.5 | |
| 16 | Average | 3.133333 | 3.208333 | |
| 17 | Median | 3 | 2.9 | |
| 18 | Maximum | 4.2 | 6.3 | |
| 19 | Minimum | 2.4 | 0.7 | |
| 20 | | | | |

Column labels

Selected columns

FIGURE 9. 19

2. **Click the Insert tab, and in the Charts group click the Dialog Box Launcher.** The Insert Chart dialog box that opens displays the different chart types. Here you select the Chart type you want to create and the Chart sub-type. It gives you the chance to consider a wide variety of chart subtypes.

3. **Close the dialog box. On the Insert tab, in the Charts group click Line. From the displayed gallery line chart types point to the first chart in the second row — Line with Markers; and then click this chart type.** This chart type is created and placed on the worksheet.. Three new contextual Chart Tools tabs display that are used to help you design or modify your charts—Design, Layout, and Format.

4. **Click the Chart Tools Layout tab.** Here you can change several options for formatting the chart such as adding a chart title or axis labels, moving the placement of the legend, or adding data labels.

5. **On the Layout tab, in the Labels group, click Chart Title and then click Above Chart. In the formula bar type:** Monthly Rainfall **and then press** Enter⏎. The title is added to the chart. You can also select the text displayed on the chart—Chart Title—and type a new title for your chart.

6. **On the Layout tab, in the Labels group, click Axis Titles, point to Primary Vertical Axis Title and then click Rotated Title. In the formula bar type: Inches and then press** [Enter ⏎]. The label is added to the left side of the chart along the vertical axis. The bottom of a line or column chart lists the categories of data—months in this example. In charts, this is called the Category axis or sometimes the X-axis. The left side of the chart is a series of increasing numbers that represent the values in the cells you selected—this is the Vertical (Value) axis or sometimes the Y-axis. A dot on the chart—called a data marker--represents one of the values in one of the cells you selected, as shown in Figure 9.20.

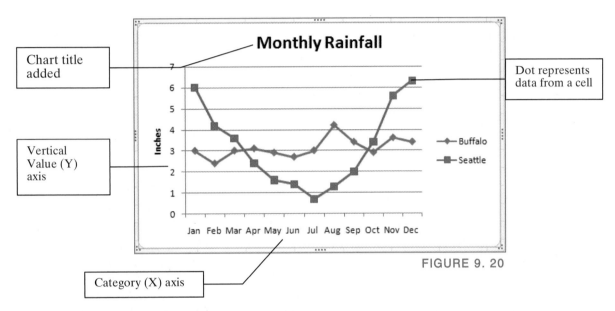

FIGURE 9. 20

7. **On the Layout tab, in the Labels group, click Legend. Click Show Legend at Bottom** The legend defines the codes used in the chart. In this case, it shows the color and shape of the dots used for each city. Differently shaped dots are used so you can tell the difference when the chart is printed in black and white.

8. **Click the Chart Tools Design tab, and in the Location group click Move Chart.** Here you have the option of placing the chart in its own worksheet or placing it next to the data in the current worksheet. You would place the chart on its own worksheet if you planned to print it out separately or if the chart has a lot of small details. In this case, you will keep the chart in the Rainfall worksheet.

9. **Confirm that Rainfall is selected next to Object in and then click OK.** The chart stays as an object on the worksheet. The sizing handles on the corners and sides are represented by a set of dots in the corner and the middle of the side. You can change the size of the chart or move the whole chart.

10. **Move the pointer onto an empty part of the chart to the right of the title. Hold down the left mouse button and drag the pointer to the location shown in Figure 9.21. The upper-left corner of the dotted line should be in middle of cell D2.** An outline, as shown in Figure 9.21,

indicates the intended position of the chart. When you release the mouse pointer, the chart will be positioned in the location indicated by the outline.

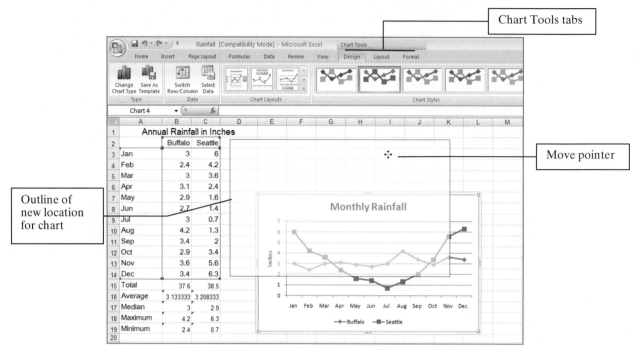

FIGURE 9. 21

11. **Drag the lower-right corner sizing handle down toward K16, as shown in Figure 9.22.** The chart is located next to the table of data. The cell references are provided as a convenient reference. The chart is not actually in any of the cells, but is in a layer that is on top of the worksheet row and column grid. The chart makes it easier to see the differences in the rainfall patterns between Buffalo, where the rainfall is fairly constant each month, and Seattle, where the rainfall is much higher in the winter months but low in the summer.

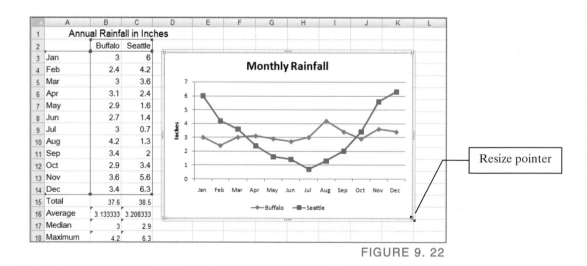

FIGURE 9. 22

12. **Click the title.** A box surrounds the title to indicate that it is selected.

13. **Click in the title to place the insertion point in the title and then edit it to read** Annual Rainfall.

14. **Save your changes to the** *Rainfall* **workbook and leave the file open to continue to the next part of this lesson.**

A line chart is useful for showing how things change with time. Column charts are useful for making comparisons of different values in the same category. In this exercise, you look at the same data with a column chart to compare the rainfall month by month

## To Change the Chart Type

1. **With the** *Rainfall* **workbook open, click the chart to select it. Click the Chart Tools Design tab, and in the Type group click Change Chart Type to display the Change Chart Type dialog box.**

2. **On the left side of the dialog box click Column. In the displayed gallery on the right point to the image in column 1 row 1 to display the ScreenTip—Clustered Column.**

3. **Click Clustered Column and then click OK.** Vertical columns replace the lines and you can compare the amount of rainfall each month with side-by-side columns, as shown in Figure 9.23.

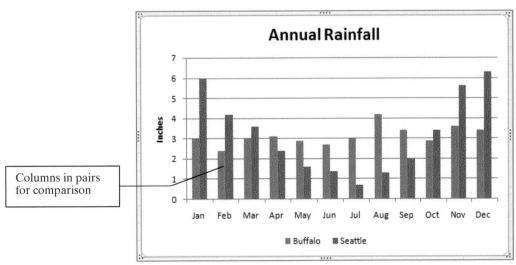

FIGURE 9. 23

4. **The line chart type is best for this example.** On the Quick Access toolbar, click the Undo button to return the line chart.

5. **Leave the** *Rainfall* **workbook open to continue to the next part of this lesson.**

Pie charts are not generally used to compare one group of data with another. A pie chart is used when you want to show how parts contribute to a whole. Consequently, you select a range of cells to use as labels and another range of cells that contain the data. The data in the selected range of cells should add up to all of something, for example, all of the rainfall in Seattle in a year. In this exercise, you will use a pie chart to show how much the rainfall in each month contributes to the total annual rainfall for Seattle.

## To Create a Pie Chart

1. **With the *Rainfall* workbook open, select cells A3 through A14.** These cells will be used as labels.

2. **Hold down Ctrl and drag across cells C3 through C14.** Two non-adjacent cell ranges are selected, as shown in Figure 9.24. In this case, the column heading, Seattle, was not selected because you will only use one column of data and the city will be identified in the title.

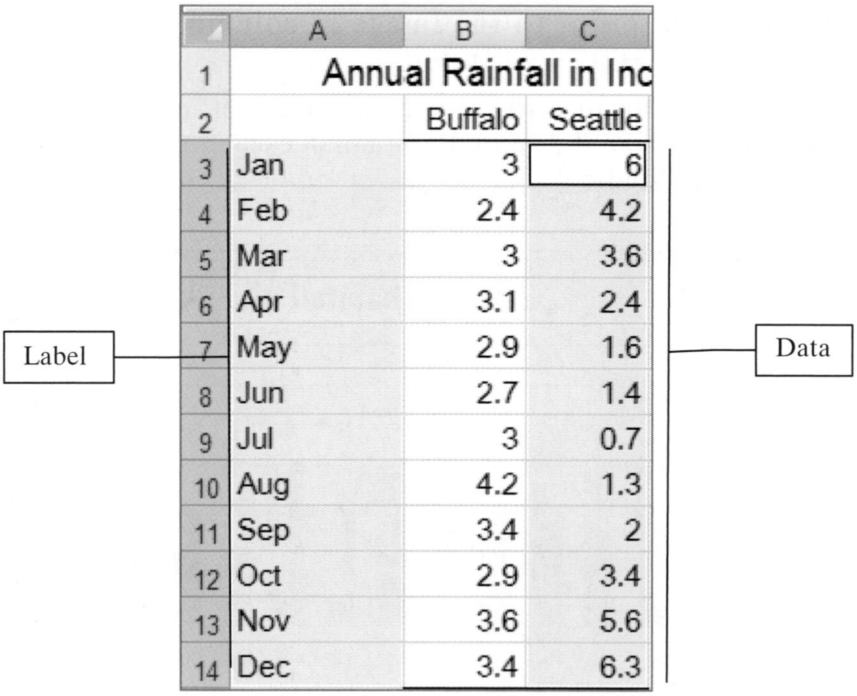

|  | A | B | C |
|---|---|---|---|
| 1 | Annual Rainfall in Inc | | |
| 2 | | Buffalo | Seattle |
| 3 | Jan | 3 | 6 |
| 4 | Feb | 2.4 | 4.2 |
| 5 | Mar | 3 | 3.6 |
| 6 | Apr | 3.1 | 2.4 |
| 7 | May | 2.9 | 1.6 |
| 8 | Jun | 2.7 | 1.4 |
| 9 | Jul | 3 | 0.7 |
| 10 | Aug | 4.2 | 1.3 |
| 11 | Sep | 3.4 | 2 |
| 12 | Oct | 2.9 | 3.4 |
| 13 | Nov | 3.6 | 5.6 |
| 14 | Dec | 3.4 | 6.3 |

Label — Data

FIGURE 9. 24

3. **Click the Insert tab, and in the Charts group, click Pie, and then in the gallery under 3-D Pie click the first item — Pie in 3-D.** A pie chart displays on the worksheet.

4. **Click the Chart Tools Layout tab, and in the Labels group click Legend.** The legend identifies the pie slices by color. The legend is selected to display by default. If you did not want to display a legend, you could click None. Leave the legend showing on the right.

5. On the Layout tab, in the Labels group, click Data Labels. At the bottom of the list click More Data Label Options Each slice of the pie may be labeled with values from the table. In a line chart, the labels would be next to each dot on the line.

6. In the Format Data Labels dialog box, under Label Contains, click Percentage and remove the check next to Value. Under Label Position click Outside End. Close the Format Data Labels box, The percentage of the total is placed next to the slice and each label box is selected as indication by the resizing handles.

7. On the Layout tab, in the Labels group, click Chart Title and then click Above Chart In the Formula bar type: Seattle Rainfall and press [Enter ↵]

8. Drag the chart to a position below the line chart. Place its upper-left corner in D17. If necessary, drag the sizing handle on the lower-right corner to K33.

9. Click the legend and drag the upper middle sizing handle up until the color for *Dec.* displays at the end of the legend. The bottom of the pie chart should not extend below row 33 and the right side should not extend past column K, as shown in Figure 9.25.

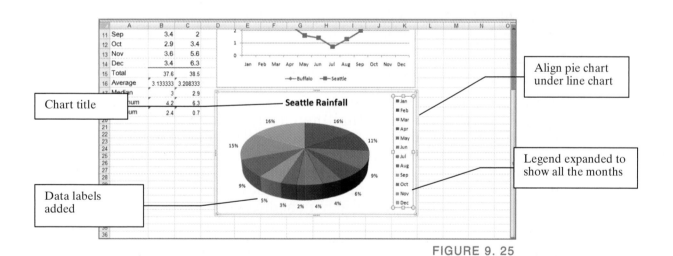

FIGURE 9. 25

10. Save your changes to the *Rainfall* workbook and leave the file open to continue to the next lesson.

## MODIFYING CHARTS

There are several techniques available for modifying a chart. When a chart is active, the Ribbon bar includes *Design, Layout* and *Format* tabs. These contextual tabs enable you to change the chart type, chart location, data source used for the chart, or other chart options. On the Layout Tab, in the Current Select group, click the list arrow in the box at the top of the group to select the element on your chart that you want to format or modify. You can also right-click on an area of the chart and choose a command from a shortcut menu. As you move your mouse pointer over a chart, the name of each chart component displays in a ScreenTip. For example, if you want to change the font size of the Value Axis, point to that area on the chart. When the Value Axis ScreenTip displays, right-click and choose Format Axis from the shortcut menu. Make the desired changes in the dialog box and then click OK.

# LESSON 5: Analyzing Data with Charts

Patterns in the data are much easier to perceive when you use charts. It is also possible to spot anomalies that could be produced by errors in the data or by unexpected events.

In this exercise, you learn about using charts to draw conclusions about the data. You change data to simulate a common data entry error and how it affects the chart.

### To Change Data in the Table to Simulate an Error

1. **With the *Rainfall* workbook open, click C6.** A common error people make when typing data is reversing the digits.

2. **Type: 6.2 and press Enter ↵.** This replacement simulates an error that someone could make if they mistakenly typed 6.2 instead of 2.4.

3. **Notice both charts are immediately updated, but the change is much more readily apparent in the line chart, as shown in Figure 9.26.** This data point for April rainfall in Seattle is out of line with the overall shape of the curve. If you see a difference like this from the overall trend, you should check the accuracy of the data. Do not change the data to conform to the trend unless you are sure an error has been made. Changing unexplained data differences is bad science because it could hide an important discovery.

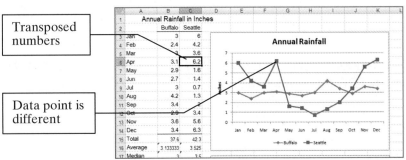

FIGURE 9. 26

4. **Click C6, type: 2.4, and press** [Enter↵]. The data is returned to its previous value. Notice that the August rainfall in Buffalo is significantly higher than the other months.

5. **Select B10, type: 2.4, and press** [Enter↵]. Does this data point look more like the others? When you see a data point that appears to be significantly different than the others, check the source of the data to confirm its accuracy.

6. **Click B10, type: 4.2, and press** [Enter↵]. In this case, the number is correct. If the data is accurate, it may indicate something unusual. This is one method that scientists use to focus their research.

7. **Leave the *Rainfall* workbook open to continue to the next part of this lesson.**

If a table of data represents how something changes with time, the data represents a value at a particular moment in time. You do not know what the values are between the data points or beyond either end of the chart. However, you can use a chart to make educated guesses. If you use the existing data to estimate an unknown value that would lie between two known data points, it is called ***interpolation***. If you extend the trend of the line into the future or the past, it is called ***extrapolation***.

In this exercise, you use a chart to estimate unknown values.

### To Interpolate and Extrapolate Data

1. **With the *Rainfall* workbook open, select B6.** Observe that the rainfall for April in Buffalo was 3.1 inches. This implies that the average for each week during that month was approximately 3/4 inches (3.1 divided by 4 weeks).

2. **Click B7.** Observe that the rainfall in Buffalo in May was 2.9 inches. This implies that the average for each week during May was also 3/4 inches. If someone asked you to guess how much rain fell on average in one particular week in Buffalo that was in April or May, you could guess that it was about 3/4 inches. It might actually have been zero, 2, or 3, but you know it was not more than 3.1, so your guess would not be far off. This is an example of interpolation. See Figure 9.27.

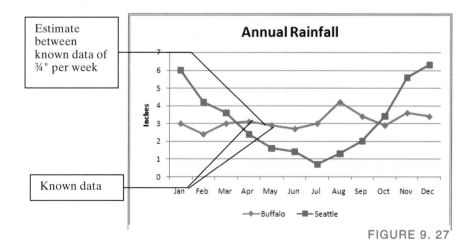

FIGURE 9. 27

---

3. **Notice the trend of rainfall for Seattle from July to December.** The amount of rain steadily increases by about one inch of rain each month. If you choose to extend this trend for six months into the future, you would estimate the rainfall next July to be 12 inches, which is clearly incorrect. This type of estimate is an extrapolation. Extrapolation is much less reliable than interpolation, as you can see from this example in which we chose to extend a portion of a line that was rising and ignored the overall pattern of annual rise and fall. See Figure 9.28.

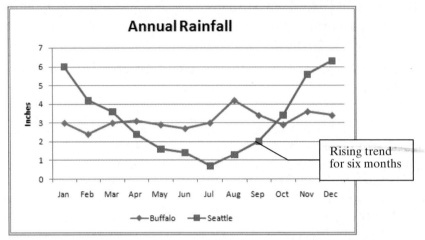

FIGURE 9. 28

4. **Click cell A1. Click the Insert tab, and in the Text group, click Header & Footer. Add your name, class, and date to the Header.** When a chart is selected, it is possible to print the chart on its own page. To prepare to print the entire worksheet, a cell in the worksheet must be active.

5. **Click cell A1 to close Header & Footer. On the status bar click the Normal button. Click the Page Layout tab, and in the Page Setup click Margins and then click Custom Margins. In the displayed Page Setup dialog box, on the Margins tab, change the Top margin to .75 and the Bottom margin to .50. Center the page Horizontally on the page. Click OK.**

6. **Click the Office button, point to Print and from the displayed list click Print Preview Be sure that the worksheet fits on one page.** The worksheet displays in Landscape orientation because the original file included that setting. The table of data and its two charts should fit on one page, as shown in Figure 9.29. The value axis on the line chart may display as 0 through 8 by twos, and the month names along the category axis may display at an angle. This setup is fine as long as both charts and the table of data display on one page.

## If you have problems...

If the worksheet data and charts will not print on one page, close the Print Preview window and adjust the size of the charts slightly to ensure that they will both print with the data on one page. If you cannot adjust the charts to a suitable size and still see all of the data—the months in the pie chart legend, for example—then display the Page Setup dialog box, click the Page tab, and choose the Fit to option. Preview the worksheet again before printing.

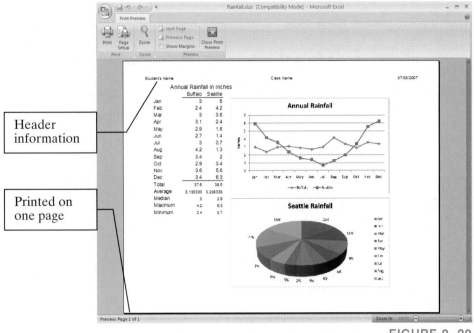

FIGURE 9. 29

7. **Print the worksheet with its two charts.**

8. **Save the *Rainfall* workbook. Close the workbook and close Excel 2007.**

## SUMMARY

In this project, you learned the basic rules for creating formulas in spreadsheets. You learned the symbols used in a spreadsheet and how to use parentheses to control the order of operation. You also learned the difference between relative cell references and absolute cell references. With relative cell references, when a formula is copied to another cell, the reference changes to reflect the cell that is in the same relative position to the solution cell. An absolute cell reference always refers to the same cell when the formula is copied into other cells. An absolute cell reference is indicated by dollar signs to the left of the column letter and row number. You practiced using the fill handle to copy a formula to adjacent cells.

You learned how to use functions to determine the AVERAGE, MEDIAN, MINIMUM, and MAXIMUM of a series of numbers. Functions such as these use arguments, which are the cells that contain the values needed to calculate the results. When you use these functions, it is important to recognize what they can tell you about the data and the limitations of each.

Finally, you created two charts to graphically represent numbers and create a visual display of the data. Line charts are often used to show trends when something changes over time. Column charts are often used to make direct comparisons between two or more sets of values, and pie charts are used to show how parts contribute to the whole. You examined the charts to look for patterns and potential errors. You also observed the data points between known points, which is called interpolation, and beyond either end of the chart, which is called extrapolation.

You can extend your learning by reviewing concepts and terms and by practicing variations f skills presented in the lessons

## KEY TERMS

# KEY TERMS

| absolute reference | chart | fill handle |
|---|---|---|
| arguments | circular reference | interpolation |
| AutoFill | extrapolation | relative reference |

# CHECKING CONCEPTS AND TERMS

## SCREEN ID

Label each element of the screen shown in Figure 9.30.

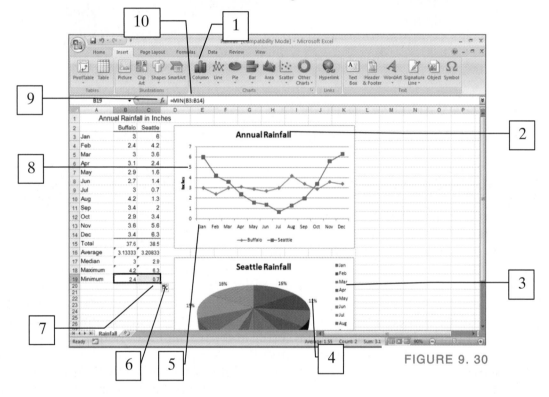

FIGURE 9. 30

_____ A. AutoFill options

_____ B. Category axis

_____ C. Chart title

_____ D. Column chart button

_____ E. Data label

_____ F. Fill handle

_____ G. Function argument

_____ H. Insert Function button

_____ I. Legend

_____ J. Value axis

## MULTIPLE CHOICE

**Circle the letter of the correct answer for each of the following.**

1. If the value in cell A1 is 12, B1 is 4, and C2 is 2, which of the following formulas will produce a result of 2? _____. [L1]

   a. =A1+B1+C2
   b. =A1/B1+C2
   c. =A1*C2/B1
   d. =A1/(B1+C2)

2. If cell D7 has the formula, =B3, and you fill the formula into cell D8, which of the following equations represent the formula in D8? _____ [L1]

   a. =D8
   b. =B4
   c. =C3.
   d. =D9

3. The function that is so commonly used that it has its own button on the Home tab is the _____ function. [L2]

   a. AVERAGE
   b. COUNT
   c. MIN
   d. SUM

4. The inputs required by a function are called _____. [L3]

   a. data
   b. arguments
   c. insights
   d. inputs

5. If two columns of data each containing ten rows of data have the same SUM, AVERAGE, and MEDIAN, which of the following conclusions will always be correct? _____ [L3]

   a. The total of both columns is the same
   b. The patterns of variation within the data is the same

   c. The value of any one of the items in the column will be close to the average
   d. If the data varies with time, the same pattern is likely to continue in the future

6. If a group raised money by doing seven different fund-raisers, the best chart to show how each fund-raiser contributed to the total money raised is a _____ chart. [L4]

   a. bar
   b. column
   c. line
   d. pie

7. If you have data that shows the population of your city for each of the last fifty years and you want to look for a trend, the best chart for this purpose would be a _____ chart. [L4]

   a. bar
   b. column
   c. line
   d. pie

8. If you are running a contest between two groups and you have a table that shows how the two groups did in each of eight categories, the best chart to use that will show how the two groups compared in each category would be a _____ chart. [L4]

   a. area
   b. column
   c. line
   d. pie

9. If you have census data that shows the population of your county every ten years for the last one hundred years and you want to estimate the population for a year during that period that was not a census year, this type of estimate is called _____ and your confidence of its accuracy is fairly _____. [L5]

  a. extrapolation, high
  b. extrapolation, low
  c. interpolation, high
  d. interpolation, low

10. If you have census data that shows the population of your county every ten years for the last one hundred years and you want to estimate the population of the county one hundred years from now, this type of estimate is called _____ and your confidence of its accuracy is fairly _____. [L5]

  a. extrapolation, high
  b. extrapolation, low
  c. interpolation, high
  d. interpolation, low

## DISCUSSION

1. In this project, you saw how the rainfall in two cities appeared to be the same at first when you compared the SUM, AVERAGE, and MEDIAN functions, but by using other functions and charts, different patterns appeared. What would be another example of two groups of data that might appear to be the same at first glance, but have different patterns of variation? [L3]

2. In this project, you saw what could happen if you try to extrapolate part of a pattern. Do you think we may be doing this by extrapolating the recent warming trend in the world's temperature? What is the pattern of world temperature? [L5]

3. Some people use charts to exaggerate variations. The way they do this is to change the scale on the value axis so that it does not start at zero. For example, if the murders in a city for the last four years were 103, 97, 98, and 102, the line chart would look fairly flat and you might conclude that there has not been a big change. If the value axis labels start at 95 and stop at 105, the line chart looks like there was a big drop and then a steady increase. Have you seen this type of chart? If so, what was the chart and did it give a false impression? Do you think it is ethical to use a chart in this manner? [L4]−[L5]

## SKILL DRILL

Skill Drill exercises reinforce project skills. Each skill reinforced is the same, or nearly the same, as a skill presented in the project. Detailed instructions are provided in a step-by-step format.

In these exercises, you create a table that uses formulas and functions to calculate the payments and monthly balances on a car loan. To complete the Skill Drill exercises, open the Excel workbook *EX_0904* and save a 97-2003 compatible file and name it **Loan**. Do all the exercises in sequence to complete the worksheet and the analysis. Be sure to save your changes and close the workbook if you need more than one work session to complete the desired exercises. Continue working on the *Loan* workbook instead of starting over with the original file. Print copies of the worksheets if your instructor requires it. All of these exercises can be completed using Microsoft Office XP or later versions. Instructions throughout the exercises are based on a Windows XP operating system, running Microsoft Office 2007.

## 1. Using Formulas

The PMT function uses arguments that are all based on the same unit of time. If you make monthly payments, the PMT function needs the number of payments and the interest rate for one month. In this exercise, you enter formulas, plus calculate monthly interest rates, months in the loan period, the total amount paid, and the total interest paid.

1. Open the *Loan* workbook and Click **B5**. The annual interest rate is in cell B4. To calculate the monthly interest rate, you need to divide the value in cell B4 by 12.

2. Type **=B4/12** and click **Enter** on the formula bar.

3. Format cell B5 to Percent Style with two decimal places. The correct value is 0.65%. This is the interest rate you would pay on the unpaid balance for one month.

4. Click **B7**. Type **=B6*12** and click **Enter** on the formula bar. This formula calculates the number of months in the loan by multiplying the number of years in B6 by the number of months in a year.

5. Click **B9**. Type **=B7*B8** and click **Enter** on the formula bar. This formula multiplies the number of monthly payments times the amount of the payment. Because there is no value yet in B8, the value in B9 is zero.

6. Click **B10**. Type **=B9-B3** and press [Enter ←]. This formula calculates the total interest paid on the loan by subtracting the *Loan Amount* from the *Total Paid*. The amount currently displays as ($25,000.00), which is the way Excel represents a negative number. This number is negative because the *Total Paid* cell — B9 — displays zero.

7. Display the Header area and add your name, class name, and the date in the Header. Display the Page Setup dialog box, and on the **Margin** tab, center the worksheet **Horizontally**. On the **Page** tab, click the **Fit to** option under *Scaling*.

8. On the status bar click the **Normal** button to return to the Normal view. Save the *Loan* workbook and leave it open to continue with the next Skill Drill.

## 2. Using the PMT Function

In this exercise, you use the PMT function to calculate the monthly payment for the car loan.

1. With the *Loan* workbook open, click **B8**. Click the **Insert Function button** on the formula bar.

2. In the Insert Function dialog box, click the *Or select a category* arrow and click **Financial**. Scroll down the list of functions in the *Select a function* box and click **PMT**. Click **OK**.

3. The Function Arguments dialog box opens. The first three arguments are indicated in bold and the last two are normal. The *Fv* (future value) and *Type* (used to indicate if the payment will take place at the beginning or end of the period) arguments are optional.

4. Click the *Rate* box and type **B5**, which is the monthly rate you calculated.

5. Click the *Nper* box and type **B7**, which is the number of months.

6. Click the *Pv* box and type **B3**, which is the present value of the loan amount..

7. Click **OK**. The payment that will pay off the loan is calculated and placed in the cell. This function calculates a value that is the opposite sign of the loan amount. In this case, the cell is formatted to show negative numbers as red with parentheses.

8. Double-click **B8**. Edit the formula to place a minus sign (a dash) between the equal sign and the PMT function. Click the **Enter** button on the formula bar. The Payment should be $607.39 and the total of all the payments in B9 should be $29,154.89.

9. Save the Loan workbook. Leave the file open if you plan to work on the next exercise.

## 3. Using Relative and Absolute Cell References in Formulas

In this exercise, you use relative and absolute formulas to fill in a payment table to see how the balance of the loan will decrease over the 48 months of the loan.

1. With the *Loan* workbook open, click **G4**. Observe that this cell contains a formula that references the loan amount in B3.

2. Click **E5**. The cells in this column should all show the payment that is calculated in B8. Type **=$B$8** and click the **Enter** button on the formula bar. The value from B8 is shown in E5.

3. Click **F5**. The interest that must be paid is calculated by multiplying the balance from the previous month by the monthly interest rate. Type **=G4*$B$5** and click **Enter** on the formula bar. The interest due on the loan after one month is 161.46.

4. Click **G5**. The new balance is calculated by taking the balance from the previous month, adding the amount of interest, and then subtracting the payment. Type **=G4+F5−E5** and then click **Enter** on the formula bar. The balance after one month is $24,554.06.

5. The formulas in cells E5, F5, and G5 are designed with a mix of relative and absolute cell references so they may be filled into the cells below to complete a table. You will do this in the next exercise.

6. Save the *Loan* workbook and leave the workbook open to continue with the next exercise.

## 4. Filling Dates and Formulas

A date is just a number that is formatted to display as a date. However, there are special programs built into spreadsheets to help fill dates in common intervals, such as months that are not always the same length. You may use the right mouse button when you drag the fill handle of a cell with a date in it to see a shortcut menu of options.

1. With the *Loan* workbook open, click **D5**.

2. Position the mouse pointer on the fill handle. Use the right mouse button instead of the left to drag the fill handle down to D52. When you release the mouse button a shortcut menu displays. On this shortcut menu click **Fill Months** from the list. The last payment date is 12/15/2008.

3. Select cells **E5** through **G5**. You can fill several formulas at once by first selecting the cells you want to copy and then using the one fill handle on the right-most cell.

4. Use the left mouse button to drag the fill handle on the corner of **G5** downward to **G52** and then release the mouse button. All three columns are filled at once. The balance value in G52 should be 0.00.

5. Save your changes and leave the *Loan* workbook open to continue with the next exercise.

## 5. Evaluating Data in a Table

One of the great strengths of spreadsheets is their ability to recalculate many formulas that depend upon a few variables to see what happens if you change those variables.

1. With the *Loan* workbook open, observe the contents of cells B3 and B9. Cell B3 contains the original loan amount and B9 shows the total you pay by the end of the loan period, which is the original amount of the loan plus the interest. You pay back $29,154.89 for an original loan of $25,000. The total interest for the loan is in cell B10.

2. Click **B6**. One way to lower the monthly payment for a car loan is to increase the number of years to pay back the loan. Type **5** and press [Enter ←].

3. Notice that all the formulas that depend on this cell were recalculated. The monthly payment in B8 dropped over $100 per month, but the total amount paid for the loan in B9 increased by more than one thousand dollars.

4. Scroll to the bottom of the table and observe the balance on the loan in G52. If you sell the car after four years, you would still owe $5,800.71, which reduces the amount of money you would get from the sale of the car.

5. Preview the worksheet and make sure it displays on one page. Print the worksheet (optional).

6. Click **B6** and type **4** to return the loan to a four-year term. Save your changes and leave the *Loan* workbook open to continue with the next exercise.

## 6. Evaluating a Table with a Chart

A chart of the monthly interest will reveal how much of the monthly payment goes toward paying the interest and how this decreases during the life of the loan.

1. With the Loan workbook open, select **D5** through **D52**. Hold the [Ctrl] key and drag across cells **F5** through **F52** to select two non-adjacent columns of data.

2. Click the **Insert tab** and in the **Charts group** click Line and then click the Line with Markers chart type.

3. On the Chart Tools Layout Table, in the Labels group click **Chart Title** and then click **Above Chart**. In the formula bar type `Monthly Interest` and then press [Enter ←].

4. In the **Labels group** click **Legend** and then click **None** to remove the legend from the chart. When only one type of data is charted a legend is unnecessary.

5. Click the **Chart Tools Design tab** and in the **Location group** click **Move Chart**. In the New sheet text box type `Monthly Interest` and then click **OK**.

6. The chart is placed on a separate sheet named Monthly Interest. Examine the chart, which shows that over $160 of the first payment goes toward paying interest, but it decreases each month to less than $20 near the end of the loan period.

7. Display the Page Setup dialog box. Click the **Header/Footer tab**, and then click the **Custom Header** button. Add your name to the Left section, class name in the Center section and date in the Right section. and then click **OK**

twice. to a Custom Header for this worksheet and then print it (optional). To add information to the header or footer of a chart sheet, it is necessary to use the Custom Header and Footer dialog box.

8. Save your changes. Close the workbook and close Excel.

## CHALLENGE

Challenge exercises expand on or are somewhat related to skills presented in the lessons. Each exercise provides a brief narrative introduction, followed by instructions in a numbered-step format that are not as detailed as those in the Skill Drill section.

Each exercise is independent of the others, so you may complete the exercises in any order.

### 1. Filling a Series

The AutoFill option has several useful choices. You can fill a series of dates or numbers. Some series, such as population, grow by a percentage of the previous number. The result is growth that is not a straight line. In this exercise, you use the fill feature to estimate future population of a city. In some computer labs, the right mouse button is disabled for security purposes. You will learn an alternative method for filling series of numbers that works for some of the series.

1. Locate and open the **EX_0905** workbook and save it as a 97-2003 compatible file and name it **Population**. The population of the United States is increasing at a rate of approximately 1% of the previous population each year. You will fill a table of years and population estimates that extrapolates this trend to the year 2050.

2. Click **A4**. Type **1998** and then press Enter ↵. You can fill a series of numbers that increases by the same amount each time by providing an example of the first two numbers in the series.

3. Select cells **A3** through **A4** and release the mouse button. The pair of cells has one fill handle in the lower-right corner of cell A4.

4. Drag the fill handle in A4 down to A56. A sequence of numbers that represents the years from 1997 through 2050 is filled into this column.

5. Click **Undo** on the Quick Access toolbar. You will learn a shortcut using the right mouse button.

6. Click **A4**. Use the right mouse button and drag the fill handle to A56. Release the mouse button and select **Fill Series** from the top of the shortcut menu. The same series of years fills the column.

7. Click **B3**. Use the right mouse button to drag the fill handle down to B56. Release the mouse button. Click **Series** at the bottom of the shortcut menu. The Series dialog box opens.

8. In the Series dialog box, click **Growth** under Type. Click the **Step value** box and type **1.01**. Click **OK**. The population in 2050 will be approximately 440 million if this extrapolation is correct.

9. Add your name, class name, and date to the header and center the worksheet horizontally.

10. Save the *Population* workbook. Print the worksheet if directed by your instructor and then close it.

## 2. Using Column or Bar Charts for Comparisons

A bar chart is similar to a column chart except the bar chart is oriented horizontally. Both are used for making comparisons and are often used when time is not used as the category.

1. 1. Open **EX_0906** and save it as 97-2003 compatible file and name it `Utility Chart`.

2. Select **A4** through **A11**. Hold down Ctrl and drag across **F4** through **F11**.

3. On the Insert tabclick the **Column** chart button and then click the **Clustered Column** chart subtype.

4. Remove the legend.

5. Add a **Chart title**: `May Utilities by Store`.

6. Drag the chart to a location below the table. The bottom of the chart should not extend below row 29 and the right side of the chart should not extend beyond column H.

7. Repeat steps 2 through 6 except choose a bar chart. Use the first chart sub-type in the first row. (Hint: to see the bar chart options, from any of the chart buttons click **All Chart Types** to open the Insert Chart dialog box.)

8. Drag the bar chart below the column chart. The bottom of the chart should not extend below row 47 and the right side of the chart should not extend beyond column H.

9. Click on any cell in the table. Add your name, class, and date to the header. Center the worksheet horizontally on the page. Print the worksheet with the two charts (optional).

10. Save the *Utility Chart* workbook. Close the file and then close Excel.

## 3. Using Absolute and Relative References and Functions

Net pay for employees is the result of the amount of pay multiplied by the hours worked, less taxes that are deducted for federal, social security (FICA), Medicare, state, and others. In this Challenge exercise, you use formulas that incorporate a combination of relative and absolute cell references. You then use the AVERAGE function to determine the average salaries for the six-month period.

1. Open **EX_0907** and save it as a 97-2003 compatible file and named it `Payroll.`

2. Select cell **B5** and type `=B3*$B$15`. In cell **B6**, type `=B3*.20`.

3. In cell **B7**, type `=B3*B16`, press F4, and then press Enter↵. F4 applies the absolute reference symbols to cell B16.

4. Select cells **B5:B7** and use the fill handle in the lower-right corner of cell **B7** to copy the formulas to the right to column G. Format the numbers with the Comma Style and no decimals.

5. Select cell **B8**. Write a formula that will multiply the salaries by an absolute reference to the Medicare tax percent (refer to the *Fixed Percentages* table in the worksheet). Use the fill handle to copy the formula to the right to column G. Use the same format for these cells as applied in the previous step.

6. Sum the deductibles in each column in row 9. Notice that the empty cell in row 4 prevents the Sum function from accidentally selecting the salaries in row 3.

7. Calculate the net salary figures by writing a formula in cell **B11** that takes the salaries for the month and subtracts the deductibles for the month. Copy the formula to cells C11 through G11.

8. In cell **B16**, change the State Tax to 6%. The worksheet is recalculated. The net salary for June should be *$1,773,694*.

9. In cell **H3**, use the AVERAGE function to determine the average gross salary expense for the first six months of the year. Copy this down column H through H11. In cells H4 and H10, the *#DIV/0!* error code displays, which happens when a number is divided by zero (0). In this case, it is because there are no values in rows 4 or 10. Delete the error code in these two cells.

10. Add a Bottom Border to the figures in row 8. Format cells H5:H9 with the Comma Style and no decimals.

11. Add your name, class name, and date to the header. Change the page orientation to Landscape and center the worksheet horizontally.

12. Save the *Payroll* workbook and then print it (optional). Press ⌃Ctrl + ⌐. In the Page Setup dialog box, fit the formulas to one page and print the formulas. Return the worksheet to the results. Close the file and close Excel.

## DISCOVERY ZONE

Discovery Zone exercises require advanced knowledge of topics presented in *Essentials* lessons, application of skills from multiple lessons, or self-directed learning of new skills. Each exercise is independent of the others, so you may complete the exercises in any order.

### 1. Using Goal Seek

In some cases, you know what the outcome of a calculation should be, but you do not know the input values that will produce that result. For example, you may know that you can afford a monthly car payment of $350, but you do not know how much you can borrow at the current interest rates for that monthly payment. For this type of problem, you can use the Goal Seek feature.

In this exercise, you use Goal Seek to learn how this type of feature works

1. Open **EX_0908** and save it as `Goal Seek`. This file has the formulas used to determine the monthly payment for a car loan. In this example, you know you can only afford a monthly car payment of $350.

2. Click **B6**. Click the **Data tab**, and in the **Data Tools group** click **What-If Analysis** and then click **Goal Seek**. The Goal Seek dialog box opens.

3. Confirm that the *Set cell* box shows B6. Click the **To value box** and type `350`. Click the **By changing cell** box and type **B1**. Click **OK**.

4. The program tries a variety of numbers in cell B1 until it gets close to the value you specified. The result in B1, which is a little over 14,400, is the amount you could borrow if the other arguments for the PMT function are not changed. Click **OK**. Add your name, class name, and date in the header and center the

worksheet horizontally. Print this worksheet if your instructor requires it. Save your changes, close the *Goal Seek* workbook, and close Excel

## 2. Tracking Grades

Excel is a great tool for recording and tracking grades for classes. In this Discovery Zone exercise, you will calculate the total points accumulated, plus the average, minimum, and maximum points scored for each assignment. You will also count the number of students and the number of non-zero scores for each assignment.

1. Open **EX_0909** and save it as a 97-2003 compatible file and name it **Class Scores**. Take a moment to explore this worksheet. Student scores are recorded in rows 3 through 21. The total possible points for each assignment are recorded in row 2.

2. Click cell **C3**. Click the **View tab**, and in the **Window group** click, click the **Freeze Panes** button and then from the list click **Freeze Panes**. This will keep the column headings and the student names in column B on the screen as you scroll across the worksheet. When you are working with a large worksheet, it is helpful to have the column and row headings displayed at all times.

3. In cell B22, type **=COUNTA** ( and then drag the range B3:B21, and press ⌷Enter ↵⌷. When you use a function, you can enter the function and its arguments directly in the results cell and drag to select the cell range to include in the argument. The closing parenthesis is added by the program when you press ⌷Enter ↵⌷.

4. Click cell **C22** and display the Insert Function dialog box. Under *Statistical functions*, select **COUNTIF**. In the *Function Argument* box, enter **C3:C21** as the range. In the *Criteria* box, type **>0** and click **OK**. Copy this function across row 22 to cell AC22. This is a specialized count function that counts cells when a specified condition is true. In this manner, you can determine how many students completed each assignment—zero (0) indicates the assignment was not completed.

5. In cell **C23**, enter the **AVERAGE** function for the grades in column C. Similarly, enter the **MIN** function in cell C24 and the **MAX** function in cell C25. Copy these three functions across to column AC. Be sure that to only include the student scores in the range arguments.

6. In cell **AD3**, use the Sum function to calculate the total score for *David*. Fill this function down column AD.

7. In cell **AE3**, calculate what percent of the total possible points in cell AD2 is contained in cell AD3. Use an absolute cell reference where needed so this formula can be copied down column AE. Format the results as a percent with no decimals and then copy it down the column.

8. Fill the formulas from rows 22 through 25 through to column AE. Save your changes.

9. Preview the worksheet and view the second page. Notice how the student names display on the second page of the printout. Close the Preview window. Display the Page Setup dialog box. Add your name, class, and date to the header. Click the Sheet tab. Notice that column B is set to repeat at the left of the worksheet. Print the worksheet (optional)

10. Save the *Class Scores* workbook. Close the file and then close Excel.

# UNIT 2: USING PRODUCTIVITY SOFTWARE

## Microsoft Office 2007 IC³

### Project 10: Creating and Delivering Presentations

**LESSON 1** Creating a Presentation and Working in Different Views

| | | |
|---|---|---|
| 2-4.1.1 | 2-4.1.3.2 | 2-4.1.8 |
| 2-4.1.2 | 2-4.1.3.3 | |
| 2.4.1.3.1 | 2-4.1.4 | |

**LESSON 2** Adding Data Elements to a Presentation

| | |
|---|---|
| 2-4.1.1 | 2-4.1.3.6 |
| 2-4.1.3.5 | 2-4.1.5 |

**LESSON 3** Applying a Theme (Design) and Adding Footers

| | | |
|---|---|---|
| 2-4.1.1 | 2-4.1.3.7 | 2-4.1.6 |

**LESSON 4** Enhancing a Presentation with Graphics

| | | |
|---|---|---|
| 2-4.1.1 | 2-4.1.3.4 | 2-4.1.5 |

**LESSON 5** Animating a Presentation

| | |
|---|---|
| 2-4.1.1 | 2-4.1.7 |

**LESSON 6** Creating Speaker Notes and Handouts

| | |
|---|---|
| 2-4.1.1 | 2-4.1.9 |

**LESSON 7** Previewing and Navigating a Slide Show Presentation

| | | |
|---|---|---|
| 2-4.1.1 | 2-4.1.10 | 2-4.1.11 |

# PROJECT 10

# CREATING AND DELIVERING PRESENTATIONS

IN THIS PROJECT, YOU LEARN HOW TO:

- Create a Presentation and Work in Different Views
- Add Data Elements to a Presentation
- Apply a Theme (Design) and Add Footers
- Enhance a Presentation with Graphics
- Animate a Presentation
- Create Speaker Notes and Handouts
- Preview and Navigate a Slide Show Presentation

# WHY WOULD I DO THIS?

In your personal or professional life, you may be asked to make a presentation to a group. Presentation software can help you get organized, stay on track, cover all the important information, and have fun at the same time. Microsoft Office PowerPoint is a presentation graphics program that helps you convey information to an audience. With it, you can create visually appealing slides, handouts for the audience, and notes for the presenter.

Presentations are delivered using transparencies displayed using a flatbed overhead projector or, more commonly, an electronic slide show that uses a projector connected to a computer to display each screen. Using an electronic slide show provides more options because you can animate slides and graphics, which helps control the pace of delivery and creates additional visual interest for the audience. Data elements such as charts and tables can also be added to slides.

In this project, you create a PowerPoint presentation by importing an outline, adding, deleting, and modifying slides. You apply a design, and add graphics, a chart and a table. Finally, you animate the slides, create speaker notes and handouts, and then preview and navigate the slide show.

# VISUAL SUMMARY

In this project, you create a presentation to train others to create an effective presentation. When you are done, you will have created a complete presentation with all of the elements that are typically used. Figure 10.1 shows audience handouts that you create as part of this project.

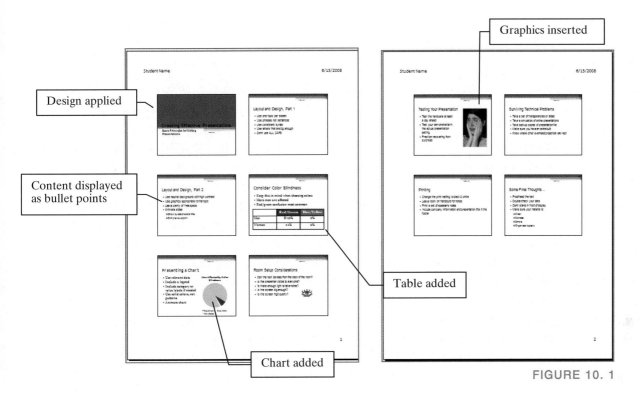

FIGURE 10. 1

You also create speaker notes to use during the presentation to provide the speaker with reminders about additional information that needs to be covered. Figure 10.2 is an example of one of the speaker notes that is created

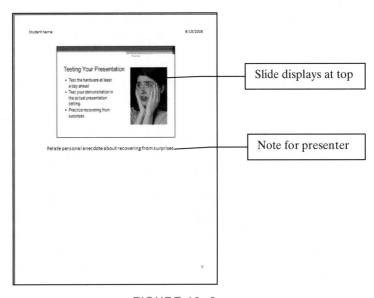

FIGURE 10. 2

# LESSON 1: Creating a Presentation and Working in Different Views

When you create a presentation, start with the content. Answer the questions: What needs to be covered and in what order should the information be presented? PowerPoint has three main views: Normal, Slide Sorter, and Slide Show. The **Normal view** includes a panel on the left with a **Slides tab** and an **Outline tab**, a **Notes pane** at the bottom, and a **Slide pane** in the middle- right. You can enter content on the Slide pane or in the Outline tab. The panel on the left can display the content as thumbnail slides or as a text outline. This helps you focus on the flow of ideas. The slide pane in the center helps you focus on one particular topic at a time. As you create your outline, you may find that you want to add notes to yourself to help you remember things you want to say when you cover a particular topic. Notes can be added as you create the slides by inserting comments in the notes pane of the Normal view. The **Slide Sorter view** is used to examine the overall flow of ideas and rearrange slides. The **Slide Show view** is used to present the information to your audience.

In this lesson, you create a presentation by importing an outline that was created in Microsoft Office Word 2003. You will then edit the content and rearrange the slides. All of these exercises can be completed with Microsoft Office 2007. Instructions throughout the lessons are based on the Windows XP operating system, running Microsoft Office 2007. Your screen may differ slightly from the figures shown, even if you are running Office 2007.

## To Create a Presentation and Import an Outline

1. **Start PowerPoint 2007.** PowerPoint opens in Normal view, and the first slide displays the title slide *layout*, which is the arrangement of *placeholders*. Placeholders are preformatted areas that define the type of information to place in each area on the slide. They contain instructions about how to proceed. For example, the title slide displays *Click to add title*, and the second placeholder displays *Click to add subtitle.*

2. **Click in the *Click to add title* placeholder and type:** `Creating Effective Presentations.` Notice that on the Home tab, in the Font group the Font Size box displays *44*, the Font box displays *Calibri (Headings)*, and the *Center* alignment button is selected. Also notice that as you type on the slide, the same text displays in the Slides tab or Outline tab on the left, depending on which tab is currently selected.

3. **Click in the *Click to add subtitle* placeholder and type:** `Basic Principles for Making Presentations.` The subtitle for your presentation is added. Notice that on the in the Font group the Font Size box displays *32*, the Font box displays *Calibri (body)*, and the *Center* button is again selected. Each placeholder is preformatted for the font, font size, and alignment. This text wraps to two lines.

4. **If necessary, click the Slides tab at the top of the Slides/Outline panel on the left side of the screen.** A thumbnail of the slide displays as shown in Figure 10.3.

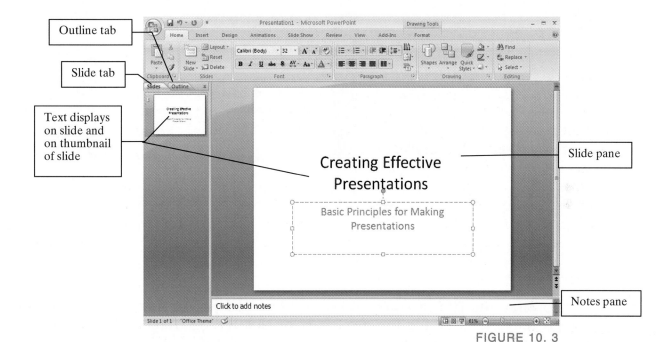

Outline tab

Slide tab

Text displays on slide and on thumbnail of slide

Slide pane

**Creating Effective Presentations**

Basic Principles for Making Presentations

Notes pane

FIGURE 10. 3

5. **On the Home tab, in the Slides group click the New Slide button arrow. At the bottom of the displayed gallery click Slides from Outline.** The Insert Outline dialog box displays. This is similar to the Open dialog box and is used to locate files on your computer. To successfully insert a file into a PowerPoint presentation it must already be in an outline format using appropriate heading styles.

6. **Navigate to the student files for this chapter, select *PP_1001*.doc and then click the Insert button.** The content of the file is inserted and placed on seven slides. The status bar displays *Slide 2 of 8*. The content on each slide displays as a bulleted list. Subtopics are indented and display a different bullet symbol.

7. **Click the Outline tab on the left side of the window.** The content of the outline can be read and you can see the overall flow of topics as shown in Figure 10.4. There is a separate scroll bar for each area in the Normal view. The buttons at the bottom of the slide pane scroll bar are used to move between slides.

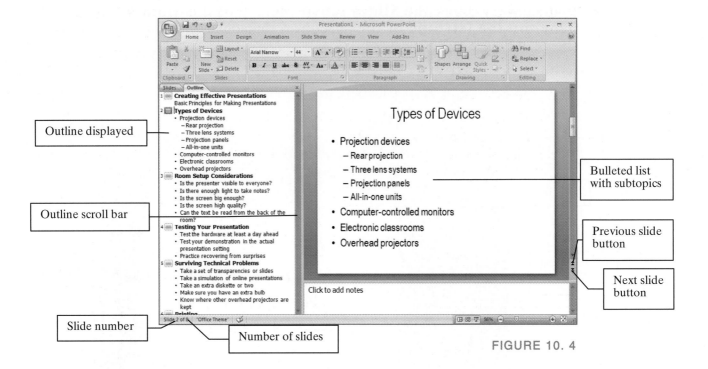

Outline displayed

Outline scroll bar

Slide number

Number of slides

Bulleted list with subtopics

Previous slide button

Next slide button

FIGURE 10. 4

8. **Save the file in your folder as Effective Presentations and leave it open for the next part of this lesson.** If the file extensions are not hidden for known file types, the PowerPoint 2007 file extension—*.pptx*—will be added to the end of the file name.

You can alter a presentation by typing on the slide, or by typing in the outline view. When you create a presentation, you want to make sure each bullet point on a slide relates to the main slide topic. Inserting an outline is an easy method for inserting content, and then you can edit the material to suit the audience. You can also insert slides, delete slides, edit content, or rearrange topics on a slide. In the next part of this lesson, you review the slides you have inserted, delete a slide, edit other slides, add some notes to the notes pane, and insert a new slide.

## To Edit a Presentation

1. **Click the slide 2 icon on the outline tab.** The entire slide 2 topic is selected. This topic concerns different types of projector options. The audience to whom the presentation will be made will be using laptop computers with connected projectors, so these issues do not need to be covered.

2. **Press Delete.** The slide is removed and the remaining slides are renumbered. The new slide 2 discusses room setup issues.

3. **Read the content of slide 2 and then click in the notes pane at the bottom of the Normal view and type:** `Tip: To test if a slide can be read from the back of the room, print the slide and place it on the floor. If you can read it from a standing position, it will probably be large enough to read from the back of the room.` This tip is placed in the notes area as shown in Figure 10.5, and will display on the speaker notes when they are printed. This note creates a reminder for the presenter that will be used when the presentation is made.

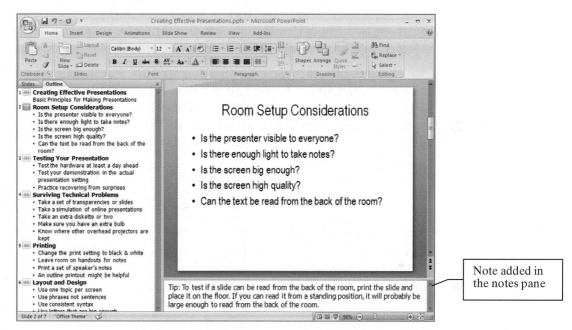

Note added in the notes pane

FIGURE 10.5

4. **Click the Next Slide button at the bottom of the slide pane scroll bar and then read the contents of slide 3.** Slide three recommends practicing your presentation in the setting where it will be given at least a day ahead. If this is not possible, you should plan to arrive at the presentation location early enough to test your slide show with the equipment and in the room where it will be given.

5. **Click in the notes pane and type** `Relate personal anecdote about recovering from surprises.` Including relevant personal stories during a presentation captures the attention of your audience and increases motivation.

6. **Click the Next Slide button and read the contents of slide 4; on the slide, select the third bulleted item by clicking on the bullet and type:** `Take backup copies of presentation file.` Whenever you use audiovisual equipment, it is a good idea to be prepared with a backup plan in case of technical problems. All of the items listed on this slide are tips for recovering from potential technical problems.

7. **Click the Next Slide button and read the contents of slide 5; on the outline tab, select the last bullet and type:** `Include company information and presentation title in footer.` This replaces the selected bullet point. The presentation can be created or edited in either the outline tab or on the slide pane. Which one you use is a matter of personal preference. As you type in one area, the same words appear in the other area on the window. Notice that the bulleted items do not include periods, even when they are complete sentences.

8. **Click the Next Slide button and read the contents of slide 6; click to the right of** *Design* **in the title placeholder and type a comma and then type** `Part 1.` All of these points are important to basic slide design, but there are additional design issues that need to be included. To do this you will insert a duplicate of this slide, alter the title, and change the content.

   **On the Home tab, in the Slides group, click the New Slides button arrow and at the end of the displayed gallery click Duplicate Selected Slides.** A duplicate of slide 6 is inserted following slide 6 and displays as slide 7 as shown in Figure 10.6. Alternatively, on the Slides/Outline panel, right-click the slide you want to duplicate, and then click Duplicate Slide from the shortcut menu.

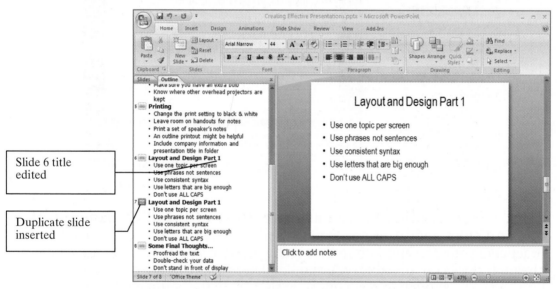

FIGURE 10. 6

9. Select *1* in the title of slide 7 and type 2. Select the entire bulleted list, type: `Use neutral background with high contrast` and then press [Enter ↵]. The previous list is removed and the first item in a new list is added. Pressing [Enter ↵] moves the insertion point to the next line and a new bullet displays. The bullet remains gray until you type the next item.

10. **Following the same process, enter the next three points on slide 7:**

    `Use graphics appropriate to the topic`

    `Leave plenty of free space`

    `Animate slides`

11. **Press** Enter↵ **and then press** Tab, **type:** `Show bullets one at a time`, **press** Enter↵ **and type:** `Dim previous point`. Two subpoints are added under *Animate slides*. Pressing Tab indented the bullet point to the next level, the same as in an outline. Notice that a different bullet symbol and font size are used for the subpoints.

12. **Click the Next Slide button and read the contents on slide 8. Click at the end of the last bullet point on slide 8, press** Enter↵ **and type:** `Make sure your material is`: A new bullet point is added at the end of this slide that requires subpoints.

13. **Press** Enter↵, **press** Tab, **and then type:** `Clear`. The subpoint is indented under the last bullet point.

14. **Press** Enter↵ **and type:** `Concise`, **press** Enter↵ **and type:** Simple, **press** Enter↵ **and type:** `Organized logically`. Four subpoints are added under the last bullet point on slide 8 as shown in Figure 10.7. Presentations use a basic outline format with a hierarchical structure.

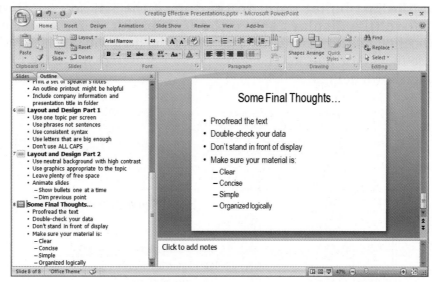

FIGURE 10. 7

15. **Save your changes to the** *Effective Presentations* **file and leave it open for the next part of this lesson.**

---

TO EXTEND YOUR KNOWLEDGE...

## USING BULLETS OR NUMBERS

The most common slide layout is a bulleted list. You can disable the bullets by clicking the Bullets button on the Home tab in the Paragraph group. If a list of items is sequential, you can change the bullets to numbers by clicking the Numbering button on the Home tab in the Paragraph group. If content has already been entered, you must select the list of items before changing the format from bullets to numbers or to no bullets.

---

Normal view is used for creating and editing the presentation. Here you can add notes to the notes pane and review the general flow of information by scrolling through the outline tab. After you have created the basic content you should review the overall flow of ideas and make any organizational changes that are necessary. If you need to reorganize topics within a slide, display the slide in the slide pane and drag the bullet point up or down to move it within the slide. To reorganize information between slides, drag a bullet point from one slide to the next in the outline tab. To rearrange the order of slides, change to the Slide Sorter view and move the entire slide from one location to the next.

## To Reorganize Topics in a Presentation

1. **Scroll to the top of the outline tab and select slide 2.** Slide 2 displays on the slide pane. The last item needs to be moved so it displays as the first item on this list.

2. **Click the bullet for the last point on the slide pane.** When you click on the bullet, the entire text of the bullet point is selected. The mouse pointer changes to a 4-way Move arrow when it is on a bullet.

3. **Drag the last bullet point to the top of the list so it is first; be sure the move line displays above the first bullet item.** As you move this item, a horizontal line displays to indicate where the item will be placed when you release the mouse button. The move pointer is used to move the item within the slide as shown in Figure 10.8.

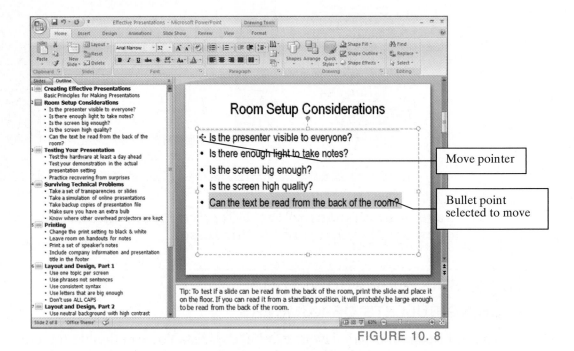

FIGURE 10. 8

4. **Release the mouse button.** The bullet point moves to the top of the list.

5. **Scroll down the outline so that slides 6 and 7 are displayed.** Items can also be moved between slides using the outline pane.

6. **In the outline tab, click the bullet next to the first item listed on slide 6.** *Use one topic per screen* is selected and the mouse pointer changes to a 4-way Move arrow.

7. **Move the selected item so it is the first topic on slide 7.** The move line displays. When you release the mouse button the selected item displays at the location indicated by the line.

8. **Click the Undo button on the Quick Access toolbar.** The move is undone and *Use one topic per screen* redisplays as the first item on slide 6.

9. **Click the View tab, in the Presentation Views group, click Slide Sorter.** In Slide Sorter view, slides display in horizontal rows as shown in Figure 10.9. The active slide—slide 6— has a border around it. This view may be used to rearrange the order of the slides.

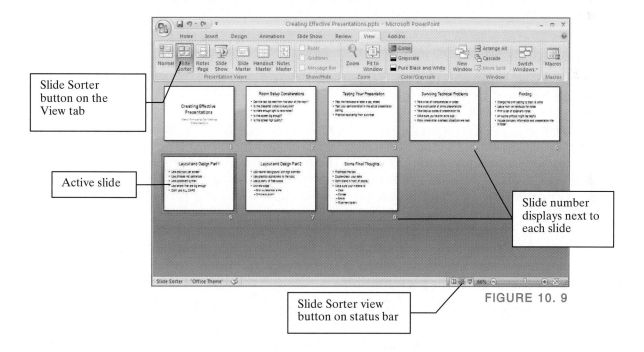

FIGURE 10. 9

10. **Click slide 6 and drag it to a position between slide 1 and slide 2.** As you move, a vertical line displays between slide 1 and 2 to indicate where the selected slide will be placed when you release the mouse button.

11. **Drag slide 7 so it is between slide 2 and slide 3.** This places the slides concerning layout and design at the beginning of the presentation. Notice that the remaining slides are renumbered as shown in Figure 10.10.

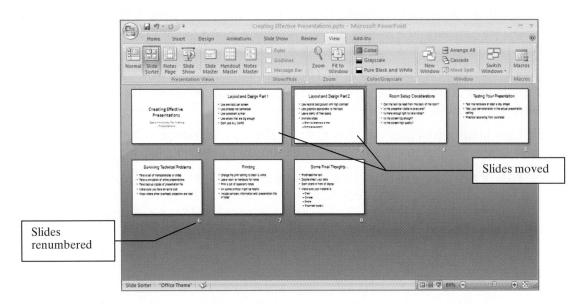

FIGURE 10. 10

12. Save your changes to the *Effective Presentations* file and leave it open for the next lesson.

## LESSON 2: Adding Data Elements to a Presentation

Data can be added to a presentation with a table or a chart. A table gives you a side-by-side comparison of related data, whereas a chart provides a graphical representation of numerical information. A chart or a table can be displayed on a separate slide, or on a slide with a list of related bullet points.

In this lesson, you will add a table and a chart to your presentation to demonstrate to your audience how these data tools can be used. The information used for the table and the chart concerns color blindness, which is something that needs to be considered when you select colors to use in your presentation.

### To Add a Table

1. **With the *Effective Presentations* file open in the Slide Sorter view, on the View tab in the Presentations Views group, click Normal, and then select slide 3.** To create a table you will insert a new slide. New slides are inserted following the active side. The slide layout determines the type of data that will be displayed.

2. **Click the Home tab, and in the Slides group, click New Slide to insert a new slide 4. In the Slides group click Layout.** When you click the top of the New Slide button, the same type of slide is inserted as was used previously— *Title and Text*. In the Layout gallery you can select the type of layout that you want to apply to the slide. You can also select the layout by clicking the New Slide button arrow.

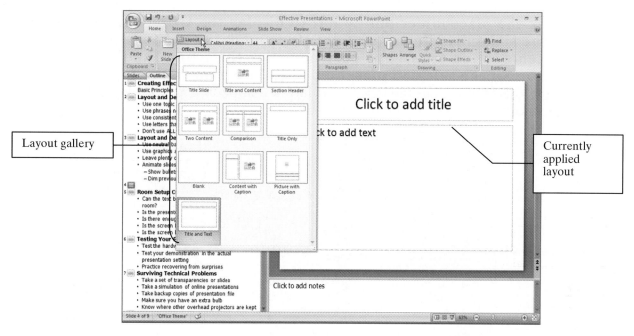

FIGURE 10. 11

3. **In the second row click Two Content.** This layout has a placeholder for a title at the top and two panes with six content icons that you can choose from to add content to the slide as shown in Figure 10.12. When you point to each of the six icons, a ScreenTip displays the type of content that will be added when you click that option. Your choices include: table, chart, SmartArt graphic, picture, clip art, or media clip.

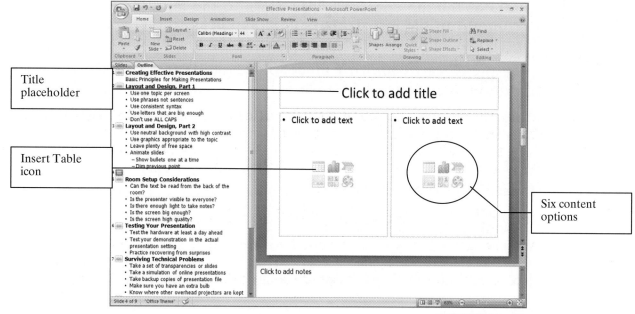

FIGURE 10. 12

4. **Click the placeholder on the left to display the sizing handles. Point to the sizing handle on the right side and drag to the right edge of the placeholder on the right side. Then click the sizing handle on the bottom of the selected placeholder and drag up to the middle of the slide.** This repositions the box on the left to a horizontal shape under the Title placeholder as shown in Figure 10.13.

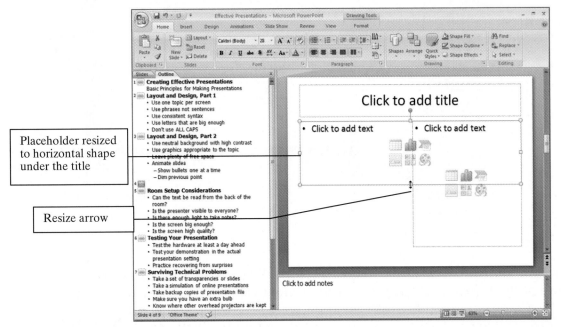

FIGURE 10. 13

5. **Click the placeholder on the right. Point to the sizing handle in the middle of the top edge and drag down to the middle of the slide. Then point to the left sizing handle and drag to the left until the lower placeholder is the same width as the placeholder on the top.**

6. **Click the *Click to add title* placeholder and type:** Consider Color Blindness.

7. **Press** [Ctrl] + [Enter←] **to move to the bullet list placeholder on the top and then enter the following three bullet points:**

Keep this in mind when choosing colors

More men are affected

Red/green confusion most common

Pressing [Ctrl] + [Enter←] can be used to move the insertion point from the title placeholder to the text placeholder on the slide. If you are in the bottom text placeholder, using this keyboard shortcut inserts a new slide with the same slide layout

8. In the placeholder on the bottom, click the Insert Table icon. In the Insert Table dialog box change the Number of columns box to 3 and the Number of rows box to 3 as shown in Figure 10.14.

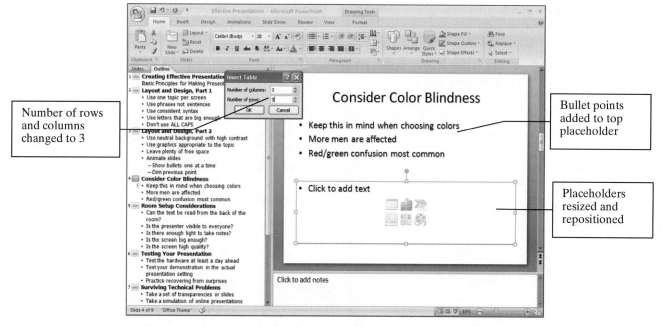

FIGURE 10. 14

9. **Click OK.** A table grid displays on the lower half of the slide in the content placeholder.

10. **Starting in the second cell in the top row of the table, type the data in the table as shown below. Use** [Tab] **to move between cells in the table grid.**

|         | Red/Green | Blue/Yellow |
|---------|-----------|-------------|
| Men     | 8-10%     | 2%          |
| Women   | <1%       | 0%          |

As you enter data, the text will wrap if necessary, and the cell sizes will adjust to accommodate the data.

11. **Point to the center sizing handle on the lower edge of the table and drag down to expand the table to fill the space. Select the content in the last two columns, and then click the Home tab, and in the Paragraph group click the Center button.** Cells in a PowerPoint table can be aligned and formatted similar to formatting a table in Word.

12. **Click in the Red/Green cell. On the Home tab in the Drawing group, click the Shape Fill button. From the displayed gallery, under Standard colors, click the second color—Red.**

13. Click the Blue/Yellow cell and repeat this process to change the color of the cell to Blue found under the Standard Colors.

14. Select the Red/Green and Blue/Yellow cells, and then on the Home tab, in the Paragraph group, click the Align Text button and from the displayed gallery click Middle. The content of both cells is centered vertically within the cell.

15. Select all of the cells in the table. On the Home tab, in the Font group, click the Font Size arrow and change the font size to 28 as shown in Figure 10.15.

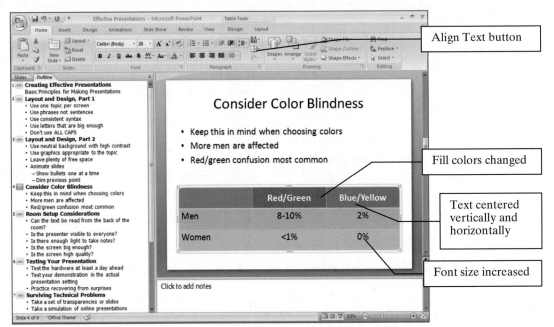

FIGURE 10. 15

16. Select the last two rows in the table, and change the Shape Fill color to white. Then click the first cell in the table and change the fill color to white.

17. Click any cell in the table. On the Table Tools Layout tab, in the Table group, click Select and then click Select Table.

18. Click the Table Tools Design tab, and in the Table Styles group, click the Borders button arrow and then click All Borders. Click outside the table to deselect.

19. Save your changes to the *Effective Presentations* file and leave it open for the next part of this lesson.

The default chart used in PowerPoint is a column chart, which is used to compare two or more sets of data, such as sales for different products, divisions, or time frames. The chart type can be changed to a pie chart, a line chart, or any of the other available chart type. You can also import charts from Microsoft Office Excel. This eliminates the need to recreate the chart and reduces the chance of error. In PowerPoint, charts are manipulated using the same techniques you used in Excel. Charts may be presented with or without related bullet points.

1. With the *Effective Presentations* file open, be sure that slide 4—*Consider Color Blindness*—is the active slide.

2. Click the Home tab, and in the Slides group click the New Slide arrow. From the displayed gallery click Two Content.

3. Click the title placeholder and type: `Presenting a Chart`.

4. Click the text placeholder on the left and type the following points:

   `Use relevant data`

   `Include a legend`

   `Include category or value labels if needed`

   `Use solid colors, not patterns`

   `Animate chart`

5. In the content placeholder on the right, click the Insert Chart icon. In the displayed Insert Chart dialog box, accept the default Column Chart type and click OK. An Excel window displays with data entered as sample data for a chart as shown in Figure 10.16. The Excel window may display side-by-side with the PowerPoint window, rather than on top of it.

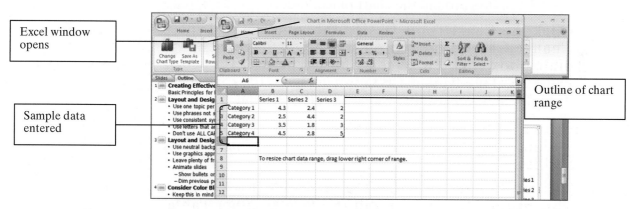

Excel window opens

Sample data entered

Outline of chart range

FIGURE 10. 16

6. In the Excel worksheet click cell B1—*Series1* and type Men, press ⏎ Enter and type 8, press ⏎ Enter and type 2, press ⏎ Enter and then type 90. The data related to color blindness in men is entered in column B in the worksheet. The chart on the slide changes as you enter data in the datasheet.

7. Click cell A2—*Category1*, type: Red/Green and press ⏎ Enter, type: Blue/Yellow, press ⏎ Enter and type: Not Affected. The labels for the data are added to the datasheet. The remaining columns and rows will not be used in this chart, so they need to be removed.

8. **In the worksheet, point to the lower right corner of the data range outline and drag up so that the outlined area only includes cells A1 though B4** The extraneous data is excluded from the chart range and the chart on the slide displays only one color for the three columns that display. When you resize the chart data area you can drag in one direction at a time. If you need to change both the width and the height of the chart data area, first change one dimension, release the mouse and then change the other deminsion.

9. **Close the Excel Chart worksheet. Save your changes to the *Effective Presentations* file and leave it open to continue to the next part of this lesson.** The Excel worksheet that is used to create the chart in PowerPoint is saved as part of the PowerPoint file.

After you create a chart, you may need to modify it in some manner. In this example, the chart type needs to be changed to a pie chart because the data displays a whole population—men—and the percent that are affected by color blindness. You will also add a chart title, move the legend, change the orientation of the pie, and change the color of the pie pieces.

### To Modify a Chart

1. **With slide 5 of *Effective Presentations* displayed, click the chart to make it active and notice that three Chart Tools contextual tabs display: Design, Layout and Format.** When the chart area is active a frame border displays around the chart placeholder.

2. **Click the Chart Tools Design tab, and in the Type group, click the Change Chart Type button. In the displayed Change Chart Type dialog box click Pie in the Chart type list.** The default pie type is selected in the Chart sub-type area as shown in Figure 10.17. The chart types that are available in Excel are also available in PowerPoint.

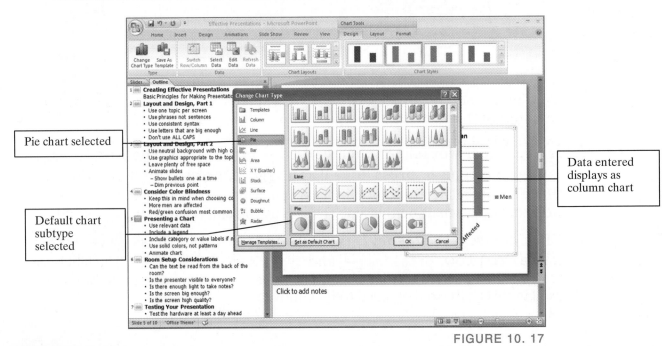

FIGURE 10. 17

3. **Click OK.** The data in the chart displays as a pie chart and the labels that displayed on the category axis now display in a legend.

4. **Right-click the chart title**—*Men*—**and from the displayed shortcut menu click Edit Text. In the chart title box, edit the title to read Men Affected by Color Blindness. Select the chart title text, right-click and on the Mini toolbar, change the font size to 20.**

5. **Click the Chart Tools Layout tab, and in the Labels group, click Legend. From the displayed gallery, click Show Legend at Bottom.** The legend displays along the bottom of the chart area as shown in Figure 10.18.

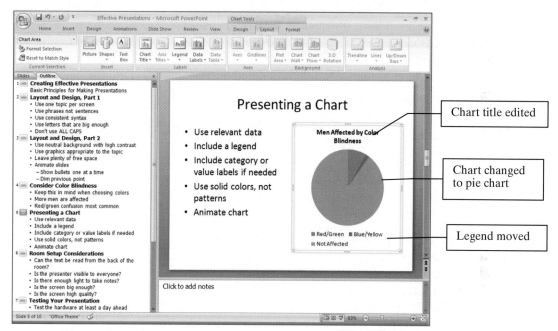

FIGURE 10. 18

6. **On the chart, right-click the pie and select Format Data Series from the shortcut menu.**

7. **In the displayed Format Data Series dialog box, be sure Series Options is selected. On the right side, under Series Options, change the *Angle of first slice* box to 120 *Degrees.*** This action places the first slice of the pie at the lower right.

8. **Click Close. Click the largest piece of the pie to select the pie.** The largest pie piece is selected and displays selection handles around its perimeter. To change the colors used in the pie, first select the piece you want to change.

9. Right-click the large pie piece and choose Format Data Point from the shortcut menu. In the left panel click Fill. In the right panel of the Format Data Point dialog box, click Solid fill. Next to Color click the arrow, and then in the first column click the fourth color—*White, Background 1, Darker 25%.* A muted color is selected, as shown in Figure 10.19, to de-emphasize the 90% that are not affected by color blindness.

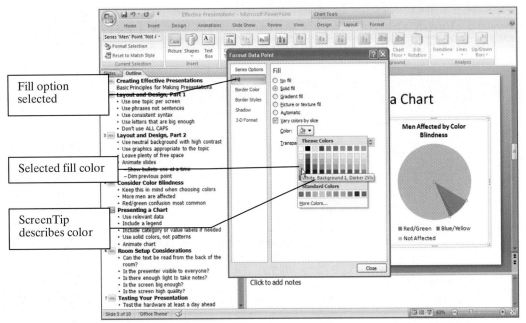

FIGURE 10. 19

10. **Click Close. Click the 8% piece to select it, right-click the selected piece, click Format Data Point. Click Fill and then click the Color arrow. Under Standard colors click Red.** Notice that the colors in the legend change when you change the colors of the pie pieces.

11. **With the Format Data Point dialog box displayed, click the smallest pie piece and change the color to Yellow.** You can format more than one data point when this dialog box is open. Simply click on the next part of the chart that you want to change and then make the necessary changes in the Format Data Point dialog box

12. **Close the Format Data Point dialog box. Click slide 5 on the outline tab to deselect the chart.** The colors of the pie pieces are changed as shown in Figure 10.20.

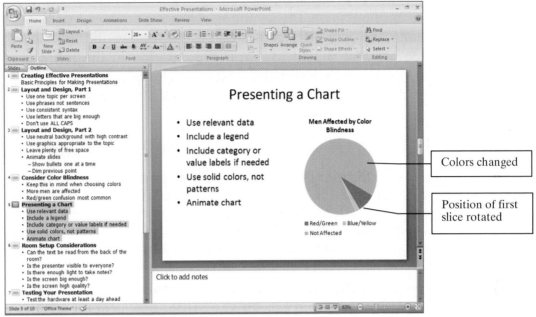

FIGURE 10. 20

13. **Save your changes to the *Effective Presentations* file and leave it open to continue to the next lesson**.

---

## TO EXTEND YOUR KNOWLEDGE...

### USING OTHER CONTENT

When you add content elements to a presentation you can choose from a variety of slide layout arrangements for a combination of text and content. In this lesson, you explored two of the content types that can be added to a presentation. In the Common Elements section of this textbook, you inserted pictures and clip art objects in Microsoft Office Word; they work in a similar manner in Microsoft Office PowerPoint. Microsoft Office 2007 also includes SmartArt Graphics that can be used to insert a variety of charts such as relationship, pyramid, hierarchy charts and many other options to diagram processes and lists.

---

## LESSON 3: Applying a Theme (Design) and Adding Footers

---

After the content is written and organized, apply a theme to create a uniform image for the presentation. When you select a theme, keep in mind the environment in which the presentation will be made and the equipment that will be used. When using a rear-projection device, the edges of the screen are usually black, so a design with a dark or black background works best. If you are using a traditional front projection device, a light or white background may be preferable. Room lighting has a great impact on a presentation. If possible you want to dim the lights just in front of the screen to avoid having a glare on the screen. This is not always possible, however, and if you use a dark slide background, the light glaring on the screen can make the slides hard to read. This is one of the reasons you should test your presentation in the room in which it will be given—to see how it will look with the available lighting controls.

In this lesson, you add a theme, change the design background on a slide, and add information to the footer area of the slides.

### To Apply a Theme and Change the Background

1. **With the *Effective Presentations* file open, click the Design tab. In the Themes group click the More button to display the Themes gallery.** The currently applied design shows at the top, followed by Custom Themes (if any) and then *Built In* themes. The currently applied theme does not include any graphics or background design elements. When you change a theme it can affect the font and font size, background color, if any, and other graphic design elements.

2. **Slowly move the mouse pointer over the theme templates to display the Live Preview feature on the slide.** Live preview enables you to preview a slide theme. After a few moments the slide theme displays on the currently active slide. If you don't like your first selection, simply move to another theme. When you point to a theme a ScreenTip displays its name. Some themes may make your content unreadable.

3. **In the last row, point to the next to last theme—Urban as shown in Figure 10.21.**

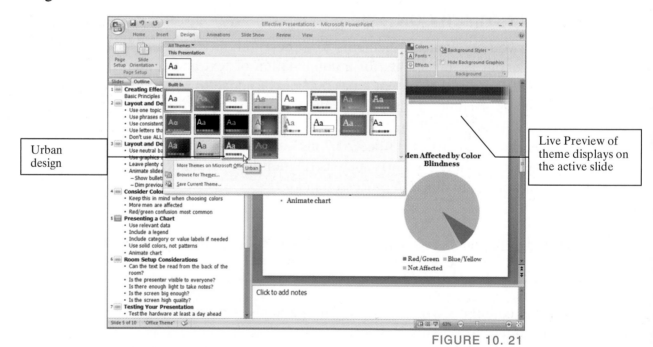

FIGURE 10. 21

4. **Click Urban to apply it to the slides. Click Slide1. On the Design tab, in the Themes group, click Colors to display the Colors gallery.** Different theme color palettes can be applied.

5. **In the displayed Colors gallery click Flow. On the left side click the Slides tab so you can see the effect on all of the slides.** The slides are updated to reflect the color change.

6. **Click slide 2 to make it the active slide.** On the Design tab, in the Background group, click the Dialog Box Launcher to display the Format Background dialog box as shown in Figure 10.22.

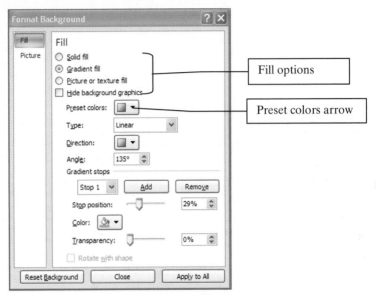

FIGURE 10. 22

7. **Click the Gradient fill option—click the Preset colors arrow and click on a pattern to see how the slide is affected. Experiment with other settings in this box to see the variations you can have.**

8. **Click the Reset Background button to return the background to its previous color. Click the Gradient fill and then click the Preset colors button and then in the second row click the second setting—Ocean. Click Close.** If you create a color pattern and click Apply to All, the background will be applied to all the slides.

9. **Save your changes to the *Effective Presentations* file and leave it open for the next part of this lesson.**

The background elements for the design you selected are controlled in the ***Slide Master view***. Use the slide master to change the font, font size, bullet symbols, and graphics for the design you selected. There is a slide master for the title slide and other slide masters for each slide layout. You can also change the font or font size for the information in the footer area by selecting the footer placeholder in the slide master.

## To Add a Footer and Use the Slide Master

1. **With the *Effective Presentations* file open, in the outline tab click slide 2 to make it the active slide.**

2. **Click the Insert tab, and in the Text group click Header & Footer.**
The Header and Footer dialog box displays as shown in Figure 10.23. Here you can add the date and/or time to be updated automatically each time the file is opened, or as a fixed value that does not change. You can also display a slide number or a customized footer by typing text in the Footer text box.

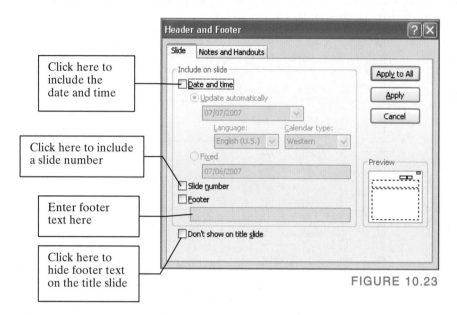

Click here to include the date and time

Click here to include a slide number

Enter footer text here

Click here to hide footer text on the title slide

FIGURE 10.23

3. **Be sure the Slide tab is selected and then clear the check mark from the Date and time check box (if necessary); click the Slide number check box, click the Footer check box and then type your name in the text box.** The preview area displays a dark border around the areas on the slide that are reserved for this information. The location of the date and time, slide number, and footer are determined by the theme that you select. In the Urban theme, the information in the footer displays at the top of the slide rather than the bottom. This change only affects the slides.

4. **Click Apply to All. The text is added to all of the slides.** With this theme the slide number displays in the upper right corner of each slide and the text in the footer box displays just below the graphic at the top of the slide.

5. **Click the View tab, and in the Presentation Views group click Slide Master.** The Urban design Slide Master displays the font, font size, and bullet symbols that are set for each level for this slide design and layout. To change any of these elements, select the level you want to affect and then use the formatting commands on the Mini toolbar or on the Home tab to make changes. Changes made to the slide master affect all slides that use the same layout in this presentation.

6. **In the panel on the left, point to the last slide thumbnail to display the ScreenTip—** *Title and Slide Layout: used by slide(s) 2-3, 6-10.* This ScreenTip tells you which slides will be affected by changes that you make to this slide layout.

7. **Right-click the** *Second level* **on the slide master and point Bullets to display the Bullets submenu.**

8. **In the displayed submenu, in column 3 Row 2 click the bullet option to change the second level bullets.** The bullet used for the second level bullet is changed as shown in Figure 10.24.

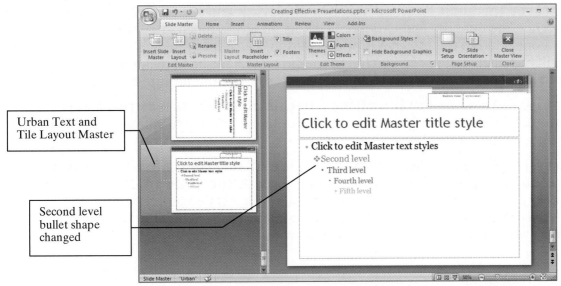

FIGURE 10. 24

9. **In the Close group click Close the Master View, and then click slide 10 to see the effect of the change in the second level bullet.**

10. **Save your changes to the _Effective Presentations_ file and leave it open to continue to the next lesson.**

## LESSON 4: Enhancing a Presentation with Graphics

Clip art, pictures, or custom drawings created with the drawing tools can be added to an existing slide. You can also change the slide layout to include content and select the type of content you want to add, similar to the way you added the table and chart. If you change the slide layout to include a contents placeholder, then the placeholder will determine where the graphic is placed. If you add the graphic to an existing slide you can move it around on the slide and position it anywhere on the slide. Graphics are added to illustrate a point, add humor, or create interest, but should not be added simply for the sake of adding a graphic. They should be relevant to the topic and enhance the idea that is being presented. Drawing tools can also be used to demonstrate a process or work flow.

In this lesson, you add clip art images that are included with your student files to two of the slides.

1. **Click slide 6. Click the Insert tab, and in the Illustrations group click Picture.** The Insert Picture dialog box displays. If you are connected to the Internet, the quantity and variety of clip art images is much greater than if you are not connected to the Internet. For this reason, two clip art images that are available when you are connected to the Internet have been included with your student files so that you can complete this lesson without an Internet connection.

2. **Navigate to your student files for this chapter, select the *Eyes* image file, and then click Insert.** An image of an eye is inserted in the middle of the screen.

3. **Drag the image to the lower-right side of the slide next to the last two bullet points. Click on another part of the slide to deselect the picture.** The graphic is moved to the right of the last two bullet points and deselected as shown in Figure 10.25. This graphic is also available as a clip art image when you are connected to the Internet.

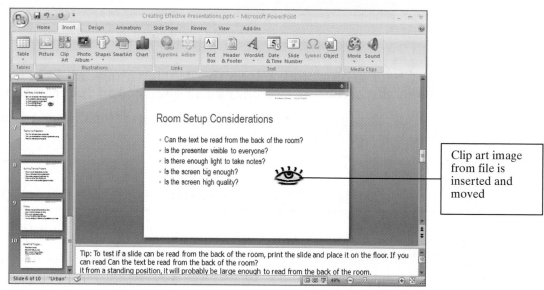

Clip art image from file is inserted and moved

FIGURE 10. 25

4. **Select slide 7. Click the Home tab, and in the Slides group click the Layout button.** By clicking the Layout button you can select a different layout for this slide.

5. **Click the Two Content layout.** The layout of slide 7 changes; the bullet points display on the left and a content placeholder displays on the right side of the slide.

6. **Click the Insert Picture from File icon on the content placeholder. In the Insert Picture dialog box, navigate to the student files, select the** *Surprise* **image file, and then click Insert.** An image of a surprised face is inserted on the right side of the slide.

7. **Hold down** Ctrl **and move the upper-right sizing handle to enlarge the image so it fills the right side of the slide. Move the image as necessary to align it to the right of the bullet points as shown in Figure 10.26.** Using the Ctrl key causes the image to remain centered in the space as it is enlarged.

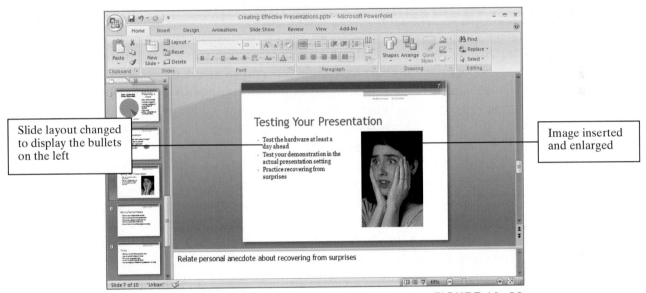

Slide layout changed to display the bullets on the left

Image inserted and enlarged

FIGURE 10. 26

8. **Save your changes to the** *Effective Presentations* **file and leave it open for the next lesson.**

### USING A BLANK SLIDE, OR A TITLE ONLY SLIDE

If you want to create a drawing using the drawing tools, choose the Title Only or Blank slide layout options. This creates a slide without any placeholders (except perhaps for a title), which enables you to use all of the drawing tools and images to create a drawing, flowchart, diagram, map, or other illustration to demonstrate an important point or concept

# LESSON 5: Animating a Presentation

A *slide transition* is the change from one slide to the next. Transitions control the direction, timing, speed, and manner in which slides appear on the screen. **Animations** are added to control the direction, timing, speed and manner in which bullet points and other objects appear on a slide. With animations you can also control the order in which items appear on the screen. Transitions and animations add motion to a presentation, which helps to keep the viewer's interest.

There is a wide variety of transitions and animations from which to choose. Animation schemes may include a slide transition, animation of the title slide, and a different animation of bullet points. After you have selected an animation scheme, you can customize it for specific slides as needed. When you add transitions and animations to slides there is a tendency to want to try one of everything, which results in a disjointed presentation that can be annoying. It is best to use consistent or complementary transitions and animation schemes. You may want to select a different transition for the opening and ending slides, or for slides that you want to stand out.

In this lesson, you will apply animations and transitions to the *Effective Presentations* slides.

## To Add Animations and Transitions

1. **With the *Effective Presentations* file open, on the status bar click the Slide Sorter button to display all slides, and then press Ctrl + A. You** can add animations or transitions in Normal view or in Slide Sorter view, but it is easier to see the transition demonstrated on multiple slides in Slide Sorter view. All of the slides are selected so the transition you choose will be applied to all of the slides.

2. **Click the Animations tab, and in the Transition to this Slide group, click the More arrow to display the Transition Schemes as shown in Figure 10.27. Scroll the list.** The transitions are grouped in categories—*No Transition, Fades and Dissolves, Wipes, Push and Cover, Stripes and Bars, and Random.* All are considered slide design elements. The most recently used animation schemes are listed first. You can select the *No Transition* option, or choose an option from any categories.

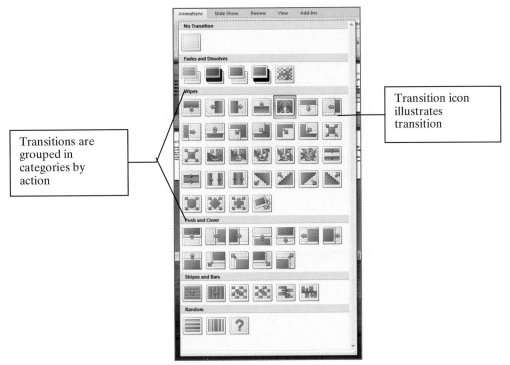

Transitions are grouped in categories by action

Transition icon illustrates transition

FIGURE 10. 27

3. **Scroll the list to view the transition categories; point to (do not click) several different transitions and read the ScreenTip that describes each.** A ScreenTip describes the actions that will take place..

4. **Under the *Stripes and Bars* category click the *Blinds Horizontal*.** The transition is applied and starts to demonstrate the action of horizontal blinds. The transition continues in this manner across all of the selected slides. You can press Esc at any time to stop the demonstration.

5. **In the Transitions to this Slide group, click the Transition Speed box arrow and then click Medium.**

6. **Double-click slide 1. This will make it the active slide and change the view to Normal view.** The title slide is selected so that you can set an animation for this slide.

7. **On the Animations tab, in the Animations group, click Custom Animation.** The Custom Animation task pane displays on the right as shown in Figure 10.28. Here you select the animation style you want to use, set the speed of the animation, add sound if appropriate, and then apply it to the slides. The default is for the animation to advance when you click the mouse, but you can set it to advance automatically after so many seconds or minutes. This is a useful feature to use if you are running a presentation on a kiosk at a trade show, or some other venue where you want to use the presentation to attract the interest of potential customers.

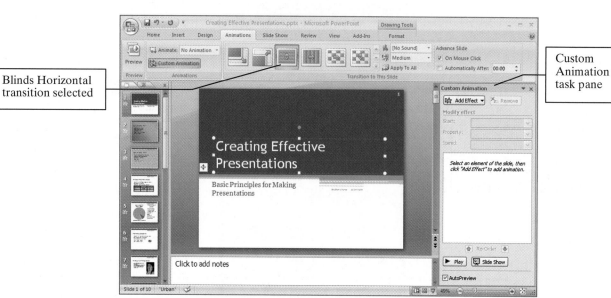

Blinds Horizontal transition selected

Custom Animation task pane

FIGURE 10. 28

8. **Click the title. In the Custom Animations task pane, click the Add Effect button. Point to Entrance and at the bottom of the display list click More Effects.** The effects are divided into categories—*Basic, Subtle, Moderate, and Exciting.* When you click an animation, and if the Preview Effect is checked, it is applied to the selected slide and the animation is demonstrated on that slide.

9. **Scroll the list as needed and from the Exciting category click Flip and then click OK. Click the Speed arrow and then click to Medium. Click the Start arrow and then click With Previous so the animation starts when the slide show starts and will not need to wait for your mouse click. Click the Play button to demonstrate the animation.**

10. **Click slide 2, and click in the bullet list. In the Custom Animation task pane, click the Add Effect button. Point to Entrance and then click More Effects. From the Basic list click Wipe and then click OK.**

11. **Click the Direction arrow and click From Left.** The Start defaults to On Click which will allow the presenter to reveal a point in the discussion by clicking the mouse button.

12. **Click the Slide Show button and click the mouse through the bullet list to display each bullet, Press Esc following the review of the slide.**

13. **Close the task pane; save your changes to the *Effective Presentations* file and leave it open to continue to the next lesson.**

### CUSTOM ANIMATIONS

You can animate charts, tables, clip art, and other objects on your slide separately. This gives you the option of using a different animation effect for the object and enables you to control the timing of the object. Objects display with the slide when it appears on the screen. If you want to have the object come onto the screen at a specific time, you first apply a custom animation and then set the sequence of that object within all of the other slide elements. The Custom Animation task pane is used for this purpose.

# LESSON 6: Creating Speaker Notes and Handouts

After the content is created, consider what needs to be printed. It is useful for the presenter to have a set of *speaker notes*—the slide content is printed on the top of each page, and any notes about specific comments to make during the presentation display on the bottom of the page. If appropriate, you can also print audience *handouts*, which display from one to nine slides to a page. Handouts have three main functions. They provide a printout of the slides, which:

- gives the audience a place to take notes
- avoids having people write what is displayed on the screen
- helps in case someone is unable to see the screen clearly

In this lesson you will create speaker notes and audience handouts.

### To Create Speaker Notes and Handouts

1. **With the *Effective Presentations* file open, click slide 6 and then click the View tab, and in the Presentation View group, click Notes Page.** The full page view of the notes page displays for slide 6. This is one of three slides that will contain notes. The default font size is 12 point, which may be too small to see easily when you are glancing at your notes during a presentation.

2. **On the View tab, in the Zoom group, click Zoom and then select 66% and click OK.** Changing the zoom makes it easier to read the content of the note. Depending on your screen size and resolution you may prefer a higher zoom such at 100%

3. **On the bottom of the slide, click the edge of the note placeholder to select it—make sure a solid border displays around the perimeter. Click the Home tab and in the Font group, click the Increase Font Size button two times.** You can select the text in the note placeholder, or click the edge of the note placeholder to select the note. When a solid border displays around the perimeter of the placeholder, changes you make will affect the contents. The font size is increased to 16 pt as shown in Figure 10.29. Each time

you click the Increase Font Size button, the font size of the selected text is increased to the next size available for that font. The Decrease Font Size button is used in a similar manner to reduce the font size of selected text.

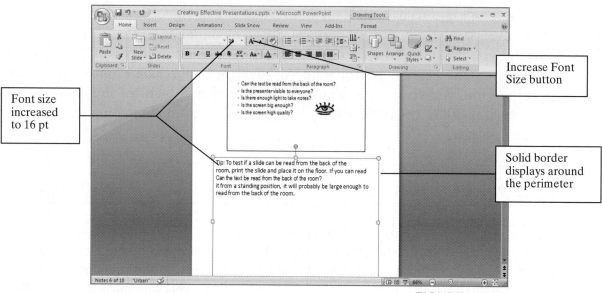

Font size increased to 16 pt

Increase Font Size button

Solid border displays around the perimeter

FIGURE 10. 29

4. **Click the Next Slide button, select the note for slide 7 and increase the font size to 16 pt.**

5. **On the right of the screen, drag the vertical scroll box until the ScreenTip reads:** *Notes 2 of 10: Layout and Design, Part 1.* As you drag the scroll box, ScreenTips display the number and title of the note (or slide). This helps you navigate to a specific slide in the presentation.

6. **Click in the notes area, change the font size to 16 pt and then type:** Guideline: `limit slides to 6 lines per slide, and 6 words per line.` Notes can also be typed directly in the notes area in the Notes Page view.

7. **Click the Insert tab, and in the Text group click Header & Footer.** The Header and Footer dialog box displays the Notes and Handouts tab as shown in Figure 10.30. Here you control the content of the header and footer areas on notes and on handouts. The *Date and time* check box is not selected by default; if selected it would display in the right corner of the header. The *Page number* check box is selected and will display on the right side of the footer. Content can be added to the *Header* box or *Footer* box, which displays on the left of each area.

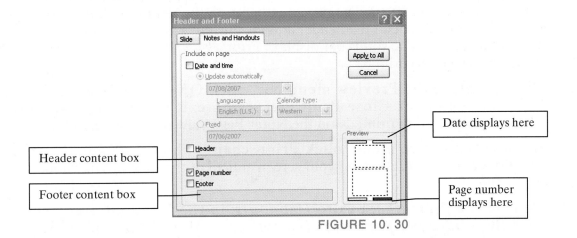

FIGURE 10. 30

8. **Place a checkmark in the Date and Time box and be sure Update automatically is selected. Place a check mark in the Header box and type your name as the Header. Be sure the Page Number box is selected and then clear the Footer check box (if necessary). Click Apply to All.** The current date displays on the right side of the header, the page number on the right side of the footer, and your name on the left side of the header.

9. **Click the Office button and click Print.** The Print dialog box controls what is printed. First determine what you want to print: slides, an outline, handouts, or notes pages. Then decide if the items need to be printed in color, or if they should be printed in *grayscale*—shades of gray to represent colors—or pure black and white. Third, limit the items printed to just the pages you need. Finally, preview the selection before you print it.

10. **Click the *Print what* arrow and select *Notes Pages*; click the Color/grayscale arrow and click *Pure Black and White*; under *Print range* click Slides, and then type 2,6–7 to print the notes pages for slides 2, 6, and 7.** Compare your selections with those in Figure 10.31.

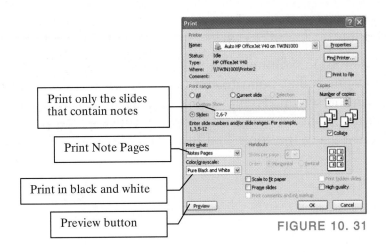

FIGURE 10. 31

11. **Click Preview.** Notice that the Preview window displays the notes page for: *Layout and Design, Part 1*. The page number is on the right side of the footer, your name is on the left side of the header and the current date displays on the right side of the header. The status bar displays *Print: Page 1 of 3*, because you selected three notes pages to print.

12. **Click Print on the Preview menu bar, click OK in the Print dialog box, and then click Close Print Preview to exit the Preview window.** Three notes pages are printed and the Notes Page view returns to your screen.

13. **Display the Office menu, click Print; change the print range to All.** The Print dialog box returns to your screen and all of the slides are included in the print range.

14. **Change the *Print what* box to *Handouts*; in the Handout area, make sure the *Slides per page* box displays *6*, the Horizontal option is selected, and *Frame_slides* is selected; change the *Color/grayscale* box to *Grayscale*, and then click *Preview*.** The first of two handout pages displays with six slides shown. Notice that the page number shows in the right side of the footer and the date and your name display in the header.

15. **Click Print, and then click OK. Click Close Print Preview to exit the Preview window. On the status bar click the Normal button. Save the *Effective Presentations* file and leave it open for the next lesson.**

---

## TO EXTEND YOUR KNOWLEDGE...

### USING HANDOUTS TO TAKE NOTES

When you print handouts, if you select the three slides to a page option, three slides display on the left and lines are printed on the right to provide a place to take notes about the topics on each slide. This is a good option to use when you expect your audience to take notes.

---

## LESSON 7: Previewing and Navigating a Slide Show Presentation

When you deliver your presentation, you may simply click the mouse button to advance from slide to slide and from one bullet point to the next, or you can click the Forward arrow button that appears on the screen. To move to a specific slide, display the shortcut menu, which provides several options for navigating between slides.

In this lesson, you practice using the tools that are available to you during the slide show.

1. **With the *Effective Presentations* file open, click slide 1, and then click the Slide Show button; move the mouse over the lower left corner of the screen. After the title displays on the screen click the mouse to move to slide 2. Move the pointer over the lower left corner of the screen.** The second slide fills the screen and the title displays. Four buttons appear in the lower-left corner of the screen—a Forward arrow, a Back arrow, a pencil, and a menu button, as shown in Figure 10.32. You can display a shortcut menu by clicking the menu button or by right-clicking anywhere on the screen. Clicking on the screen with the left mouse button has the same effect as clicking the Forward arrow—it causes the next bullet point, object, or slide to display. The Back arrow removes the most recent action.

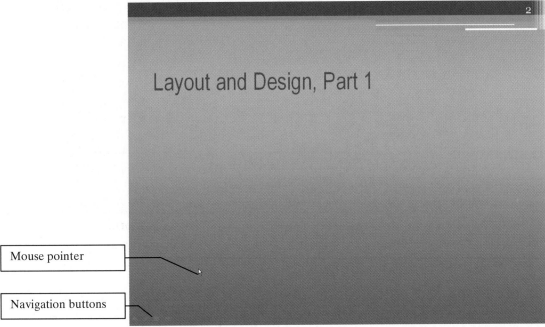

Layout and Design, Part 1

Mouse pointer

Navigation buttons

FIGURE 10. 32

2. **Click the Forward arrow on the lower-left corner of the slide to display the first bullet point.** Adding animations gives you the opportunity to control the pace of the presentation. As each bullet point is presented, you can take the time to expand on that point and add some examples. Be sure you do not read the slides to your audience. You should be prepared with more content than what is displayed. The points on the slide are summary ideas to help keep you and your audience on track.

3. **Continue with the forward arrow until you advance to Slide 3.Click the left mouse button in an open space on the slide.** The fourth slide appears on the screen using the Horizontal Blinds transition applied to the slides. Here you can see that the placement of the title and bullet points needs to be adjusted. It is always a good idea to preview your slides to see if there are any design issues that need to be fixed.

4. **Point to the lower left corner of the screen and click the Back arrow two times to return to Slide 2.**

5. **Right-click on the screen and point to Go to Slide from the shortcut menu. A list of slides by title displays as shown in Figure 10.33.** You can click on any of the displayed titles to move to a specific slide in your presentation. This *is useful if* someone asks you a question and you want to move to a slide that addresses the question that was asked.

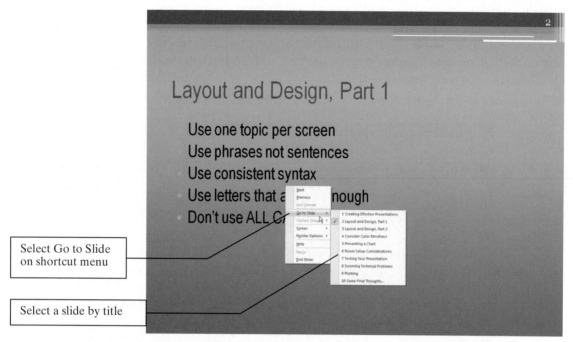

FIGURE 10. 33

6. **Click *6 Room Setup Considerations***

7. **Click the Menu button on the lower-left corner of the screen and, from the displayed shortcut menu, click Last Viewed.** Slide 2 returns to your screen. In this manner, you can move back to the slide that was previously shown and then move forward from that point. If you click Previous, the previous action is removed. When slides are animated, this simply removes the previous bullet point.

8. **Use the Forward arrow or simply click the mouse to continue through to the end of the presentation.** At the end of the presentation a black screen displays and *End of slide show, click to exit* appears at the top.

9. **Click to end the slide show and return to the Normal view.** You can press Esc at anytime to end a slide show.

10. **Click Slide 4. Click the bullet list, and then click the top middle sizing handle and drag down slightly until the bullet points do not overlap the title text. Be sure there is a solid border around the bullet list, and then click the Home tab and in the Font group click the Increase Font button as needed to increase the font size to 28 pt.**

11. Click the title and use the bottom middle sizing handle to drag the title up away from the bullet points.

12. Click slide 5 and use the techniques you just practiced to increase the font size of the bullet list to 28 pt. Then click slide 7 and change the font size on the bullet list to 28 pt.

13. Save your changes to the *Effective Presentations* file and then close it. Close PowerPoint.

## SUMMARY

In this project, you learned to use PowerPoint to create slides to show an audience during a presentation. Slide presentations help the presenter get organized, stay on track, and create a visual focus for the audience. Slides usually contain a title, which is the main topic for that slide, and several bullet points to expand or explain the main topic on the slide. You learned how to enter content and add data in the form of tables or charts. You added clip art and pictures to increase the viewer's interest, add humor, or illustrate a point. Drawing tools can alsobe used to create a diagram, illustrate a process, or create a flowchart.

After the content was added and organized, you applied a design to create a uniform impression for the slide show. Animations and slide transitions were applied to create movement by controlling the direction, timing, speed, and manner in which slides and bullet points or other objects are displayed during the presentation. Color designs and animation help keep the attention of the audience.

Finally, you created audience handouts and speaker notes for the presenter. Slides are typically presented using an overhead projector that is connected to the computer.

## KEY TERMS

| | | |
|---|---|---|
| animations | Normal view | Slide pane |
| dim | Notes pane | Slide Show view |
| grayscale | Outline/Slides tabs | Slide Sorter view |
| handouts | placeholders | slide transition |
| layout | Slide Master view | speaker notes |

# CHECKING CONCEPTS AND TERMS

## SCREEN ID
Label each element of the screen shown in Figure 10.34.

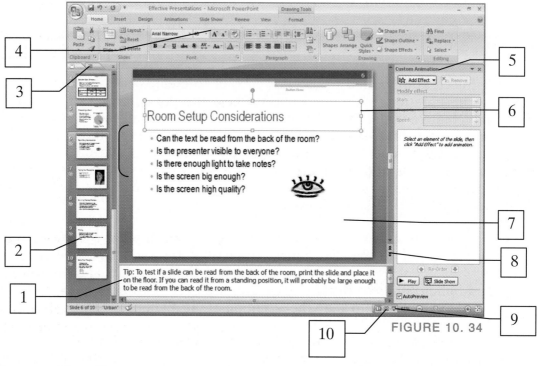

FIGURE 10. 34

_____ A. Increase Font Size button

_____ B. Next Slide button

_____ C. Notes pane

_____ D. Outline tab

_____ E. Custom Animation task pane

_____ F. Slide pane

_____ G. Slide Show button

_____ H. Slide Sorter button

_____ I. Thumbnail slides

_____ J. Title placeholder

## MULTIPLE CHOICE

**Circle the letter of the correct answer for each of the following.**

1. To reorganize slides it is best to use the _____ view [L1]
   a. Normal
   b. Slide Sorter
   c. Notes Pages
   d. Slide Master

2. You may want to add graphics to your slides for any of the following reasons expect _____. [L4]
   a. to illustrate a point
   b. to create interest
   c. to add humor
   d. to include a graphic on every slide

3. To add a data element to your slides select a layout that includes a _____ placeholder. [L2]

   a. auxiliary
   b. basic
   c. content
   d. data

4. To control how bullet points appear on the screen, select a (n) _____. [L5]

   a. Animation Scheme
   b. Slide Transition
   c. Bullet Transition
   d. Exhibition Control

5. When using a slide presentation, make sure you do the following _____. [L1, L5, L7]

   a. stand in front of the display so people won't see any errors you have made
   b. read the slides to your audience in case they can't see them
   c. have only one topic per slide
   d. add a different animation on every slide to keep people's interest

6. When applying a design to a presentation the most important factor to keep in mind is _____. [L3]

   a. the environment in which the presentation will be given
   b. how many printouts you have to make to be sure you don't run out of ink
   c. the number of people who will be attending the presentation

   d. what you will wear that day so you do not clash with the presentation background

7. Presentations can help with all of the following except?[L1]

   a. organize your content
   b. speak clearly
   c. stay on track during your presentation
   d. give the audience a visual focus

8. Notes for the speaker can be added in the _____.[L1, L6]

   a. Normal view
   b. Slide Sorter view
   c. Notes Pages view
   d. a or c, but not b

9. Audience handouts are provided for all of the following reasons except _____. [L6]

   a. to people feel like they are part of a group
   b. to remove the need to write what is displayed on the screen
   c. to provide a place to take notes
   d. in case someone is unable to see the screen

10.    In a slide show, to return to the slide that was just viewed prior to the current slide, display the menu and select. [L7]

   a. Back
   b. Last Viewed
   c. Previous
   d. Return

## DISCUSSION

1. Discuss how PowerPoint can help you communicate information to others. Give examples of when you might use it in school, business, or personal situations [L1]−[L7]

2. Think about presentations, seminars, or lectures you have attended. Describe circumstances where PowerPoint has been used effectively. What made it effective? Describe a situation where you think PowerPoint might have improved a presentation. What are the pros and cons of using an electronic presentation? [L1]−[L7]

3.  PowerPoint provides several different views. Describe the main purpose of the Normal view, Slide Show view, Slide Sorter view, Notes Pages view and Slide Master view.[L1, L6, L7]

## SKILL DRILL

Skill Drill exercises reinforce project skills. Each skill reinforced is the same, or nearly the same, as a skill presented in the project. Detailed instructions are provided in a step-by-step format.

Start with the first Skill Drill exercise to create and save the file that will be used in the remaining Skill Drill exercises. Complete the Skill Drill exercises in order as presented. All of these exercises can be completed using Microsoft Office XP or later versions. Instructions throughout the exercises are based on a Windows XP operating system, running Microsoft Office 2007.

### 1. Creating a Presentation and Working in Different Views

As part of the training for the sales force at your company, you have been asked to create a brief presentation to provide tips on giving presentations.

1.  Start **PowerPoint.** (If PowerPoint is already open, from the Office menu click **New** to start a blank presentation.) On the title slide type: `Tips for Making Presentations` in the title placeholder. In the subtitle placeholder, type: `How to Control the "Fear Factor".`

2.  On the **Home tab**, in the **Slides group** click **New Slide.** In the title placeholder type: `Be Prepared.` Hold down Ctrl and press Enter↵ to move to the text placeholder. Enter the following bullet points.

    `Research your customer`

    `Review your material`

    `Rehearse what you will say`

    `Create speaker notes`

3.  Click at the end of the second bullet point, press Enter↵, and then press Tab, and type: `Remove errors and typos`; press Enter↵ and type: `Proofread the slides.`

4.  Click **New Slide.** Type: Practice in the title placeholder and then add the following bullet points:

    `Practice with your slides`

    `Practice with the actual equipment`

    `Practice in front of a mirror`

    `Practice in front of a friend`

    `Practice in the actual room`

5. Add a fourth slide and type: `Relax` in the title placeholder and add the following bullet points:

`Have fun`

`Smile`

`Use humor`

`Mingle with the group beforehand`

6. Save the file in your folder with the name `Presentation Tips.`

7. Click **slide 2**. On the slide, click the bullet next to *Proofread the slides* and drag it up so it precedes *Remove errors and typos.* (Logically you need to proofread before you can remove errors and typos.)

8. Click **slide 4**, click the last bullet point and drag it up to be the first bullet point on the slide. Select *Have fun* and drag it down to be the last bullet point on slide 4.

9. Save the Presentation Tips file. Leave the file open if you plan to continue to another Skill Drill exercise.

## 2. Adding Data Elements to a Presentation and Working in Different Views

You need to add a chart to the presentation to point out the value of including data elements in a presentation.

1. With the *Presentation Tips* file open, be sure that **slide 4** displays in Normal view.

2. On the **Home tab**, in the **Slides group**, click the **New Slide** arrow and from the list select **Title and Content** layout.

3. Type: `Include Sales Data` in the title placeholder, and then click the **Insert Chart** icon. Select **Clustered Column Chart** and click **OK**.

4. Click *Series 1* in the Excel worksheet and type `Product A`. Click *Series 2* and type `Product B`; click *Series 3* and type `Product C`. Change the Category labels to 1st Qtr, 2nd Qtr, 3rd Qtr and 4th Qtr. Leave the data that displays as filler data.

5. Close the datasheet. Click the Product A column to select it, right-click and choose **Format Data Series**. In the Format Data Series dialog box, click **Fill** and then click **Solid Fill**. Click the **Color arrow** and under **Standard Colors** select **Orange**.

6. With the Format Data Series dialog box open, click the middle column—Product B—and change the color to **Standard Color Light Blue** then click the right column—Product C—and change the color to **Standard Color Purple**. By selecting Standard colors, the colors of the bars will not be affected by the design that is applied. Click *Close* to close the Format Data Series dialog box.

7. On the **View tab** click **Slide Sorter**. Click **slide 5,** with the chart, and move it between slides 3 and 4.

8. Save the *Presentation Tips* file. Leave the file open if you plan to do any more Skill Drill exercises.

## 3. Applying a Design and Adding Graphics

This presentation is about tips for making presentations. It is also attempting to help the sales force relax so they can be comfortable making presentations. You need to add a fun design and some funny clip art to add humor.

1. With the *Presentation Tips* file open, click the **Normal View** button if necessary and then click **slide 1**.

2. Click the **Design tab**, and in the **Theme group**, click the **More** button. Move the pointer over the various themes to see the effect on the presentation to see how they look. Try the *Metro* or the *Paper* design. Both of these present a calming image, but have a fairly dark background. Scroll the list and click the *Oriel* design. This design adds more levity to the presentation.

3. Click the **Next Slide** button. On the **Insert tab**, in the **Illustrations group**, click **Picture**. Navigate to the student folder for this chapter and then select the *Research* image. Click **Insert**. Move the image to the right of the last three bullet points.

4. Click the **Next Slide** button. On the **Home tab**, in the **Slides group**, click **Layout**, and then click the **Two Content** layout. Click the **Insert Picture from File** icon in the content placeholder, navigate to the student folder for this chapter, and then insert the *Practice* image. The image fills the right side of slide 3.

5. Click **slide 5**—titled *Relax*. Change the slide layout to **Two Content**. You would like the bullet list to be on the right side of the slide with the content on the left. Select the bullet list on the left, point to the frame of the placeholder and drag to the right frame. Then select the content placeholder, point to the edge of the frame and drag it to the left side of the slide. Adjust the two frames so they are even with each other. Follow the procedure that you have used previously to insert the Smile image from the student files on the left side of slide 5. Drag the image up so it balances the bullet points on the right.

6. Save the *Presentation Tips* file and leave it open if you plan to continue with another Skill Drill exercise.

## 4. Animating a Presentation and Previewing the Slide Show

It is time to add animations and transitions to the presentation and then test it to see how it looks in a slide show.

1. With the *Presentation Tips* file open, click the **Slide Sorter View** button. Click **slide 1**.

2. Click the **Animations tab**, and in the **Transitions to This Slide group** click the **More** button. Under the *Wipes* category, select **Wheel Clockwise, 2 Spokes**. Change **Transition Speed** to **Medium**.

3. Click **slide 2**, hold down [⇧ Shift] and click **slide 5**, so that you can apply an animation to the last four slides. Click the **More** button and under the *Wipes* category select **Wipe Box Out**. Change the Transition Speed box to **Slow**.

4. Change to the **Normal View** and click **Slide 1**. In the **Animations group** click **Custom Animation**. Click the Title on slide 1 and then in the Custom Animations task pane, click the **Add Effects** button. Click **Entrance** and then click **More Effects**. In the Basic Category click **Fly In** and then click **OK**. Change the Start to **With Previous**, the Direction to **From Top-Left** and the Speed to **Slow**.

5. Click the subtitle on **slide 1** and using the same procedure add an entrance effect of **Unfold**.

6. Click **slide 2**, and click in the bullet list to make it active. In the **Animations group**, click the **Animate box arrow**, and under Wipe click **By 1st Level Paragraph**. Click **slide 3** and follow the same process to apply the Wipe By 1st Level Paragraph animation, and then apply this same animation to the bullet list on **slide 5**.

7. Click **slide 1,** click the **Slide Show** button on the status bar. Click the mouse to move through the presentation and each of the bullet points.

8. Save the Presentation Tips file, and leave it open if you plan to continue to another Skill Drill exercise.

### 5. Creating Handouts

Now that you have completed the presentation, you can create any speaker notes or handouts that may be necessary.

1. With the *Presentation Tips* file open, click the **Insert tab** and in the **Text group** click **Header & Footer**. On the **Slide** tab, place a check marks in the *Slide number* check box, and then click **Don't show on title slide**. This places numbers on all of the slides except the title slide.

2. Click the **Notes and Handouts** tab. Clear the check mark from the *Date and time* check box (if necessary). Check the *Header* box, type: **Presentation Tips for Sales Staff**. Check the *Footer* box, type your name. Clear the *Page number* check box, and then click **Apply to All.**

3. From the **Office** menu click **Print**. In the *Print what* box select **Handouts.** In the *Slides per* page box select **6**; be sure that the **Frame slides** check box is selected and **Color** is selected, and then click **Preview.**

4. Click **Print**, and then click **OK** in the Print dialog box. Click the **Close Print Preview** button to return to Normal view. Save the *Presentation Tips* file and close it.

## CHALLENGE

Challenge exercises expand on or are somewhat related to skills presented in the lessons. Each exercise provides a brief narrative introduction, followed by instructions in a numbered-step format that are not as detailed as those in the Skill Drill section.

Each exercise is independent of the others, so you may complete the exercises in any order.

### 1. Creating a Sales Training Presentation

As part of the sales training program at your company, you have been asked to create a presentation about the selling process.

1. Start **PowerPoint** (If PowerPoint is already open, click **New** on the Office menu to start a blank presentation.) Add the title: **Effective Sales Techniques**. In the subtitle placeholder type: **Presented by:**, press ⎣Enter ⏎⎦, and type: **Sales and Marketing.**

2. On the **Home tab**, click the **New Slide arrow** and then click **Slides from Outline.** Insert file **PP_1002.** Review the content that you have just inserted.

3. In the Slide Sorter view, display the Themes Gallery. Apply the **Apex** design. Click the **Theme Colors** arrow and select the **Flow** color scheme.

4. On the **View tab** click **Slide Master.** On the Title and Text layout master, select the title text, right-click and then click **Format Text Effects.** Select **Shadow** and then click the **Presets** button and click **No Shadow.** Click **Text Fill**, click **Solid Fill**, and then change the color to **Orange.** Click **Close** to close the Format Text Effects dialog box.

5. Select the text in the first level bullet and increase the font size once. Increase the font size for the second level bullet once. Close the Master View. On the Title slide, change the Font Color for the title to Orange.

6. Apply the **Rise Up** animation to both the title and subtitle on the Title slide and the **Faded Zoom** to the title and bullet points on the remaining slides.

7. In slide Sorter View, select all of the slides. On the Animations tab, in the Transition to This Slide group, scroll to the bottom of the slide transition gallery and select **Random Transition**, change the speed to **Medium.**

8. Click slide 1, display the slide show and pace through it until you return to the previous view (Slide Sorter view).

9. From the Insert tab click Header & Footer. Add slide numbers to the slides. On the notes and handouts, add your name to the footer and include the date.

10. Print handouts, 6 slides to a page, with frames and in grayscale.

11. Save the file as **Effective Sales**, and then close the file and close PowerPoint.

## 2. Creating a Presentation for the Alumni Travel Club

The Alumni Travel Club is planning another trip to Alaska. They asked you to create a presentation to generate interest for the trip and to inform people about what they are likely to see. You have some pictures that you included in another presentation that you want to use in this presentation.

1. Open *PP_1003*. Save it in your folder as an Office 2007 file with the name **Alaska**.

2. On **slide 1,** select the title *The Alaska Adventure* and change it to a WordArt graphic of your choice. Delete the title placeholder.

3. On the Home tab, in the Slides group, click the New Slides arrow and then click Reuse Slides. The Reuse Slides task pane opens. This is used to locate a presentation that contains slides you want to use in this presentation, similar to importing an outline from Word. Click the **Browse** button and then click **Browse File**. Navigate to the student folder, select *PP_1004* and then click **Open.**

4. The selected presentation slides display in the Reuse Slides task pane. Use the scroll bar on the right of the Reuse Slides task panes to view the slides. When you point to a slide an enlarged image of the slide displays. Click to select **slides 4, 5** and **8**—*Snow Packs Slide, Some End in Lakes, Large Animals are Common*—and then close the Reuse Slides task pane. Three slides are inserted following slide 1.

5.  Click **slides 2, 3** and **4** to see their content. With **slide 4** selected, insert a new slide and apply the **Title and Content** layout. Add the title: `Anchorage Weather in July`. Create a 2-column, 4-row table and enter the following data:

    `Average high     65º`

    `Average low      51º`

    `Average rainfall 2"`

    `Average humidity 72%`

    Hint: Use the Insert Symbol dialog box to locate a degree sign for the temperatures.

6.  Expand the table to fill the slide. Change the **Font Color** for the first row to **Black** and remove the bold format. For all the text in the table, increase the font size to fill the cells and align the text in the table so it is in the middle vertically.

7.  Insert a new slide and apply the Title and Content layout. Type: `Estimated Costs` as the title. Create a Pie in 3-D chart. Enter the data as follows in the datasheet. Series 1 is Estimated cost, the others are in rows.

|  | Estimated Costs |
|---|---|
| Air Transportation | $834 |
| Accommodation and Meals | $700 |
| Ground Transportation | $150 |
| Sightseeing Trips | $550 |

8.  On the **Chart Tools Layout tab**, click **Legend** and move the legend to the bottom of the chart.

9.  In the Slide Sorter view, move the weather table slide to follow the Places You'll Visit slide, and the chart slide to follow The Basics slide. Save the presentation.

10. Change to the Normal view. On the **Design tab** apply the **Module** design Adjust the colors and placement of the WordArt graphic on slide 1 if necessary to make it visible with this background. If necessary, adjust the placement of the title placeholder on slide 2 so it is fully displayed in the title area.

11. On the **Animations tab**, click **Custom Animation.** Click slide 5 and click the bullet list. Add an Entrance effect of Ease In. Apply the same animation to bullets on slides 7 and 9.

12. In the Slide Sorter view select all of the slides and apply the **Wipes Shape Plus** transition. Change the Speed to Slow. Click slide 1 and preview the slide show.

13. Insert a Header & Footer. Add slide numbers to the slides and your name on the footer. Click the Notes and Handouts tab and include the current date, your name in the header, and a page number.

14. Preview the handouts, 9 to a page, in Pure Black and White, and then print the handout. Save the Alaska presentation file and then close it. Close PowerPoint.

## 3. Creating a Presentation for a Historical Society

In this Challenge exercise, you will create a presentation for the local history society about census statistics gathered for a rural county in Michigan during the late 1800s.

1.  Open **PowerPoint**. In the title placeholder type `A Statistical Profile of Alcona County, Michigan*`. In the subtitle placeholder type: `*Taken from Federal Census Data 1860 to 1900.`

2.  Save the file in your folder with the name `Alcona County`.

3.  Insert a new slide and apply the **Title and Content** layout. In the title placeholder type: `Alcona County Population Growth 1860 – 1900`. Create a line chart (Line with Markers) Adjust the chart datasheet to two columns with six rows. In the first column type, `Year, 1860, 1870, 1880, 1890, 1900`. In the second column type `185, 696, 3107, 5409, 5691`. Delete any placeholder data that remains in the datasheet.

4.  Delete the legend. Display the Format Data Series dialog box for the line, and under Line Style, change the **Width** box to **3 pt**.

5.  Insert a new slide and apply the Title and Content layout. In the title placeholder type: `Percent Born in the U. S.` Create a table with 4 columns and 6 rows, and then enter the following data.

|      | U.S.  | Foreign | % U.S. |
|------|-------|---------|--------|
| 1860 | 106   | 79      | 57.3%  |
| 1870 | 382   | 314     | 54.9%  |
| 1880 | 1,626 | 1,481   | 52.3%  |
| 1890 | 2,859 | 2,550   | 52.9%  |
| 1900 | 2,684 | 2,243   | 62.2%  |

6.  Right-align the contents of the last three columns. Display the Slide Theme gallery and then apply the **Verve** Theme. Select the first row of the table, right-click then click Format Shape. Change the **Fill color** and apply the sixth color in the first row—Pink Accent 2 in the colors listed on the Fill Color gallery.

7.  In the Slide Sorter view, select all the slides. In the Transitions to This Slide group apply the **Split Horizontal In** transition to all three slides. Change the Speed to **Medium.**

8. In the Normal view, click **slide 2** and then click the chart. Display the Custom Animation task pane. On the Custom Animation task pane, click the **Add Effect** button, point to **Entrance** and then click **Wipe.**

9. Under *Modify: Wipe,* make sure the *Direction* displays **From Bottom** and change the *Speed* to **Medium.** Click the **Play** button to see how the slide transitions onto the screen first and then the chart is displayed.

10. Click **slide 3** and then click the table. On the Custom Animation task pane, click the **Add Effect** button, point to **Entrance** and then click **Blinds.**

11. Under *Modify: Blinds,* change the *Direction* to **Vertical** and the *Speed* to **Medium.** Click the **Play** button to see how the slide transitions onto the screen first, and then the table is displayed.

12. On the Insert tab click Header & Footer. Add your name to the header for the handouts. Preview the handouts with 3 to a page and then print the handout.

13. Save the *Alcona County* presentation and close the file. Close PowerPoint.

## DISCOVERY ZONE

Discovery Zone exercises require advanced knowledge of topics presented in *Essentials* lessons, application of skills from multiple lessons, or self-directed learning of new skills. Each exercise is independent of the others, so you may complete the exercises in any order.

### 1. Creating your Own Presentation

Demonstrate your mastery of PowerPoint by creating a presentation on a topic of your choice that you could present to classmates in this class. Choose a topic on which you are an expert. Make sure the topic is appropriate for a college class and follow good presentation techniques as discussed in this chapter. Include the following elements:

- Eight to ten slides
- Your name in the subtitle on the title slide
- An appropriate graphic on at least three slides
- A design with a change to the background
- Slide numbers on the slides and the title of the presentation in the footer.
- Animate the bullet points and apply transitions to the slides
- Preview the presentation and make sure it does not contain any errors
- Add notes to at least three slides and print those slides as speaker notes. Be sure to include your name in the header of the speaker notes and handouts
- Print handouts with six slides to a page

### 2. Working with Graphic Tools in PowerPoint

In this Discovery Zone exercise, you explore the use of drawing tools as graphic objects in PowerPoint. Drawing tools are useful for demonstrating a process, procedure, or relationship. Use Figure 10.35 as a guide and follow the instructions below to create a single slide.

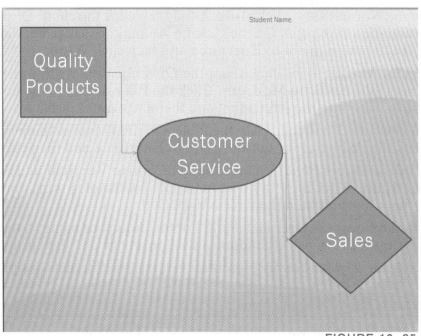

FIGURE 10. 35

Start **PowerPoint** and change the slide layout to **Blank.** On the Insert tab, in the Illustrations group click Shapes, and then click the **Rectangle.** In the upper-left corner of the slide, press ⌈⇧ Shift⌉ and draw a square that is approximately two inches on a side. Right-click the square and choose **Edit Text.** Type **Quality**, press ⌈Enter ↵⌉ and type: **Products**. Select *Quality Products* and increase the font size to 36. Resize the text box as needed to display the text on two lines as shown in Figure 10.35.

From the Shapes gallery, click the **Oval** button and draw an oval in the middle of the slide. Right-click the oval, select **Edit Text** and type: **Customer**, press ⌈Enter ↵⌉ and type: **Service**. Increase the font size to 36 and display it on two lines. On the Shapes gallery select the **Diamond** shape. Draw a diamond as shown in the lower-right corner of the slide. In a similar manner type Sales in the diamond and change the font size to 36.

From the Shapes gallery, under **Lines** locate and click the **Elbow Arrow Connector.** When you move your mouse pointer onto the screen red dots display around the object you are closest to. Click the red connector dot on the right side of the *Quality Products* square and drag down to the red connector dot on the left side of the oval. A line with an arrow connects these two dots. Follow this same procedure to add an Elbow Arrow Connector between the right side of the *Customer Service* oval and the left side of the *Sales* diamond. Compare your screen with Figure 10.35. Apply the **Trek** design.

Display the Custom Animation task pane. Click the **Quality Products** square and then click the **Add Effect** button. Point to **Entrance**, click **More Effects**, click **Diamond**, and then click **OK.** Under *Modify: Diamond*, change the *Direction* to **Out** and the *Speed* to **Medium.** In a similar manner add a custom entrance to the first elbow connector, and then to the *Customer Service* oval, the second elbow connector, and finally the *Sales* diamond. Play the animation and make sure each object is animated in order across the screen.

Add your name to the footer of the slide and then print the slide in grayscale. Save the file as Sales Process and close the file. Close PowerPoint.